Love Hina

By
Ken
Akamatsu

Vol.14

ALSO AVAILABLE FROM 🔵TOKYOPOP®

MANGA

.HACK//LEGEND OF THE TWILIGHT
@LARGE (October 2003)
ANGELIC LAYER*
BABY BIRTH*
BATTLE ROYALE*
BRAIN POWERED*
BRIGADOON*
CARDCAPTOR SAKURA
CARDCAPTOR SAKURA: MASTER OF THE CLOW*
CHOBITS*
CHRONICLES OF THE CURSED SWORD
CLAMP SCHOOL DETECTIVES*
CLOVER
CONFIDENTIAL CONFESSIONS*
CORRECTOR YUI
COWBOY BEBOP*
COWBOY BEBOP: SHOOTING STAR*
CYBORG 009*
DEMON DIARY
DIGIMON*
DRAGON HUNTER
DRAGON KNIGHTS*
DUKLYON: CLAMP SCHOOL DEFENDERS*
ERICA SAKURAZAWA*
FAKE*
FLCL*
FORBIDDEN DANCE*
GATE KEEPERS*
G GUNDAM*
GRAVITATION*
GTO*
GUNDAM WING
GUNDAM WING: BATTLEFIELD OF PACIFISTS
GUNDAM WING: ENDLESS WALTZ*
GUNDAM WING: THE LAST OUTPOST*
HAPPY MANIA*
HARLEM BEAT
I.N.V.U.
INITIAL D*
ISLAND
JING: KING OF BANDITS*
JULINE
KARE KANO*
KINDAICHI CASE FILES, THE*
KING OF HELL
KODOCHA: SANA'S STAGE*
LOVE HINA*
LUPIN III*
MAGIC KNIGHT RAYEARTH*

MAGIC KNIGHT RAYEARTH II* (COMING SOON)
MAN OF MANY FACES*
MARMALADE BOY*
MARS*
MIRACLE GIRLS
MIYUKI-CHAN IN WONDERLAND* (October 2003)
MONSTERS, INC.
PARADISE KISS*
PARASYTE
PEACH GIRL
PEACH GIRL: CHANGE OF HEART*
PET SHOP OF HORRORS*
PLANET LADDER*
PLANETES* (October 2003)
PRIEST
RAGNAROK
RAVE MASTER*
REALITY CHECK
REBIRTH
REBOUND*
RISING STARS OF MANGA
SABER MARIONETTE J*
SAILOR MOON
SAINT TAIL
SAMURAI DEEPER KYO*
SAMURAI GIRL: REAL BOUT HIGH SCHOOL*
SCRYED*
SHAOLIN SISTERS*
SHIRAHIME-SYO: SNOW GODDESS TALES* (Dec. 2003)
SHUTTERBOX (November 2003)
SORCERER HUNTERS
THE SKULL MAN*
THE VISION OF ESCAFLOWNE
TOKYO MEW MEW*
UNDER THE GLASS MOON
VAMPIRE GAME*
WILD ACT*
WISH*
WORLD OF HARTZ (COMING SOON)
X-DAY*
ZODIAC P.I. *

For more information visit www.TOKYOPOP.com

*INDICATES 100% AUTHENTIC MANGA (RIGHT-TO-LEFT FORMAT)

CINE-MANGA™

CARDCAPTORS
JACKIE CHAN ADVENTURES (November 2003)
JIMMY NEUTRON
KIM POSSIBLE
LIZZIE MCGUIRE
POWER RANGERS: NINJA STORM
SPONGEBOB SQUAREPANTS
SPY KIDS 2

NOVELS

KARMA CLUB (April 2004)
SAILOR MOON

TOKYOPOP KIDS

STRAY SHEEP

ART BOOKS

CARDCAPTOR SAKURA*
MAGIC KNIGHT RAYEARTH*

ANIME GUIDES

COWBOY BEBOP ANIME GUIDES
GUNDAM TECHNICAL MANUALS
SAILOR MOON SCOUT GUIDES

062703

Love Hina

By

Ken Akamatsu

Volume 14

Los Angeles • Tokyo • London

Translator - Nan Rymer
English Adaptation - Adam Arnold
Associate Editors - Paul Morrissey & Tim Beedle
Copy Editors - Amy Court Kaemon & Bryce P. Coleman
Retouch and Lettering - James Lee
Cover Layout - Anna Kernbaum
Editors - Mark Paniccia & Rob Tokar

Managing Editor - Jill Freshney
Production Coordinator - Antonio DePietro
Production Manager - Jennifer Miller
Art Director - Matt Alford
Editorial Director - Jeremy Ross
VP of Production - Ron Klamert
President & C.O.O. - John Parker
Publisher & C.E.O. - Stuart Levy

Email: editor@TOKYOPOP.com
Come visit us online at www.TOKYOPOP.com

A  Manga

TOKYOPOP Inc.
5900 Wilshire Blvd. Suite 2000
Los Angeles, CA 90036

ISBN: 1-59182-120-7

First TOKYOPOP printing: September 2003

10 9 8 7 6
Printed in the USA

Love Hina

The Story Thus Far...

Some promises are meant to be kept. Fifteen years ago, as a young child, Keitaro Urashima met a little girl who told him a story that if two people who love each other go to Tokyo University together, they'd live happily ever after. Keitaro's promise to the girl that they would make the legend come true has been the driving force for him to make it into Tokyo University...despite the fact that he can't remember who the girl was.

Over two years ago, Keitaro's globe-trotting grandmother left him in charge of the Hinata House, an all-girls' dormitory whose clientele was none too pleased that their live-in landlord is a man...or as close to a man as poor Keitaro can be. The lanky loser incessantly (and accidentally) crashes their sessions in the hot springs, walks in on them changing, and pokes his nose pretty much everywhere that it can get broken, if not by the hot-headed Naru, then by one of the other Hinata inmates—Kitsune, an alcoholic with a diesel libido and knack for gambling; Motoko, a swordsman who struggles with a feminine identity; Shinobu, a pre-teen princess with a colossal crush on Keitaro; Su, princess of the tropical Kingdom of Molmol with a big appetite and some mean hacker skills; Sarah, an orphaned ward resentful of being left by her globe trotting archeologist guardian, Seta; Mutsumi, an accident-prone lily also studying for her exams; Haruka, Keitaro's aunt and de facto matriarch of Hinata House; and Kanako, Keitaro's little sister with a knack for impersonations and a bizarre love for her brother.

Somehow, through their years of stumbling through one misadventure after another, the girls of Hinata House have all developed strong crushes on Keitaro. Once Keitaro had declared his feelings for Naru alone, though, the other girls teamed up to thwart their budding romance using every outrageous means at their disposal. Keitaro and Naru escaped their friends' plots and were about to cross the threshold into Tokyo U together when Keitaro was kidnapped by Seta and taken to the island of Molmol to help with a secret archaeological mission of great importance. As the Hinata House girls returned home, they saw a fax from Keitaro's grandmother stating that she would be arriving to grant Keitaro sole ownership of Hinata House in one week...providing she could meet his fiancee.

With Keitaro's star on the rise, the girls trailed him to Molmol in a last-ditch effort to capture his heart. Despite their wild machinations, the girls discovered that Keitaro's love for Naru is unshakable and they ultimately helped to bring the couple back together. Happily reunited in the tropical paradise, Naru asked Keitaro if he wanted to take their relationship to the next level...

CONTENTS

LOVE♡HINA

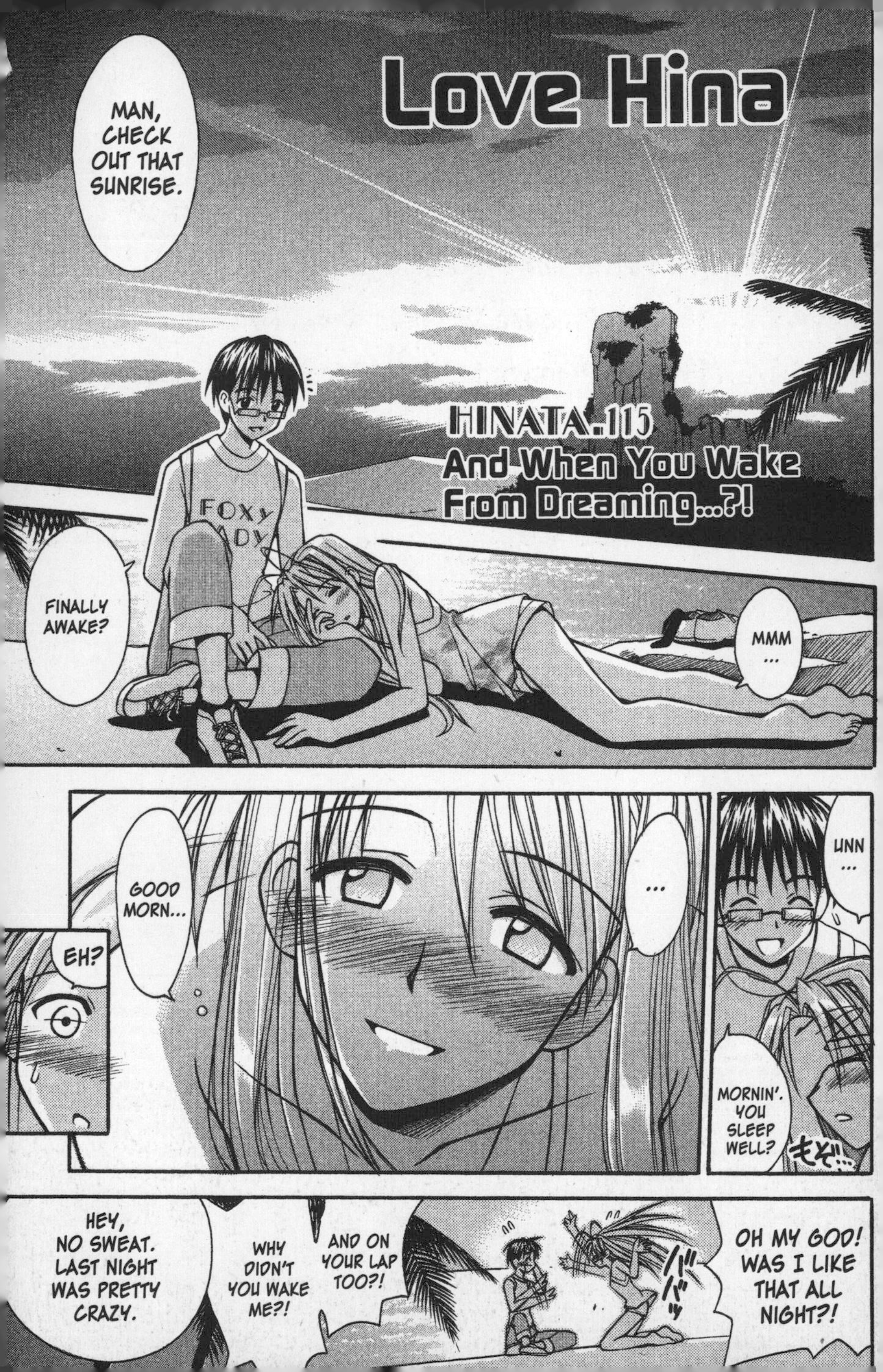
Love Hina
MAN, CHECK OUT THAT SUNRISE.
HINATA.115
And When You Wake From Dreaming...?!
MMM ...
FINALLY AWAKE?
UNN ...
MORNIN'. YOU SLEEP WELL?
もぞ...
...
GOOD MORN...
EH?
OH MY GOD! WAS I LIKE THAT ALL NIGHT?!
バババッ
AND ON YOUR LAP TOO?!
WHY DIDN'T YOU WAKE ME?!
HEY, NO SWEAT. LAST NIGHT WAS PRETTY CRAZY.

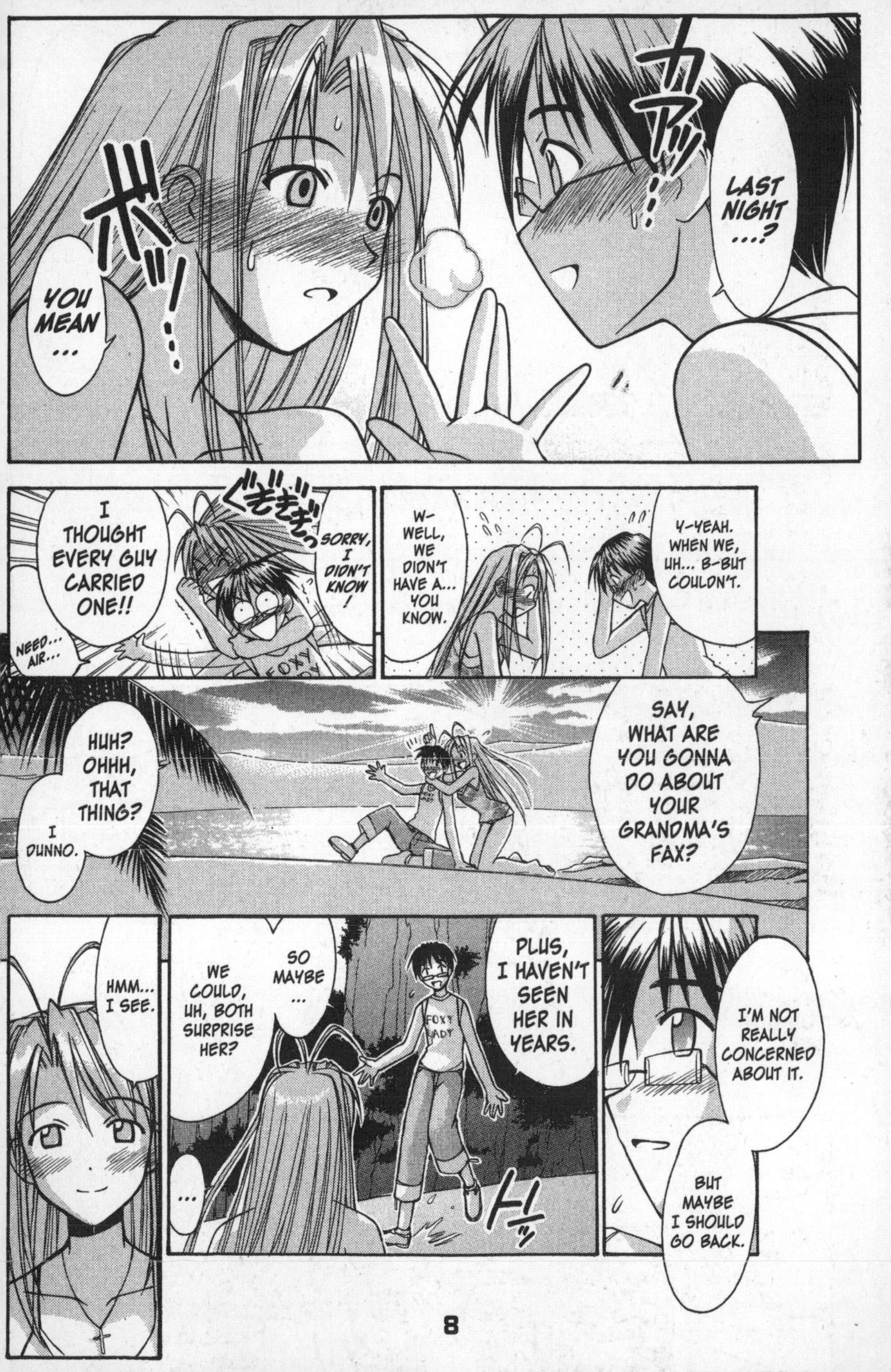
LAST NIGHT ...?
YOU MEAN ...
Y-YEAH. WHEN WE, UH... B-BUT COULDN'T.
W-WELL, WE DIDN'T HAVE A... YOU KNOW.
SORRY, I DIDN'T KNOW!
I THOUGHT EVERY GUY CARRIED ONE!!
NEED... AIR...
SAY, WHAT ARE YOU GONNA DO ABOUT YOUR GRANDMA'S FAX?
HUH? OHHH, THAT THING?
I DUNNO.
I'M NOT REALLY CONCERNED ABOUT IT.
BUT MAYBE I SHOULD GO BACK.
PLUS, I HAVEN'T SEEN HER IN YEARS.
SO MAYBE ...
WE COULD, UH, BOTH SURPRISE HER?
...
HMM... I SEE.

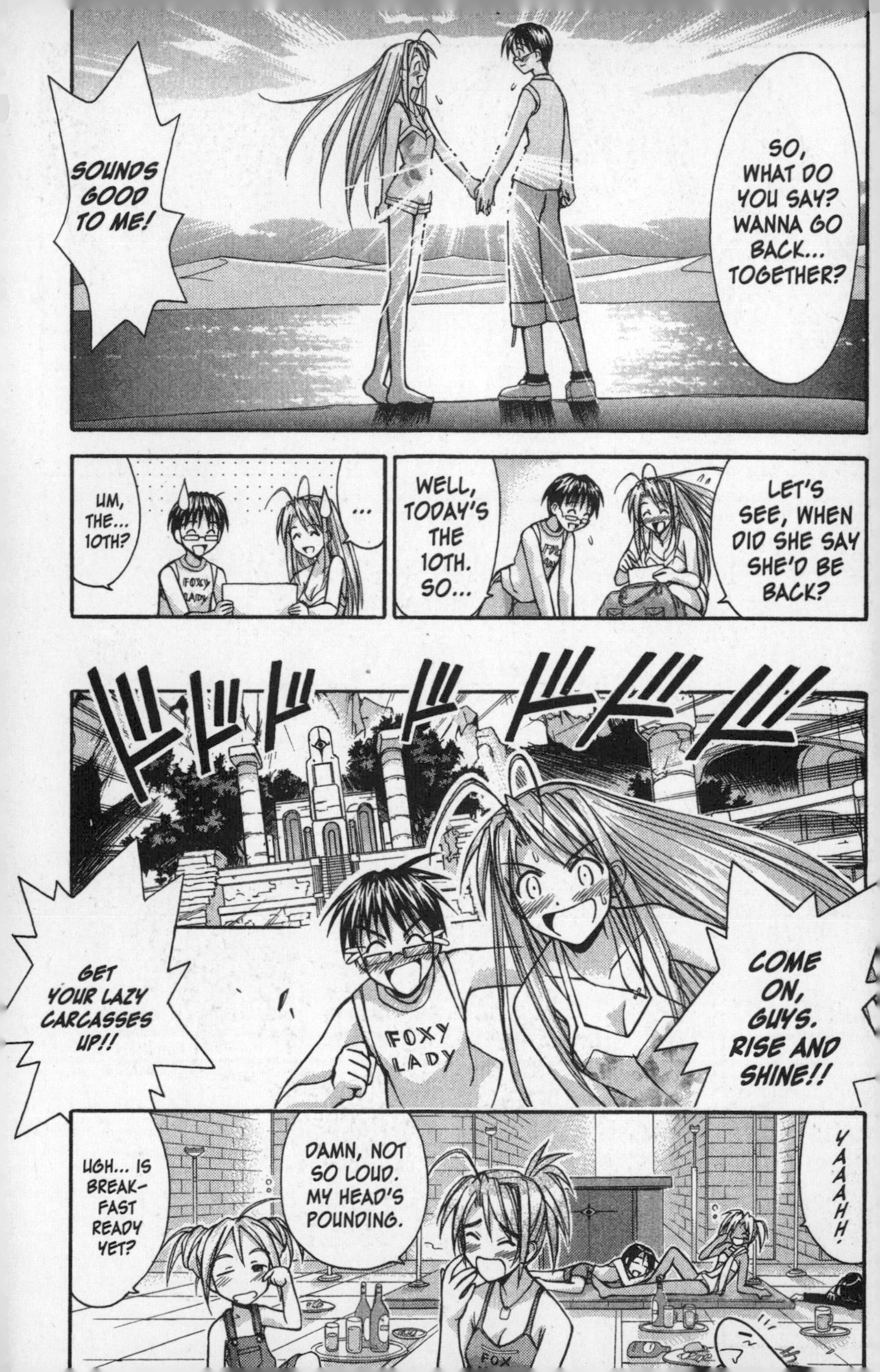
SO, WHAT DO YOU SAY? WANNA GO BACK... TOGETHER?
SOUNDS GOOD TO ME!
LET'S SEE, WHEN DID SHE SAY SHE'D BE BACK?
WELL, TODAY'S THE 10TH. SO...
...
UM, THE... 10TH?
FOXY LADY
ドドド ド ドドドド
COME ON, GUYS. RISE AND SHINE!!
GET YOUR LAZY CARCASSES UP!!
FOXY LADY
YAAAHH!
DAMN, NOT SO LOUD. MY HEAD'S POUNDING.
UGH... IS BREAK-FAST READY YET?

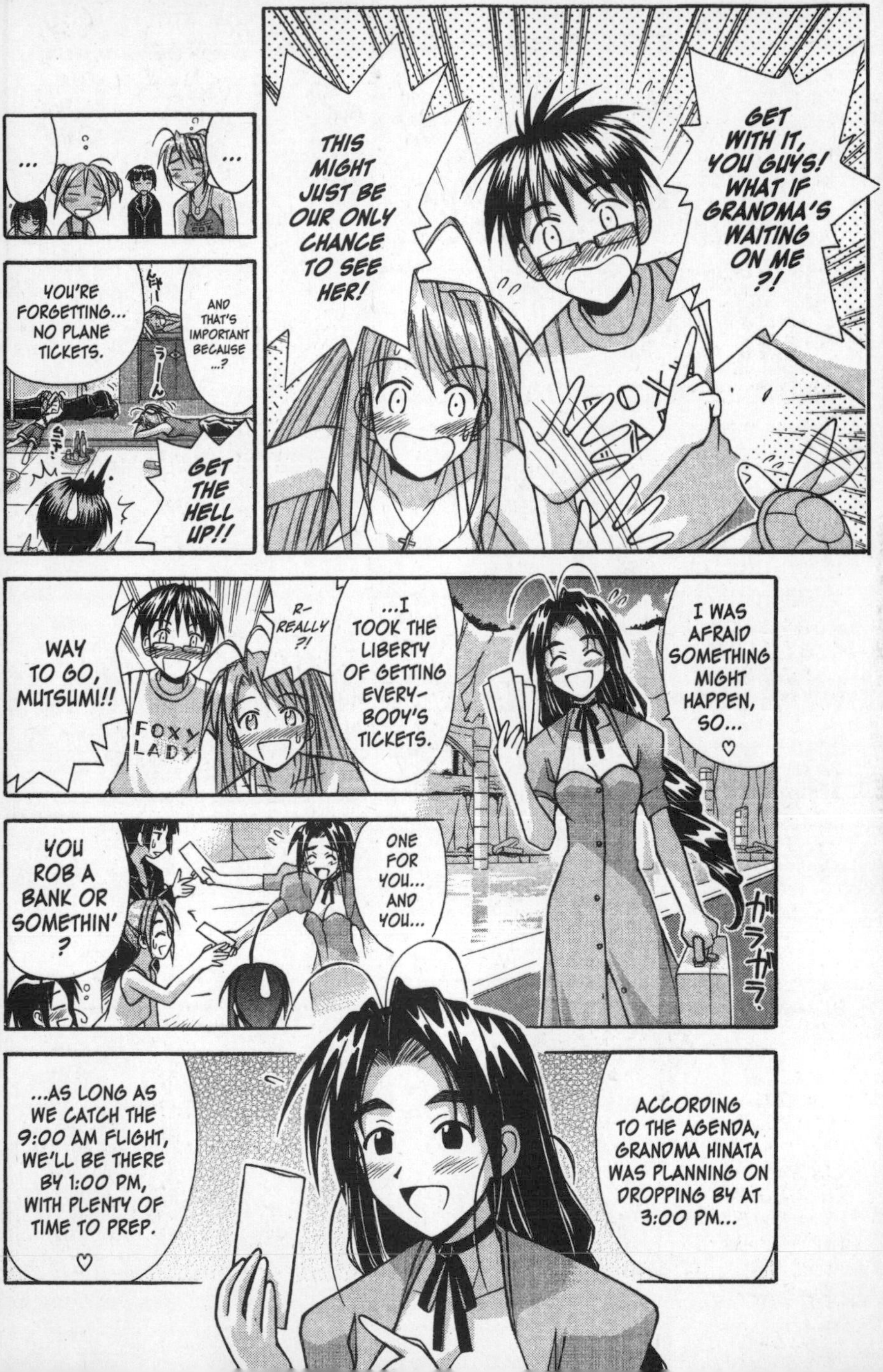
GET WITH IT, YOU GUYS! WHAT IF GRANDMA'S WAITING ON ME ?!
THIS MIGHT JUST BE OUR ONLY CHANCE TO SEE HER!
...
...
AND THAT'S IMPORTANT BECAUSE ...?
YOU'RE FORGETTING... NO PLANE TICKETS.
GET THE HELL UP!!
I WAS AFRAID SOMETHING MIGHT HAPPEN, SO... ♡
...I TOOK THE LIBERTY OF GETTING EVERYBODY'S TICKETS.
R-REALLY ?!
WAY TO GO, MUTSUMI!!
ガラガラ
ONE FOR YOU... AND YOU...
YOU ROB A BANK OR SOMETHIN' ?
ACCORDING TO THE AGENDA, GRANDMA HINATA WAS PLANNING ON DROPPING BY AT 3:00 PM...
...AS LONG AS WE CATCH THE 9:00 AM FLIGHT, WE'LL BE THERE BY 1:00 PM, WITH PLENTY OF TIME TO PREP. ♡

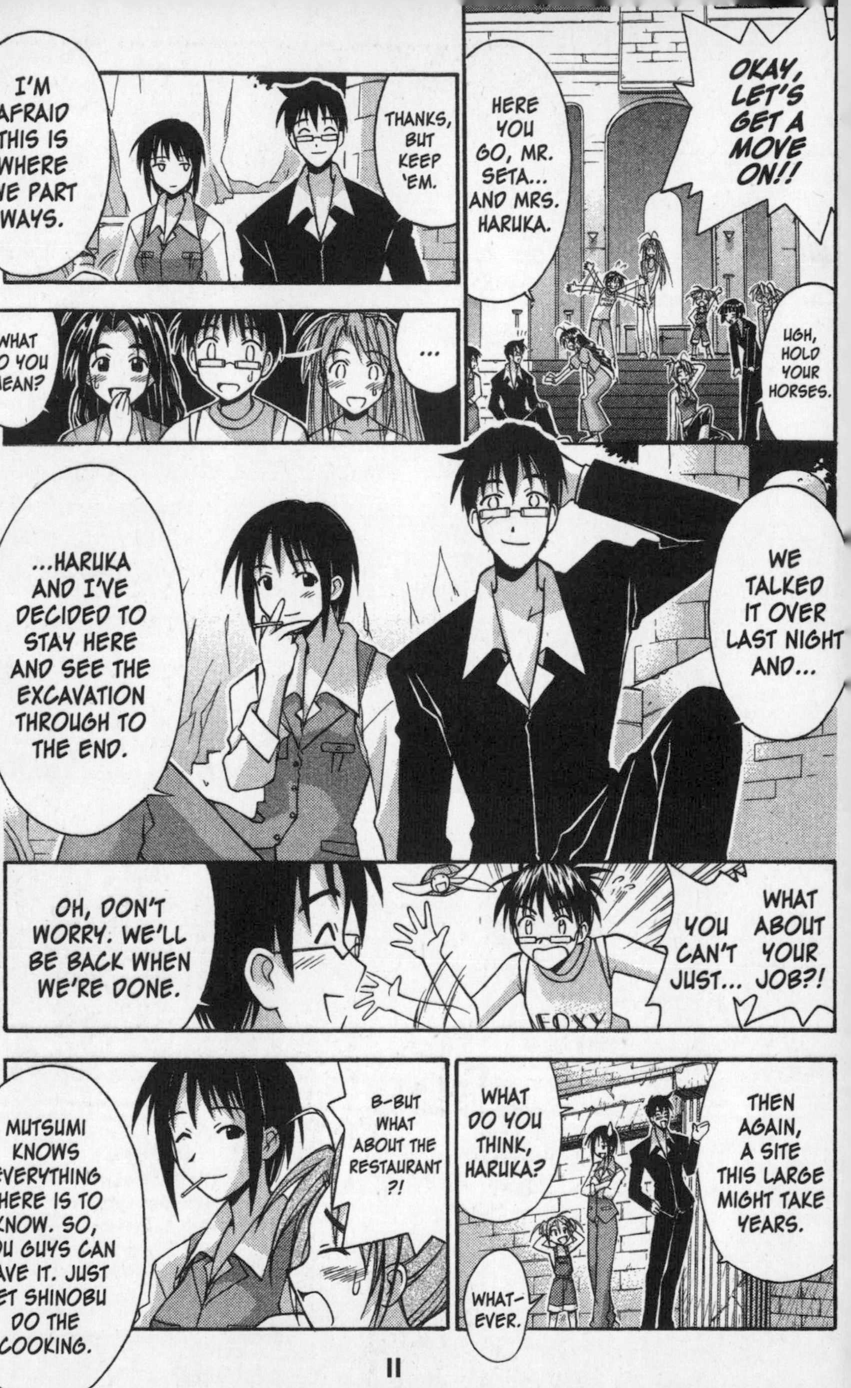
OKAY, LET'S GET A MOVE ON!!
HERE YOU GO, MR. SETA... AND MRS. HARUKA.
UGH, HOLD YOUR HORSES.
THANKS, BUT KEEP 'EM.
I'M AFRAID THIS IS WHERE WE PART WAYS.
...
WHAT DO YOU MEAN?
WE TALKED IT OVER LAST NIGHT AND...
...HARUKA AND I'VE DECIDED TO STAY HERE AND SEE THE EXCAVATION THROUGH TO THE END.
WHAT ABOUT YOUR JOB?!
YOU CAN'T JUST...
FOXY
OH, DON'T WORRY. WE'LL BE BACK WHEN WE'RE DONE.
THEN AGAIN, A SITE THIS LARGE MIGHT TAKE YEARS.
WHAT DO YOU THINK, HARUKA?
WHAT-EVER.
B-BUT WHAT ABOUT THE RESTAURANT?!
MUTSUMI KNOWS EVERYTHING THERE IS TO KNOW. SO, YOU GUYS CAN HAVE IT. JUST LET SHINOBU DO THE COOKING.

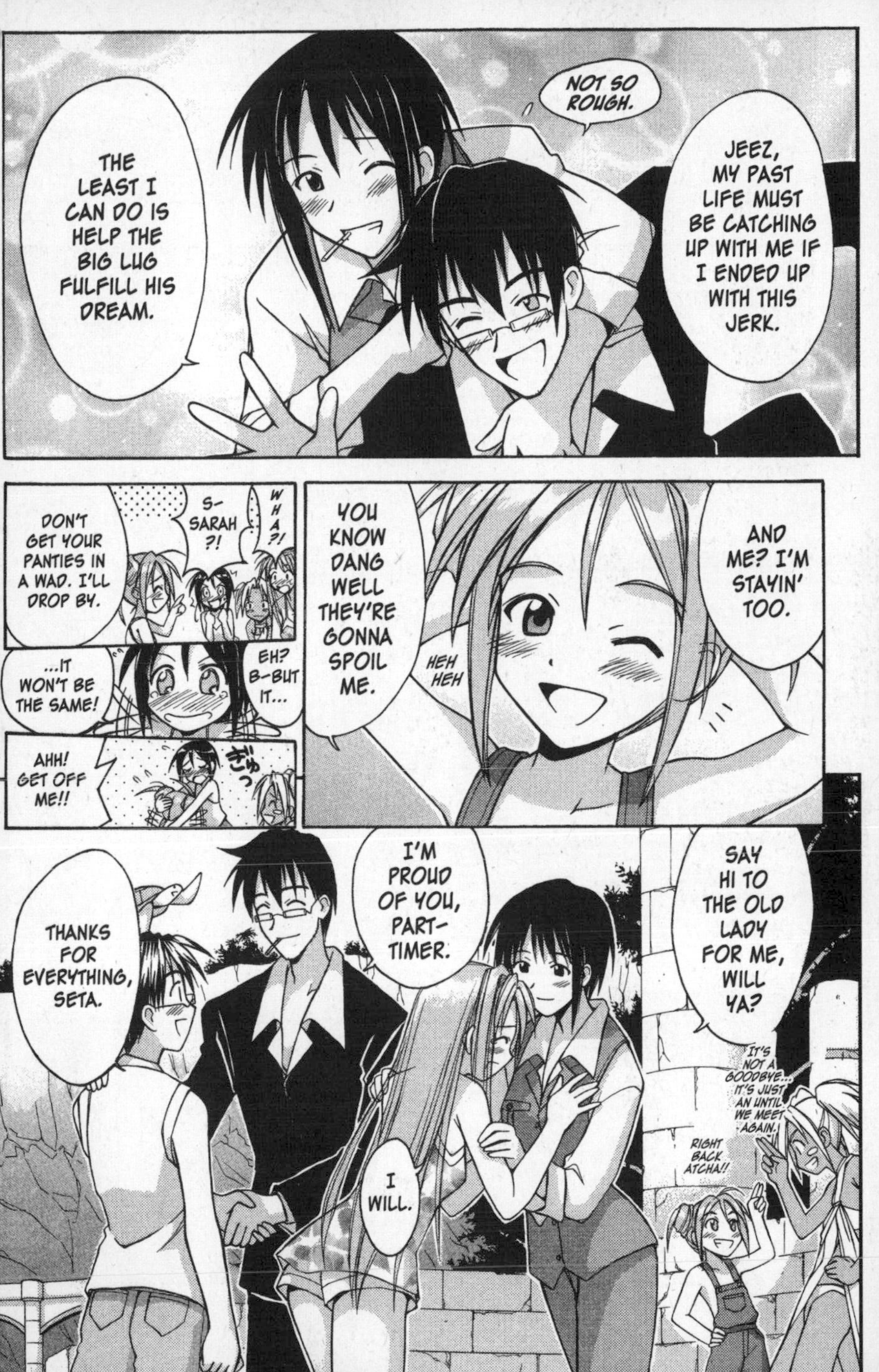
JEEZ, MY PAST LIFE MUST BE CATCHING UP WITH ME IF I ENDED UP WITH THIS JERK.
NOT SO ROUGH.
THE LEAST I CAN DO IS HELP THE BIG LUG FULFILL HIS DREAM.
AND ME? I'M STAYIN' TOO.
HEH HEH
YOU KNOW DANG WELL THEY'RE GONNA SPOIL ME.
WHA?!
S-SARAH?!
DON'T GET YOUR PANTIES IN A WAD. I'LL DROP BY.
EH? B-BUT IT...
...IT WON'T BE THE SAME!
ぎゅっ
AHH! GET OFF ME!!
SAY HI TO THE OLD LADY FOR ME, WILL YA?
IT'S NOT A GOODBYE... IT'S JUST AN UNTIL WE MEET AGAIN.
RIGHT BACK ATCHA!!
I WILL.
I'M PROUD OF YOU, PART-TIMER.
THANKS FOR EVERYTHING, SETA.

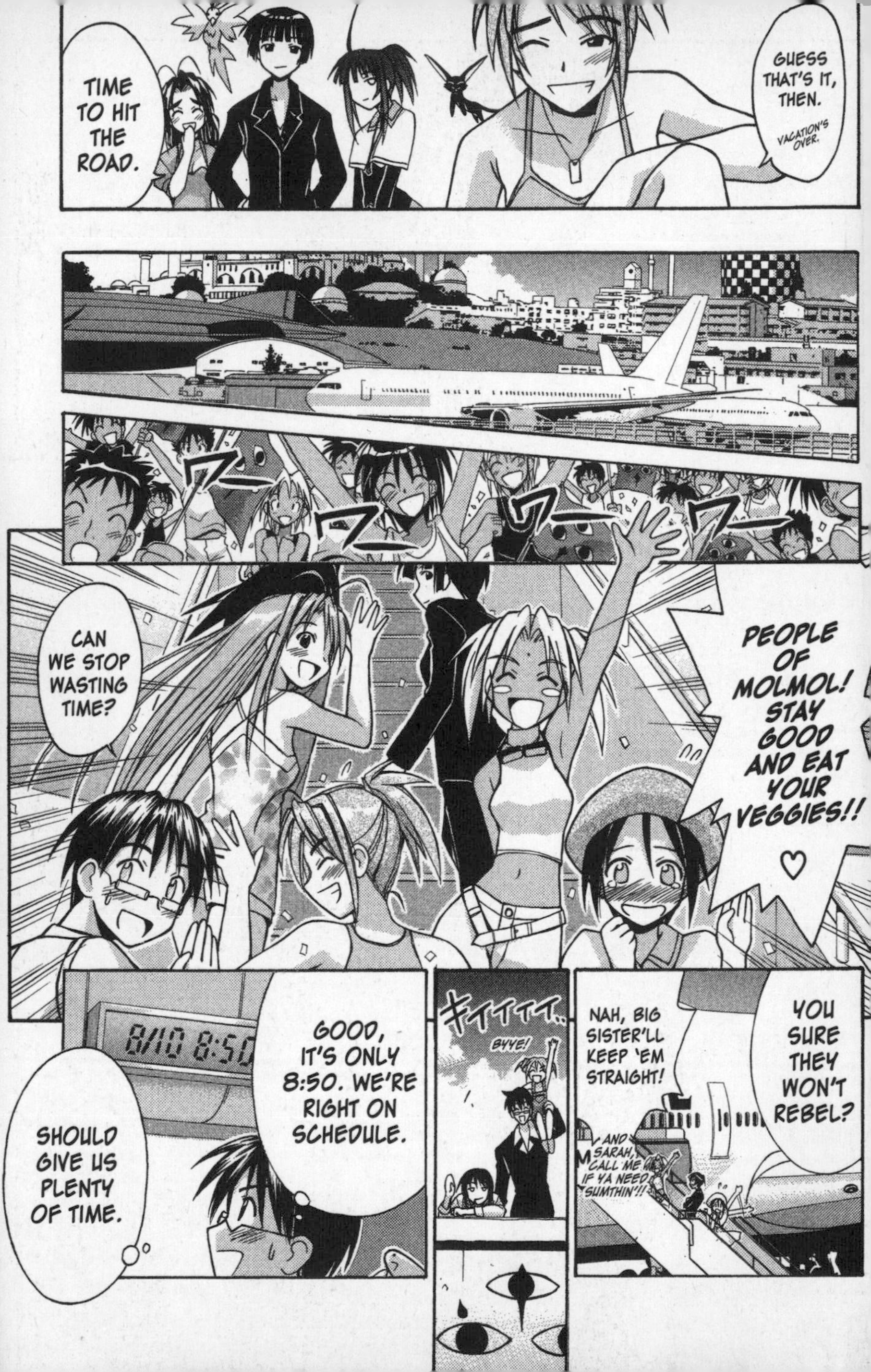
GUESS THAT'S IT, THEN.
VACATION'S OVER.
TIME TO HIT THE ROAD.
ワー
ワー
ワー
ワー
PEOPLE OF MOLMOL! STAY GOOD AND EAT YOUR VEGGIES!! ♡
CAN WE STOP WASTING TIME?
YOU SURE THEY WON'T REBEL?
NAH, BIG SISTER'LL KEEP 'EM STRAIGHT!
AND SARAH, CALL ME IF YA NEED SUMTHIN'!!
キイイイイ..
BYYE!
8/10 8:5
GOOD, IT'S ONLY 8:50. WE'RE RIGHT ON SCHEDULE.
SHOULD GIVE US PLENTY OF TIME.

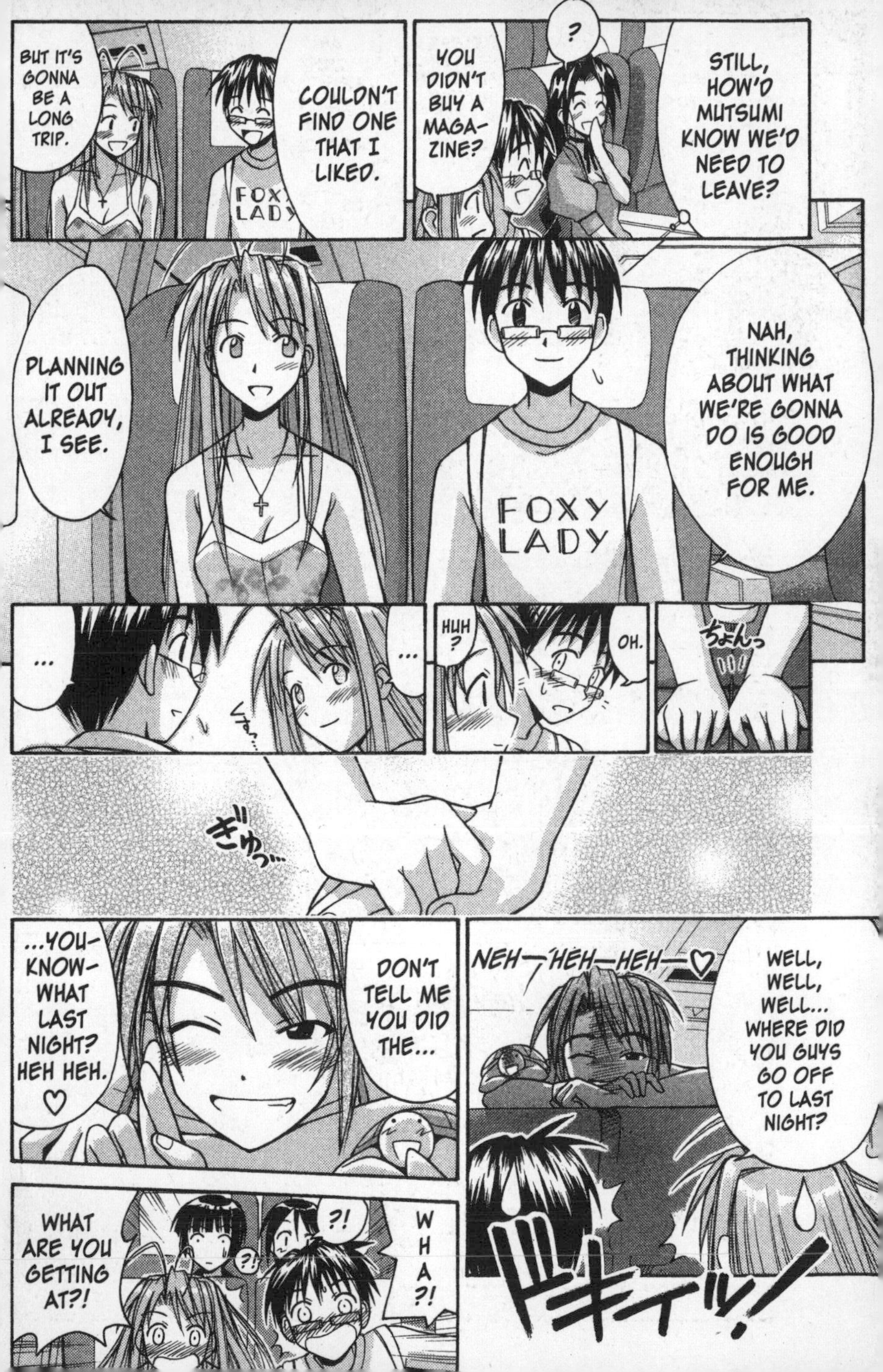
STILL, HOW'D MUTSUMI KNOW WE'D NEED TO LEAVE?
?
YOU DIDN'T BUY A MAGA-ZINE?
COULDN'T FIND ONE THAT I LIKED.
BUT IT'S GONNA BE A LONG TRIP.
NAH, THINKING ABOUT WHAT WE'RE GONNA DO IS GOOD ENOUGH FOR ME.
PLANNING IT OUT ALREADY, I SEE.
ちょんっ
OH.
HUH?
...
...
ぎゅっ...
WELL, WELL, WELL... WHERE DID YOU GUYS GO OFF TO LAST NIGHT?
NEH—HEH—HEH—♡
ドキィッ!
DON'T TELL ME YOU DID THE...
...YOU-KNOW-WHAT LAST NIGHT? HEH HEH. ♡
WHA?!
?!
?!
WHAT ARE YOU GETTING AT?!

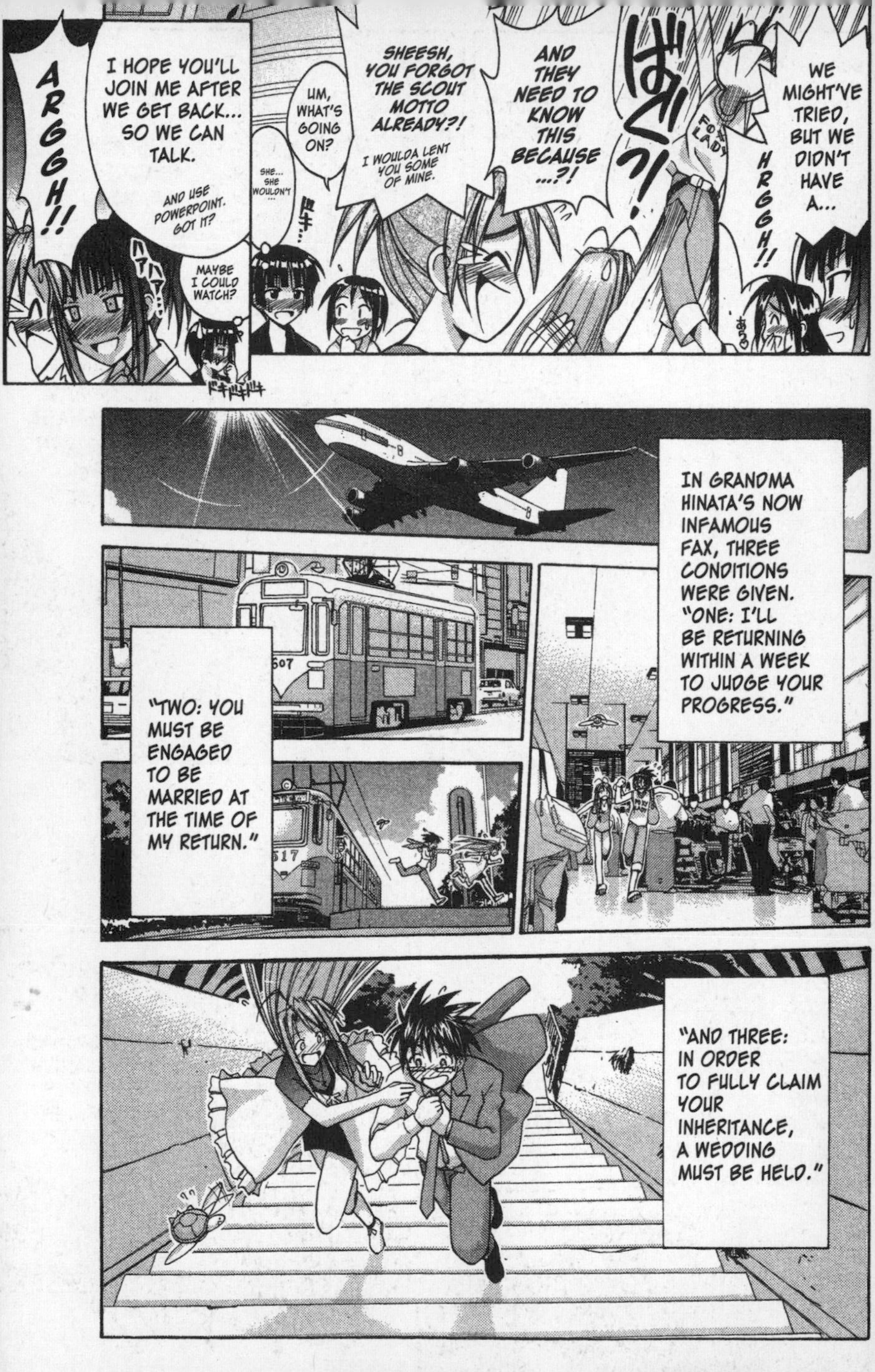

WE MIGHT'VE TRIED, BUT WE DIDN'T HAVE A...
HRGGH!!
AND THEY NEED TO KNOW THIS BECAUSE...?!
SHEESH, YOU FORGOT THE SCOUT MOTTO ALREADY?!
I WOULDA LENT YOU SOME OF MINE.
UM, WHAT'S GOING ON?
SHE... SHE WOULDN'T ...
I HOPE YOU'LL JOIN ME AFTER WE GET BACK... SO WE CAN TALK.
AND USE POWERPOINT. GOT IT?
MAYBE I COULD WATCH?
ARGGGH!!
IN GRANDMA HINATA'S NOW INFAMOUS FAX, THREE CONDITIONS WERE GIVEN. "ONE: I'LL BE RETURNING WITHIN A WEEK TO JUDGE YOUR PROGRESS."
"TWO: YOU MUST BE ENGAGED TO BE MARRIED AT THE TIME OF MY RETURN."
"AND THREE: IN ORDER TO FULLY CLAIM YOUR INHERITANCE, A WEDDING MUST BE HELD."

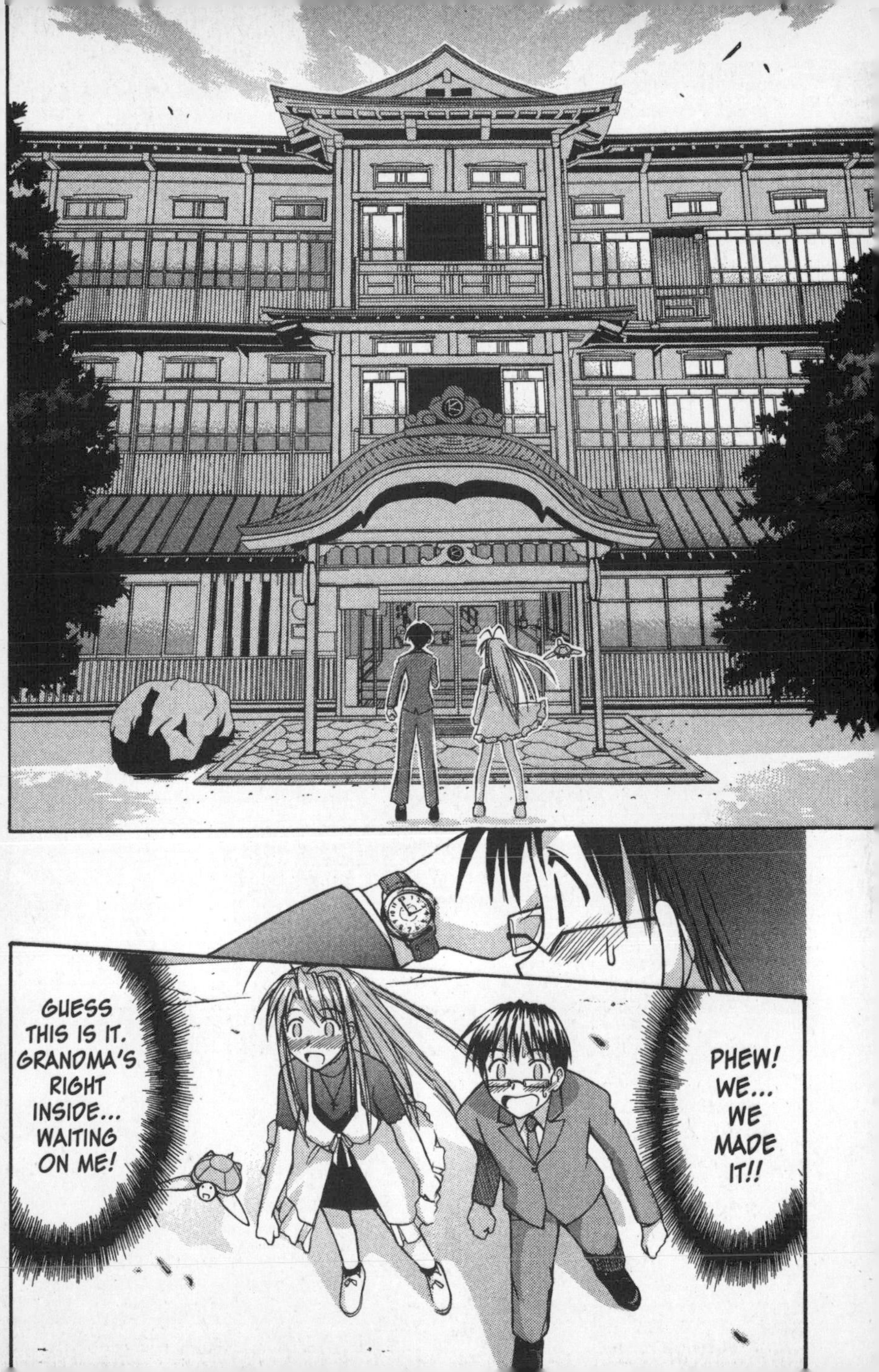
PHEW! WE... WE MADE IT!!
GUESS THIS IS IT. GRANDMA'S RIGHT INSIDE... WAITING ON ME!

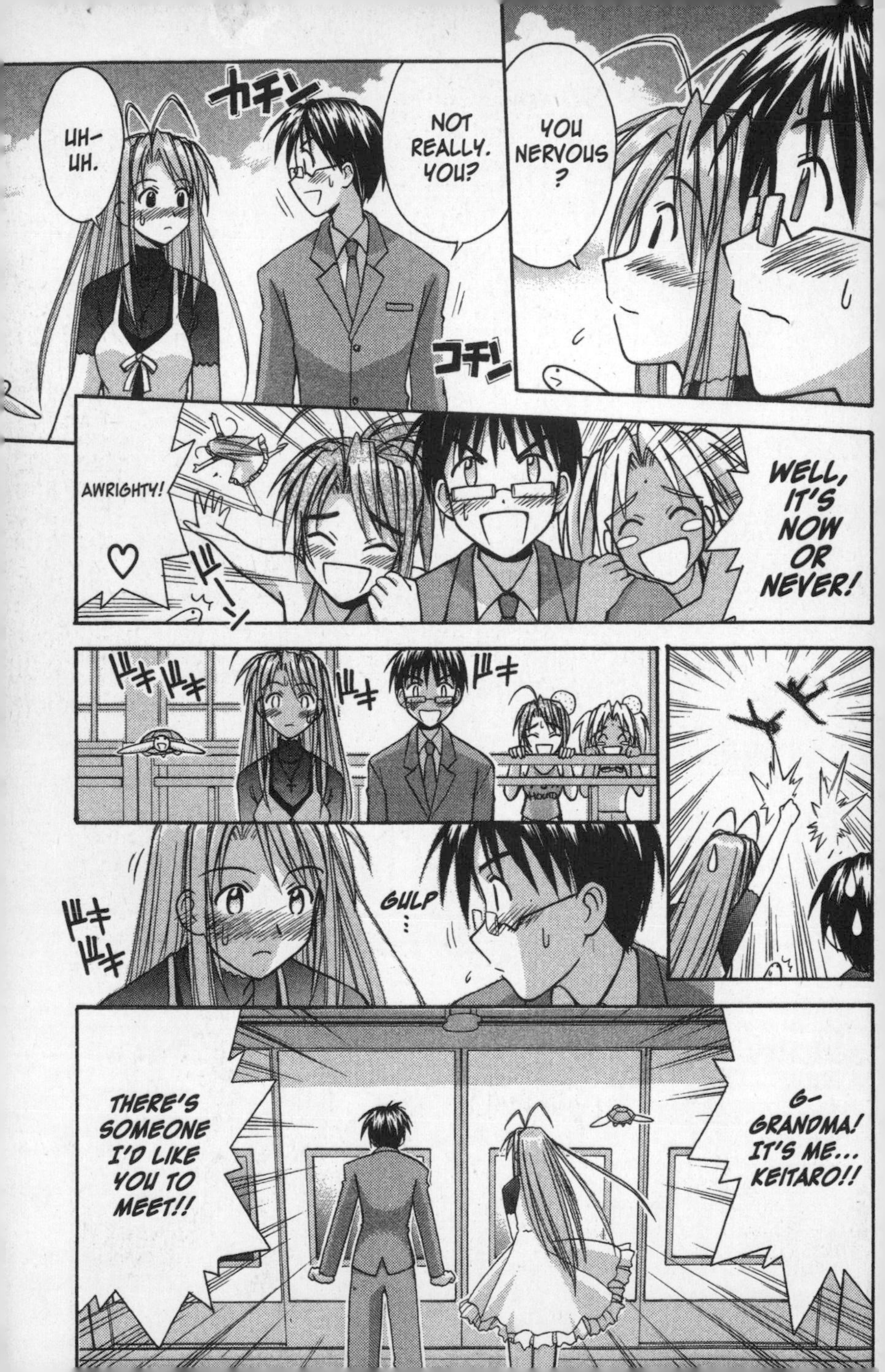
YOU NERVOUS ?
NOT REALLY. YOU?
カチン
UH-UH.
コチン
WELL, IT'S NOW OR NEVER!
AWRIGHTY!
ドーン
ドキ
ドキドキ
GULP...
ドキ ドキ
G-GRANDMA! IT'S ME... KEITARO!!
THERE'S SOMEONE I'D LIKE YOU TO MEET!!

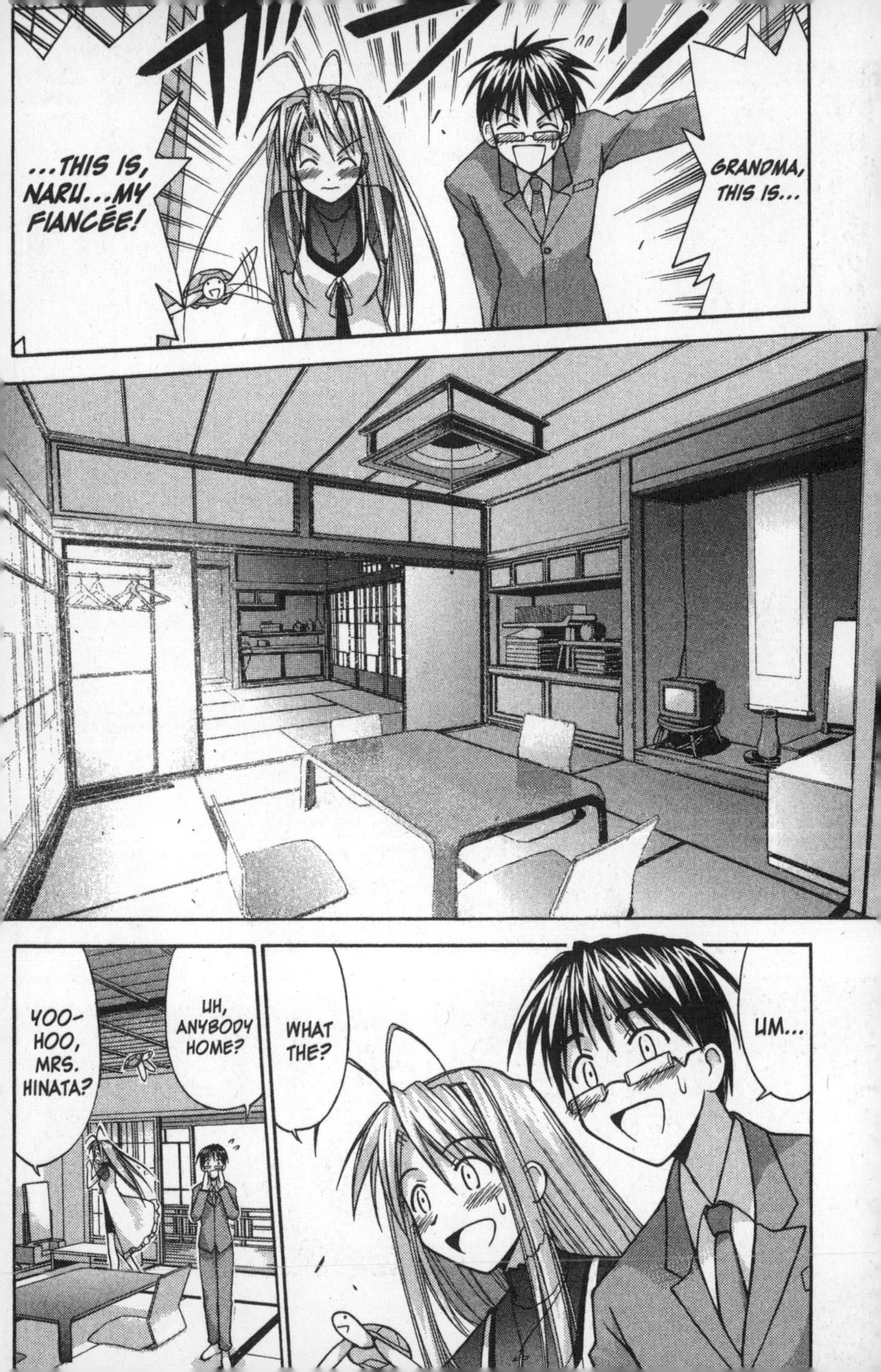
GRANDMA, THIS IS...
...THIS IS, NARU...MY FIANCÉE!
UM...
WHAT THE?
UH, ANYBODY HOME?
YOO-HOO, MRS. HINATA?

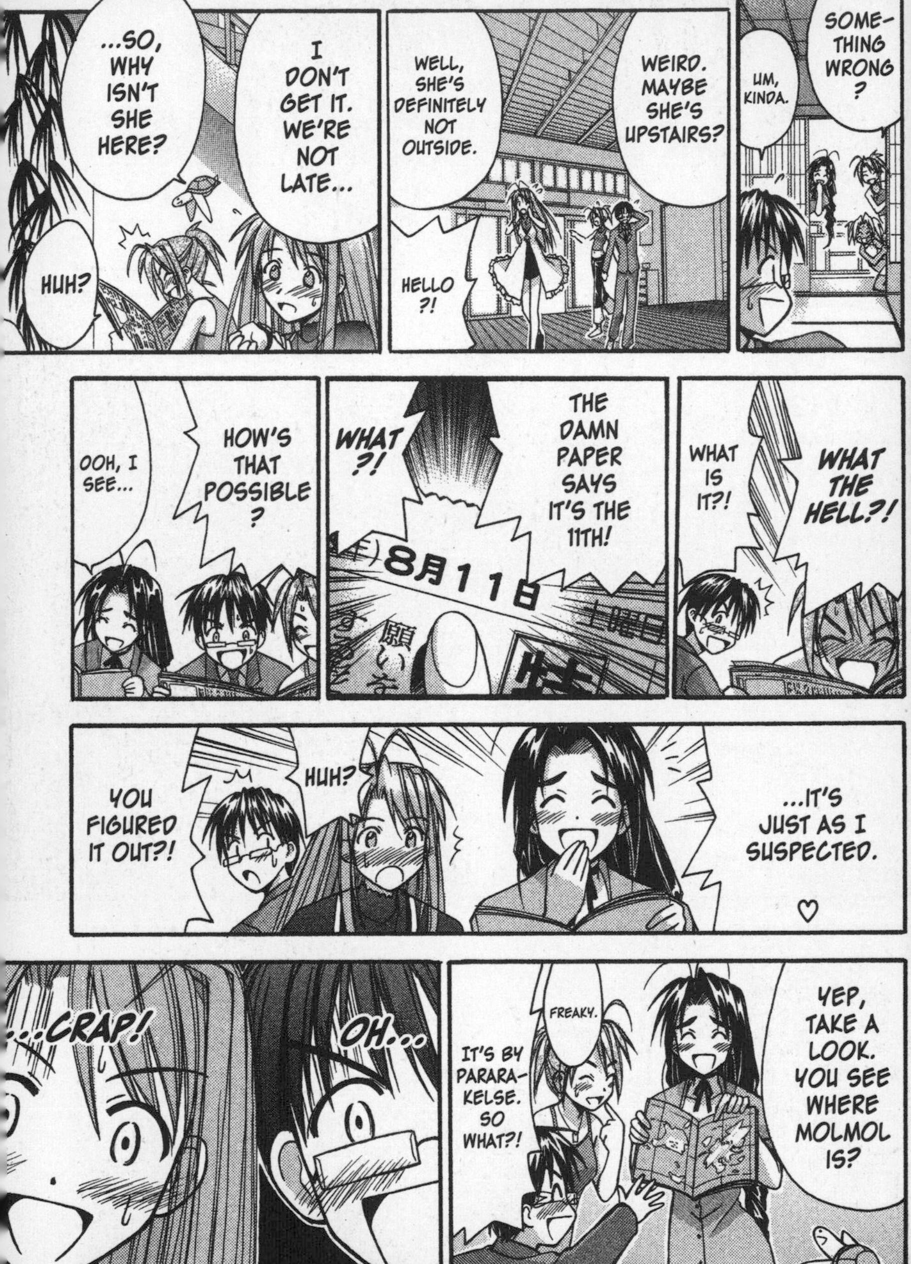
SOME-THING WRONG?
UM, KINDA.
WEIRD. MAYBE SHE'S UPSTAIRS?
WELL, SHE'S DEFINITELY NOT OUTSIDE.
HELLO?!
I DON'T GET IT. WE'RE NOT LATE...
...SO, WHY ISN'T SHE HERE?
HUH?
WHAT THE HELL?!
WHAT IS IT?!
THE DAMN PAPER SAYS IT'S THE 11TH!
WHAT?!
8月11日
HOW'S THAT POSSIBLE?
OOH, I SEE...
...IT'S JUST AS I SUSPECTED. ♡
HUH?
YOU FIGURED IT OUT?!
YEP, TAKE A LOOK. YOU SEE WHERE MOLMOL IS?
FREAKY.
IT'S BY PARARA-KELSE. SO WHAT?!
OH...
...CRAP!

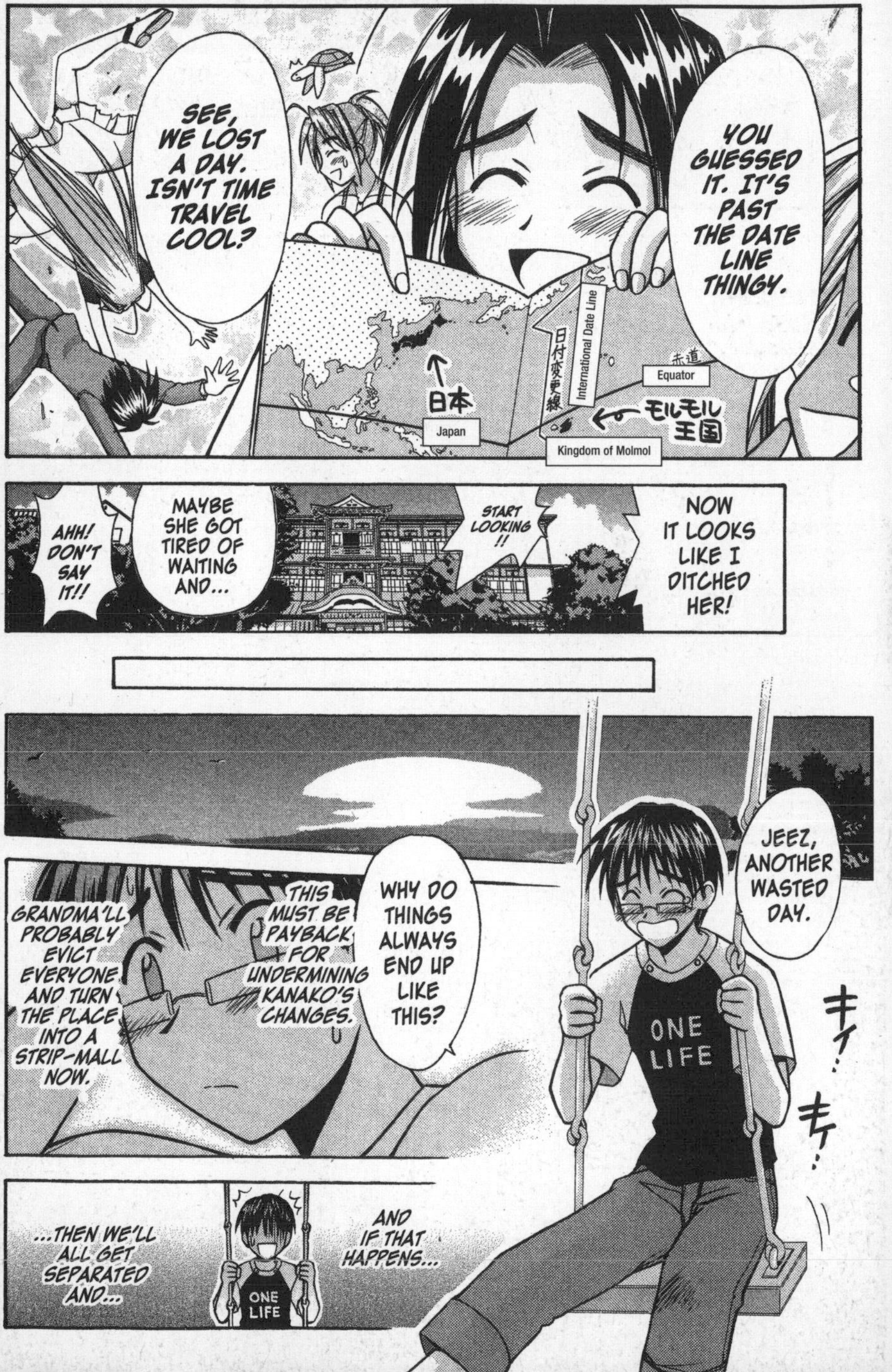
YOU GUESSED IT. IT'S PAST THE DATE LINE THINGY.
SEE, WE LOST A DAY. ISN'T TIME TRAVEL COOL?
日付変更線
International Date Line
赤道
Equator
日本
Japan
モルモル王国
Kingdom of Molmol
NOW IT LOOKS LIKE I DITCHED HER!
START LOOKING !!
MAYBE SHE GOT TIRED OF WAITING AND...
AHH! DON'T SAY IT!!
JEEZ, ANOTHER WASTED DAY.
キィ…
キィ…
ONE LIFE
WHY DO THINGS ALWAYS END UP LIKE THIS?
THIS MUST BE PAYBACK FOR UNDERMINING KANAKO'S CHANGES.
GRANDMA'LL PROBABLY EVICT EVERYONE AND TURN THE PLACE INTO A STRIP-MALL NOW.
AND IF THAT HAPPENS...
...THEN WE'LL ALL GET SEPARATED AND...
ONE LIFE

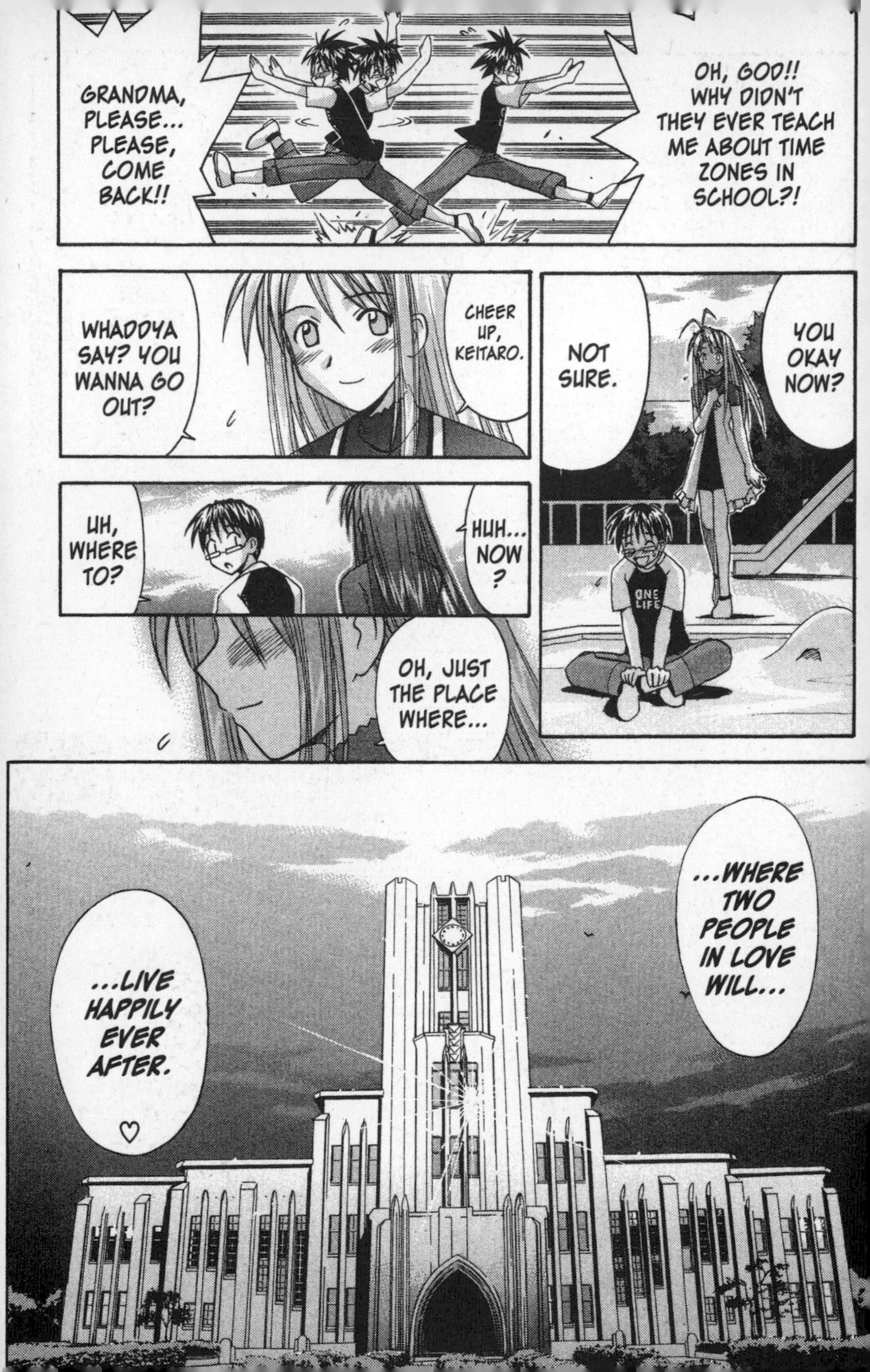
OH, GOD!! WHY DIDN'T THEY EVER TEACH ME ABOUT TIME ZONES IN SCHOOL?!
GRANDMA, PLEASE... PLEASE, COME BACK!!
YOU OKAY NOW?
NOT SURE.
CHEER UP, KEITARO.
WHADDYA SAY? YOU WANNA GO OUT?
HUH... NOW?
UH, WHERE TO?
OH, JUST THE PLACE WHERE...
...WHERE TWO PEOPLE IN LOVE WILL...
...LIVE HAPPILY EVER AFTER. ♡

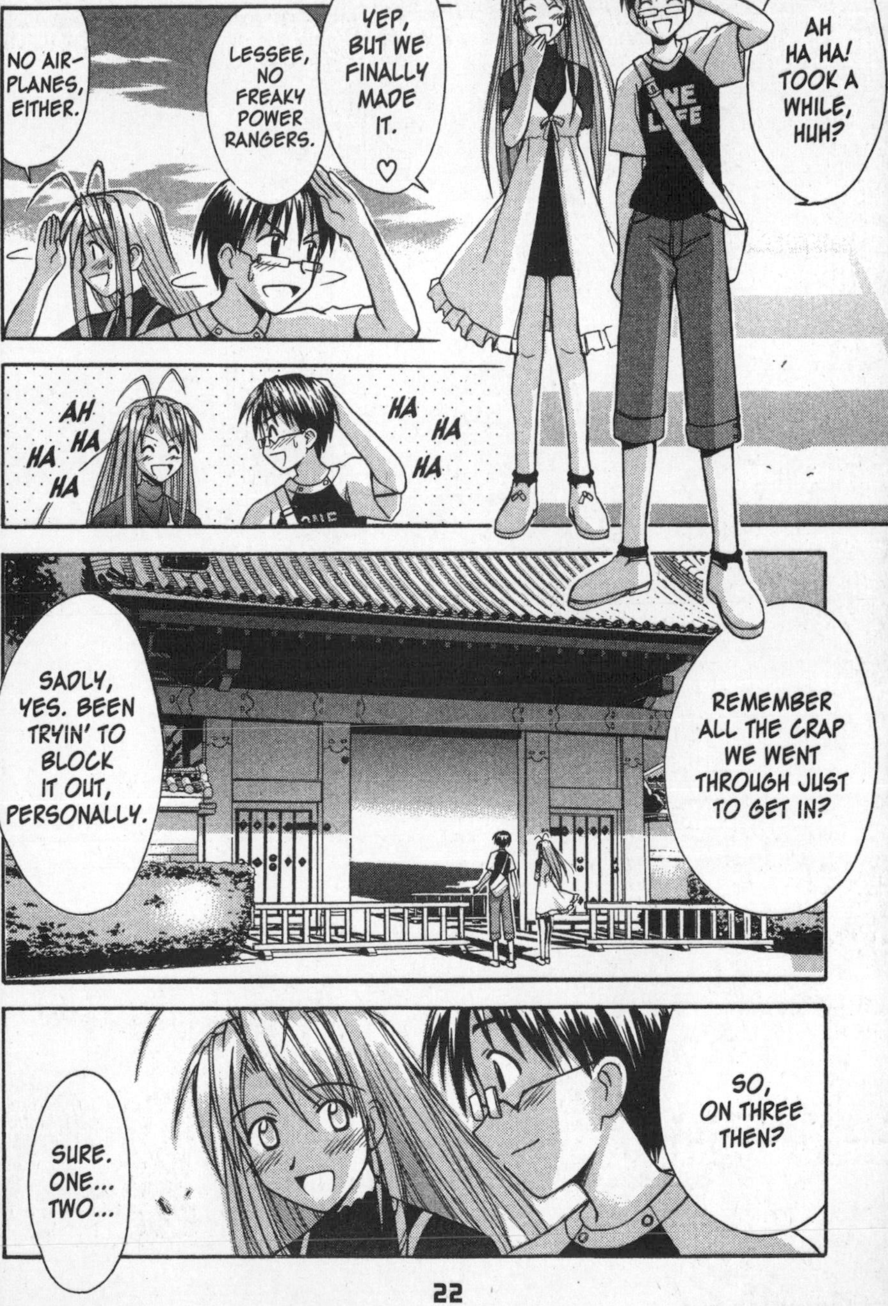
AH HA HA! TOOK A WHILE, HUH?
YEP, BUT WE FINALLY MADE IT. ♡
LESSEE, NO FREAKY POWER RANGERS.
NO AIR-PLANES, EITHER.
HA HA HA
AH HA HA HA
REMEMBER ALL THE CRAP WE WENT THROUGH JUST TO GET IN?
SADLY, YES. BEEN TRYIN' TO BLOCK IT OUT, PERSONALLY.
SO, ON THREE THEN?
SURE. ONE... TWO...

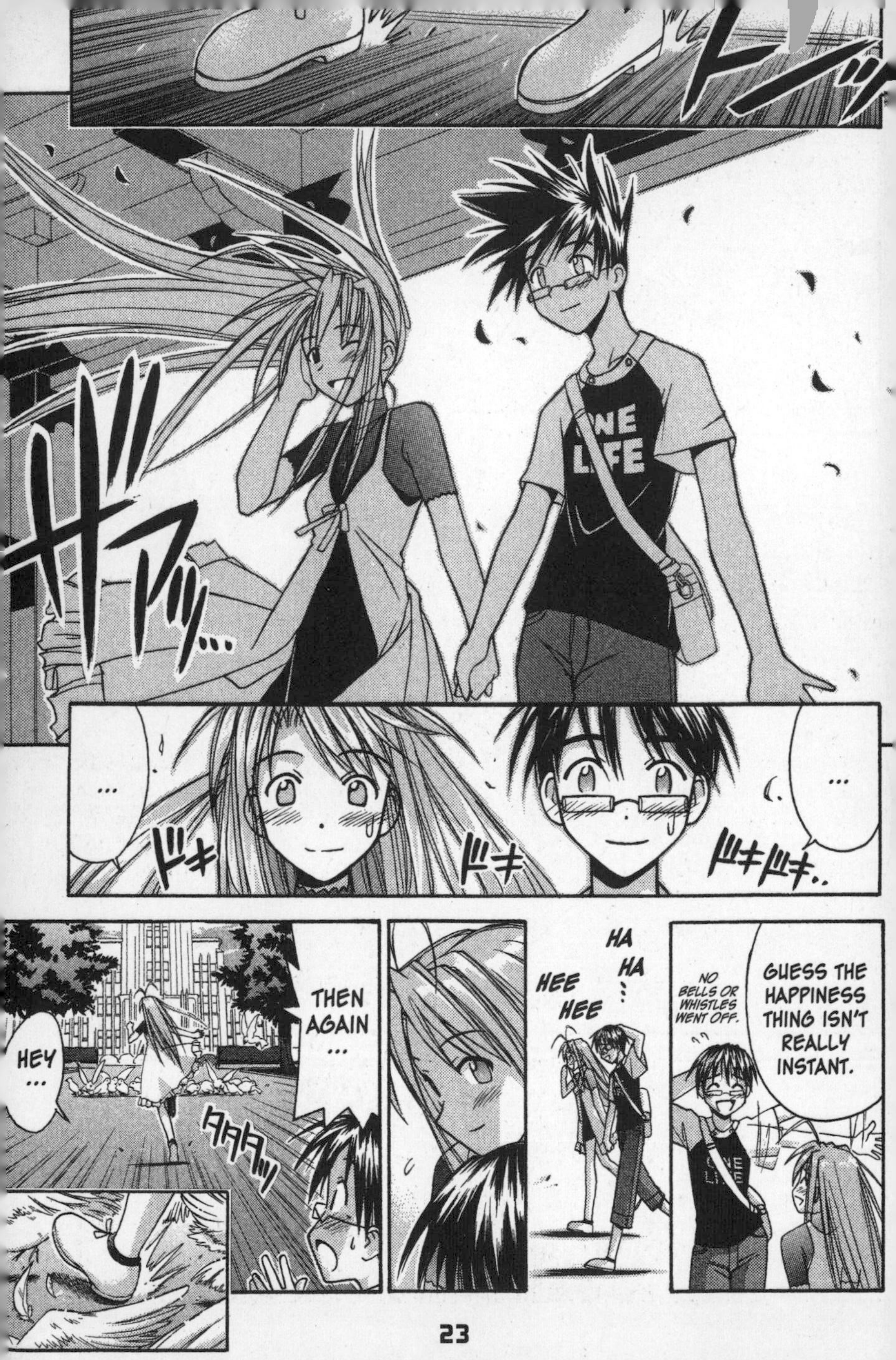

トンッ
ザァッ...
...
ドキドキ..
ドキ
ドキ
...
GUESS THE HAPPINESS THING ISN'T REALLY INSTANT.
NO BELLS OR WHISTLES WENT OFF.
HA HA
HEE HEE
THEN AGAIN ...
タタタッ
HEY ...

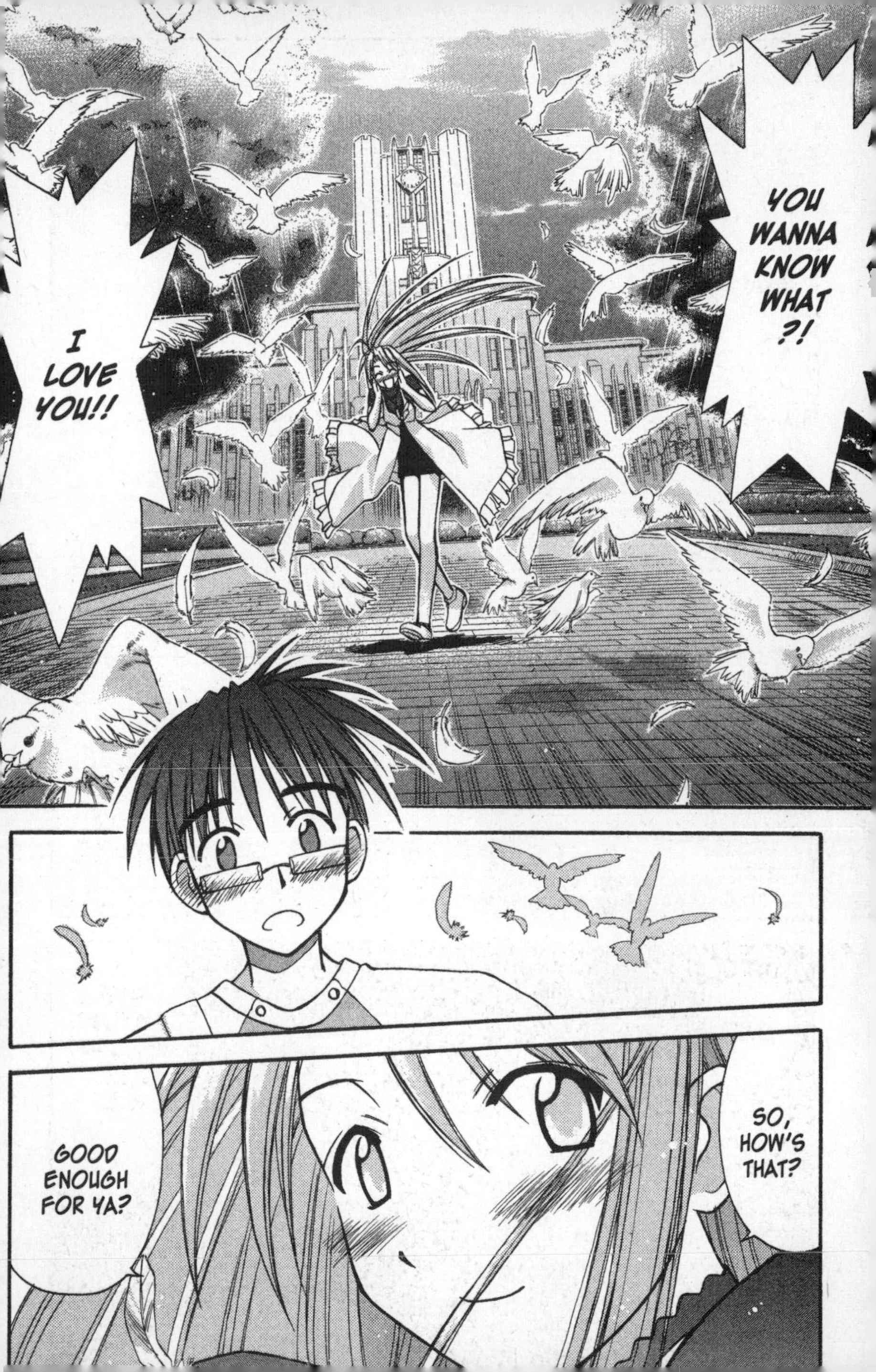
YOU WANNA KNOW WHAT?!
I LOVE YOU!!
SO, HOW'S THAT?
GOOD ENOUGH FOR YA?

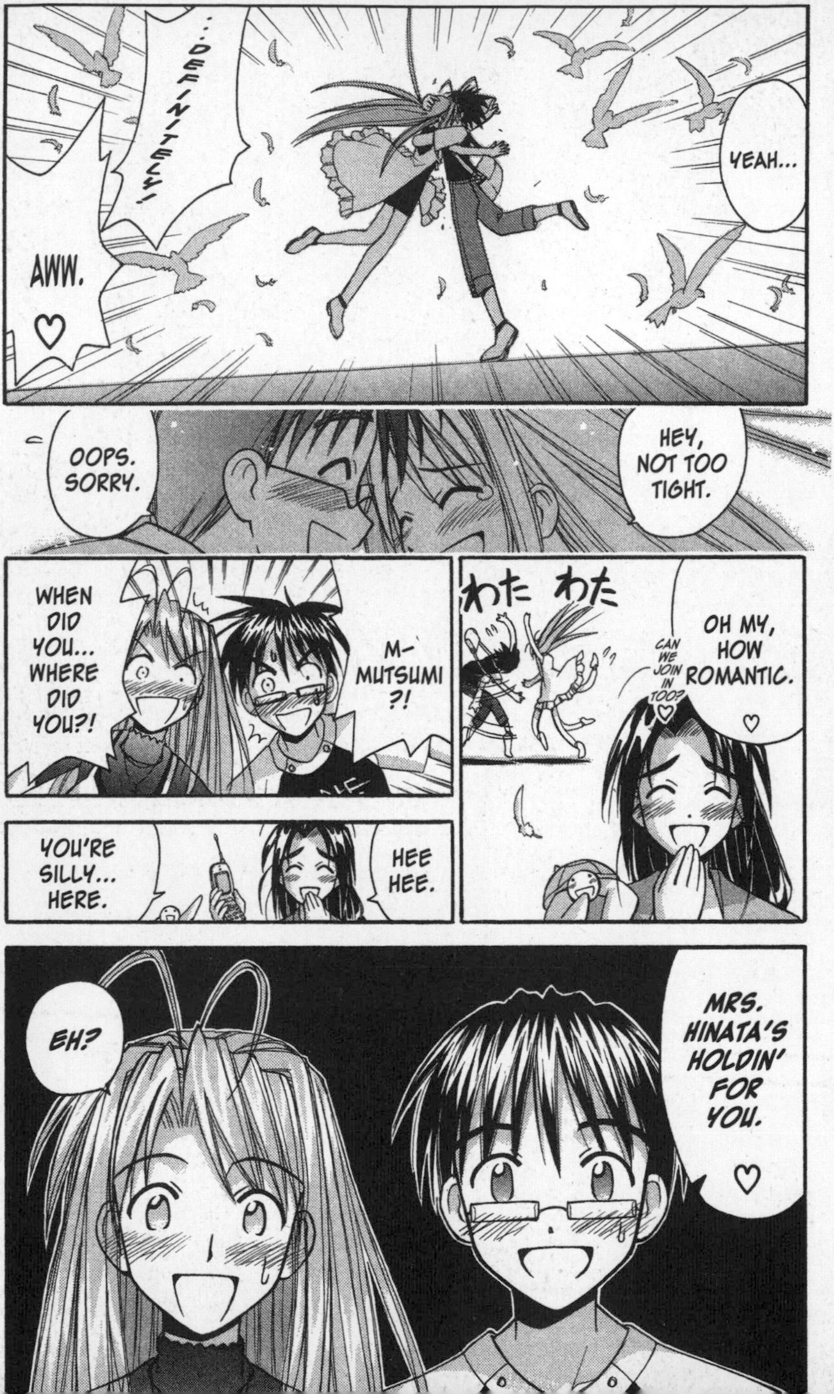
YEAH...
...DEFINITELY!
AWW. ♡
HEY, NOT TOO TIGHT.
OOPS. SORRY.
OH MY, HOW ROMANTIC. ♡
わた わた
CAN WE JOIN IN TOO? ♡
M-MUTSUMI?!
WHEN DID YOU... WHERE DID YOU?!
HEE HEE.
YOU'RE SILLY... HERE.
MRS. HINATA'S HOLDIN' FOR YOU. ♡
EH?

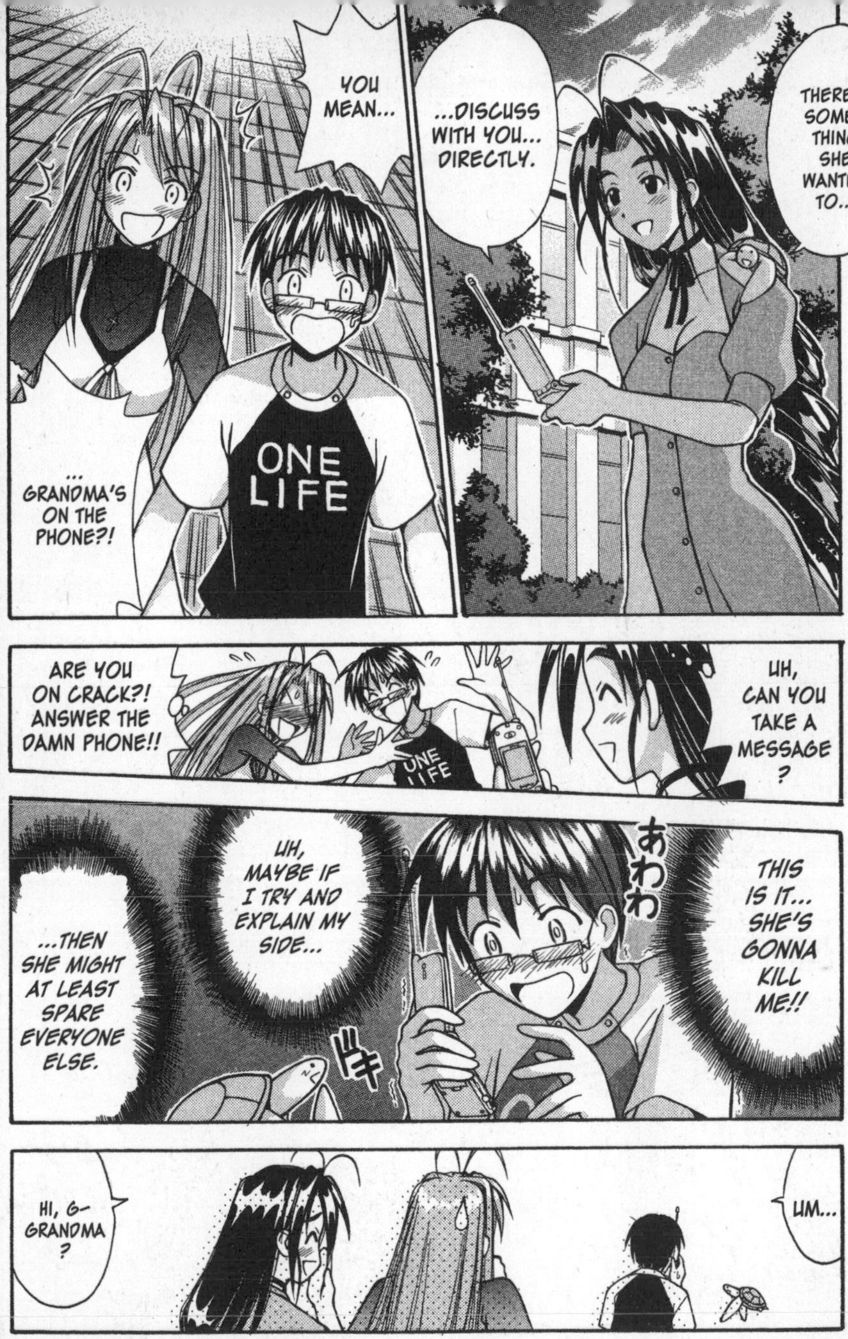
THERE'S SOME-THING SHE WANTED TO...
...DISCUSS WITH YOU... DIRECTLY.
YOU MEAN...
...GRANDMA'S ON THE PHONE?!
ONE LIFE
UH, CAN YOU TAKE A MESSAGE ?
ARE YOU ON CRACK?! ANSWER THE DAMN PHONE!!
ONE LIFE
THIS IS IT... SHE'S GONNA KILL ME!!
あわわ
UH, MAYBE IF I TRY AND EXPLAIN MY SIDE...
...THEN SHE MIGHT AT LEAST SPARE EVERYONE ELSE.
ドキ
UM...
HI, G-GRANDMA ?

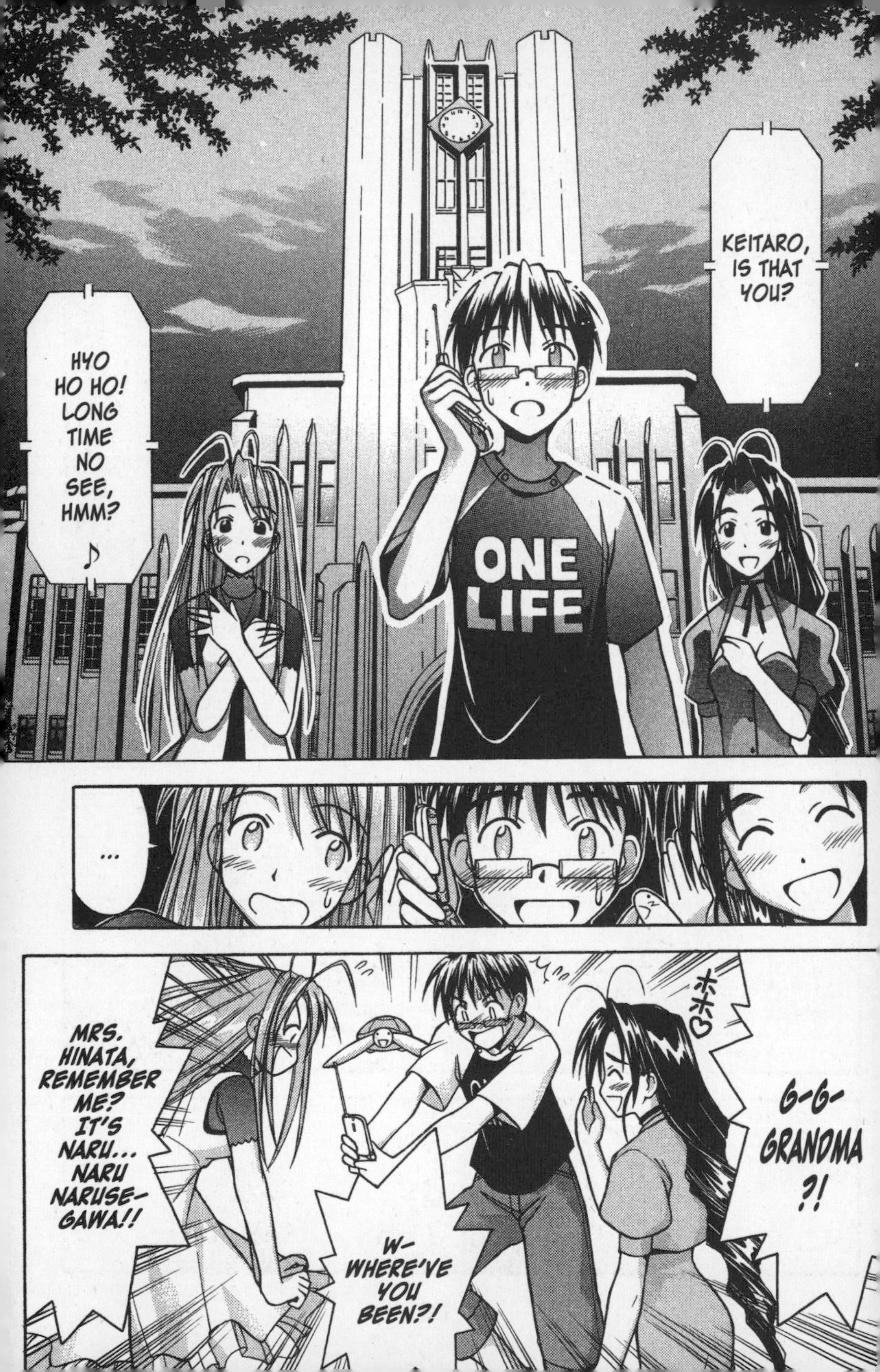
KEITARO, IS THAT YOU?
HYO HO HO! LONG TIME NO SEE, HMM? ♪
...
G-G-GRANDMA?!
W-WHERE'VE YOU BEEN?!
MRS. HINATA, REMEMBER ME? IT'S NARU... NARU NARUSE-GAWA!!

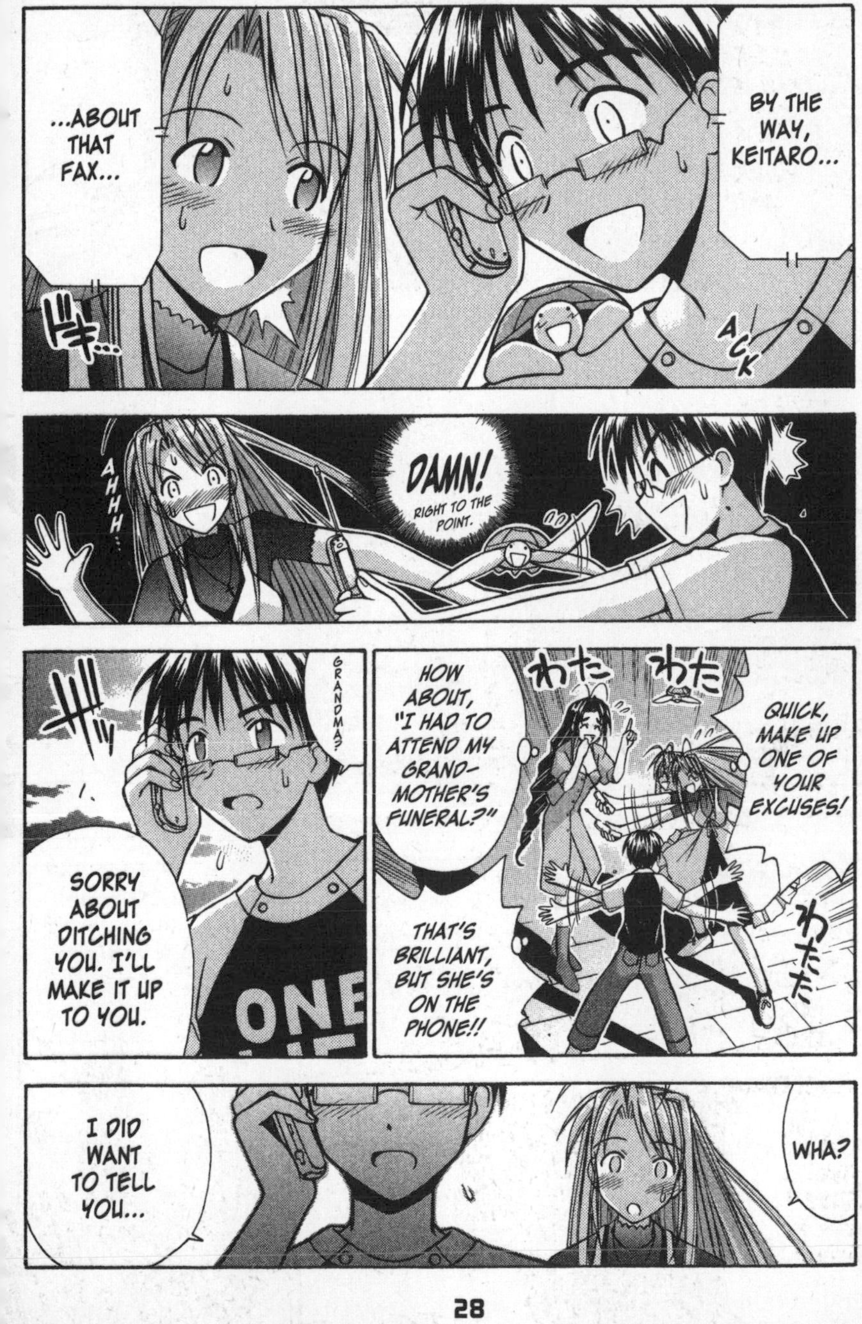
BY THE WAY, KEITARO...
ACK
...ABOUT THAT FAX...
ドキ...
DAMN!
RIGHT TO THE POINT.
AHHH...
QUICK, MAKE UP ONE OF YOUR EXCUSES!
わた わた
HOW ABOUT, "I HAD TO ATTEND MY GRAND-MOTHER'S FUNERAL?"
THAT'S BRILLIANT, BUT SHE'S ON THE PHONE!!
わたた
GRANDMA?
ガッ
SORRY ABOUT DITCHING YOU. I'LL MAKE IT UP TO YOU.
ONE
WHA?
I DID WANT TO TELL YOU...

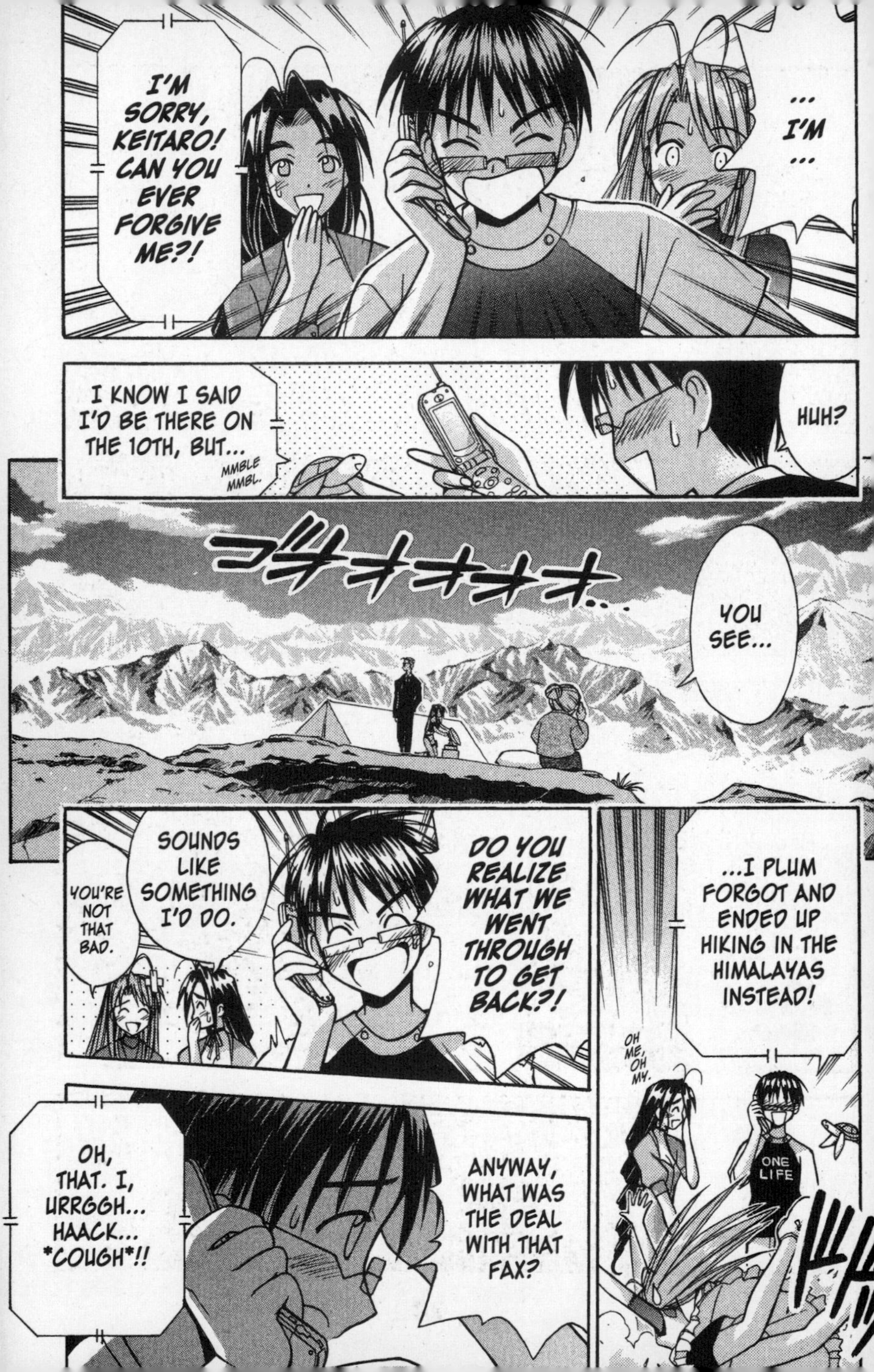

... I'M ...
I'M SORRY, KEITARO! CAN YOU EVER FORGIVE ME?!
HUH?
I KNOW I SAID I'D BE THERE ON THE 10TH, BUT...
MMBLE MMBL.
ゴサオオオオオ...
YOU SEE...
...I PLUM FORGOT AND ENDED UP HIKING IN THE HIMALAYAS INSTEAD!
OH ME, OH MY.
ONE LIFE
DO YOU REALIZE WHAT WE WENT THROUGH TO GET BACK?!
SOUNDS LIKE SOMETHING I'D DO.
YOU'RE NOT THAT BAD.
ANYWAY, WHAT WAS THE DEAL WITH THAT FAX?
OH, THAT. I, URRGGH... HAACK... *COUGH*!!

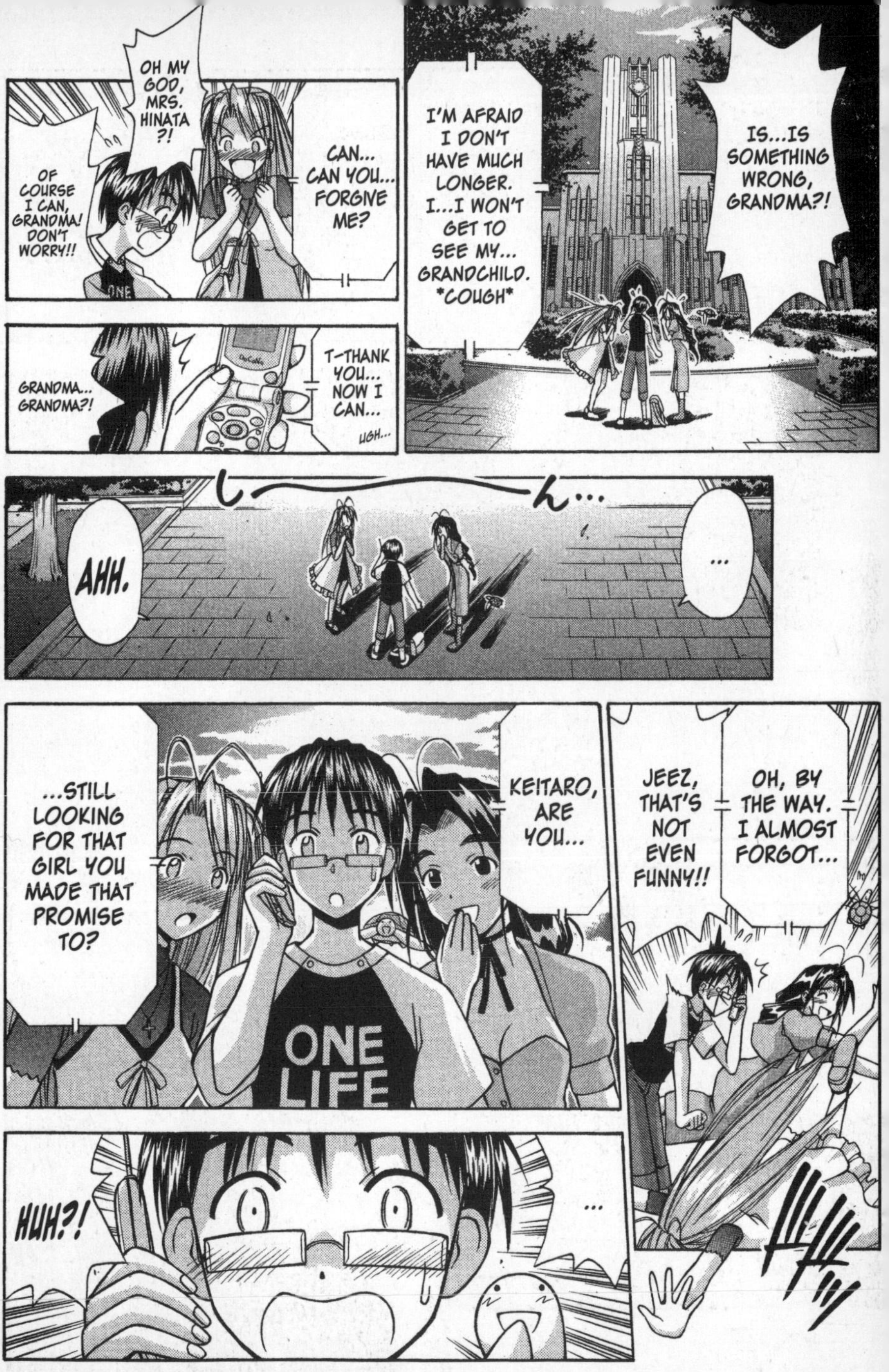
IS...IS SOMETHING WRONG, GRANDMA?!
I'M AFRAID I DON'T HAVE MUCH LONGER. I...I WON'T GET TO SEE MY... GRANDCHILD. *COUGH*
CAN... CAN YOU... FORGIVE ME?
OH MY GOD, MRS. HINATA?!
OF COURSE I CAN, GRANDMA! DON'T WORRY!!
T-THANK YOU... NOW I CAN...
UGH...
GRANDMA... GRANDMA?!
し――――ん...
...
AHH.
OH, BY THE WAY. I ALMOST FORGOT...
JEEZ, THAT'S NOT EVEN FUNNY!!
KEITARO, ARE YOU...
...STILL LOOKING FOR THAT GIRL YOU MADE THAT PROMISE TO?
...
HUH?!

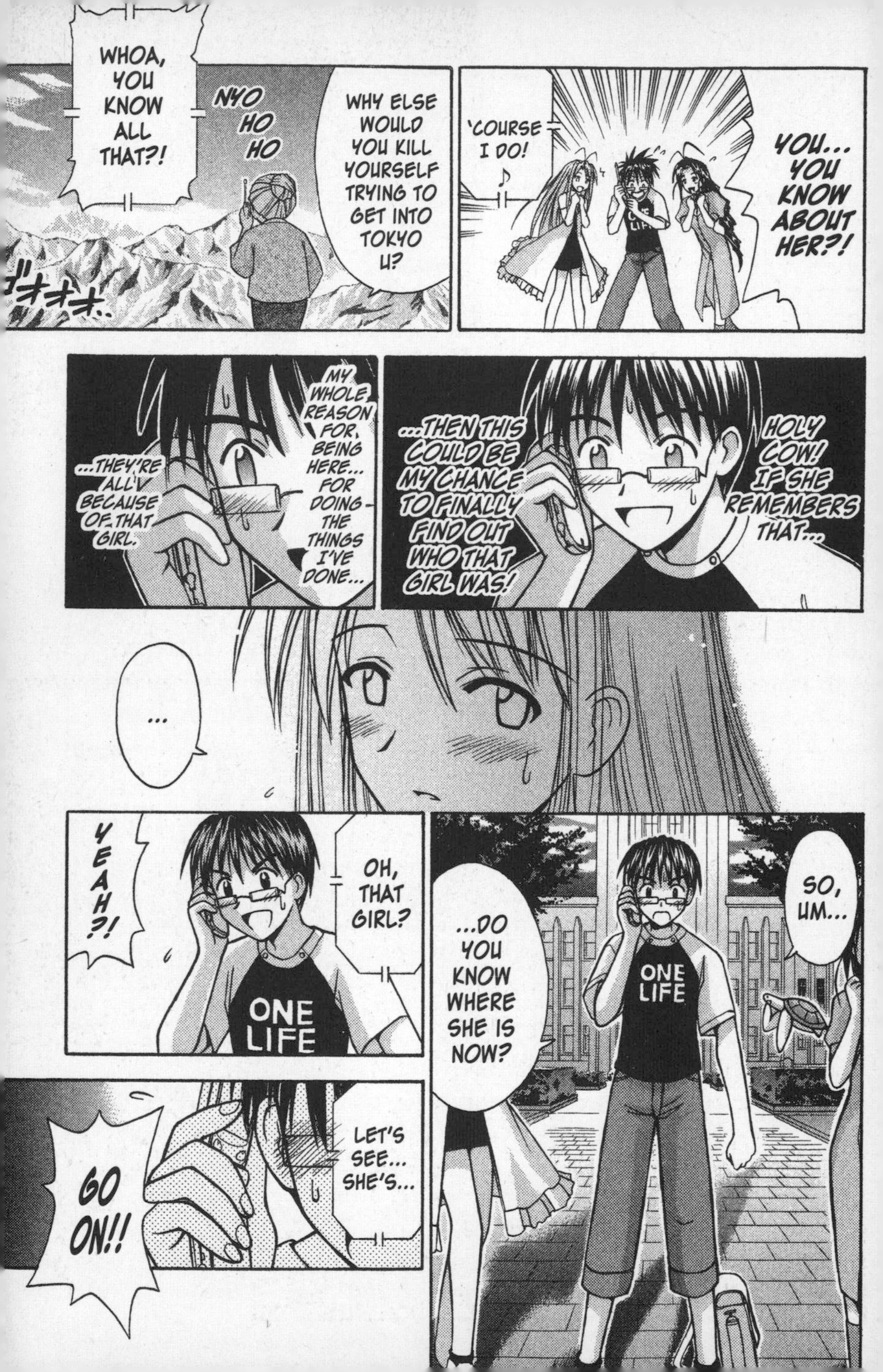
YOU... YOU KNOW ABOUT HER?!
'COURSE I DO! ♪
WHY ELSE WOULD YOU KILL YOURSELF TRYING TO GET INTO TOKYO U?
NYO HO HO
WHOA, YOU KNOW ALL THAT?!
HOLY COW! IF SHE REMEMBERS THAT...
...THEN THIS COULD BE MY CHANCE TO FINALLY FIND OUT WHO THAT GIRL WAS!
MY WHOLE REASON FOR BEING HERE... FOR DOING THE THINGS I'VE DONE...
...THEY'RE ALL BECAUSE OF THAT GIRL.
...
SO, UM...
...DO YOU KNOW WHERE SHE IS NOW?
OH, THAT GIRL?
YEAH?!
LET'S SEE... SHE'S...
GO ON!!

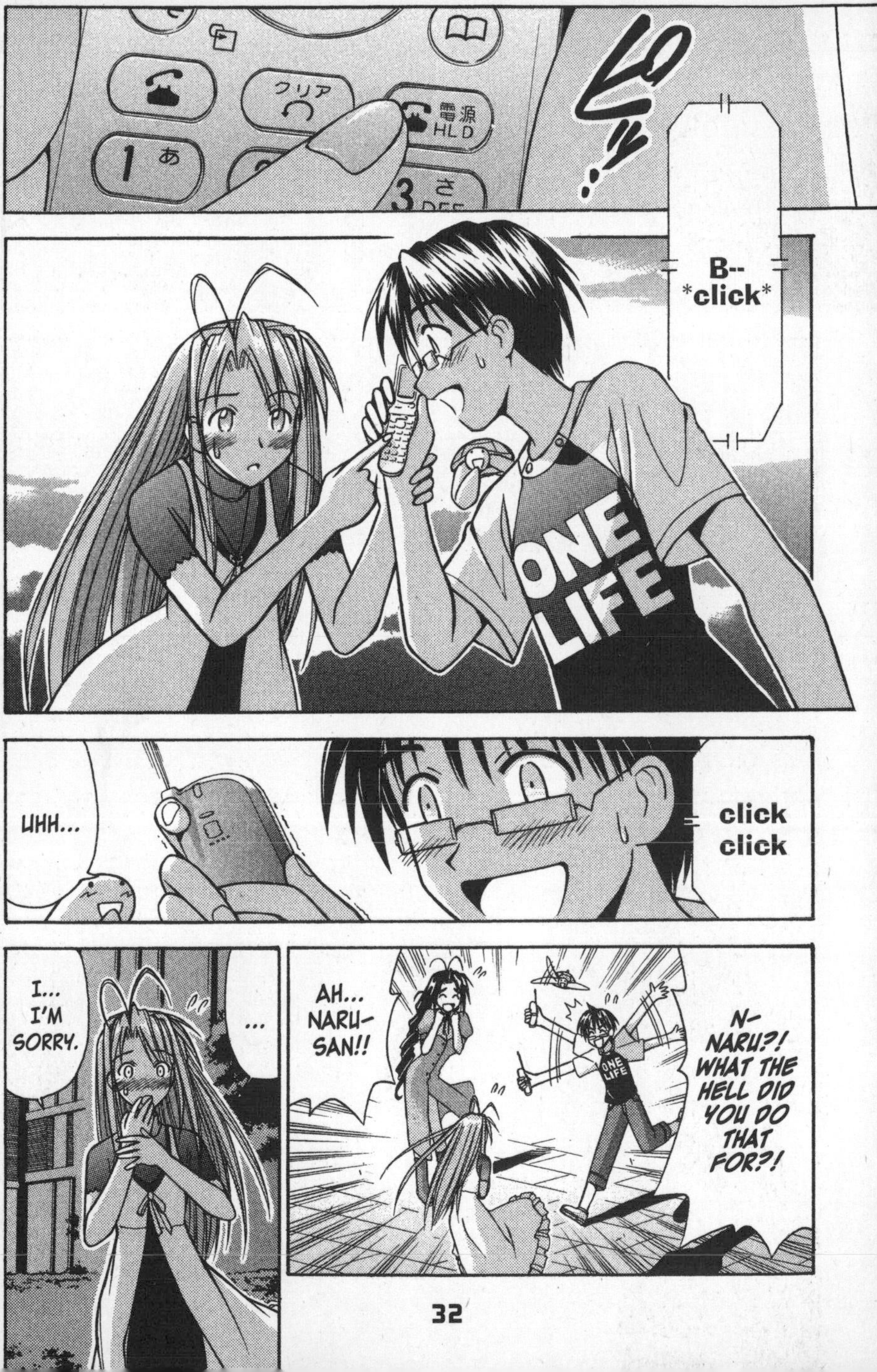
ピッ
B--
click
click
click
UHH...
N-NARU?! WHAT THE HELL DID YOU DO THAT FOR?!
AH... NARU-SAN!!
...
I... I'M SORRY.

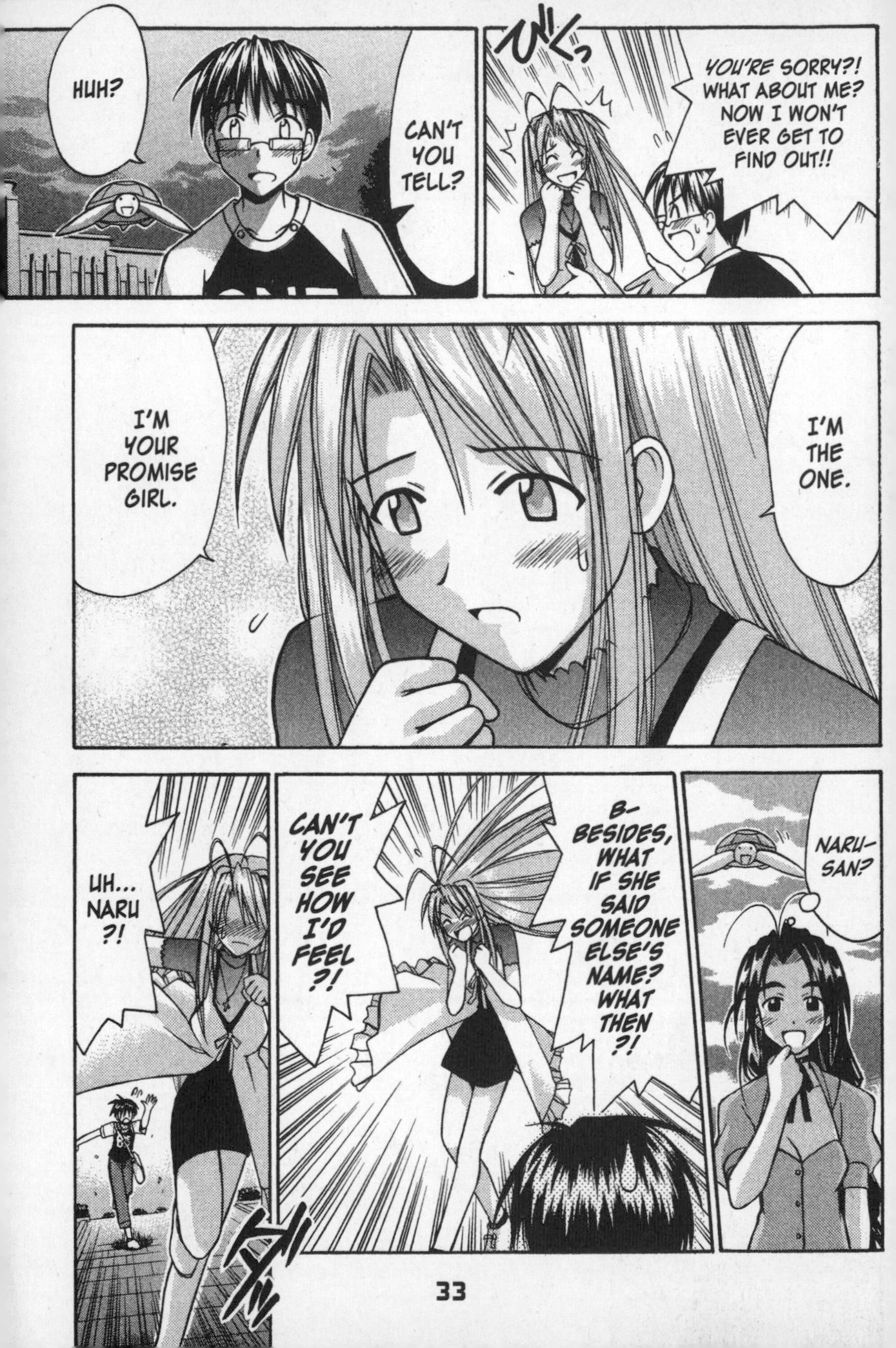
びくっ
YOU'RE SORRY?! WHAT ABOUT ME? NOW I WON'T EVER GET TO FIND OUT!!
CAN'T YOU TELL?
HUH?
I'M THE ONE.
I'M YOUR PROMISE GIRL.
NARU-SAN?
B-BESIDES, WHAT IF SHE SAID SOMEONE ELSE'S NAME? WHAT THEN?!
CAN'T YOU SEE HOW I'D FEEL?!
UH... NARU?!

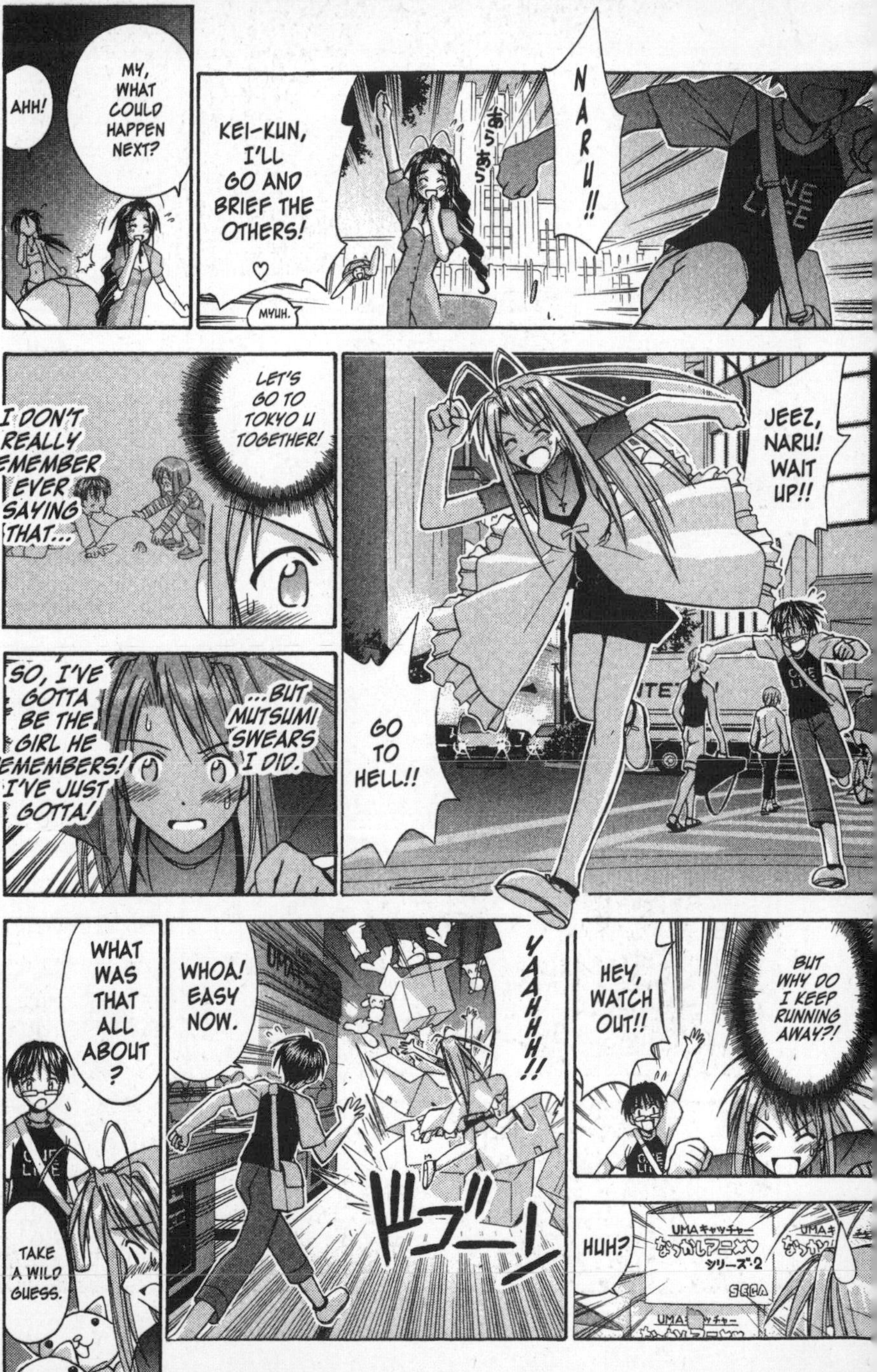
NARU!!
あらあら
KEI-KUN, I'LL GO AND BRIEF THE OTHERS! ♡
MYUH.
MY, WHAT COULD HAPPEN NEXT?
AHH!
JEEZ, NARU! WAIT UP!!
GO TO HELL!!
LET'S GO TO TOKYO U TOGETHER!
I DON'T REALLY REMEMBER EVER SAYING THAT...
...BUT MUTSUMI SWEARS I DID.
SO, I'VE GOTTA BE THE GIRL HE REMEMBERS! I'VE JUST GOTTA!
BUT WHY DO I KEEP RUNNING AWAY?!
HEY, WATCH OUT!!
HUH?
UMAキャッチャー
なつかしアニメ♥
シリーズ・2
SEGA
YAAHHH!!
WHOA! EASY NOW.
ドゴーー!
WHAT WAS THAT ALL ABOUT?
TAKE A WILD GUESS.

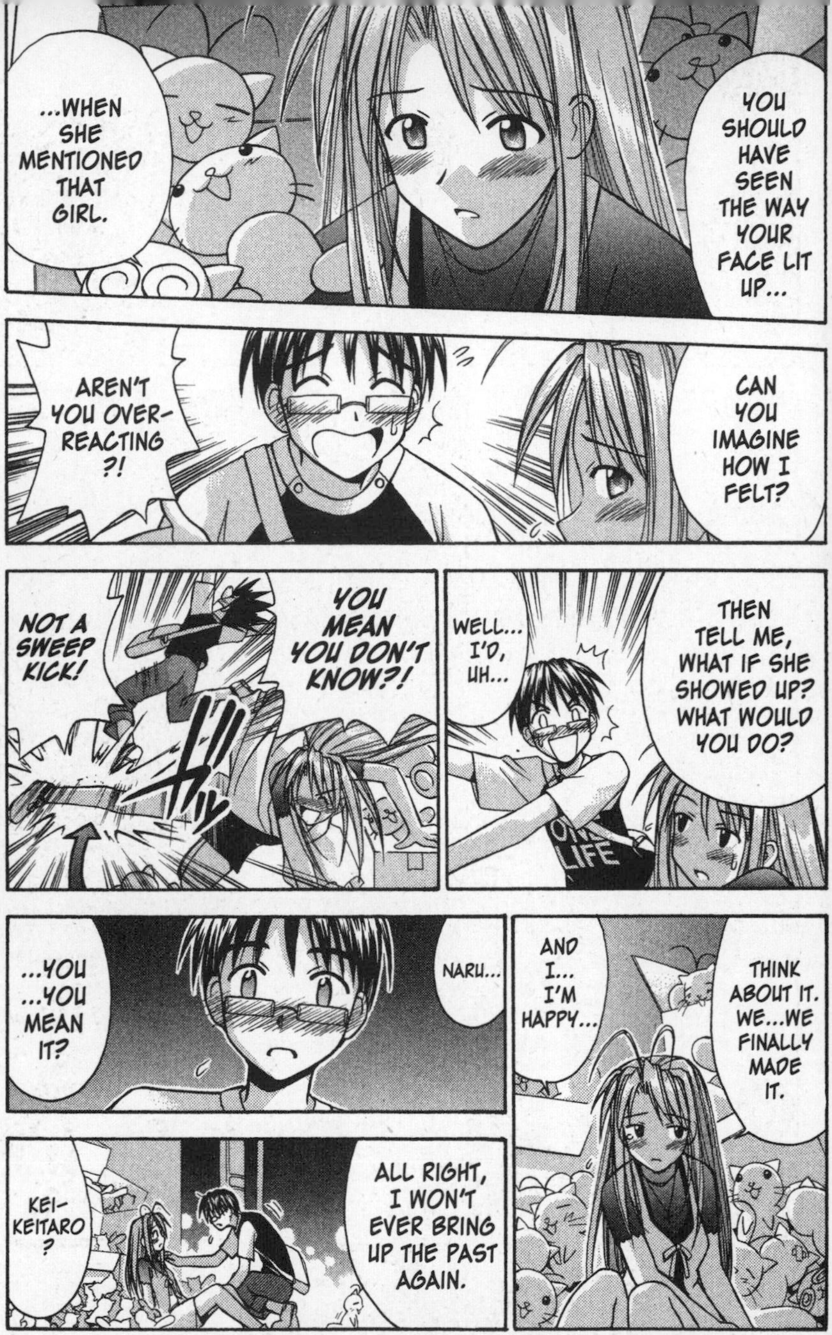
YOU SHOULD HAVE SEEN THE WAY YOUR FACE LIT UP...
...WHEN SHE MENTIONED THAT GIRL.
CAN YOU IMAGINE HOW I FELT?
AREN'T YOU OVER-REACTING ?!
THEN TELL ME, WHAT IF SHE SHOWED UP? WHAT WOULD YOU DO?
WELL... I'D, UH...
YOU MEAN YOU DON'T KNOW?!
NOT A SWEEP KICK!
THINK ABOUT IT. WE...WE FINALLY MADE IT.
AND I... I'M HAPPY...
NARU...
...YOU ...YOU MEAN IT?
ALL RIGHT, I WON'T EVER BRING UP THE PAST AGAIN.
KEI-KEITARO ?

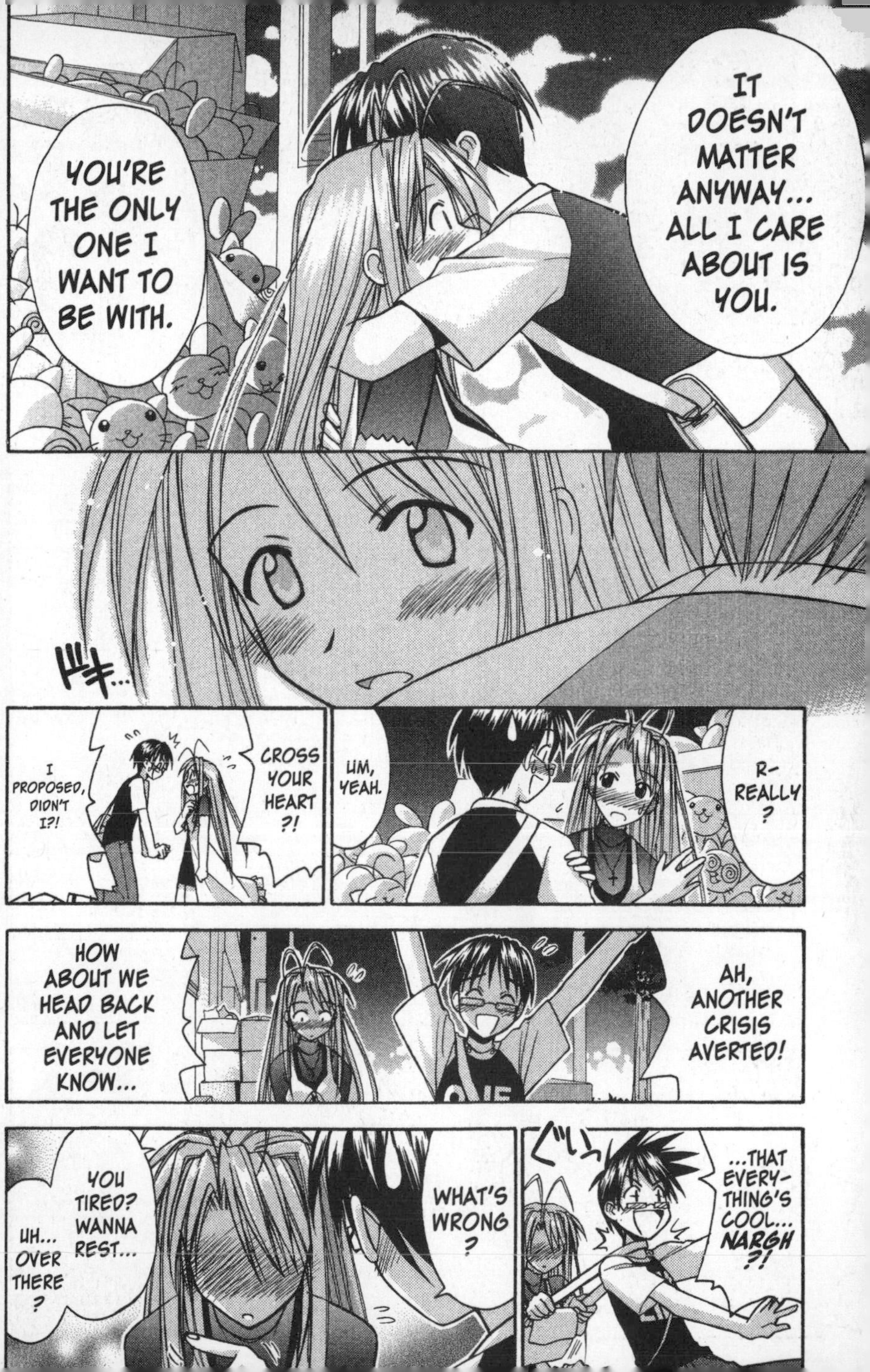
IT DOESN'T MATTER ANYWAY... ALL I CARE ABOUT IS YOU.
YOU'RE THE ONLY ONE I WANT TO BE WITH.
ドキ…
R-REALLY?
UM, YEAH.
CROSS YOUR HEART?!
I PROPOSED, DIDN'T I?!
AH, ANOTHER CRISIS AVERTED!
HOW ABOUT WE HEAD BACK AND LET EVERYONE KNOW...
ぐいっ
...THAT EVERY-THING'S COOL... NARGH?!
WHAT'S WRONG?
YOU TIRED? WANNA REST...
UH... OVER THERE?

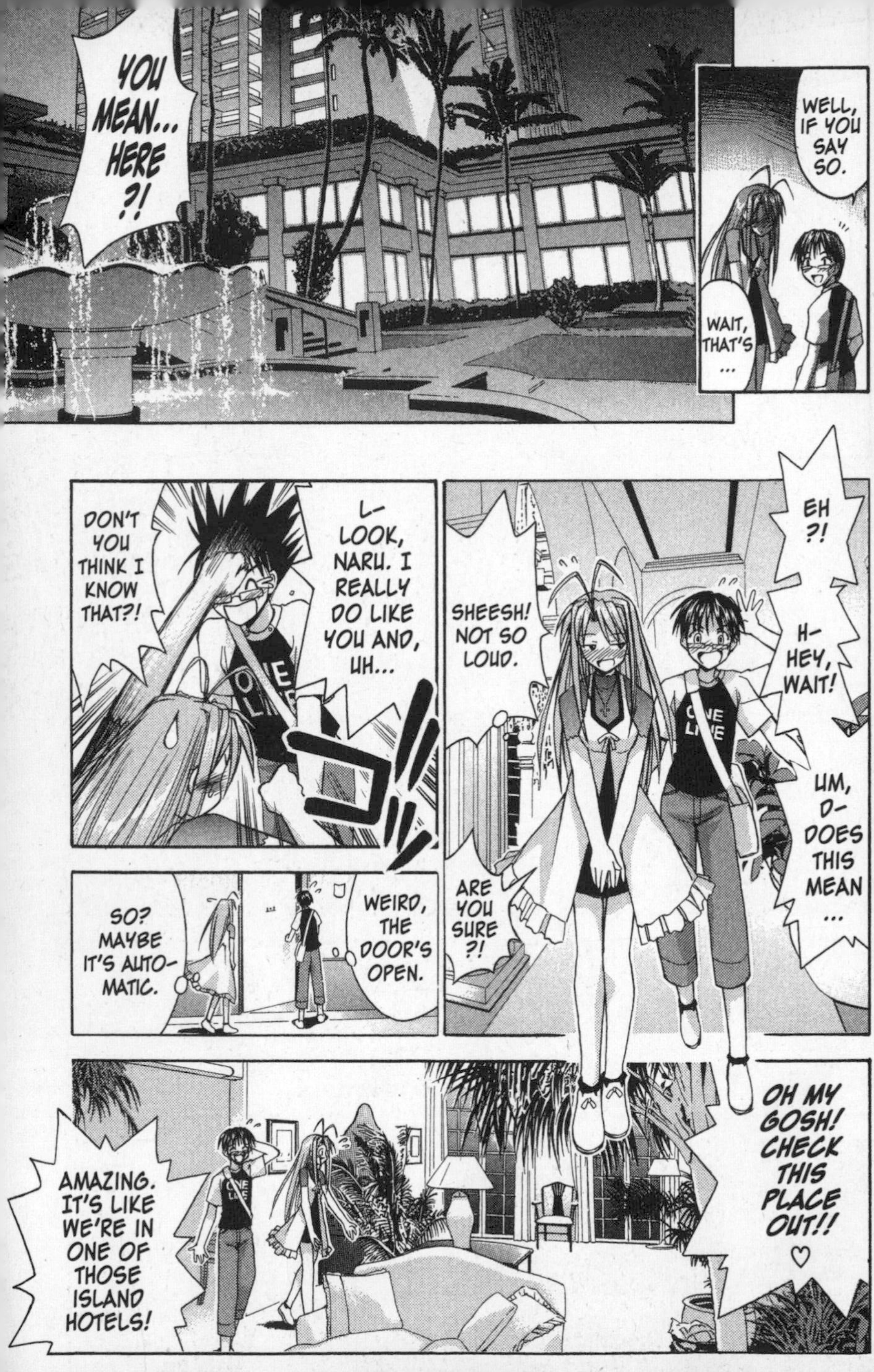
WELL, IF YOU SAY SO.
WAIT, THAT'S ...
YOU MEAN... HERE?!
EH?!
H-HEY, WAIT!
SHEESH! NOT SO LOUD.
UM, D-DOES THIS MEAN ...
ARE YOU SURE?!
L-LOOK, NARU. I REALLY DO LIKE YOU AND, UH...
DON'T YOU THINK I KNOW THAT?!
WEIRD, THE DOOR'S OPEN.
SO? MAYBE IT'S AUTO-MATIC.
OH MY GOSH! CHECK THIS PLACE OUT!! ♥
AMAZING. IT'S LIKE WE'RE IN ONE OF THOSE ISLAND HOTELS!

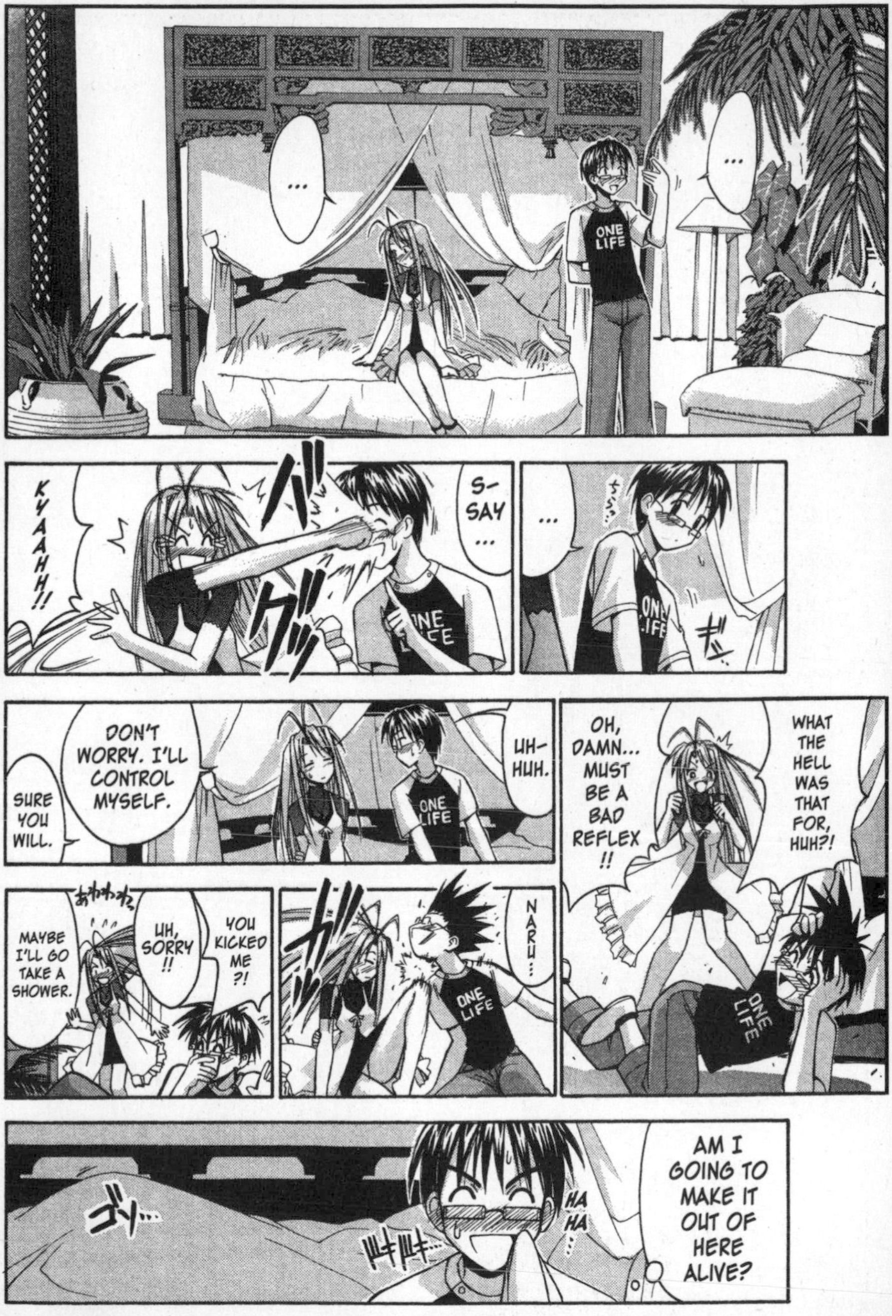
...
...
...
S-SAY ...
KYAAAHH!!
WHAT THE HELL WAS THAT FOR, HUH?!
OH, DAMN... MUST BE A BAD REFLEX !!
UH-HUH.
DON'T WORRY. I'LL CONTROL MYSELF.
SURE YOU WILL.
NARU...
YOU KICKED ME ?!
UH, SORRY !!
MAYBE I'LL GO TAKE A SHOWER.
AM I GOING TO MAKE IT OUT OF HERE ALIVE?
HA HA ...

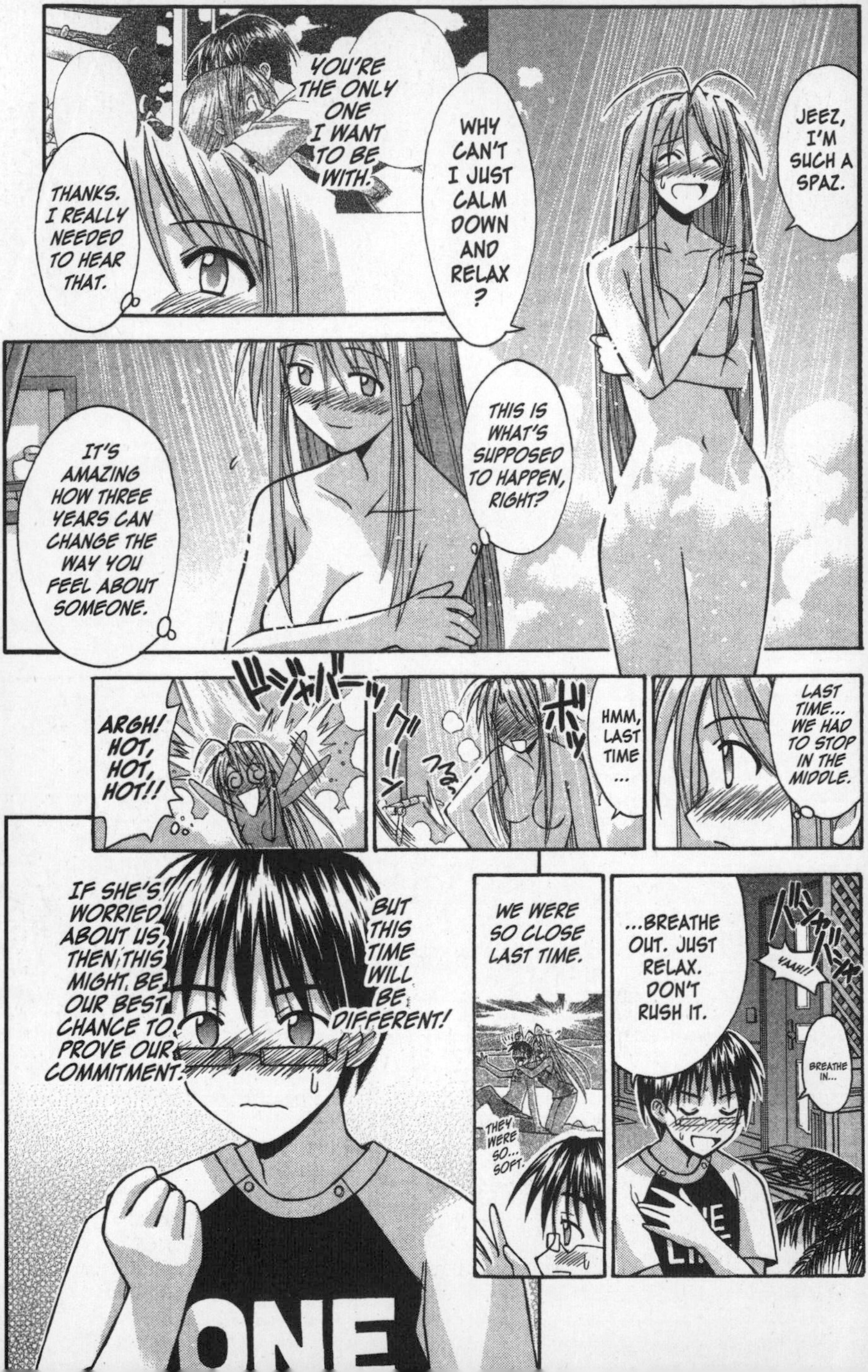
JEEZ, I'M SUCH A SPAZ.
WHY CAN'T I JUST CALM DOWN AND RELAX?
YOU'RE THE ONLY ONE I WANT TO BE WITH.
THANKS. I REALLY NEEDED TO HEAR THAT.
THIS IS WHAT'S SUPPOSED TO HAPPEN, RIGHT?
IT'S AMAZING HOW THREE YEARS CAN CHANGE THE WAY YOU FEEL ABOUT SOMEONE.
LAST TIME... WE HAD TO STOP IN THE MIDDLE.
HMM, LAST TIME ...
ARGH! HOT, HOT, HOT!!
YAAH!!
BREATHE IN...
...BREATHE OUT. JUST RELAX. DON'T RUSH IT.
WE WERE SO CLOSE LAST TIME.
THEY WERE SO... SOFT.
BUT THIS TIME WILL BE DIFFERENT!
IF SHE'S WORRIED ABOUT US, THEN THIS MIGHT BE OUR BEST CHANCE TO PROVE OUR COMMITMENT.
ONE

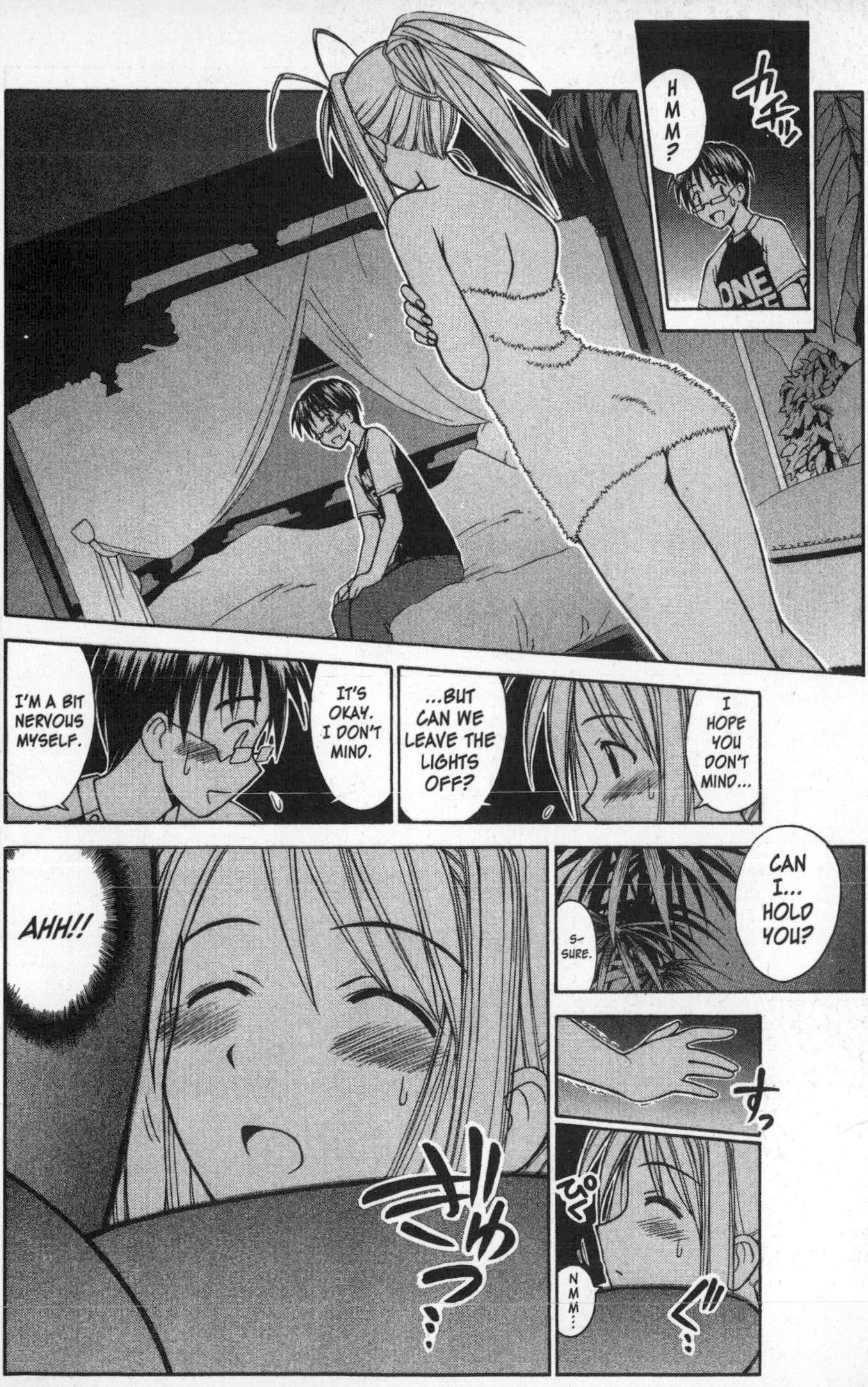
カチッ
HMMM?
I HOPE YOU DON'T MIND...
...BUT CAN WE LEAVE THE LIGHTS OFF?
IT'S OKAY. I DON'T MIND.
I'M A BIT NERVOUS MYSELF.
CAN I... HOLD YOU?
S-SURE.
すっ
ぴく
NMM...
AHH!!

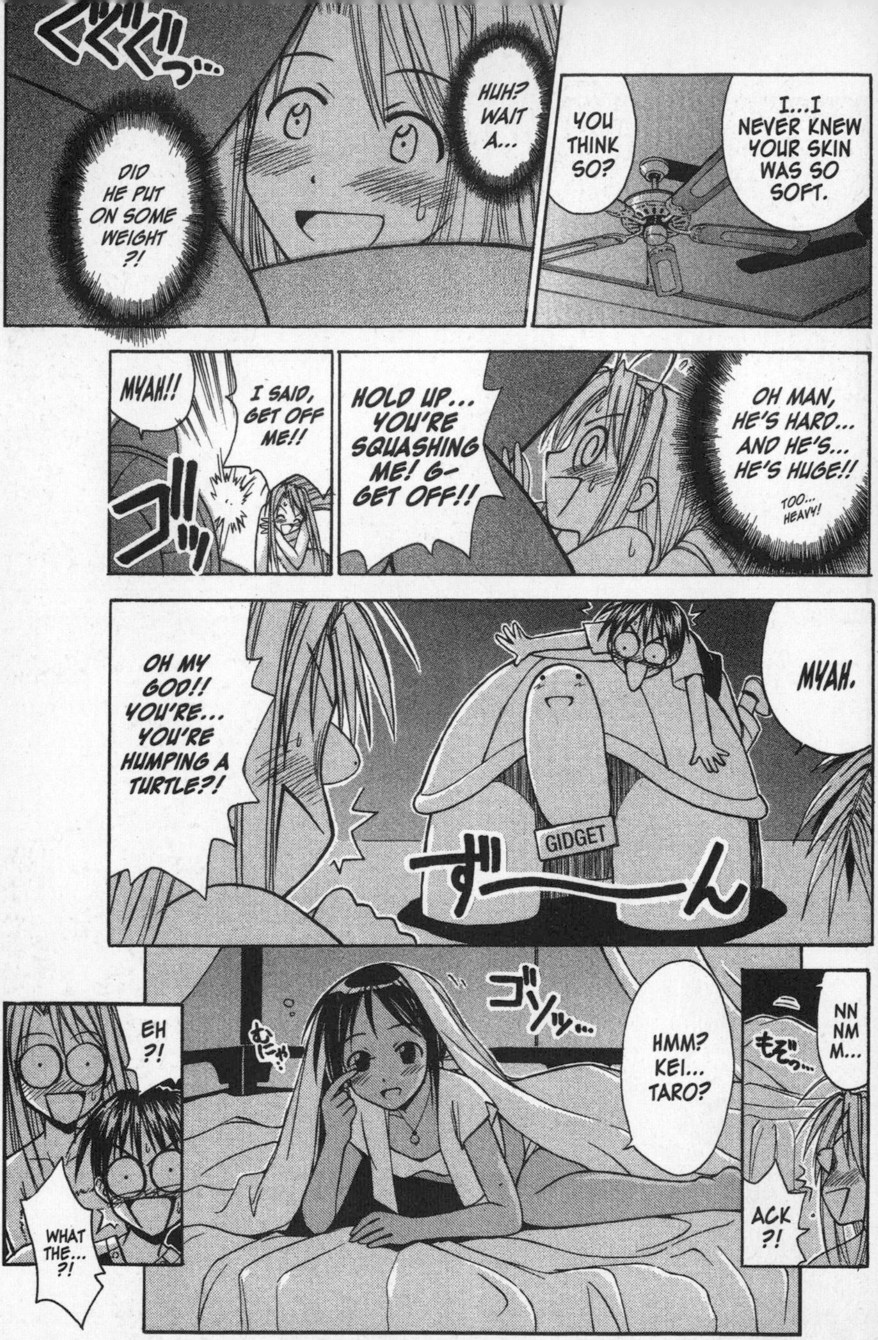
I...I NEVER KNEW YOUR SKIN WAS SO SOFT.
YOU THINK SO?
ぐぐぐ
づっ...
HUH? WAIT A...
DID HE PUT ON SOME WEIGHT ?!
OH MAN, HE'S HARD... AND HE'S... HE'S HUGE!!
TOO... HEAVY!
HOLD UP... YOU'RE SQUASHING ME! G-GET OFF!!
I SAID, GET OFF ME!!
MYAH!!
ゴッ
MYAH.
GIDGET
ず——ん
OH MY GOD!! YOU'RE... YOU'RE HUMPING A TURTLE?!
NN NM M...
もぞっ...
ACK ?!
HMM? KEI... TARO?
ゴソッ...
むにゃ
EH ?!
WHAT THE... ?!

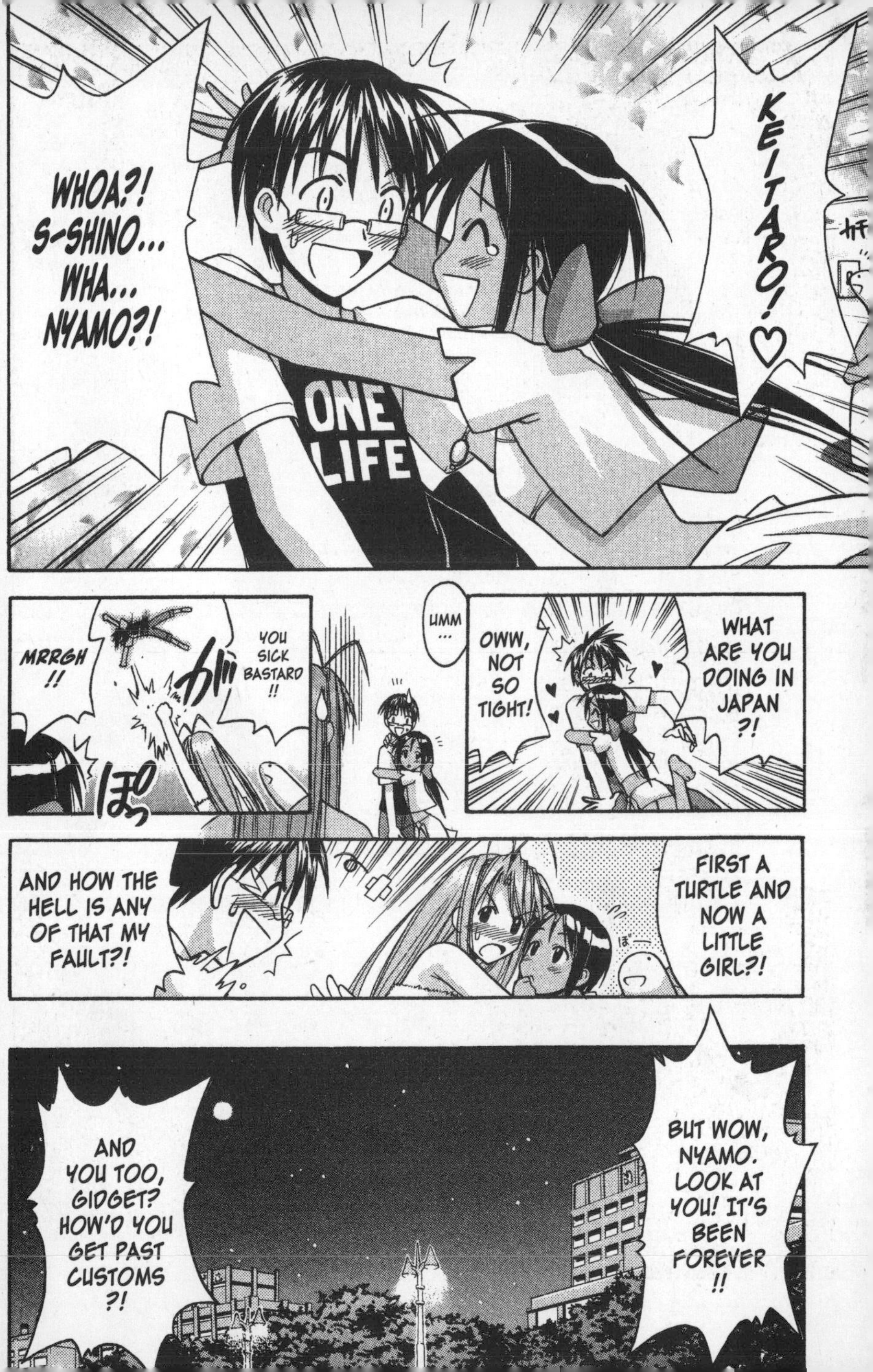
KEITARO! ♡
WHOA?! S-SHINO... WHA... NYAMO?!
WHAT ARE YOU DOING IN JAPAN ?!
OWW, NOT SO TIGHT!
UMM ...
YOU SICK BASTARD !!
MRRGH !!
FIRST A TURTLE AND NOW A LITTLE GIRL?!
AND HOW THE HELL IS ANY OF THAT MY FAULT?!
BUT WOW, NYAMO. LOOK AT YOU! IT'S BEEN FOREVER !!
AND YOU TOO, GIDGET? HOW'D YOU GET PAST CUSTOMS ?!

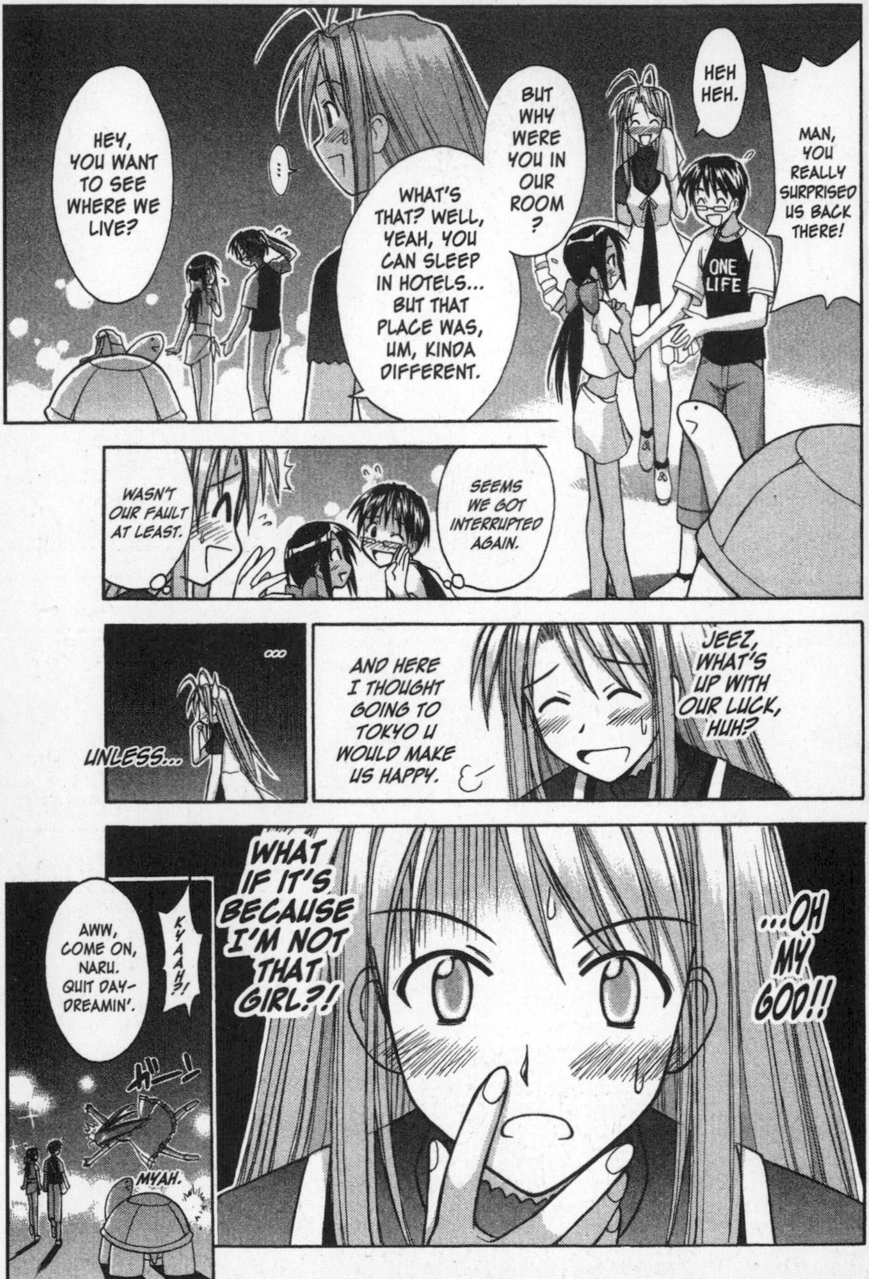
HEH HEH.
MAN, YOU REALLY SURPRISED US BACK THERE!
BUT WHY WERE YOU IN OUR ROOM?
WHAT'S THAT? WELL, YEAH, YOU CAN SLEEP IN HOTELS... BUT THAT PLACE WAS, UM, KINDA DIFFERENT.
...
HEY, YOU WANT TO SEE WHERE WE LIVE?
SEEMS WE GOT INTERRUPTED AGAIN.
WASN'T OUR FAULT AT LEAST.
JEEZ, WHAT'S UP WITH OUR LUCK, HUH?
AND HERE I THOUGHT GOING TO TOKYO U WOULD MAKE US HAPPY.
UNLESS...
...OH MY GOD!!
WHAT IF IT'S BECAUSE I'M NOT THAT GIRL?!
KYAAH?!
AWW, COME ON, NARU. QUIT DAY-DREAMIN'.
MYAH.

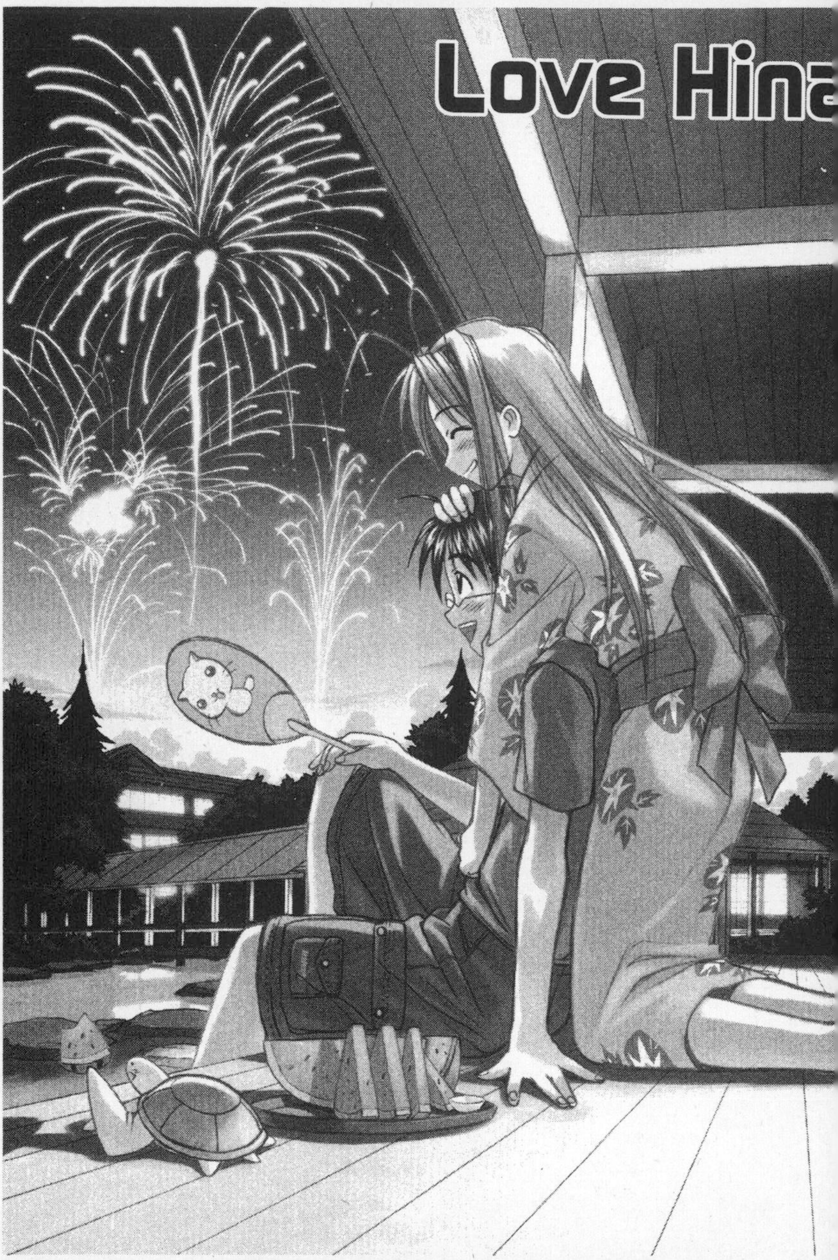
Love Hina

HINATA. 116 Secret Letter From Nyamo.

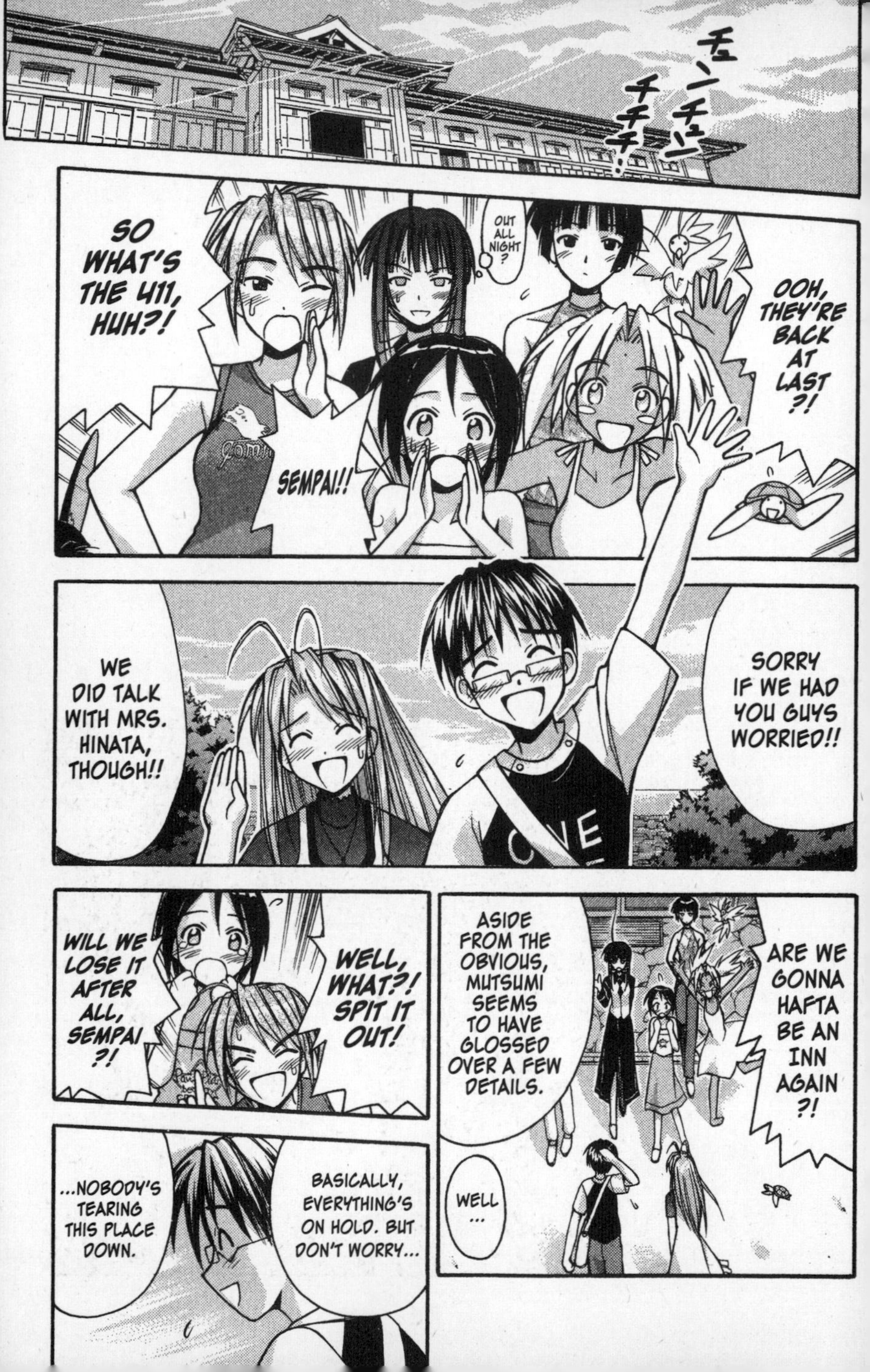

チュンチュン
チチチ！
OOH, THEY'RE BACK AT LAST?!
OUT ALL NIGHT?
SO WHAT'S THE 411, HUH?!
SEMPAI!!
SORRY IF WE HAD YOU GUYS WORRIED!!
WE DID TALK WITH MRS. HINATA, THOUGH!!
ARE WE GONNA HAFTA BE AN INN AGAIN?!
ASIDE FROM THE OBVIOUS, MUTSUMI SEEMS TO HAVE GLOSSED OVER A FEW DETAILS.
WELL...
WELL, WHAT?! SPIT IT OUT!
WILL WE LOSE IT AFTER ALL, SEMPAI?!
BASICALLY, EVERYTHING'S ON HOLD. BUT DON'T WORRY...
...NOBODY'S TEARING THIS PLACE DOWN.

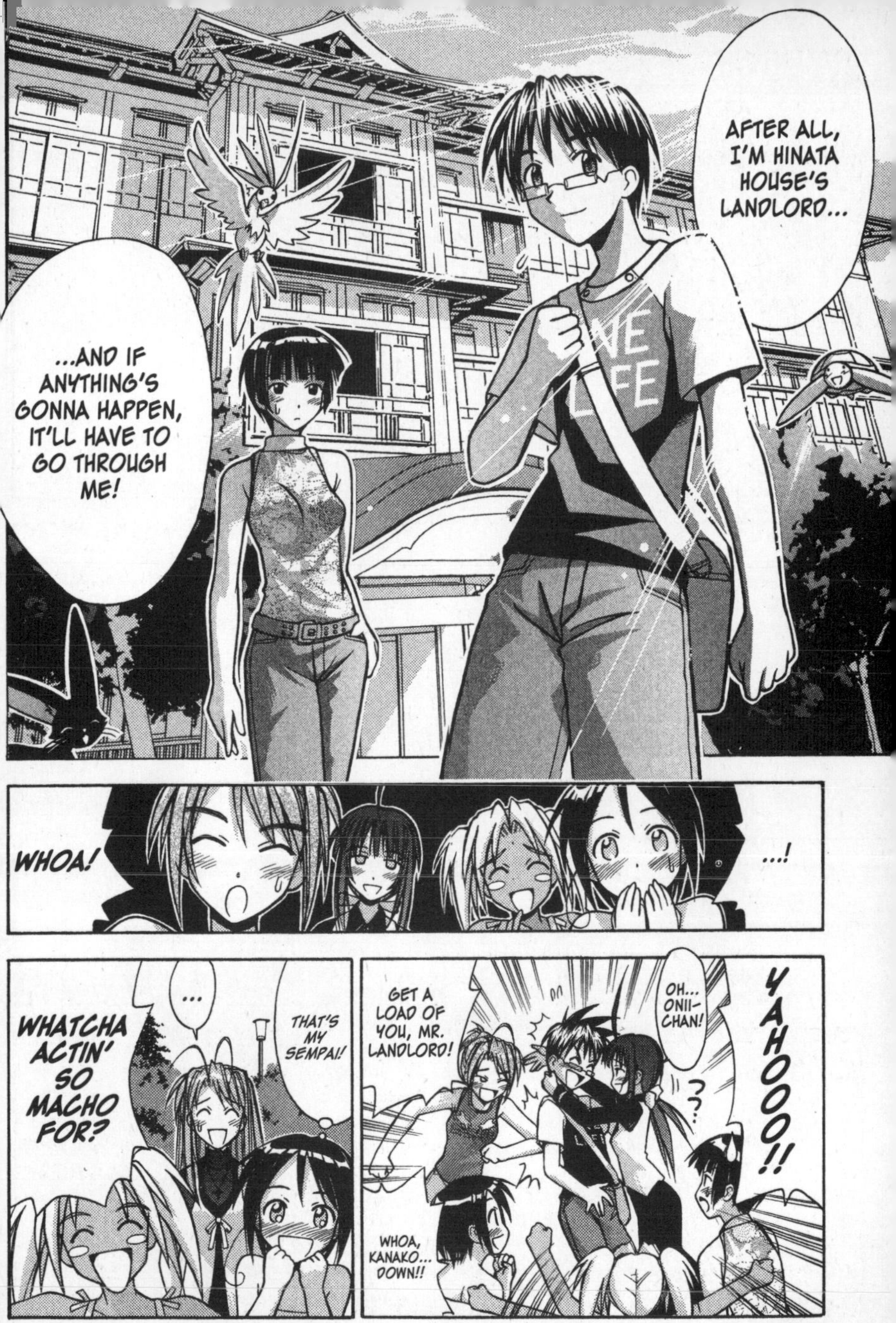
AFTER ALL, I'M HINATA HOUSE'S LANDLORD...
...AND IF ANYTHING'S GONNA HAPPEN, IT'LL HAVE TO GO THROUGH ME!
...!
WHOA!
YAHOOOO!!
OH... ONII-CHAN!
GET A LOAD OF YOU, MR. LANDLORD!
??
WHOA, KANAKO... DOWN!!
THAT'S MY SEMPAI!
...
WHATCHA ACTIN' SO MACHO FOR?

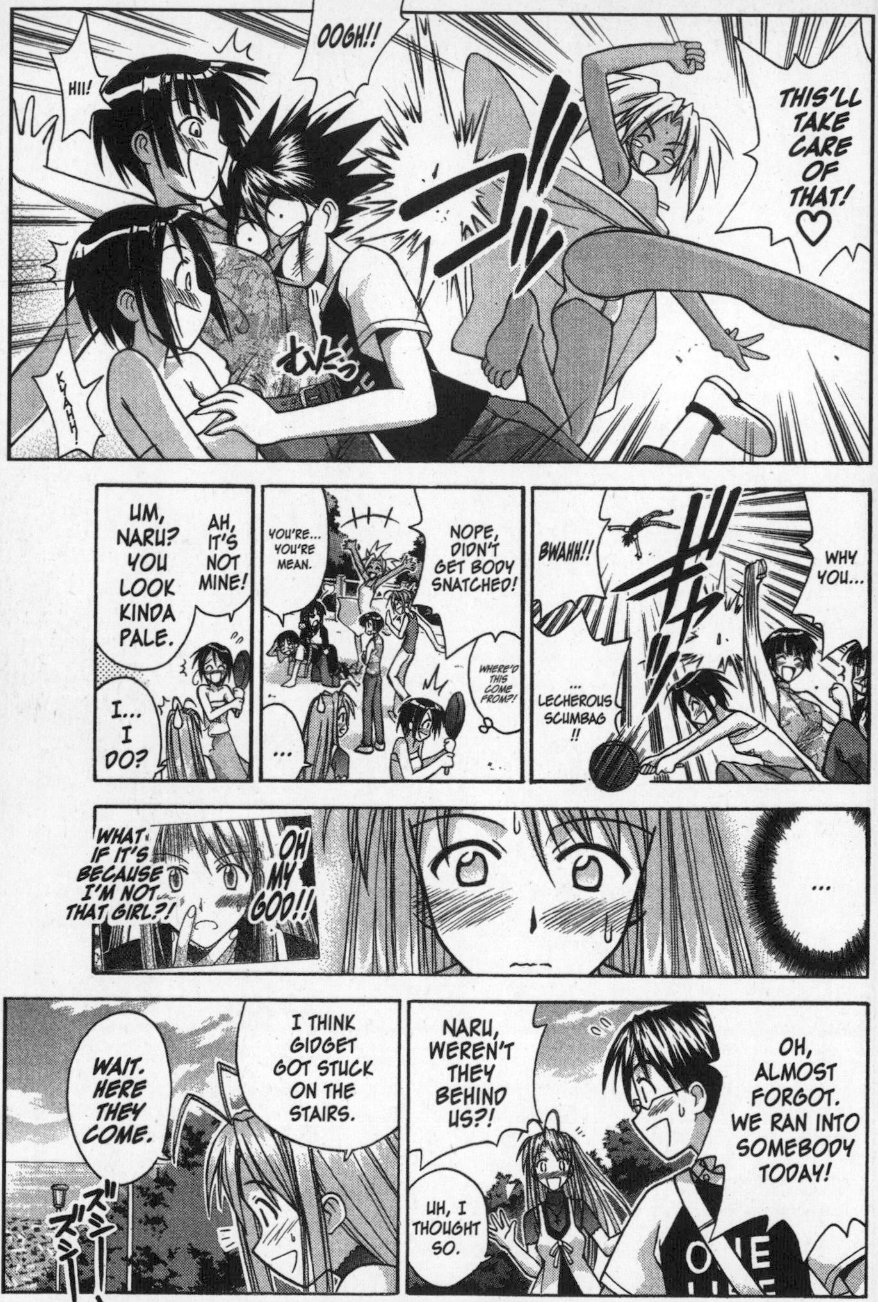
THIS'LL TAKE CARE OF THAT! ♡
OOGH!!
HII!
KYAHH!
WHY YOU...
BWAHH!!
... LECHEROUS SCUMBAG !!
NOPE, DIDN'T GET BODY SNATCHED!
YOU'RE... YOU'RE MEAN.
WHERE'D THIS COME FROM?!
...
AH, IT'S NOT MINE!
UM, NARU? YOU LOOK KINDA PALE.
I... I DO?
...
OH MY GOD!!
WHAT IF IT'S BECAUSE I'M NOT THAT GIRL?!
OH, ALMOST FORGOT. WE RAN INTO SOMEBODY TODAY!
NARU, WEREN'T THEY BEHIND US?!
UH, I THOUGHT SO.
I THINK GIDGET GOT STUCK ON THE STAIRS.
WAIT. HERE THEY COME.

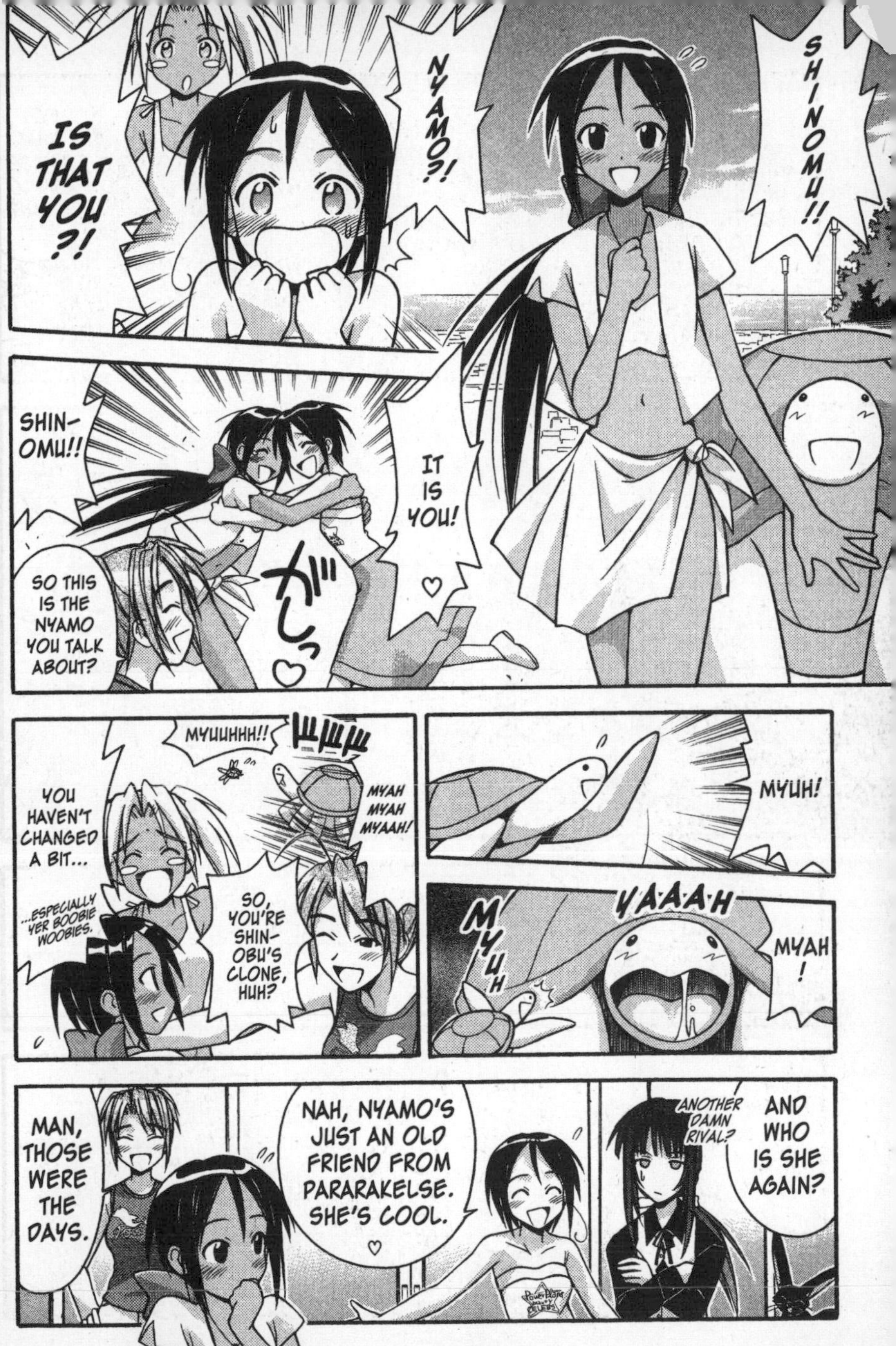
SHINOMU!!
NYAMO?!
IS THAT YOU?!
IT IS YOU! ♥
SHIN-OMU!!
がしっ
SO THIS IS THE NYAMO YOU TALK ABOUT?
MYUH!
YAAAH
MYAH!
MYUH
MYUUHHH!!
MYAH MYAH MYAAH!
YOU HAVEN'T CHANGED A BIT...
...ESPECIALLY YER BOOBIE WOOBIES.
SO, YOU'RE SHINOBU'S CLONE, HUH?
AND WHO IS SHE AGAIN?
ANOTHER DAMN RIVAL?
NAH, NYAMO'S JUST AN OLD FRIEND FROM PARARAKELSE. SHE'S COOL. ♥
MAN, THOSE WERE THE DAYS.

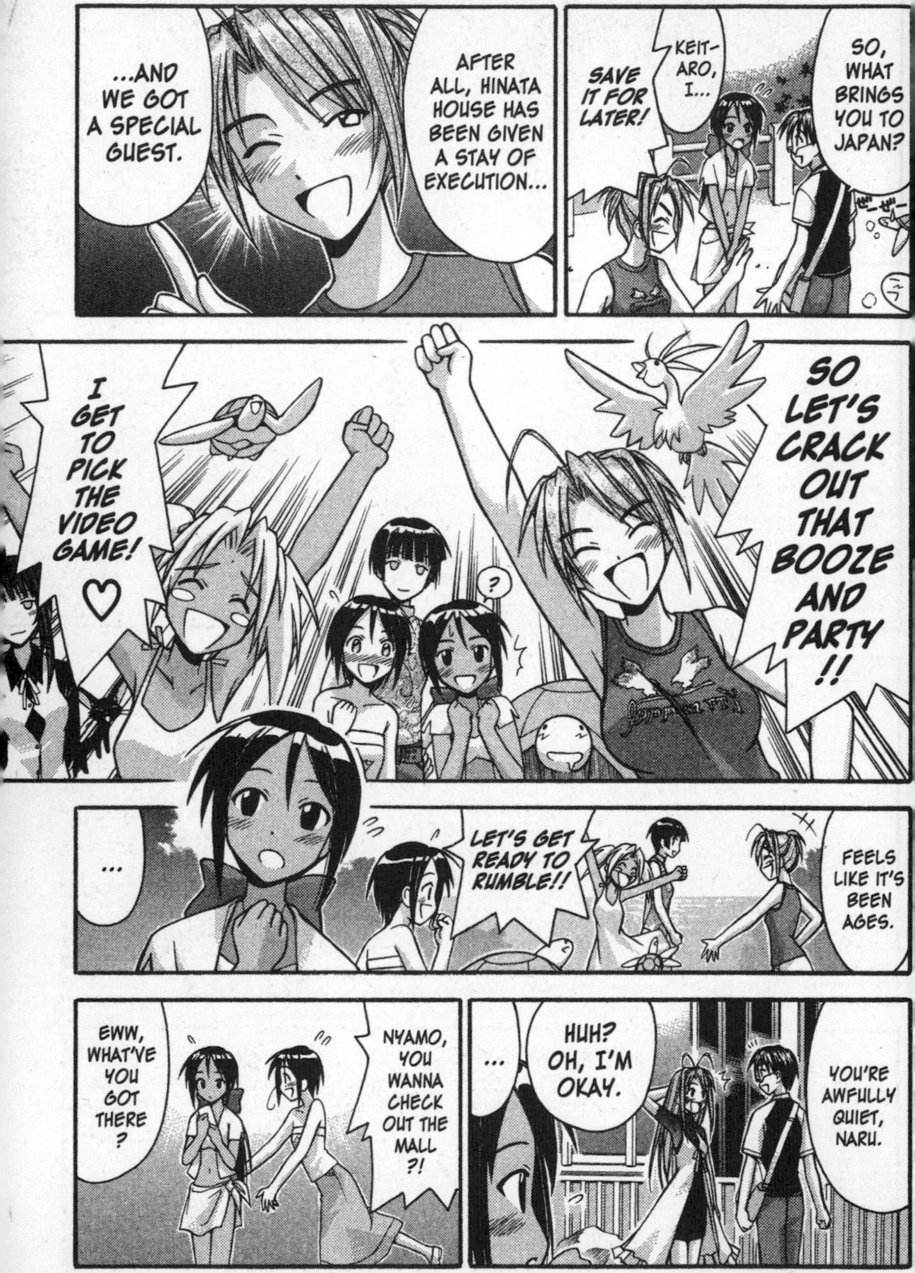
SO, WHAT BRINGS YOU TO JAPAN?
KEIT-ARO, I...
SAVE IT FOR LATER!
AFTER ALL, HINATA HOUSE HAS BEEN GIVEN A STAY OF EXECUTION...
...AND WE GOT A SPECIAL GUEST.
SO LET'S CRACK OUT THAT BOOZE AND PARTY!!
?
I GET TO PICK THE VIDEO GAME! ♡
FEELS LIKE IT'S BEEN AGES.
LET'S GET READY TO RUMBLE!!
...
YOU'RE AWFULLY QUIET, NARU.
HUH? OH, I'M OKAY.
...
NYAMO, YOU WANNA CHECK OUT THE MALL?!
EWW, WHAT'VE YOU GOT THERE?

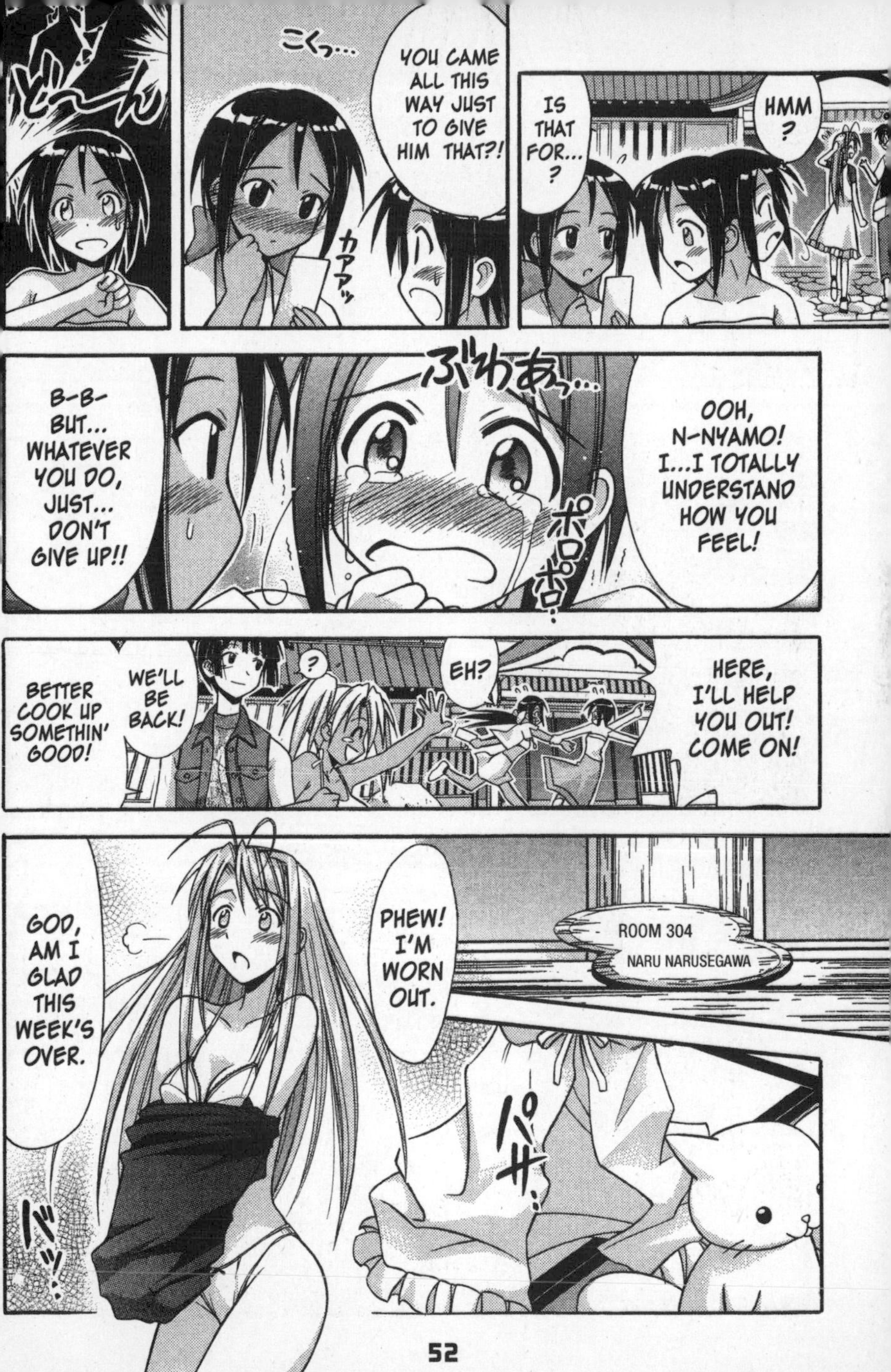
HMM ?
IS THAT FOR... ?
YOU CAME ALL THIS WAY JUST TO GIVE HIM THAT?!
こくっ...
カアアッ
どーん
OOH, N-NYAMO! I...I TOTALLY UNDERSTAND HOW YOU FEEL!
ぶわあっ...
ポロポロ...
B-B-BUT... WHATEVER YOU DO, JUST... DON'T GIVE UP!!
HERE, I'LL HELP YOU OUT! COME ON!
EH?
?
WE'LL BE BACK!
BETTER COOK UP SOMETHIN' GOOD!
ROOM 304
NARU NARUSEGAWA
PHEW! I'M WORN OUT.
GOD, AM I GLAD THIS WEEK'S OVER.
パサ...
バッ...

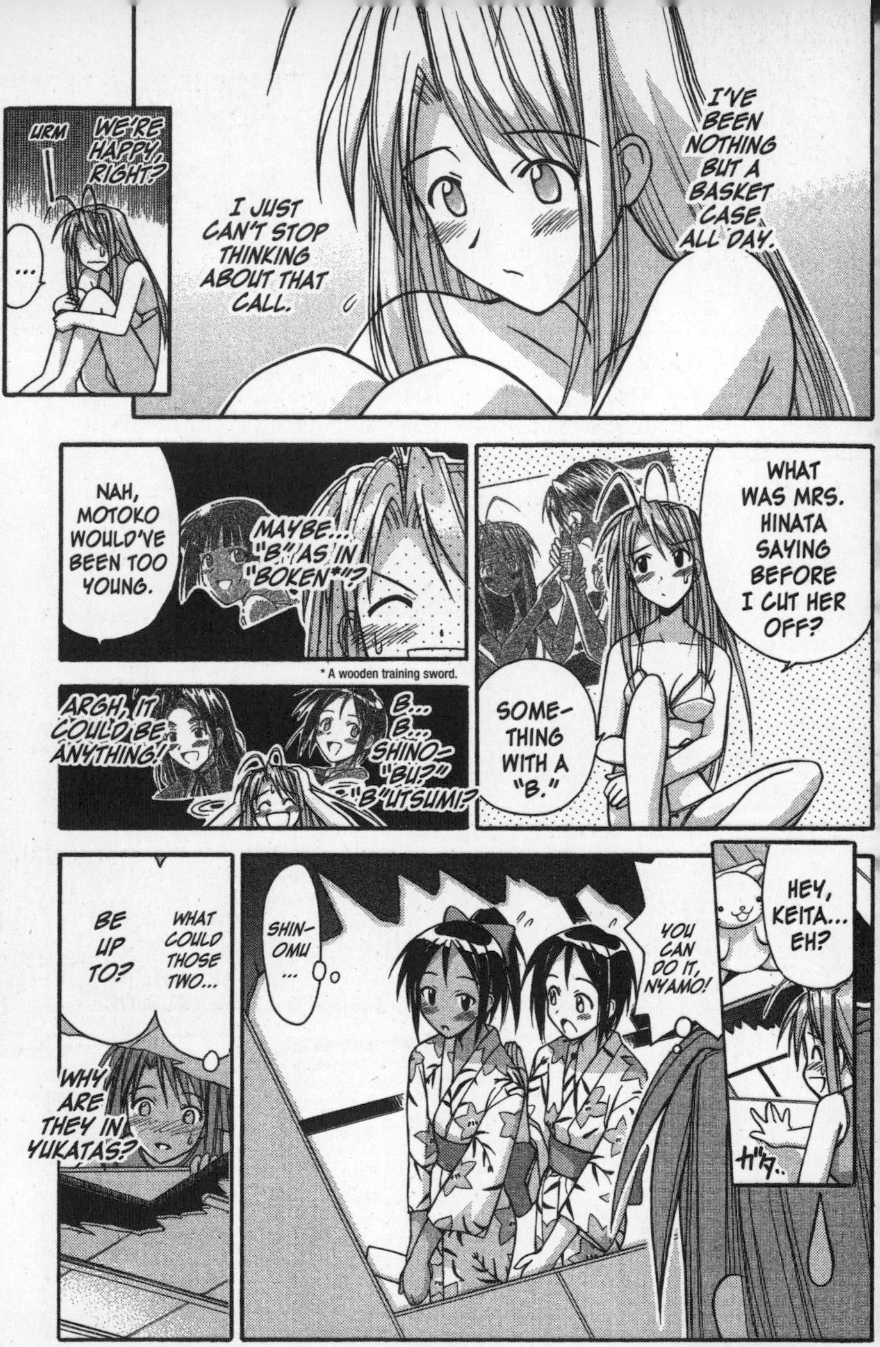
I'VE BEEN NOTHING BUT A BASKET CASE ALL DAY.
I JUST CAN'T STOP THINKING ABOUT THAT CALL.
WE'RE HAPPY, RIGHT?
URM
...
WHAT WAS MRS. HINATA SAYING BEFORE I CUT HER OFF?
SOME-THING WITH A "B."
MAYBE... "B" AS IN "BOKEN*"?
NAH, MOTOKO WOULD'VE BEEN TOO YOUNG.
B... B... SHINO-"BU?"
"B"UTSUMI?
ARGH, IT COULD BE ANYTHING!
HEY, KEITA... EH?
ガタ..
YOU CAN DO IT, NYAMO!
SHIN-OMU...
WHAT COULD THOSE TWO...
BE UP TO?
WHY ARE THEY IN YUKATAS?
* A wooden training sword.

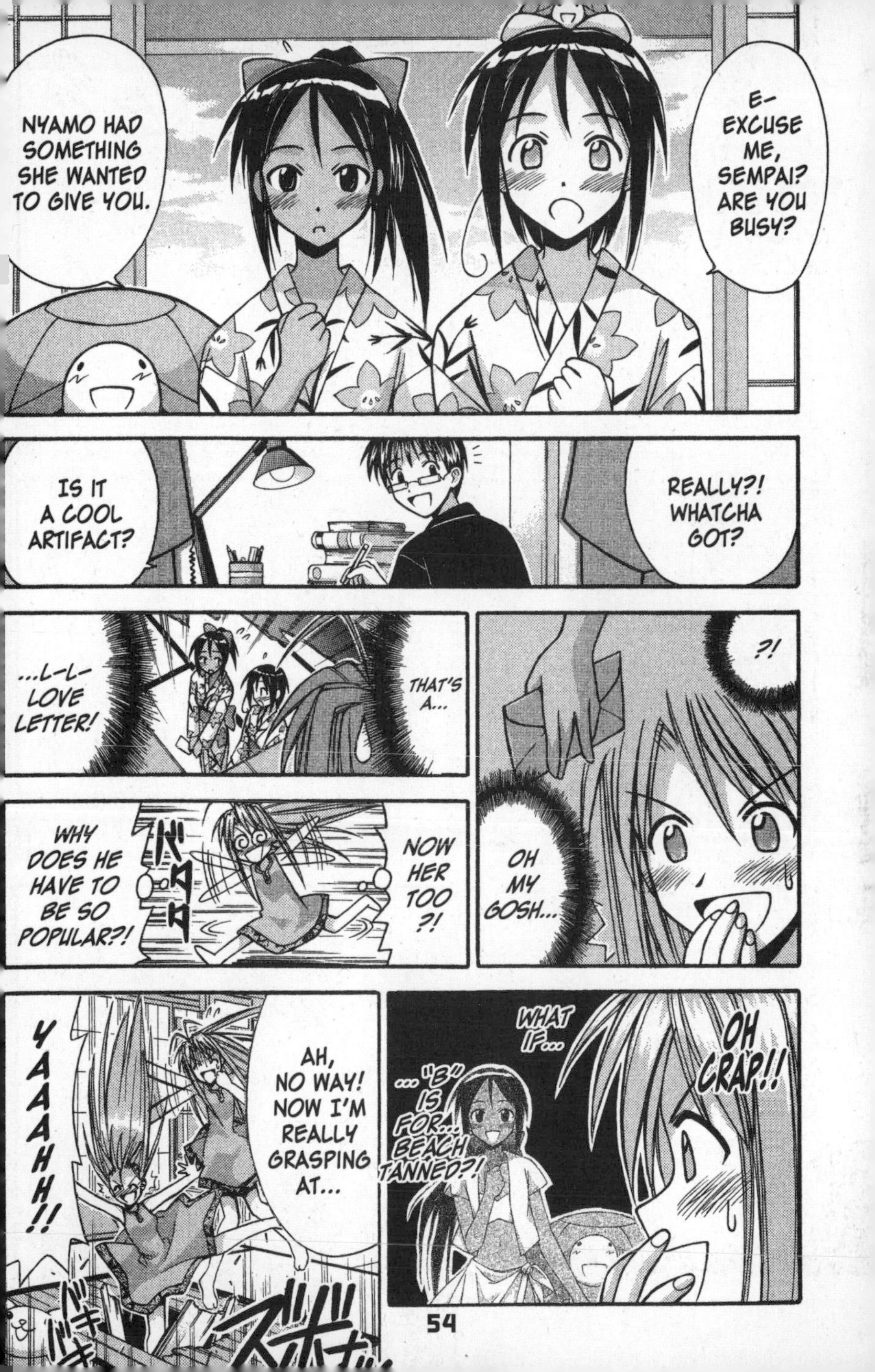
E-EXCUSE ME, SEMPAI? ARE YOU BUSY?
NYAMO HAD SOMETHING SHE WANTED TO GIVE YOU.
REALLY?! WHATCHA GOT?
IS IT A COOL ARTIFACT?
?!
OH MY GOSH...
THAT'S A...
...L-L-LOVE LETTER!
NOW HER TOO?!
WHY DOES HE HAVE TO BE SO POPULAR?!
OH CRAP!!
WHAT IF...
..."B" IS FOR... BEACH TANNED?!
AH, NO WAY! NOW I'M REALLY GRASPING AT...
YAAAAHH!!

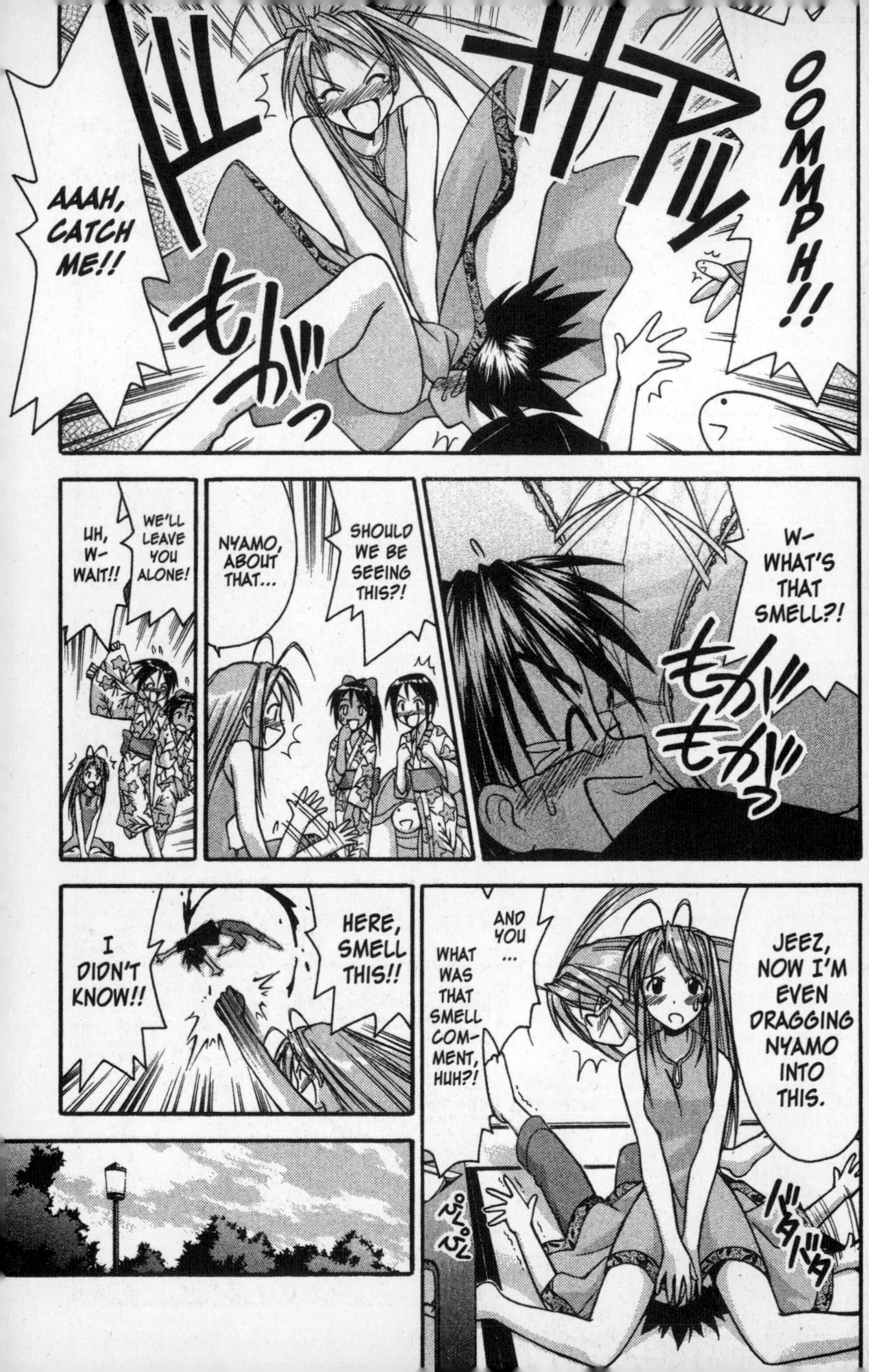
OOMMPH!!
ドサッ
AAAH, CATCH ME!!
もがっ
W-WHAT'S THAT SMELL?!
もがもがっ
SHOULD WE BE SEEING THIS?!
NYAMO, ABOUT THAT...
WE'LL LEAVE YOU ALONE!
UH, W-WAIT!!
JEEZ, NOW I'M EVEN DRAGGING NYAMO INTO THIS.
AND YOU ...
WHAT WAS THAT SMELL COMMENT, HUH?!
バタバタ
HERE, SMELL THIS!!
I DIDN'T KNOW!!

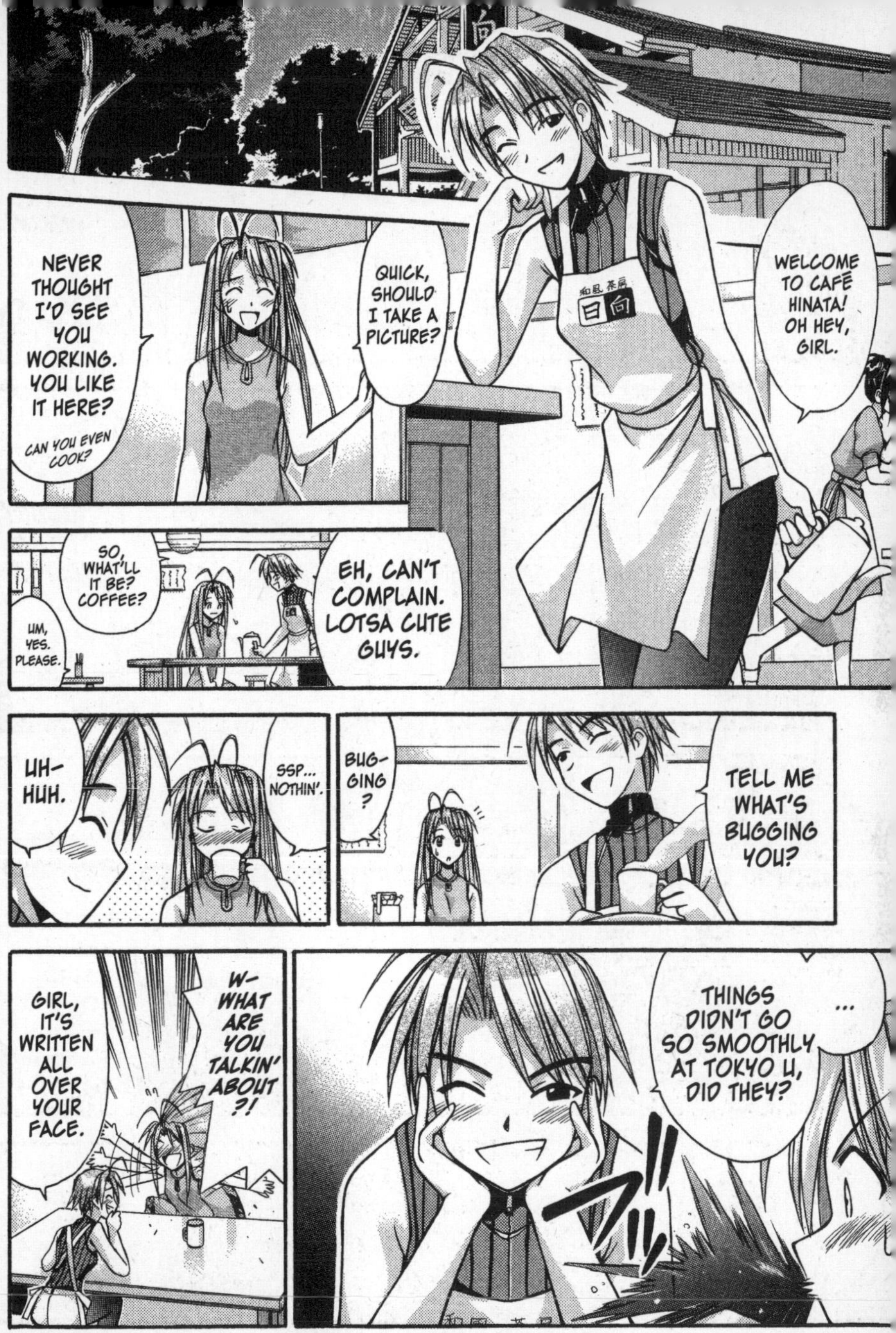
WELCOME TO CAFÉ HINATA! OH HEY, GIRL.
QUICK, SHOULD I TAKE A PICTURE?
NEVER THOUGHT I'D SEE YOU WORKING. YOU LIKE IT HERE?
CAN YOU EVEN COOK?
EH, CAN'T COMPLAIN. LOTSA CUTE GUYS.
SO, WHAT'LL IT BE? COFFEE?
UM, YES. PLEASE.
TELL ME WHAT'S BUGGING YOU?
BUG-GING?
SSP... NOTHIN'.
UH-HUH.
...
THINGS DIDN'T GO SO SMOOTHLY AT TOKYO U, DID THEY?
W-WHAT ARE YOU TALKIN' ABOUT?!
GIRL, IT'S WRITTEN ALL OVER YOUR FACE.

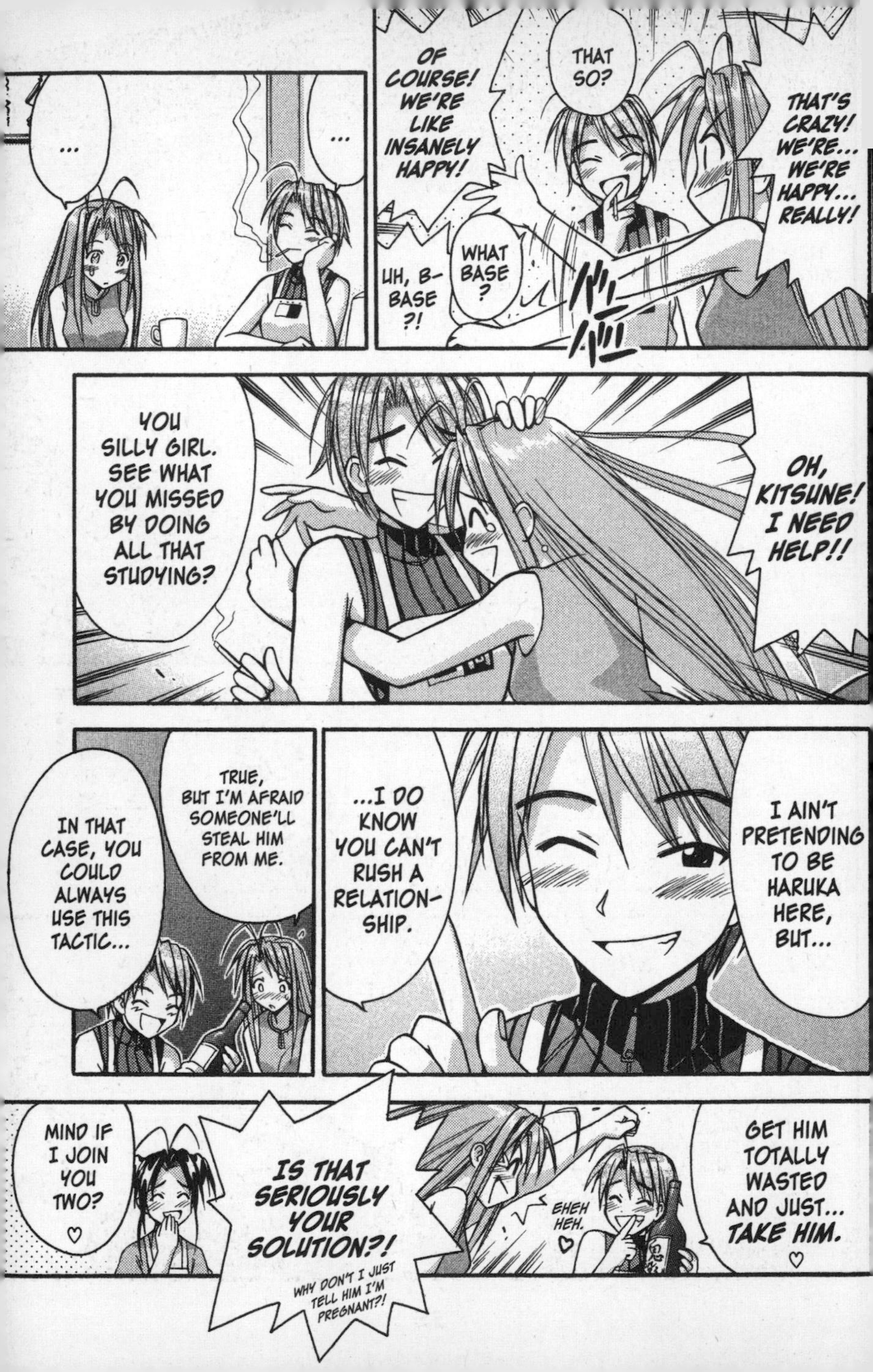
THAT SO?
THAT'S CRAZY! WE'RE... WE'RE HAPPY... REALLY!
OF COURSE! WE'RE LIKE INSANELY HAPPY!
WHAT BASE?
UH, B-BASE?!
...
...
OH, KITSUNE! I NEED HELP!!
YOU SILLY GIRL. SEE WHAT YOU MISSED BY DOING ALL THAT STUDYING?
I AIN'T PRETENDING TO BE HARUKA HERE, BUT...
...I DO KNOW YOU CAN'T RUSH A RELATION-SHIP.
TRUE, BUT I'M AFRAID SOMEONE'LL STEAL HIM FROM ME.
IN THAT CASE, YOU COULD ALWAYS USE THIS TACTIC...
GET HIM TOTALLY WASTED AND JUST... TAKE HIM. ♡
EHEH HEH. ♡
IS THAT SERIOUSLY YOUR SOLUTION?!
WHY DON'T I JUST TELL HIM I'M PREGNANT?!
MIND IF I JOIN YOU TWO? ♡

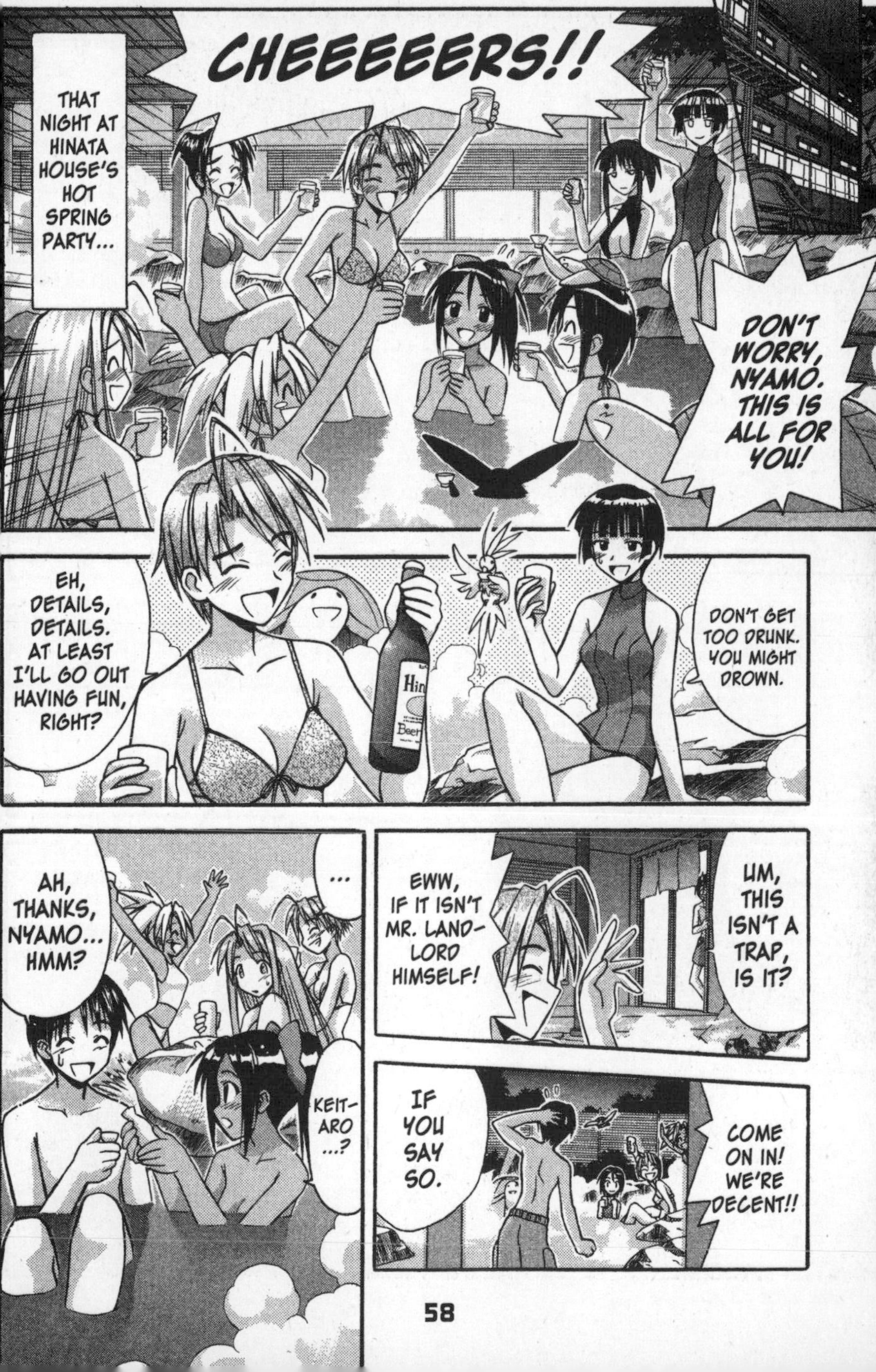
THAT NIGHT AT HINATA HOUSE'S HOT SPRING PARTY...
CHEEEEEERS!!
DON'T WORRY, NYAMO. THIS IS ALL FOR YOU!
DON'T GET TOO DRUNK. YOU MIGHT DROWN.
EH, DETAILS, DETAILS. AT LEAST I'LL GO OUT HAVING FUN, RIGHT?
UM, THIS ISN'T A TRAP, IS IT?
EWW, IF IT ISN'T MR. LAND-LORD HIMSELF!
COME ON IN! WE'RE DECENT!!
IF YOU SAY SO.
...
AH, THANKS, NYAMO... HMM?
KEIT-ARO ...?

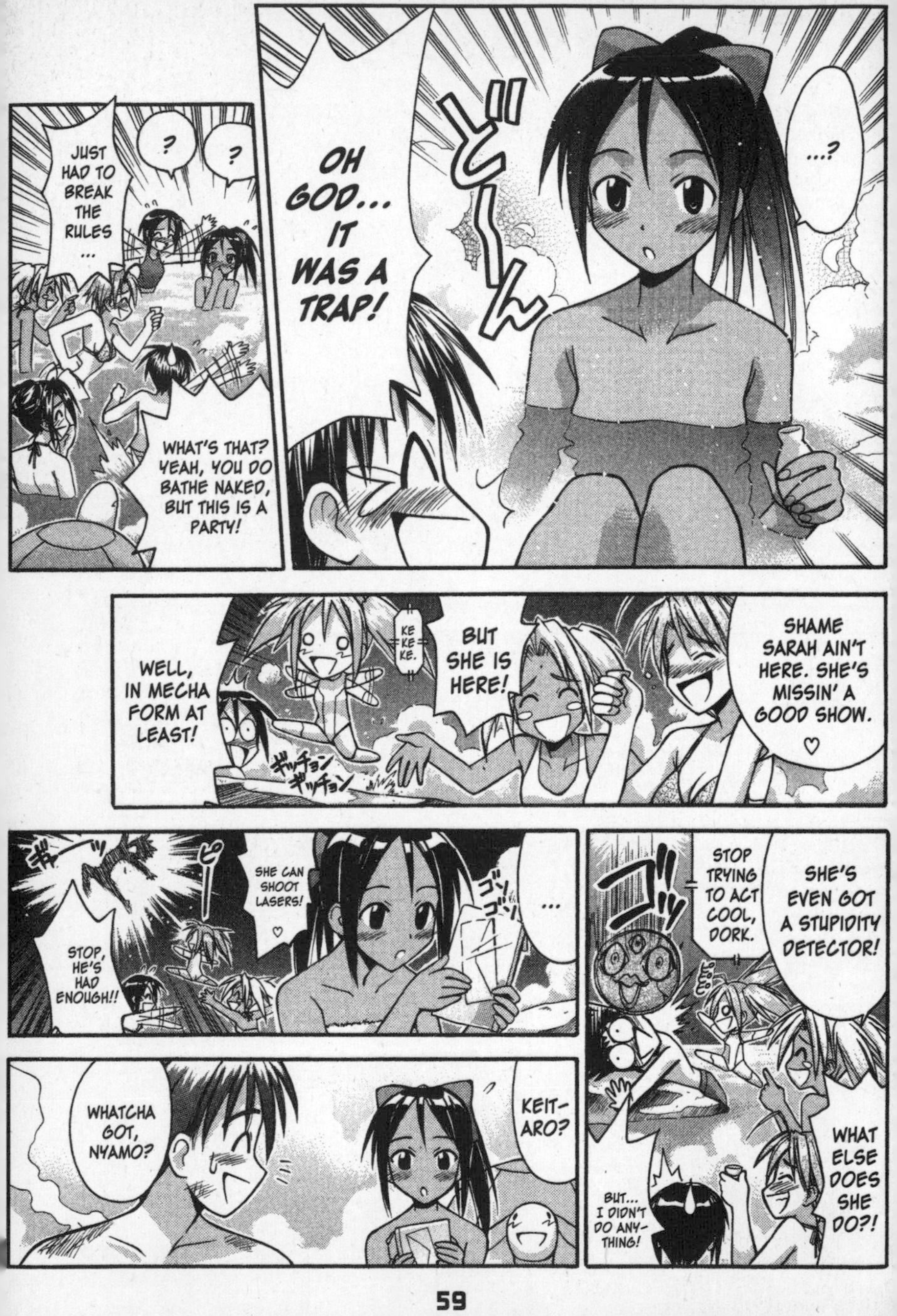
...?
どーん
OH GOD... IT WAS A TRAP!
?
?
JUST HAD TO BREAK THE RULES ...
WHAT'S THAT? YEAH, YOU DO BATHE NAKED, BUT THIS IS A PARTY!
SHAME SARAH AIN'T HERE. SHE'S MISSIN' A GOOD SHOW. ♡
BUT SHE IS HERE!
KE KE KE.
WELL, IN MECHA FORM AT LEAST!
ギッチョン ギッチョン
SHE'S EVEN GOT A STUPIDITY DETECTOR!
STOP TRYING TO ACT COOL, DORK.
ゴッ
WHAT ELSE DOES SHE DO?!
BUT... I DIDN'T DO ANY-THING!
...
SHE CAN SHOOT LASERS! ♡
ピ
STOP, HE'S HAD ENOUGH!!
KEIT-ARO?
WHATCHA GOT, NYAMO?

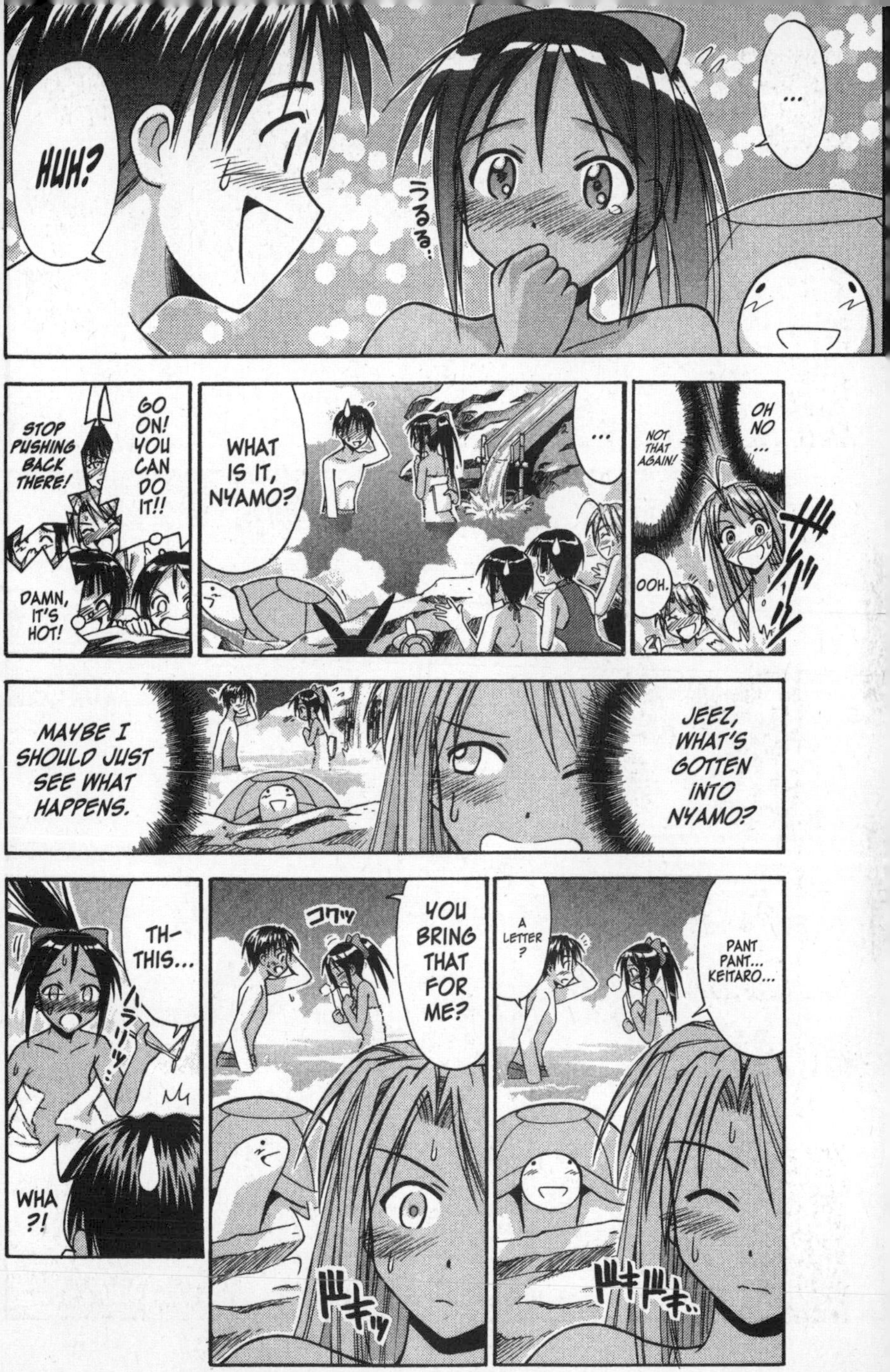
...
うるる..
HUH?
OH NO...
NOT THAT AGAIN!
OOH.
...
WHAT IS IT, NYAMO?
GO ON! YOU CAN DO IT!!
STOP PUSHING BACK THERE!
DAMN, IT'S HOT!
JEEZ, WHAT'S GOTTEN INTO NYAMO?
MAYBE I SHOULD JUST SEE WHAT HAPPENS.
PANT PANT... KEITARO...
A LETTER?
ドキドキ
YOU BRING THAT FOR ME?
コクッ
ドキッ
TH- THIS...
ハラリッ
WHA?!

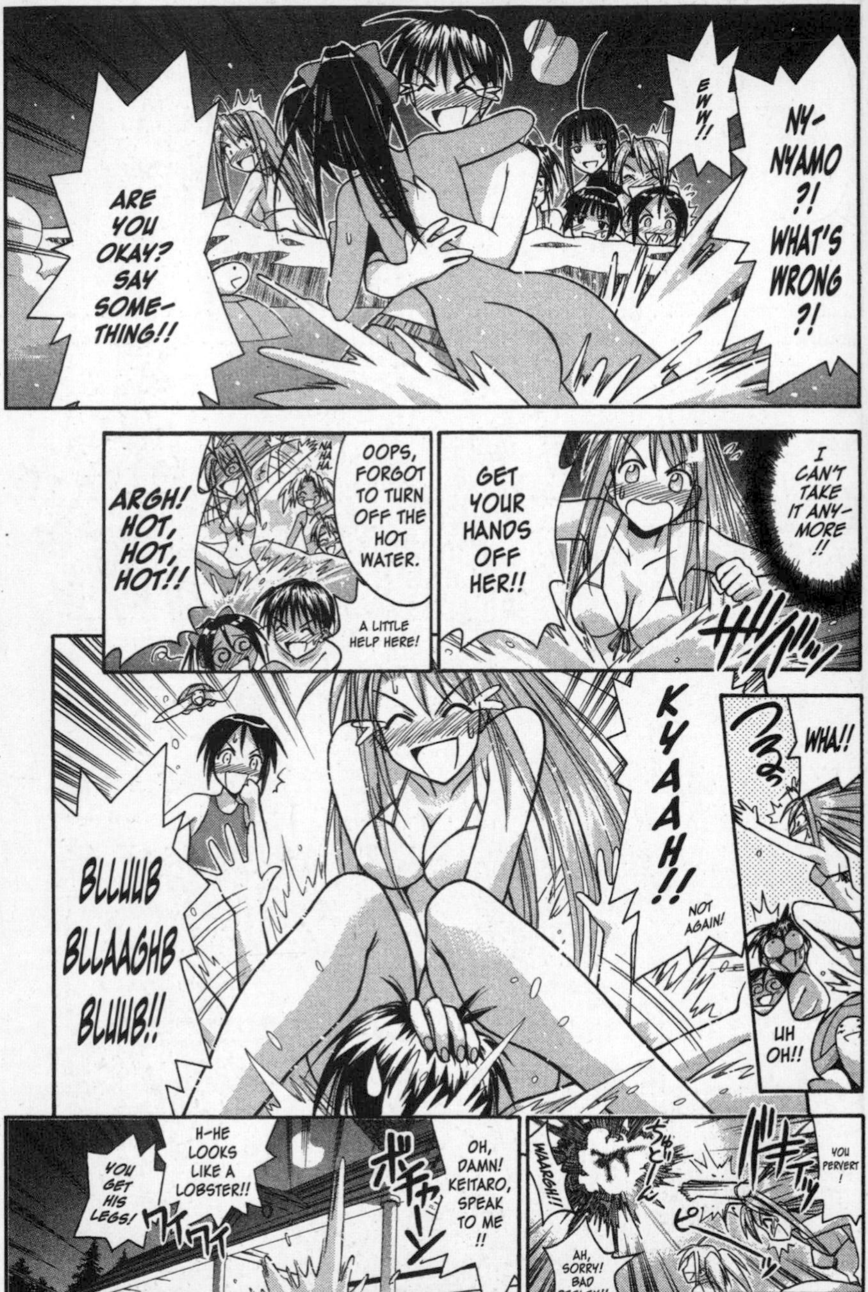
NY-NYAMO ?! WHAT'S WRONG ?!
EWW!!
ARE YOU OKAY? SAY SOME-THING!!
I CAN'T TAKE IT ANY-MORE !!
GET YOUR HANDS OFF HER!!
OOPS, FORGOT TO TURN OFF THE HOT WATER.
NA HA HA.
ARGH! HOT, HOT, HOT!!
A LITTLE HELP HERE!
WHA!!
UH OH!!
KYAAAH!!
NOT AGAIN!
BLLUUB BLLAAGHB BLUUB!!
YOU PERVERT!
WAARGH!!
AH, SORRY! BAD REFLEX!!
THAT WAS A REFLEX?!
OH, DAMN! KEITARO, SPEAK TO ME !!
H-HE LOOKS LIKE A LOBSTER!!
YOU GET HIS LEGS!

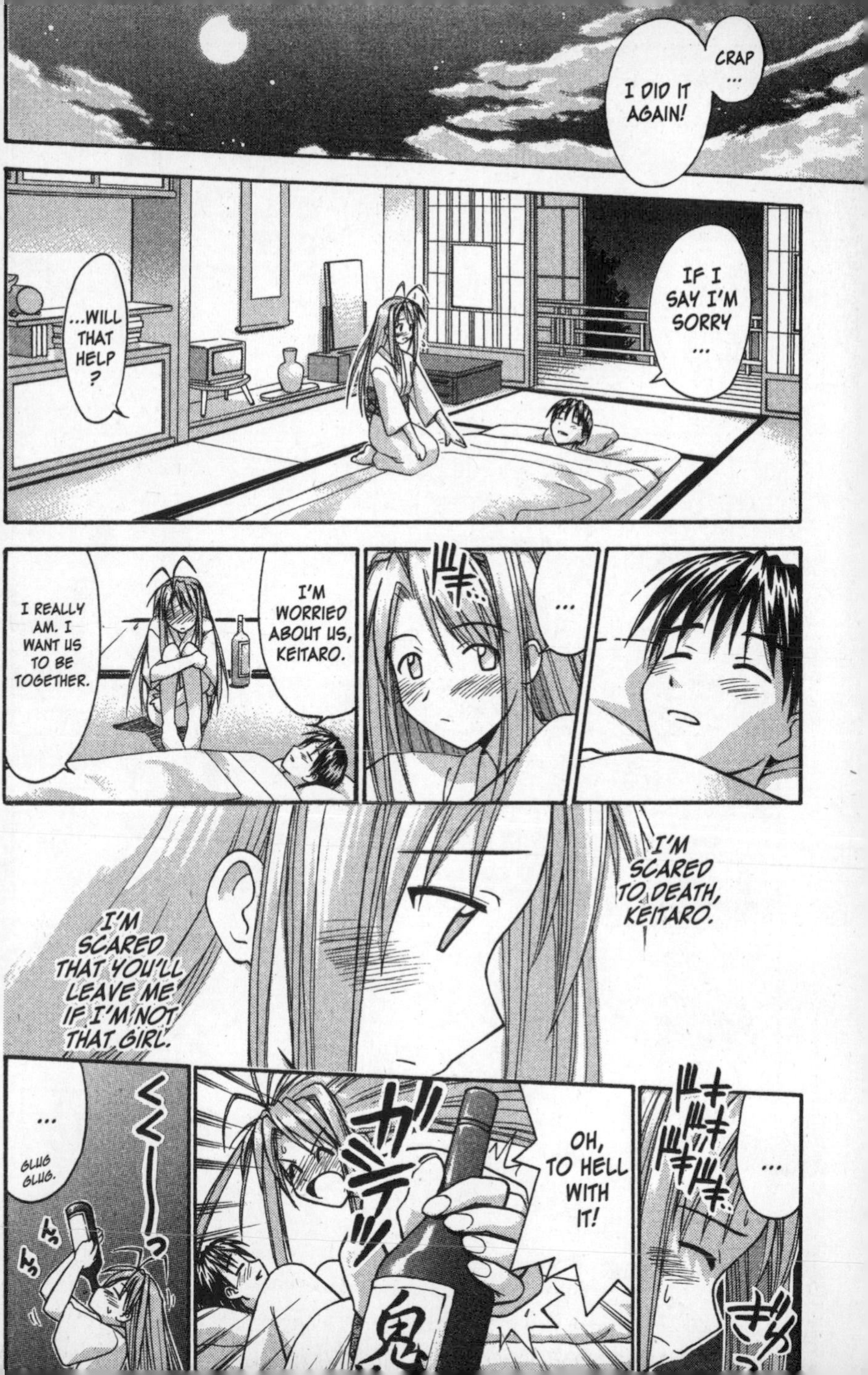
CRAP ...
I DID IT AGAIN!
IF I SAY I'M SORRY ...
...WILL THAT HELP ?
...
I'M WORRIED ABOUT US, KEITARO.
I REALLY AM. I WANT US TO BE TOGETHER.
I'M SCARED TO DEATH, KEITARO.
I'M SCARED THAT YOU'LL LEAVE ME IF I'M NOT THAT GIRL.
...
OH, TO HELL WITH IT!
...
GLUG GLUG.

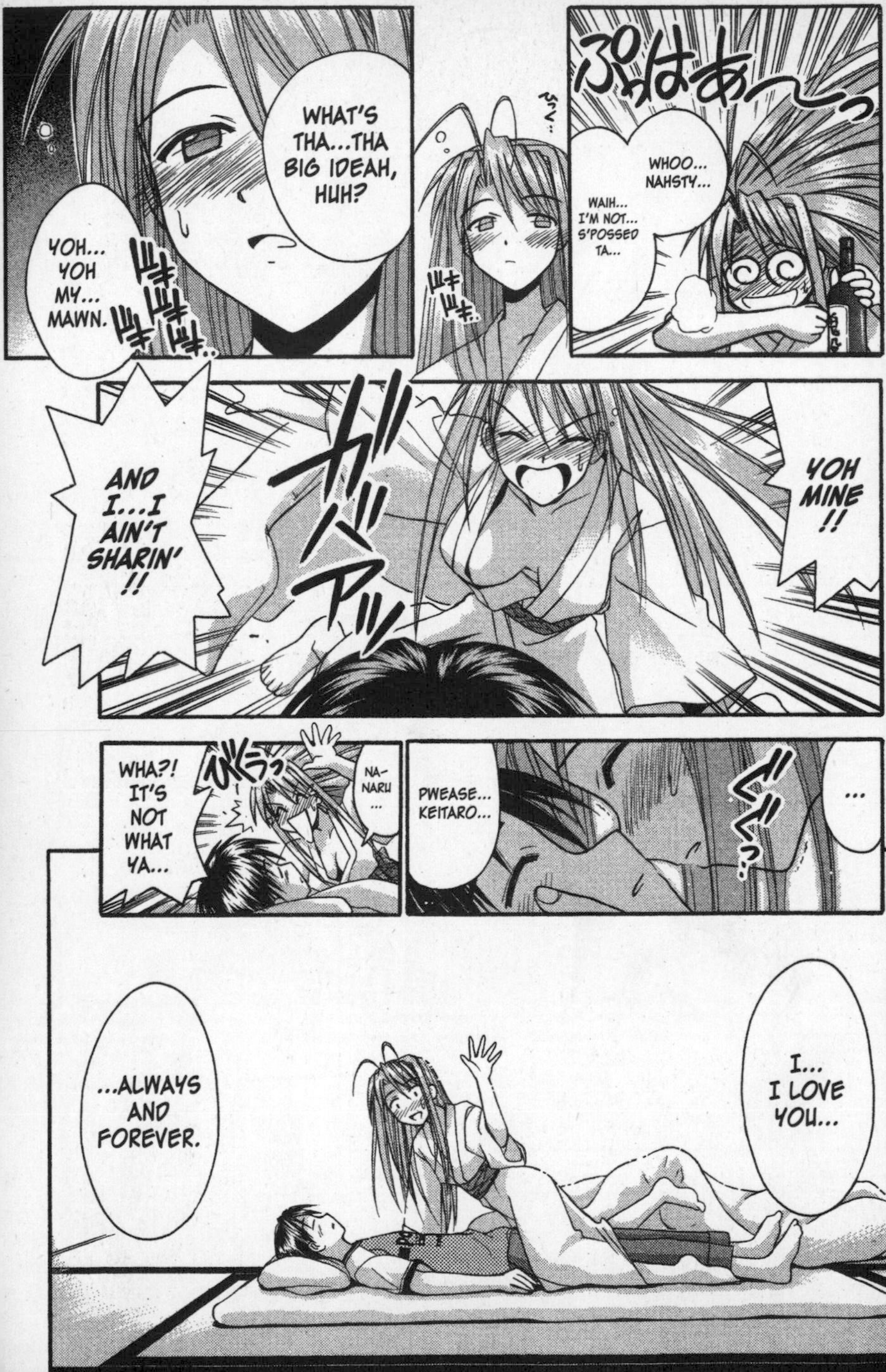
ぷはあ〜っ
WHOO... NAHSTY...
WAIH... I'M NOT... S'POSSED TA...
WHAT'S THA...THA BIG IDEAH, HUH?
YOH... YOH MY... MAWN.
YOH MINE !!
ガバアッ
AND I...I AIN'T SHARIN' !!
...
PWEASE... KEITARO...
NA-NARU ...
WHA?! IT'S NOT WHAT YA...
I... I LOVE YOU...
...ALWAYS AND FOREVER.

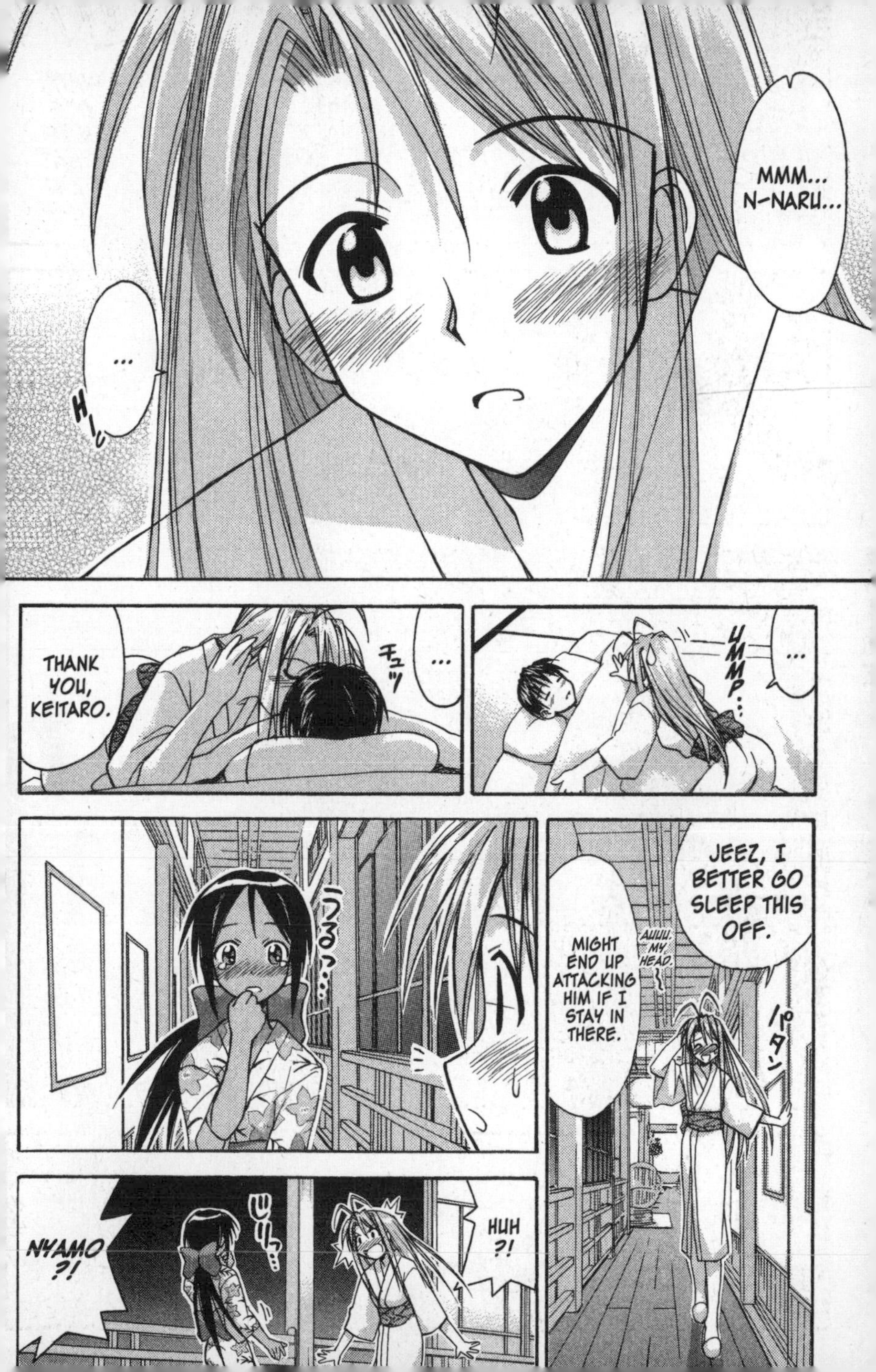
MMM... N-NARU...
...
HIC
...
UMMP...
...
チュッ
THANK YOU, KEITARO.
JEEZ, I BETTER GO SLEEP THIS OFF.
AUUU. MY HEAD.
MIGHT END UP ATTACKING HIM IF I STAY IN THERE.
パタン
うるる...
HUH ?!
NYAMO ?!

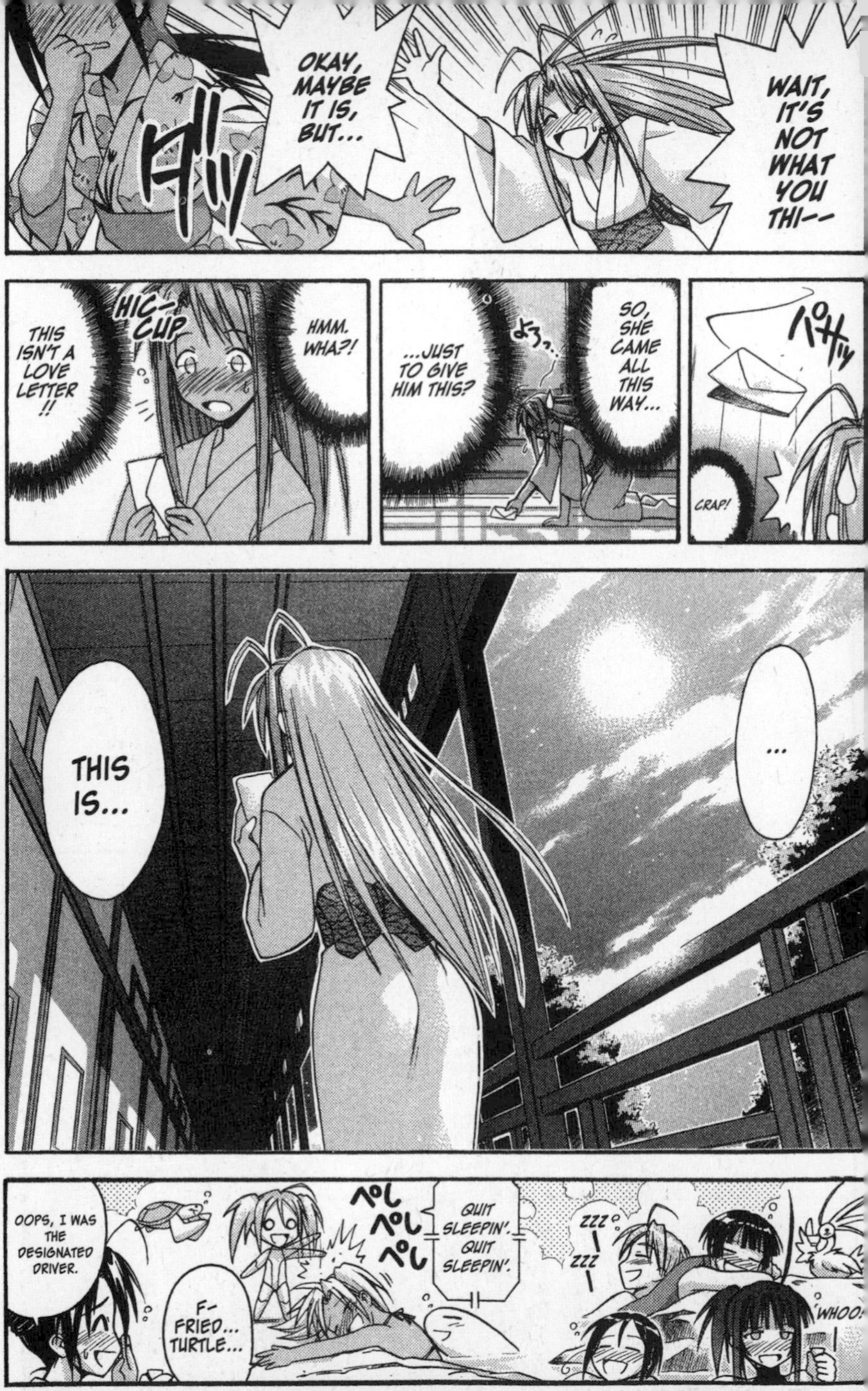
WAIT, IT'S NOT WHAT YOU THI--
OKAY, MAYBE IT IS, BUT...
パサッ
CRAP!
SO, SHE CAME ALL THIS WAY...
よろっ
...JUST TO GIVE HIM THIS?
HMM. WHA?!
HIC-CUP
THIS ISN'T A LOVE LETTER!!
...
THIS IS...
WHOO!
ZZZ ZZZ
QUIT SLEEPIN'. QUIT SLEEPIN'.
ぺしぺしぺし
F-FRIED... TURTLE...
OOPS, I WAS THE DESIGNATED DRIVER.

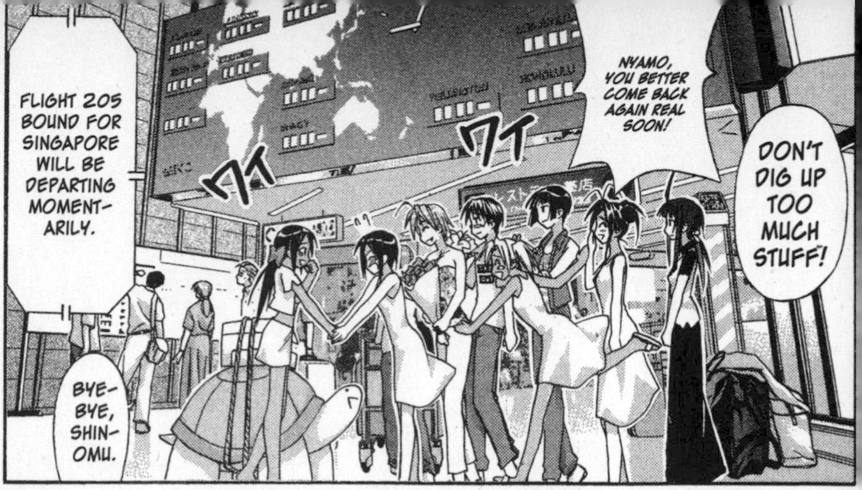
DON'T DIG UP TOO MUCH STUFF!
NYAMO, YOU BETTER COME BACK AGAIN REAL SOON!
ワイ
ワイ
FLIGHT 205 BOUND FOR SINGAPORE WILL BE DEPARTING MOMENT-ARILY.
BYE-BYE, SHINOMU.

Love Hina

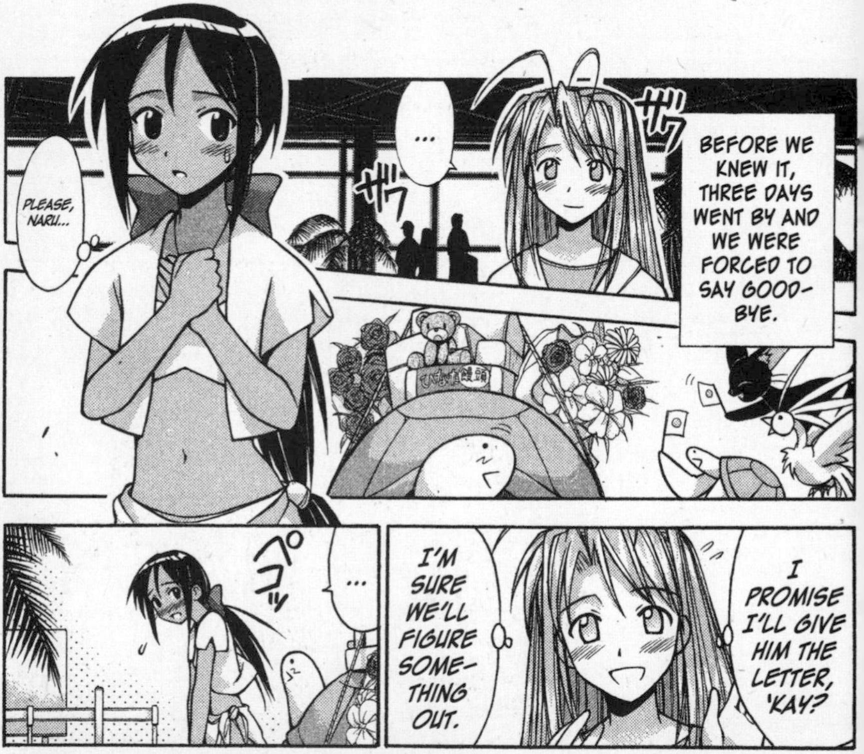
BEFORE WE KNEW IT, THREE DAYS WENT BY AND WE WERE FORCED TO SAY GOOD-BYE.
ザワ
ザワ
...
PLEASE, NARU...
I PROMISE I'LL GIVE HIM THE LETTER, 'KAY?
I'M SURE WE'LL FIGURE SOME-THING OUT.
...

HINATA..117 The Promise Girl (Part 1 of 2)

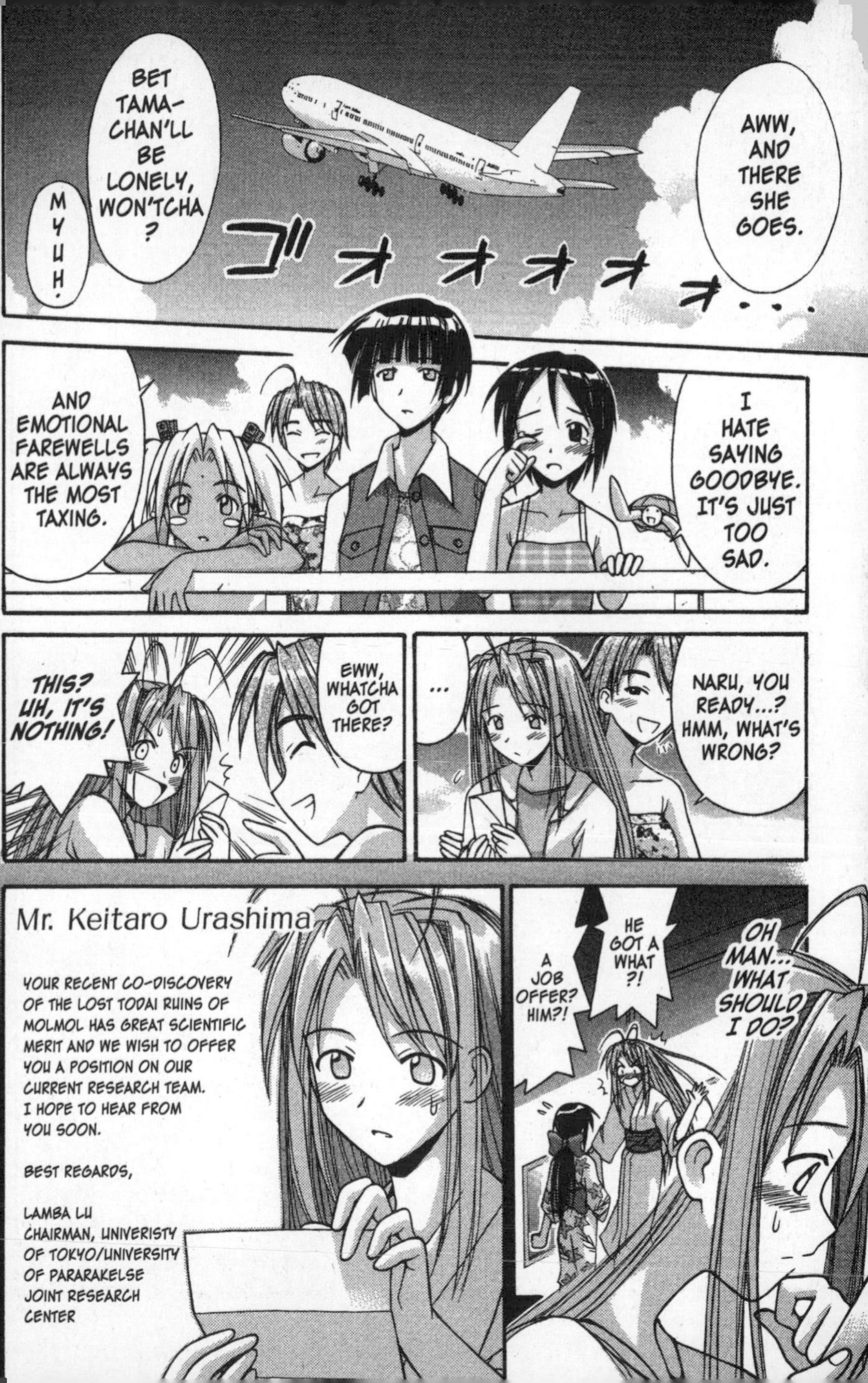
AWW, AND THERE SHE GOES.
BET TAMA-CHAN'LL BE LONELY, WON'TCHA?
MYUH.
ゴオオオオオ…
I HATE SAYING GOODBYE. IT'S JUST TOO SAD.
AND EMOTIONAL FAREWELLS ARE ALWAYS THE MOST TAXING.
NARU, YOU READY...? HMM, WHAT'S WRONG?
...
EWW, WHATCHA GOT THERE?
THIS? UH, IT'S NOTHING!
OH MAN... WHAT SHOULD I DO?
HE GOT A WHAT?!
A JOB OFFER? HIM?!
Mr. Keitaro Urashima
YOUR RECENT CO-DISCOVERY OF THE LOST TODAI RUINS OF MOLMOL HAS GREAT SCIENTIFIC MERIT AND WE WISH TO OFFER YOU A POSITION ON OUR CURRENT RESEARCH TEAM. I HOPE TO HEAR FROM YOU SOON.
BEST REGARDS,
LAMBA LU
CHAIRMAN, UNIVERISTY OF TOKYO/UNIVERSITY OF PARARAKELSE JOINT RESEARCH CENTER

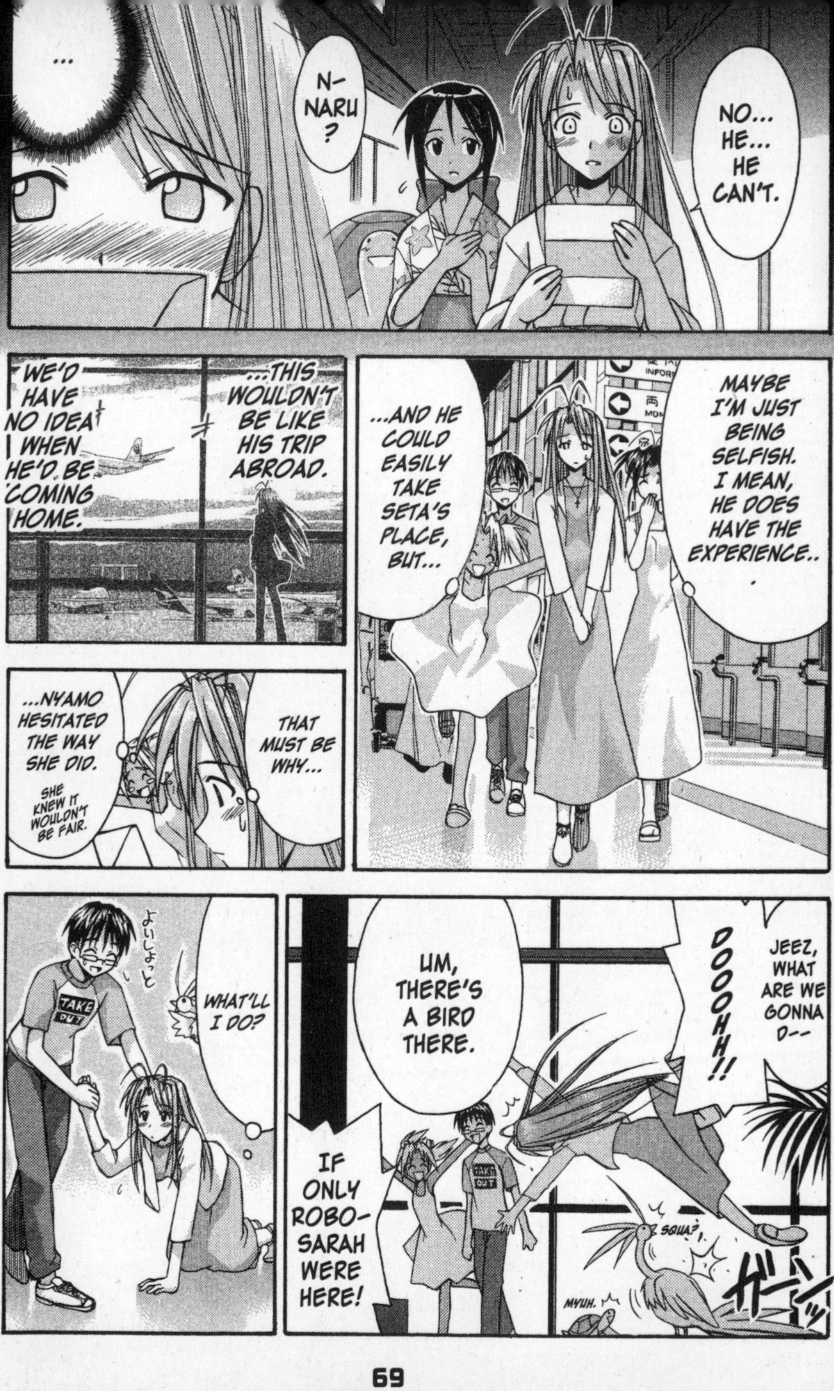

NO... HE... HE CAN'T.
N-NARU?
...
MAYBE I'M JUST BEING SELFISH. I MEAN, HE DOES HAVE THE EXPERIENCE...
...AND HE COULD EASILY TAKE SETA'S PLACE, BUT...
...THIS WOULDN'T BE LIKE HIS TRIP ABROAD.
WE'D HAVE NO IDEA WHEN HE'D BE COMING HOME.
THAT MUST BE WHY...
...NYAMO HESITATED THE WAY SHE DID.
SHE KNEW IT WOULDN'T BE FAIR.
JEEZ, WHAT ARE WE GONNA D--
DOOOOHH!!
UM, THERE'S A BIRD THERE.
TAKE OUT
IF ONLY ROBO-SARAH WERE HERE!
SQUA?!
ガバーッ
MYUH.
WHAT'LL I DO?
よいしょっと
TAKE OUT

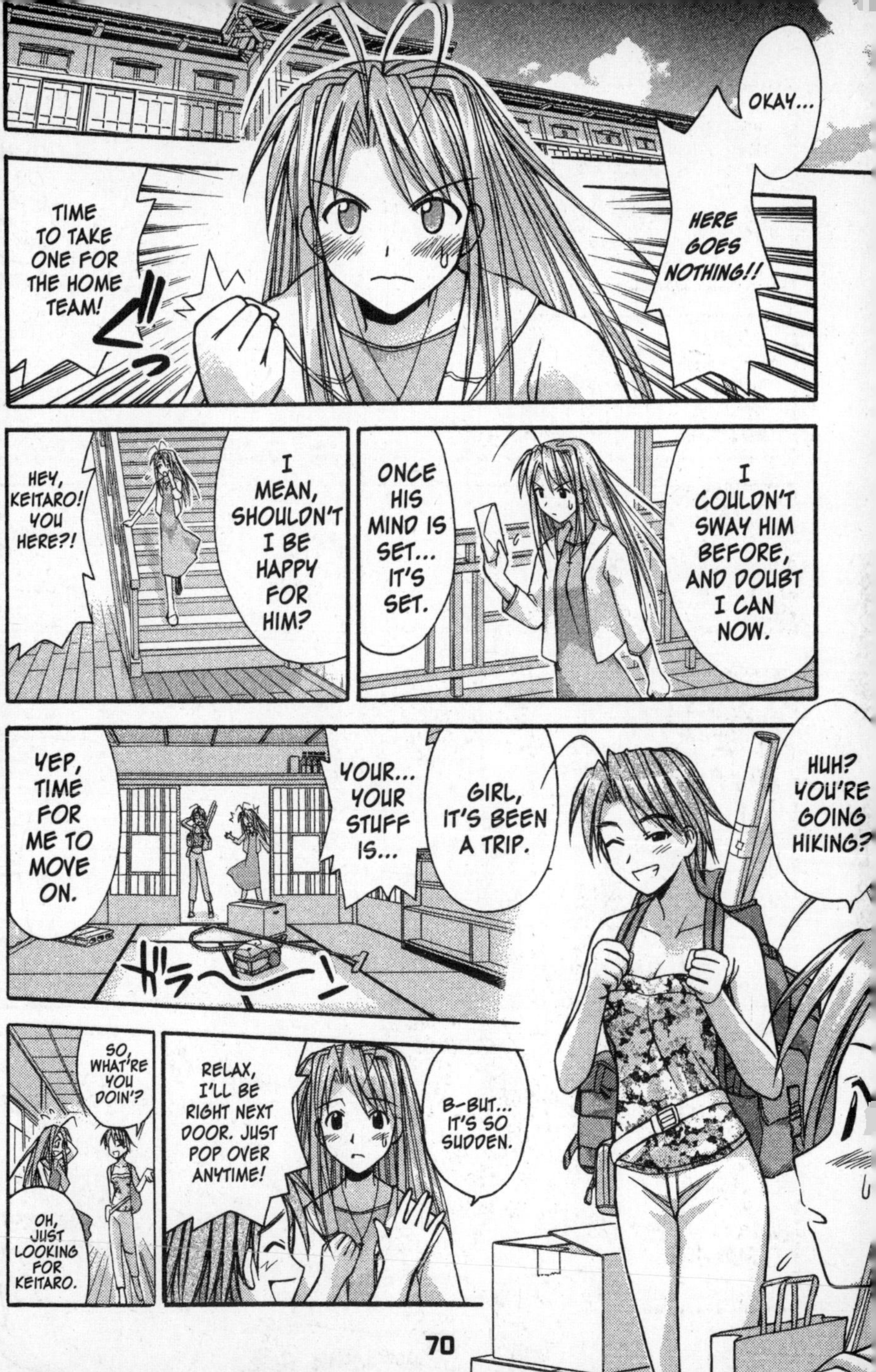
OKAY...
HERE GOES NOTHING!!
TIME TO TAKE ONE FOR THE HOME TEAM!
I COULDN'T SWAY HIM BEFORE, AND DOUBT I CAN NOW.
ONCE HIS MIND IS SET... IT'S SET.
I MEAN, SHOULDN'T I BE HAPPY FOR HIM?
HEY, KEITARO! YOU HERE?!
HUH? YOU'RE GOING HIKING?
GIRL, IT'S BEEN A TRIP.
YOUR... YOUR STUFF IS...
YEP, TIME FOR ME TO MOVE ON.
ガラ〜〜!
B-BUT... IT'S SO SUDDEN.
RELAX, I'LL BE RIGHT NEXT DOOR. JUST POP OVER ANYTIME!
SO, WHAT'RE YOU DOIN'?
OH, JUST LOOKING FOR KEITARO.

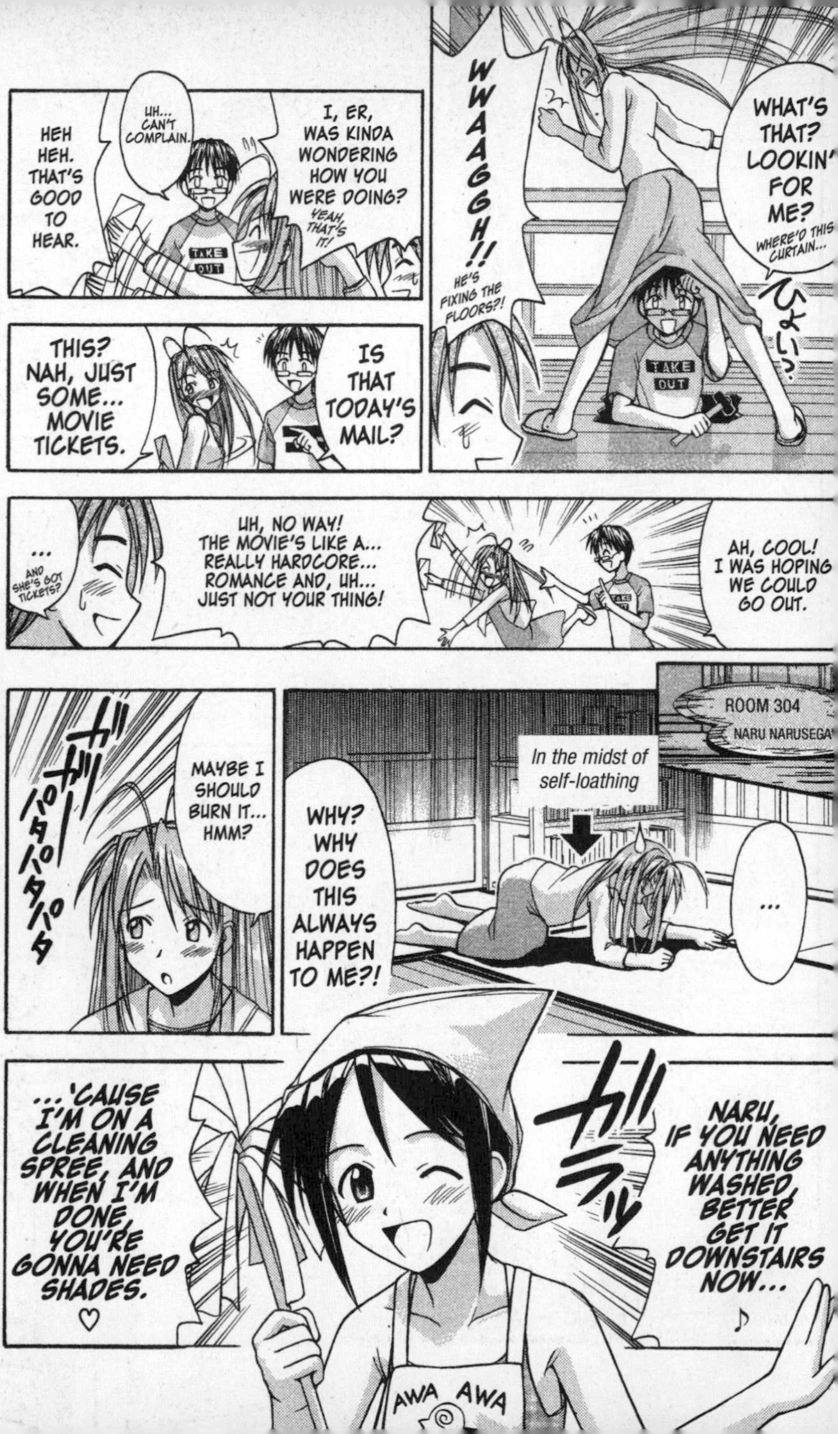
WHAT'S THAT? LOOKIN' FOR ME?
WHERE'D THIS CURTAIN...
WWAAGGH!!
HE'S FIXING THE FLOORS?!
ひょい?
UH... CAN'T COMPLAIN.
I, ER, WAS KINDA WONDERING HOW YOU WERE DOING?
YEAH, THAT'S IT!
HEH HEH. THAT'S GOOD TO HEAR.
IS THAT TODAY'S MAIL?
THIS? NAH, JUST SOME... MOVIE TICKETS.
AH, COOL! I WAS HOPING WE COULD GO OUT.
UH, NO WAY! THE MOVIE'S LIKE A... REALLY HARDCORE... ROMANCE AND, UH... JUST NOT YOUR THING!
...
AND SHE'S GOT TICKETS?
ROOM 304
NARU NARUSEGA
In the midst of self-loathing
...
WHY? WHY DOES THIS ALWAYS HAPPEN TO ME?!
MAYBE I SHOULD BURN IT... HMM?
NARU, IF YOU NEED ANYTHING WASHED, BETTER GET IT DOWNSTAIRS NOW... ♪
...'CAUSE I'M ON A CLEANING SPREE, AND WHEN I'M DONE, YOU'RE GONNA NEED SHADES. ♡
AWA AWA

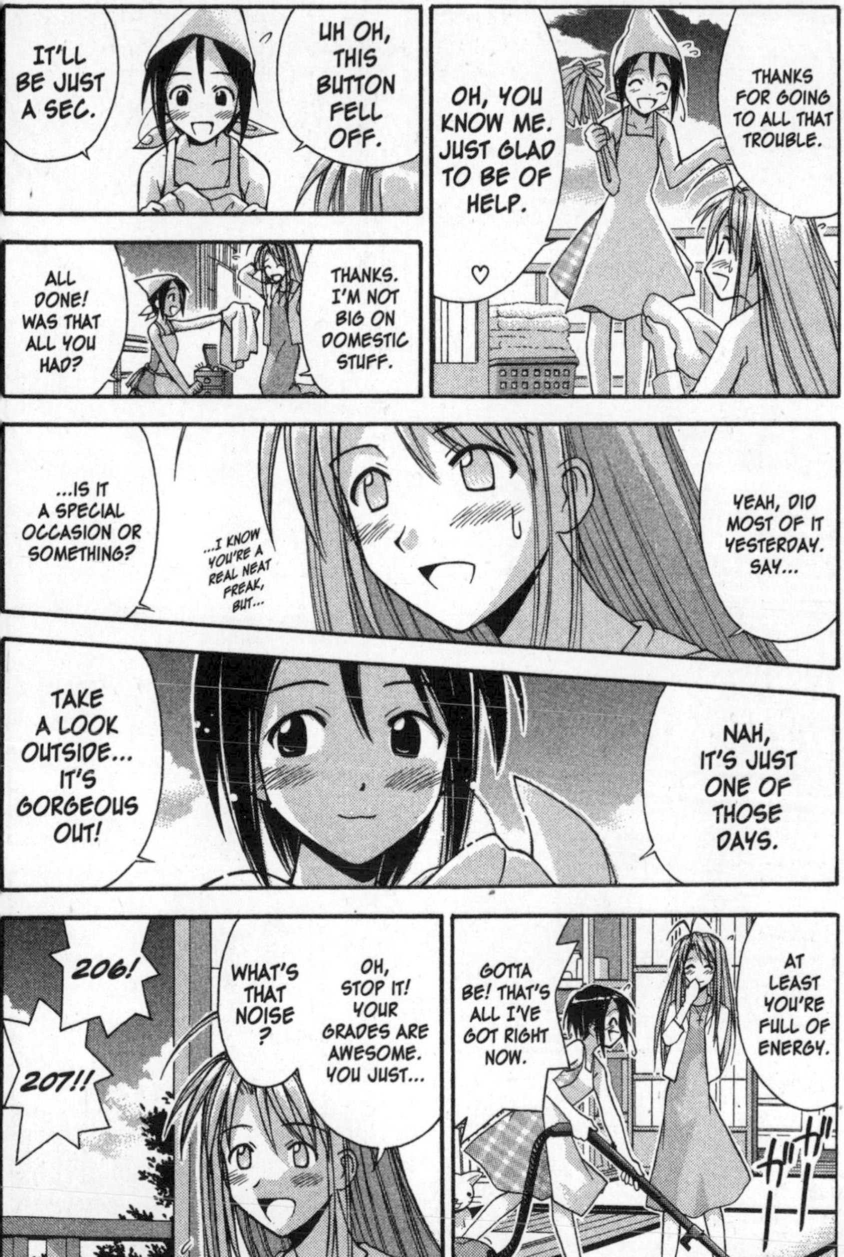
THANKS FOR GOING TO ALL THAT TROUBLE.
OH, YOU KNOW ME. JUST GLAD TO BE OF HELP. ♡
UH OH, THIS BUTTON FELL OFF.
IT'LL BE JUST A SEC.
THANKS. I'M NOT BIG ON DOMESTIC STUFF.
ALL DONE! WAS THAT ALL YOU HAD?
YEAH, DID MOST OF IT YESTERDAY. SAY...
...I KNOW YOU'RE A REAL NEAT FREAK, BUT...
...IS IT A SPECIAL OCCASION OR SOMETHING?
NAH, IT'S JUST ONE OF THOSE DAYS.
TAKE A LOOK OUTSIDE... IT'S GORGEOUS OUT!
AT LEAST YOU'RE FULL OF ENERGY.
GOTTA BE! THAT'S ALL I'VE GOT RIGHT NOW.
ガーガー
OH, STOP IT! YOUR GRADES ARE AWESOME. YOU JUST...
WHAT'S THAT NOISE?
206!
207!!

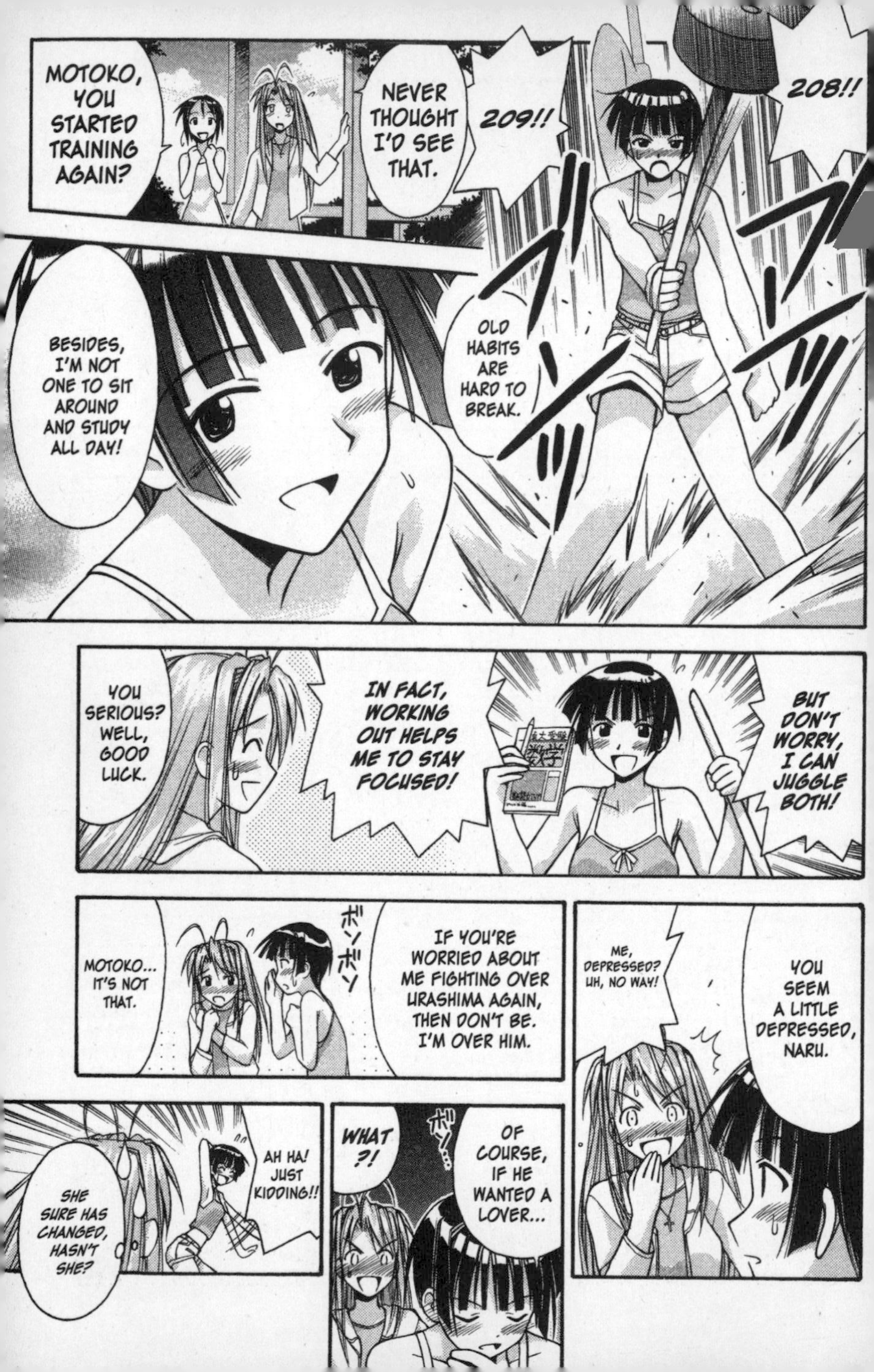
208!!
209!!
OLD HABITS ARE HARD TO BREAK.
MOTOKO, YOU STARTED TRAINING AGAIN?
NEVER THOUGHT I'D SEE THAT.
BESIDES, I'M NOT ONE TO SIT AROUND AND STUDY ALL DAY!
BUT DON'T WORRY, I CAN JUGGLE BOTH!
IN FACT, WORKING OUT HELPS ME TO STAY FOCUSED!
YOU SERIOUS? WELL, GOOD LUCK.
YOU SEEM A LITTLE DEPRESSED, NARU.
ME, DEPRESSED? UH, NO WAY!
IF YOU'RE WORRIED ABOUT ME FIGHTING OVER URASHIMA AGAIN, THEN DON'T BE. I'M OVER HIM.
ボソボソ
MOTOKO... IT'S NOT THAT.
OF COURSE, IF HE WANTED A LOVER...
ボソ...
WHAT ?!
AH HA! JUST KIDDING!!
SHE SURE HAS CHANGED, HASN'T SHE?

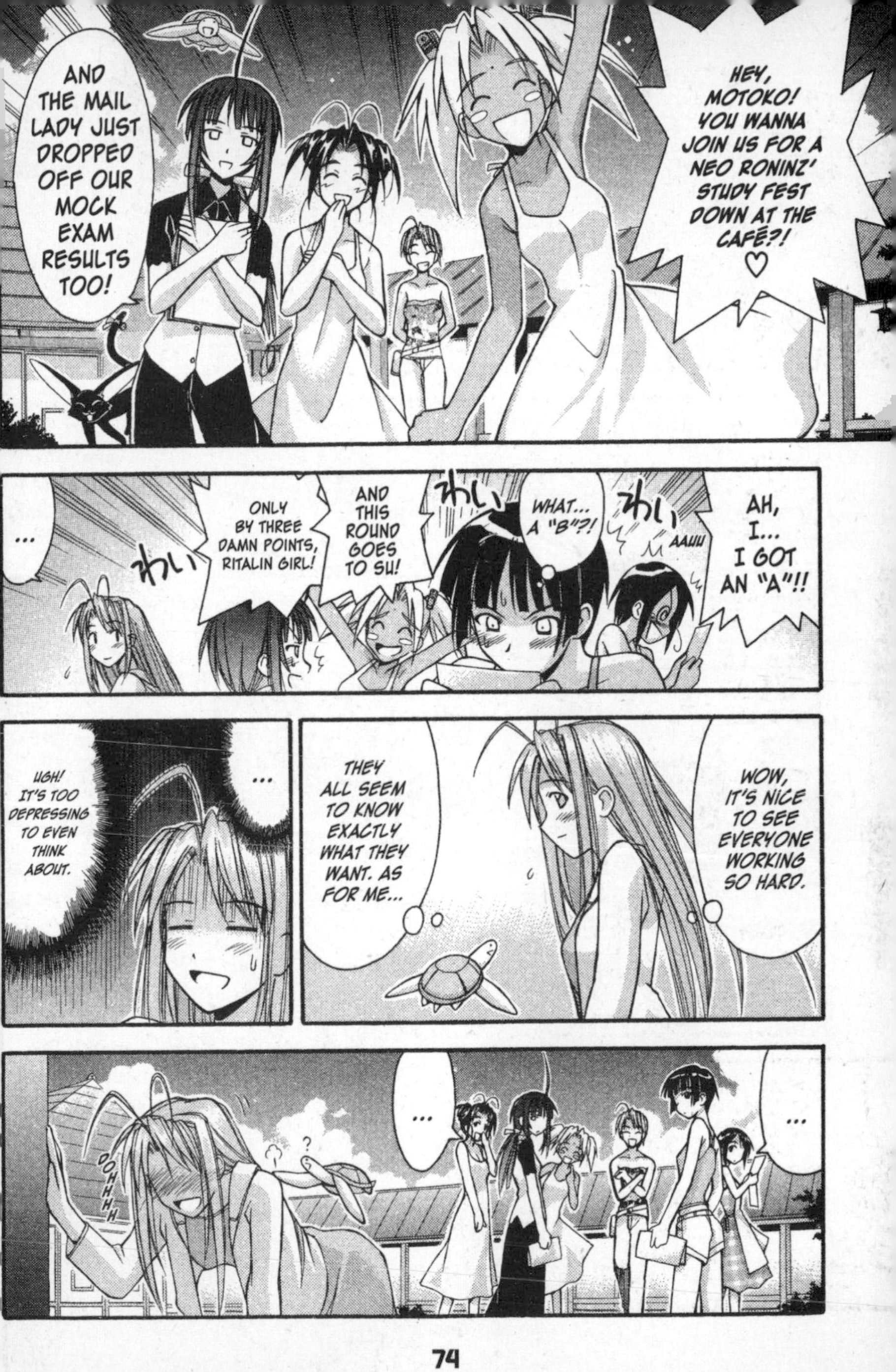
HEY, MOTOKO! YOU WANNA JOIN US FOR A NEO RONINZ' STUDY FEST DOWN AT THE CAFÉ?! ♡
AND THE MAIL LADY JUST DROPPED OFF OUR MOCK EXAM RESULTS TOO!
AH, I... I GOT AN "A"!!
AAUU
わい
WHAT... A "B"?!
わい
AND THIS ROUND GOES TO SU!
ONLY BY THREE DAMN POINTS, RITALIN GIRL!
わい
...
WOW, IT'S NICE TO SEE EVERYONE WORKING SO HARD.
THEY ALL SEEM TO KNOW EXACTLY WHAT THEY WANT. AS FOR ME...
...
UGH! IT'S TOO DEPRESSING TO EVEN THINK ABOUT.
...
...
DOHHHH

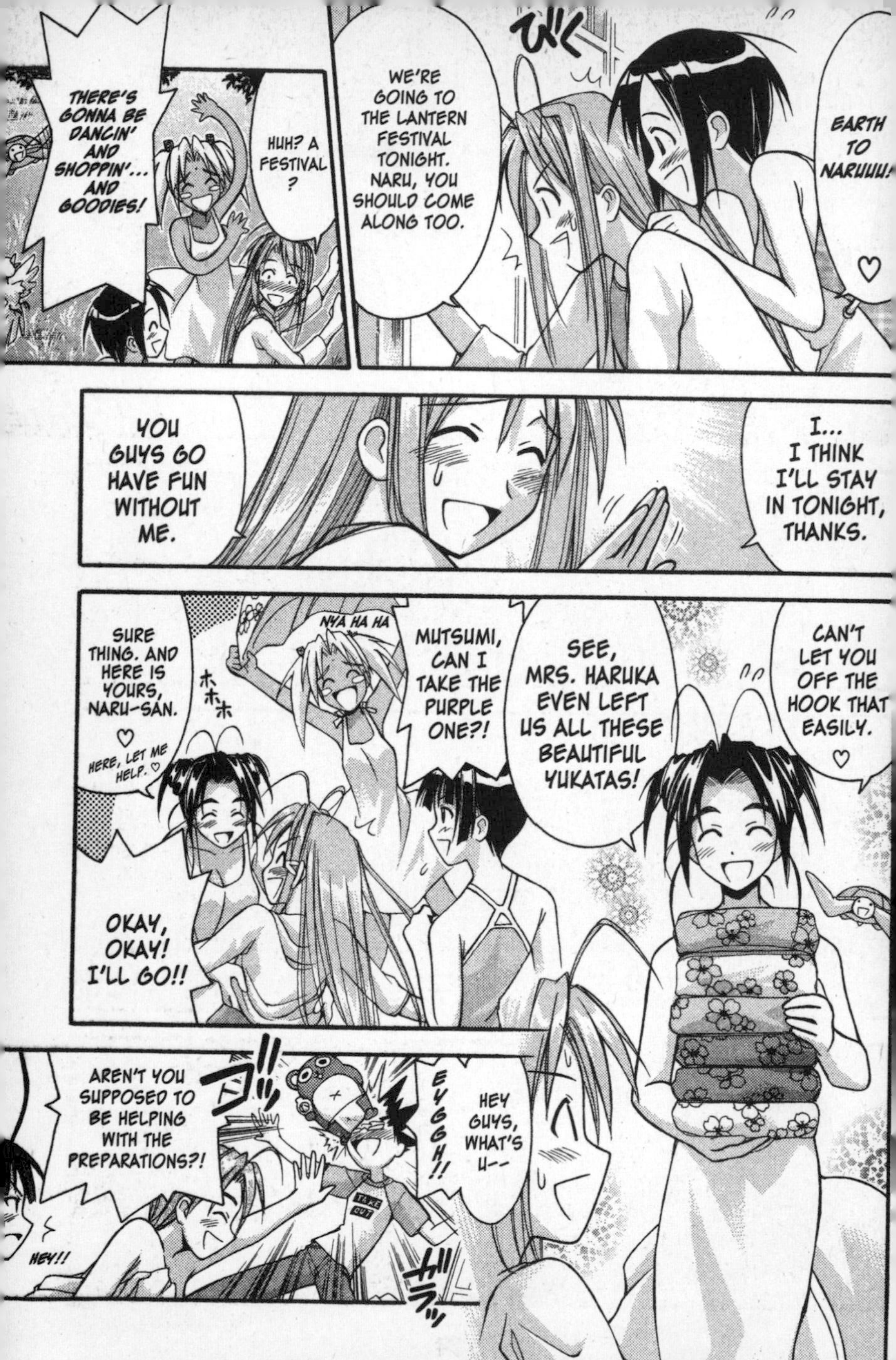
EARTH TO NARUUUU!
WE'RE GOING TO THE LANTERN FESTIVAL TONIGHT. NARU, YOU SHOULD COME ALONG TOO.
HUH? A FESTIVAL?
THERE'S GONNA BE DANCIN' AND SHOPPIN'... AND GOODIES!
I... I THINK I'LL STAY IN TONIGHT, THANKS.
YOU GUYS GO HAVE FUN WITHOUT ME.
CAN'T LET YOU OFF THE HOOK THAT EASILY.
SEE, MRS. HARUKA EVEN LEFT US ALL THESE BEAUTIFUL YUKATAS!
MUTSUMI, CAN I TAKE THE PURPLE ONE?!
NYA HA HA
SURE THING. AND HERE IS YOURS, NARU-SAN.
HERE, LET ME HELP.
OKAY, OKAY! I'LL GO!!
HEY GUYS, WHAT'S U--
EYGGH!!
AREN'T YOU SUPPOSED TO BE HELPING WITH THE PREPARATIONS?!
HEY!!

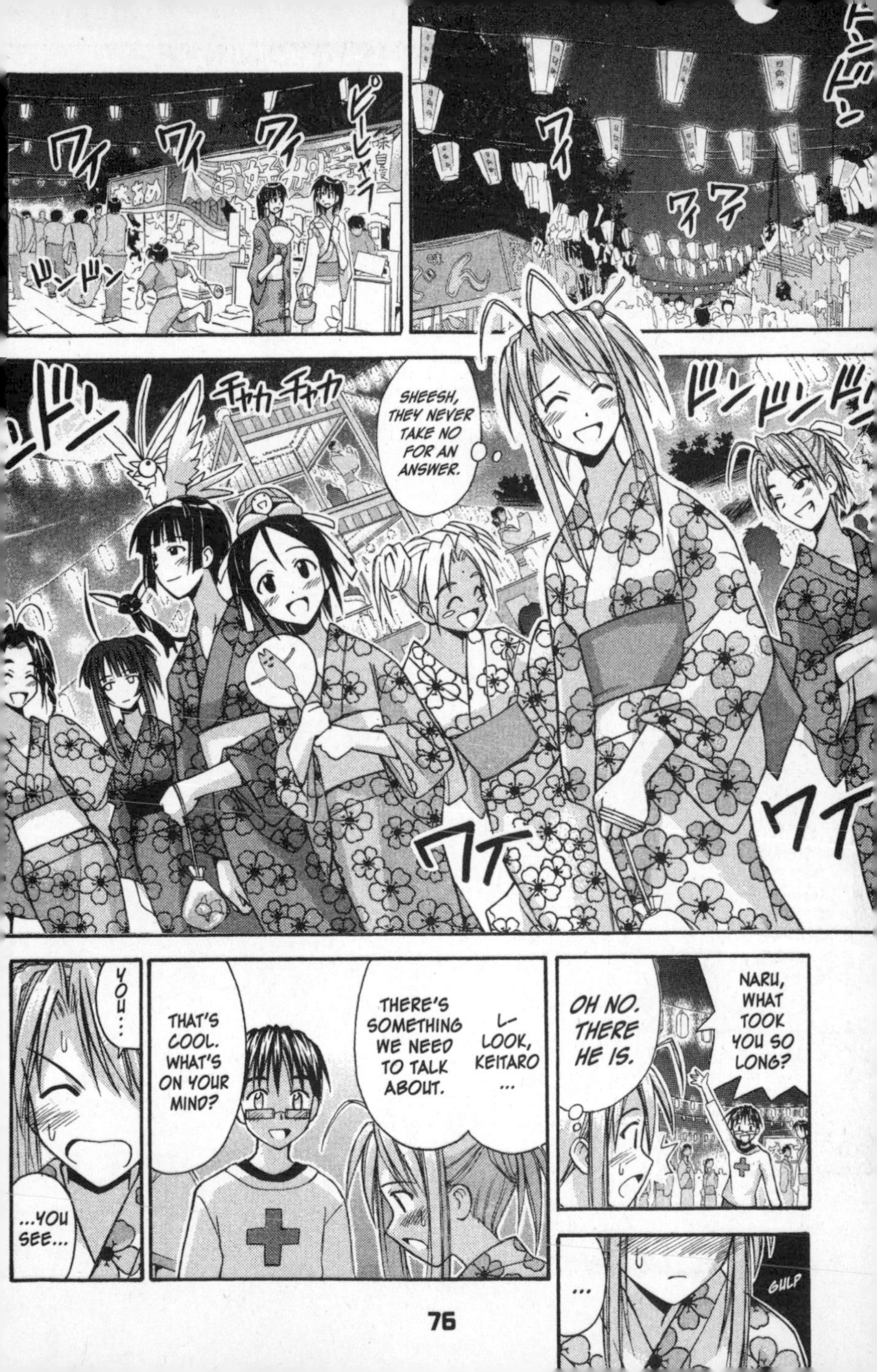
ドドン
ワイ
ワイワイ
ワイ ワイ ワイ
ピーヒャラ
ドンドン
ドドン
チャカ チャカ
SHEESH, THEY NEVER TAKE NO FOR AN ANSWER.
ドンドンドン
ワイ
ワイ
NARU, WHAT TOOK YOU SO LONG?
OH NO. THERE HE IS.
...
GULP
L-LOOK, KEITARO...
THERE'S SOMETHING WE NEED TO TALK ABOUT.
THAT'S COOL. WHAT'S ON YOUR MIND?
YOU...
...YOU SEE...

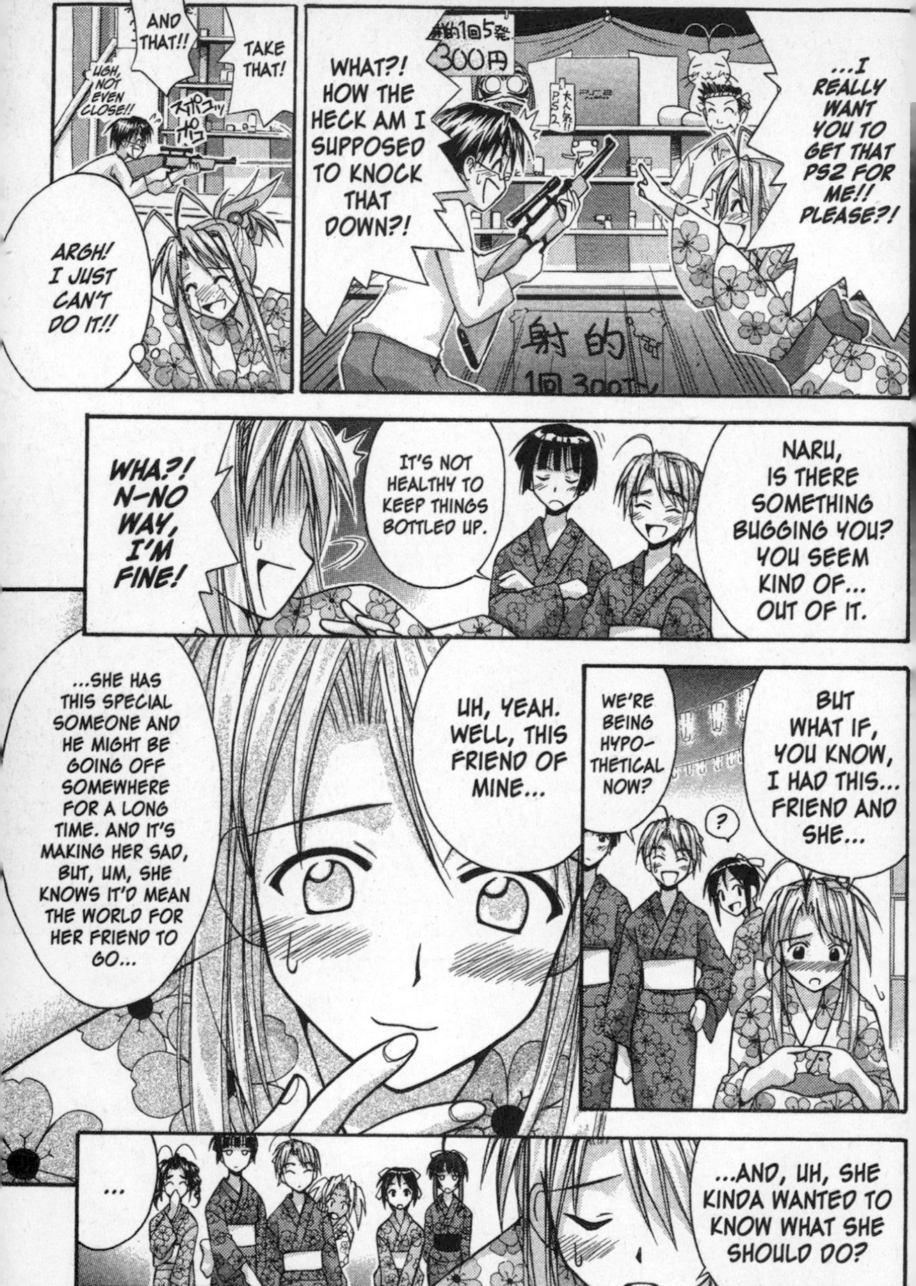
...I REALLY WANT YOU TO GET THAT PS2 FOR ME!! PLEASE?!
300円
大人気!! PS2
WHAT?! HOW THE HECK AM I SUPPOSED TO KNOCK THAT DOWN?!
AND THAT!!
TAKE THAT!
UGH, NOT EVEN CLOSE!!
スポコッ ポコ
ARGH! I JUST CAN'T DO IT!!
NARU, IS THERE SOMETHING BUGGING YOU? YOU SEEM KIND OF... OUT OF IT.
IT'S NOT HEALTHY TO KEEP THINGS BOTTLED UP.
WHA?! N-NO WAY, I'M FINE!
BUT WHAT IF, YOU KNOW, I HAD THIS... FRIEND AND SHE...
?
WE'RE BEING HYPO-THETICAL NOW?
UH, YEAH. WELL, THIS FRIEND OF MINE...
...SHE HAS THIS SPECIAL SOMEONE AND HE MIGHT BE GOING OFF SOMEWHERE FOR A LONG TIME. AND IT'S MAKING HER SAD, BUT, UM, SHE KNOWS IT'D MEAN THE WORLD FOR HER FRIEND TO GO...
...AND, UH, SHE KINDA WANTED TO KNOW WHAT SHE SHOULD DO?
...

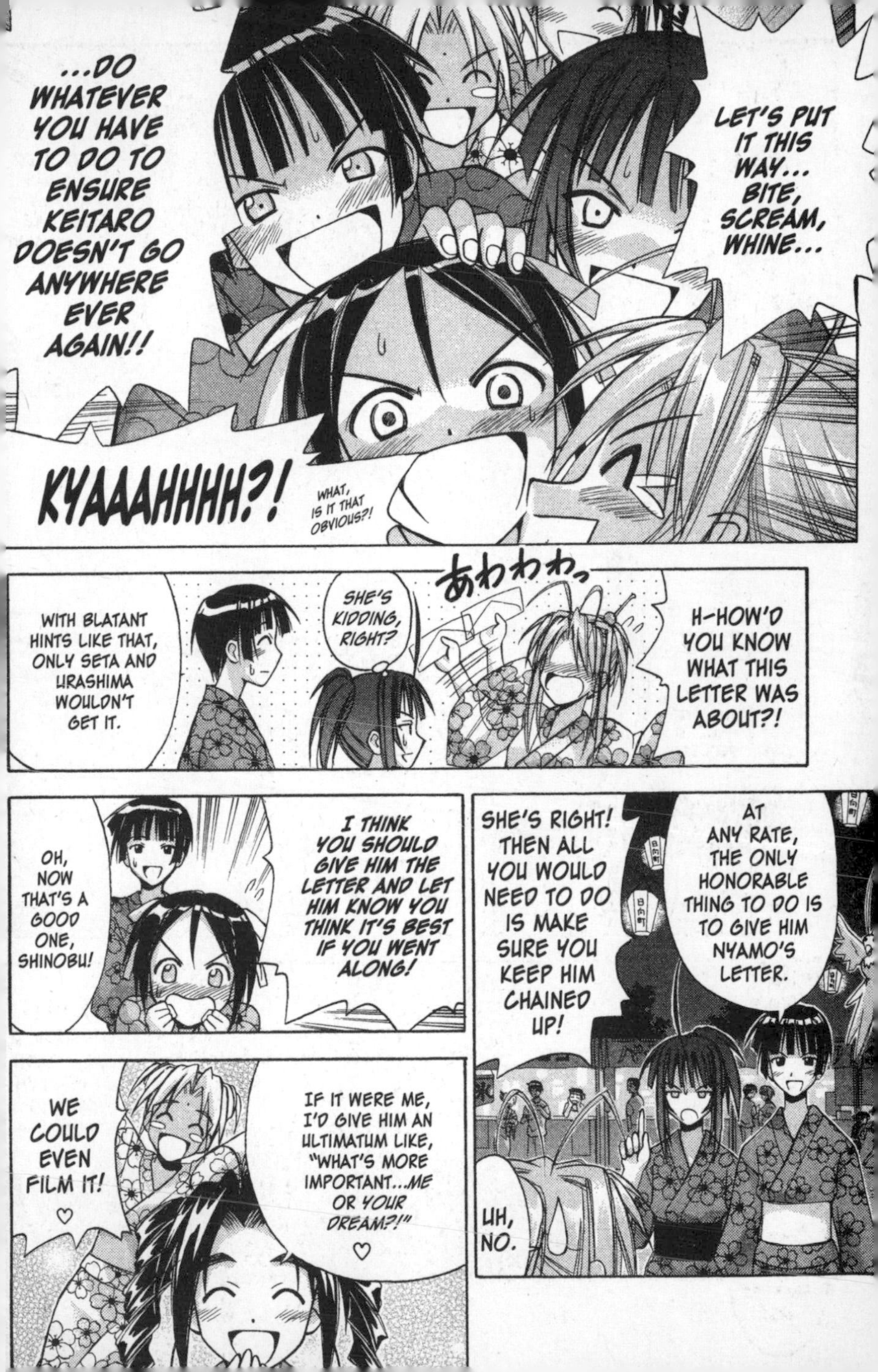
LET'S PUT IT THIS WAY... BITE, SCREAM, WHINE...
...DO WHATEVER YOU HAVE TO DO TO ENSURE KEITARO DOESN'T GO ANYWHERE EVER AGAIN!!
WHAT, IS IT THAT OBVIOUS?!
KYAAAHHHH?!
H-HOW'D YOU KNOW WHAT THIS LETTER WAS ABOUT?!
あわわわっ
SHE'S KIDDING, RIGHT?
WITH BLATANT HINTS LIKE THAT, ONLY SETA AND URASHIMA WOULDN'T GET IT.
AT ANY RATE, THE ONLY HONORABLE THING TO DO IS TO GIVE HIM NYAMO'S LETTER.
SHE'S RIGHT! THEN ALL YOU WOULD NEED TO DO IS MAKE SURE YOU KEEP HIM CHAINED UP!
UH, NO.
I THINK YOU SHOULD GIVE HIM THE LETTER AND LET HIM KNOW YOU THINK IT'S BEST IF YOU WENT ALONG!
OH, NOW THAT'S A GOOD ONE, SHINOBU!
IF IT WERE ME, I'D GIVE HIM AN ULTIMATUM LIKE, "WHAT'S MORE IMPORTANT...ME OR YOUR DREAM?!" ♡
WE COULD EVEN FILM IT! ♡

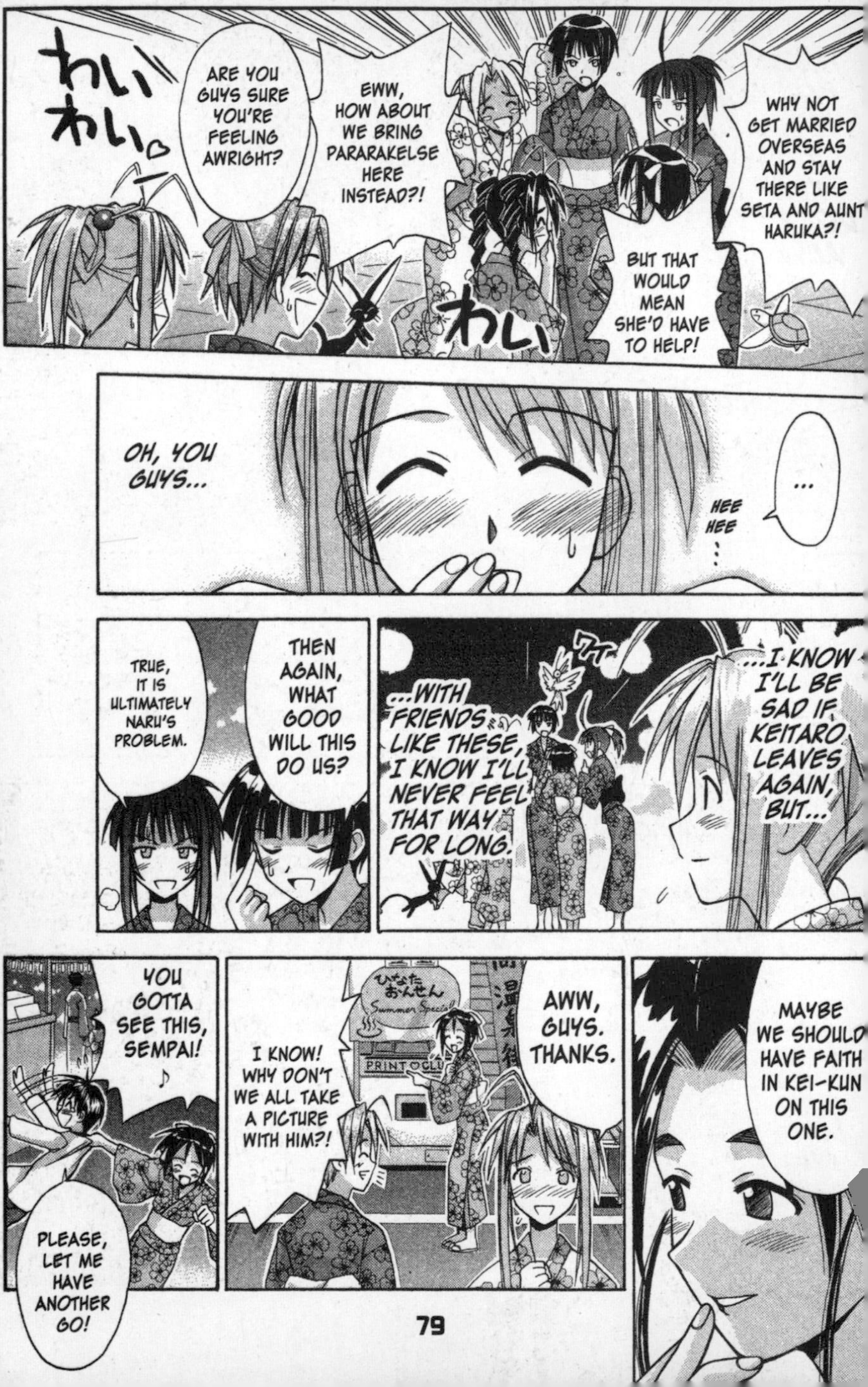
WHY NOT GET MARRIED OVERSEAS AND STAY THERE LIKE SETA AND AUNT HARUKA?!
BUT THAT WOULD MEAN SHE'D HAVE TO HELP!
EWW, HOW ABOUT WE BRING PARARAKELSE HERE INSTEAD?!
ARE YOU GUYS SURE YOU'RE FEELING AWRIGHT?
わいわい♡
わい
...
HEE HEE...
OH, YOU GUYS...
...I KNOW I'LL BE SAD IF KEITARO LEAVES AGAIN, BUT...
ワイ
...WITH FRIENDS LIKE THESE, I KNOW I'LL NEVER FEEL THAT WAY FOR LONG.
THEN AGAIN, WHAT GOOD WILL THIS DO US?
TRUE, IT IS ULTIMATELY NARU'S PROBLEM.
MAYBE WE SHOULD HAVE FAITH IN KEI-KUN ON THIS ONE.
AWW, GUYS. THANKS.
ひなた おんせん Summer Special
PRINT♡CLUB
I KNOW! WHY DON'T WE ALL TAKE A PICTURE WITH HIM?!
YOU GOTTA SEE THIS, SEMPAI! ♪
PLEASE, LET ME HAVE ANOTHER GO!

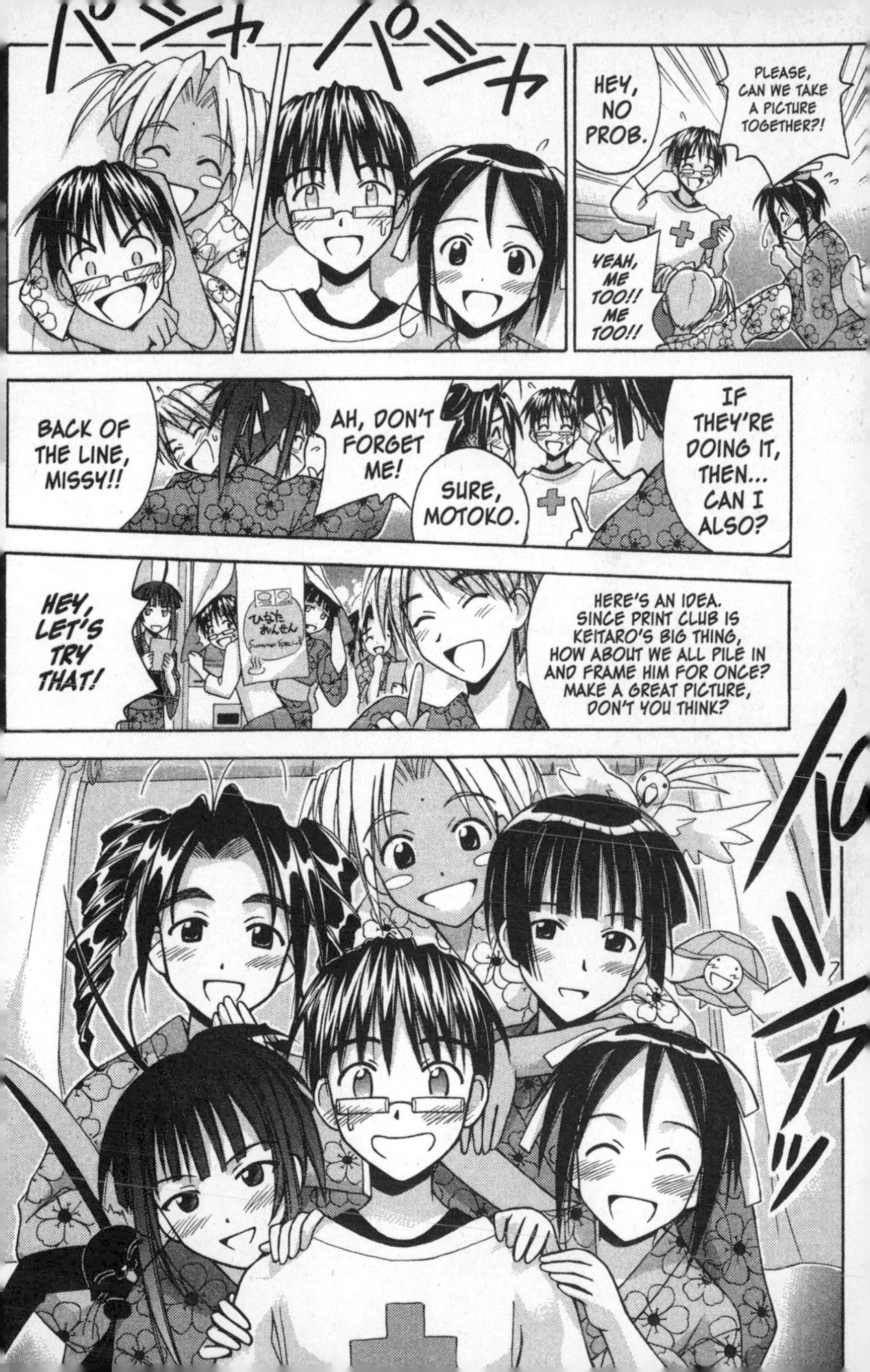
パシャ
パシャ
PLEASE, CAN WE TAKE A PICTURE TOGETHER?!
HEY, NO PROB.
YEAH, ME TOO!! ME TOO!!
IF THEY'RE DOING IT, THEN... CAN I ALSO?
SURE, MOTOKO.
AH, DON'T FORGET ME!
BACK OF THE LINE, MISSY!!
HERE'S AN IDEA. SINCE PRINT CLUB IS KEITARO'S BIG THING, HOW ABOUT WE ALL PILE IN AND FRAME HIM FOR ONCE? MAKE A GREAT PICTURE, DON'T YOU THINK?
ひなた おんせん
HEY, LET'S TRY THAT!

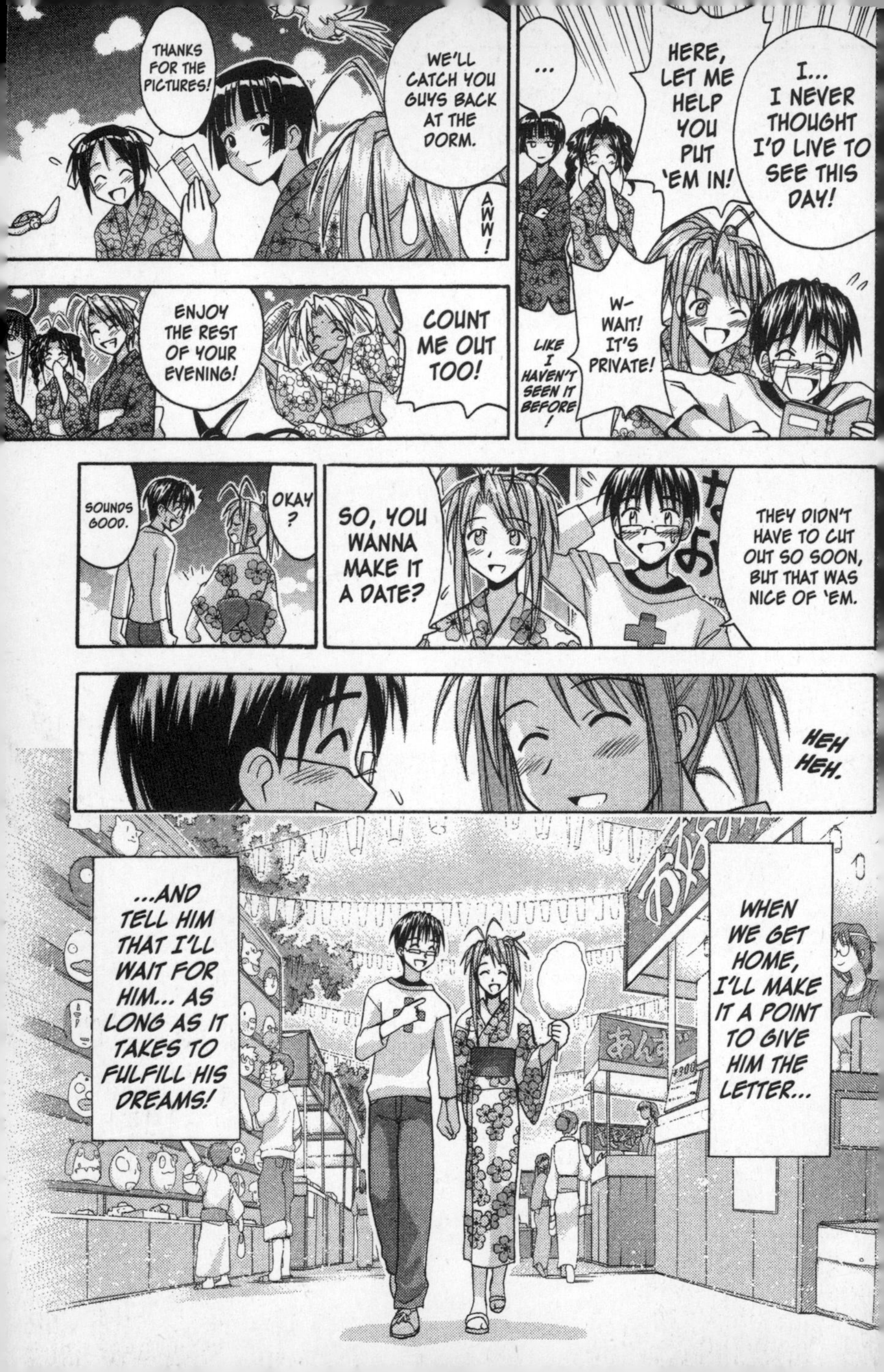

I... I NEVER THOUGHT I'D LIVE TO SEE THIS DAY!
HERE, LET ME HELP YOU PUT 'EM IN!
...
W- WAIT! IT'S PRIVATE!
LIKE I HAVEN'T SEEN IT BEFORE!
WE'LL CATCH YOU GUYS BACK AT THE DORM.
AWW!
THANKS FOR THE PICTURES!
COUNT ME OUT TOO!
ENJOY THE REST OF YOUR EVENING!
THEY DIDN'T HAVE TO CUT OUT SO SOON, BUT THAT WAS NICE OF 'EM.
SO, YOU WANNA MAKE IT A DATE?
OKAY?
SOUNDS GOOD.
HEH HEH.
WHEN WE GET HOME, I'LL MAKE IT A POINT TO GIVE HIM THE LETTER...
...AND TELL HIM THAT I'LL WAIT FOR HIM... AS LONG AS IT TAKES TO FULFILL HIS DREAMS!

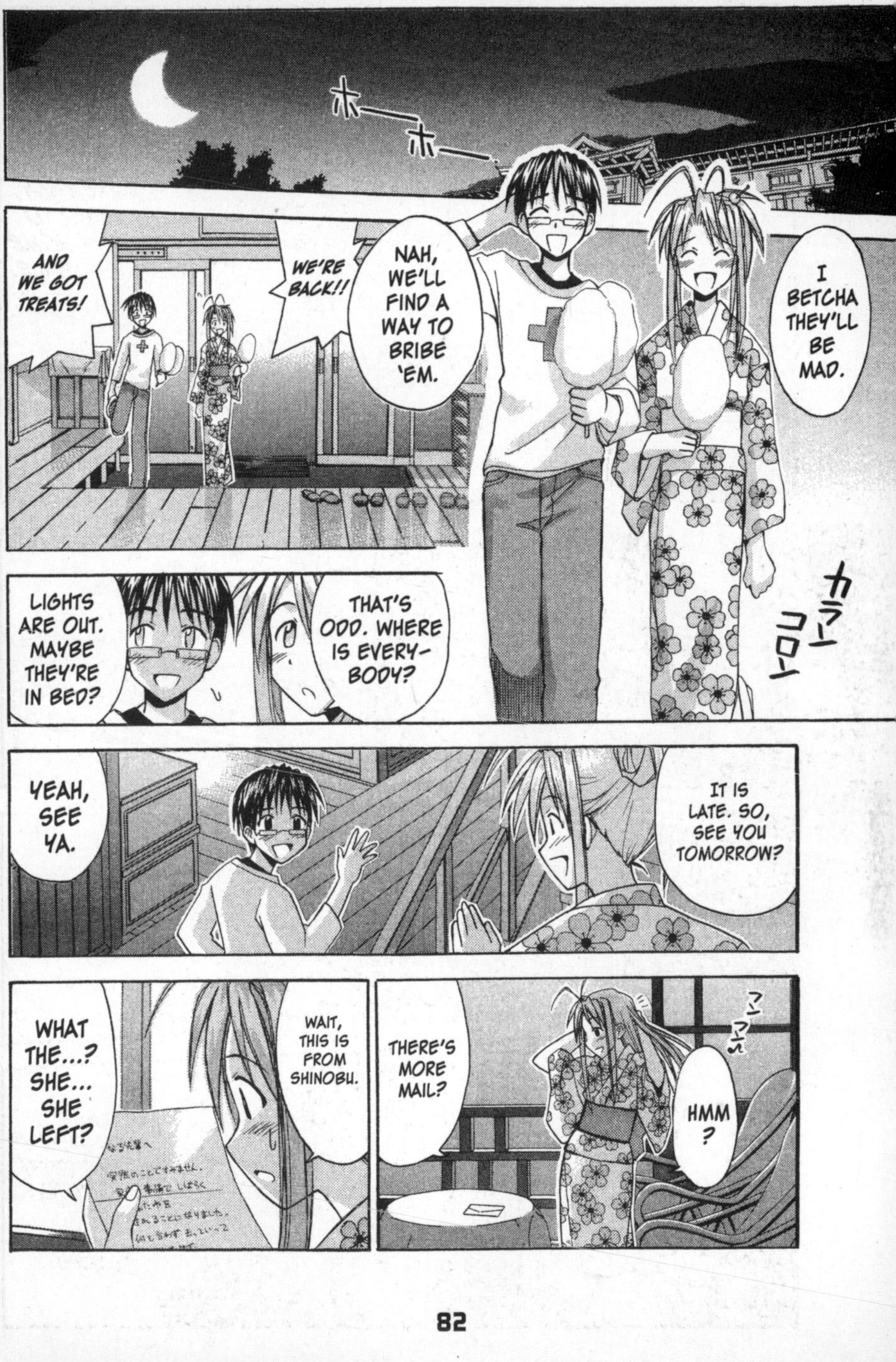
ホー
ホー
I BETCHA THEY'LL BE MAD.
NAH, WE'LL FIND A WAY TO BRIBE 'EM.
カラーン
コローン
WE'RE BACK!!
AND WE GOT TREATS!
THAT'S ODD. WHERE IS EVERY-BODY?
LIGHTS ARE OUT. MAYBE THEY'RE IN BED?
IT IS LATE. SO, SEE YOU TOMORROW?
YEAH, SEE YA.
HMM?
THERE'S MORE MAIL?
WAIT, THIS IS FROM SHINOBU.
WHAT THE...? SHE... SHE LEFT?

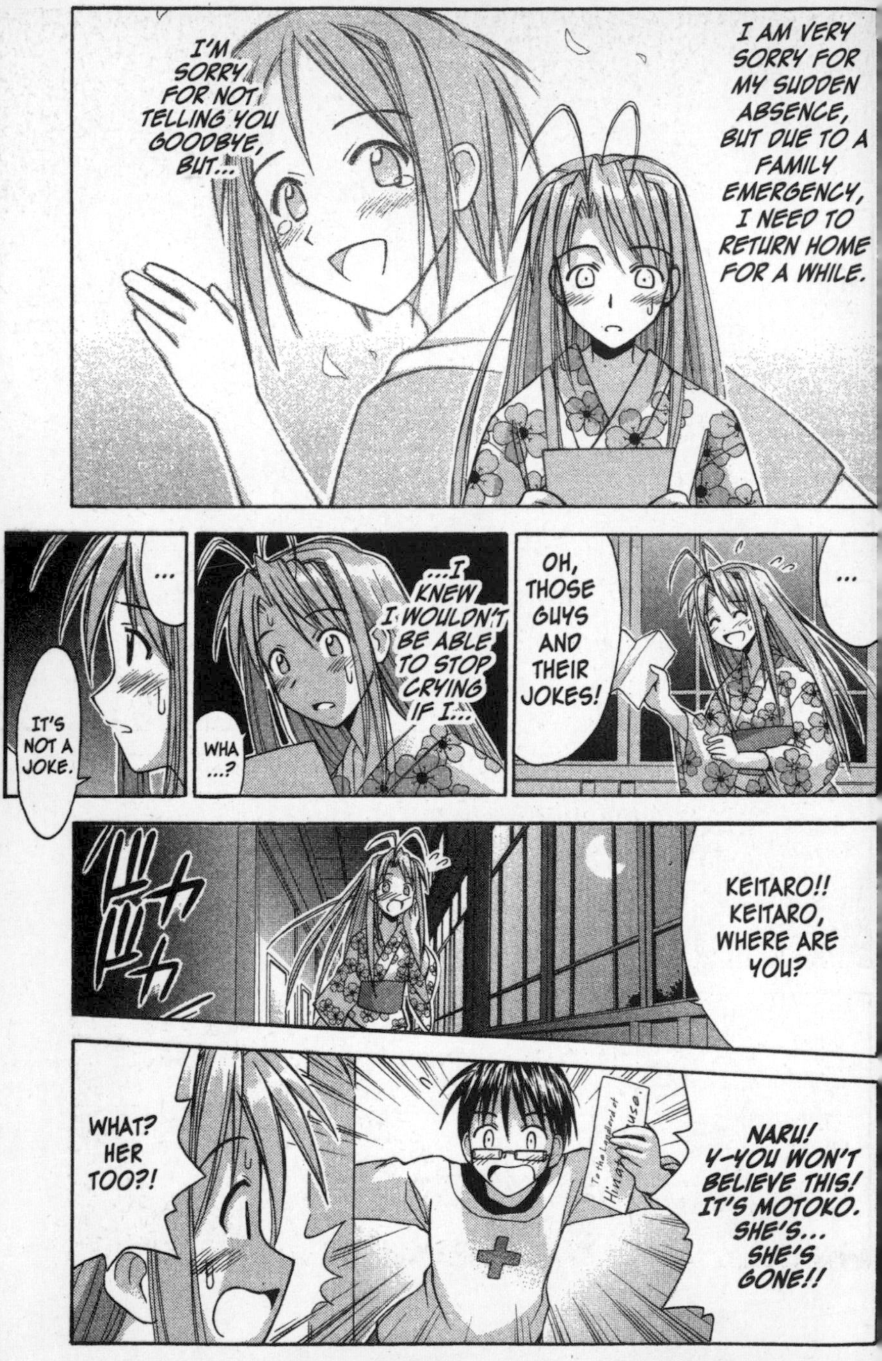
I AM VERY SORRY FOR MY SUDDEN ABSENCE, BUT DUE TO A FAMILY EMERGENCY, I NEED TO RETURN HOME FOR A WHILE.
I'M SORRY FOR NOT TELLING YOU GOODBYE, BUT...
...
OH, THOSE GUYS AND THEIR JOKES!
...I KNEW I WOULDN'T BE ABLE TO STOP CRYING IF I...
WHA ...?
...
IT'S NOT A JOKE.
KEITARO!! KEITARO, WHERE ARE YOU?
NARU! Y-YOU WON'T BELIEVE THIS! IT'S MOTOKO. SHE'S... SHE'S GONE!!
WHAT? HER TOO?!

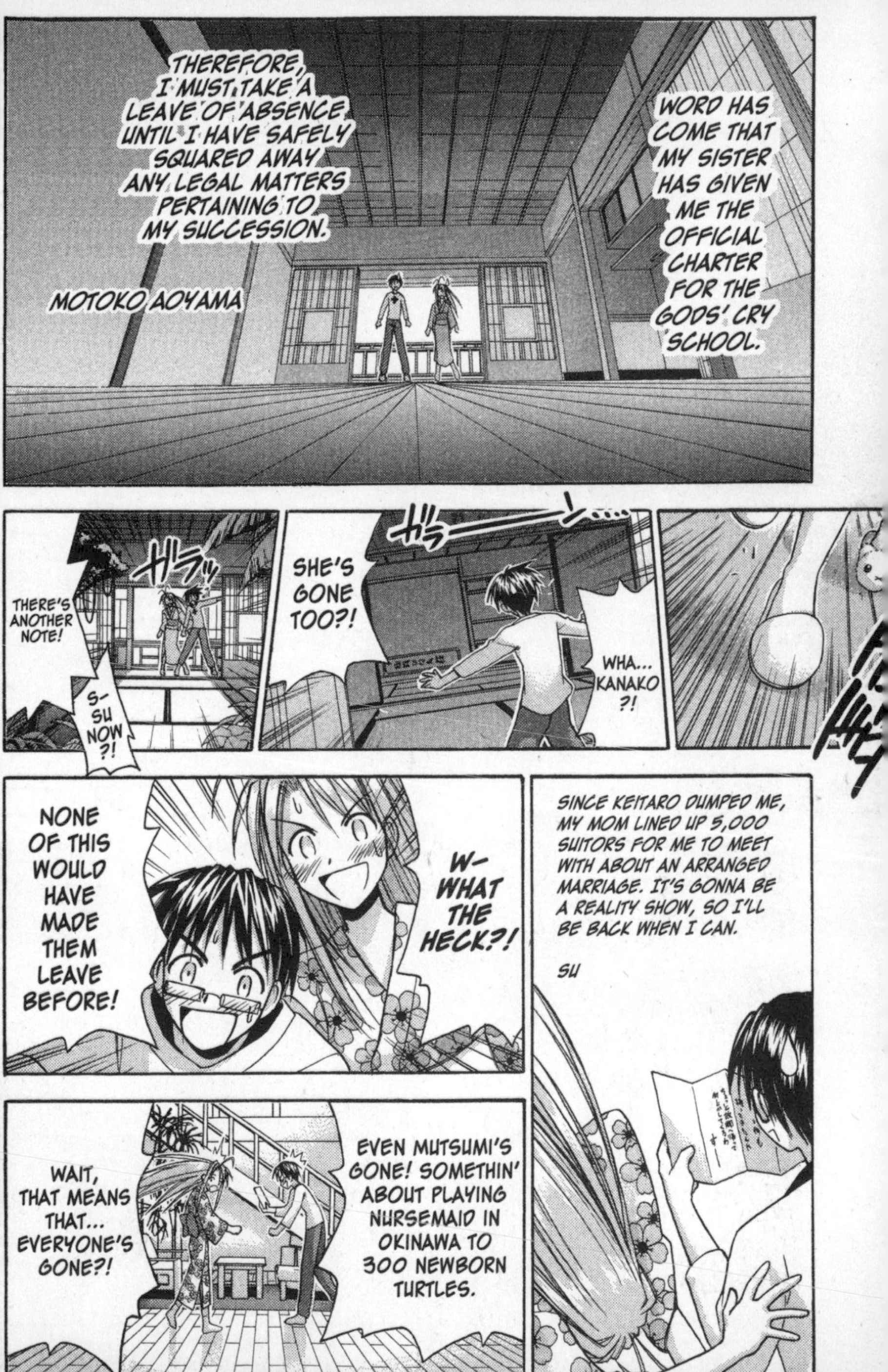
WORD HAS COME THAT MY SISTER HAS GIVEN ME THE OFFICIAL CHARTER FOR THE GODS' CRY SCHOOL.
THEREFORE, I MUST TAKE A LEAVE OF ABSENCE UNTIL I HAVE SAFELY SQUARED AWAY ANY LEGAL MATTERS PERTAINING TO MY SUCCESSION.
MOTOKO AOYAMA
ガラ——ッ…
WHA... KANAKO ?!
SHE'S GONE TOO?!
ガラッ
THERE'S ANOTHER NOTE!
S-SU NOW ?!
SINCE KEITARO DUMPED ME, MY MOM LINED UP 5,000 SUITORS FOR ME TO MEET WITH ABOUT AN ARRANGED MARRIAGE. IT'S GONNA BE A REALITY SHOW, SO I'LL BE BACK WHEN I CAN.
SU
W-WHAT THE HECK?!
NONE OF THIS WOULD HAVE MADE THEM LEAVE BEFORE!
EVEN MUTSUMI'S GONE! SOMETHIN' ABOUT PLAYING NURSEMAID IN OKINAWA TO 300 NEWBORN TURTLES.
WAIT, THAT MEANS THAT... EVERYONE'S GONE?!

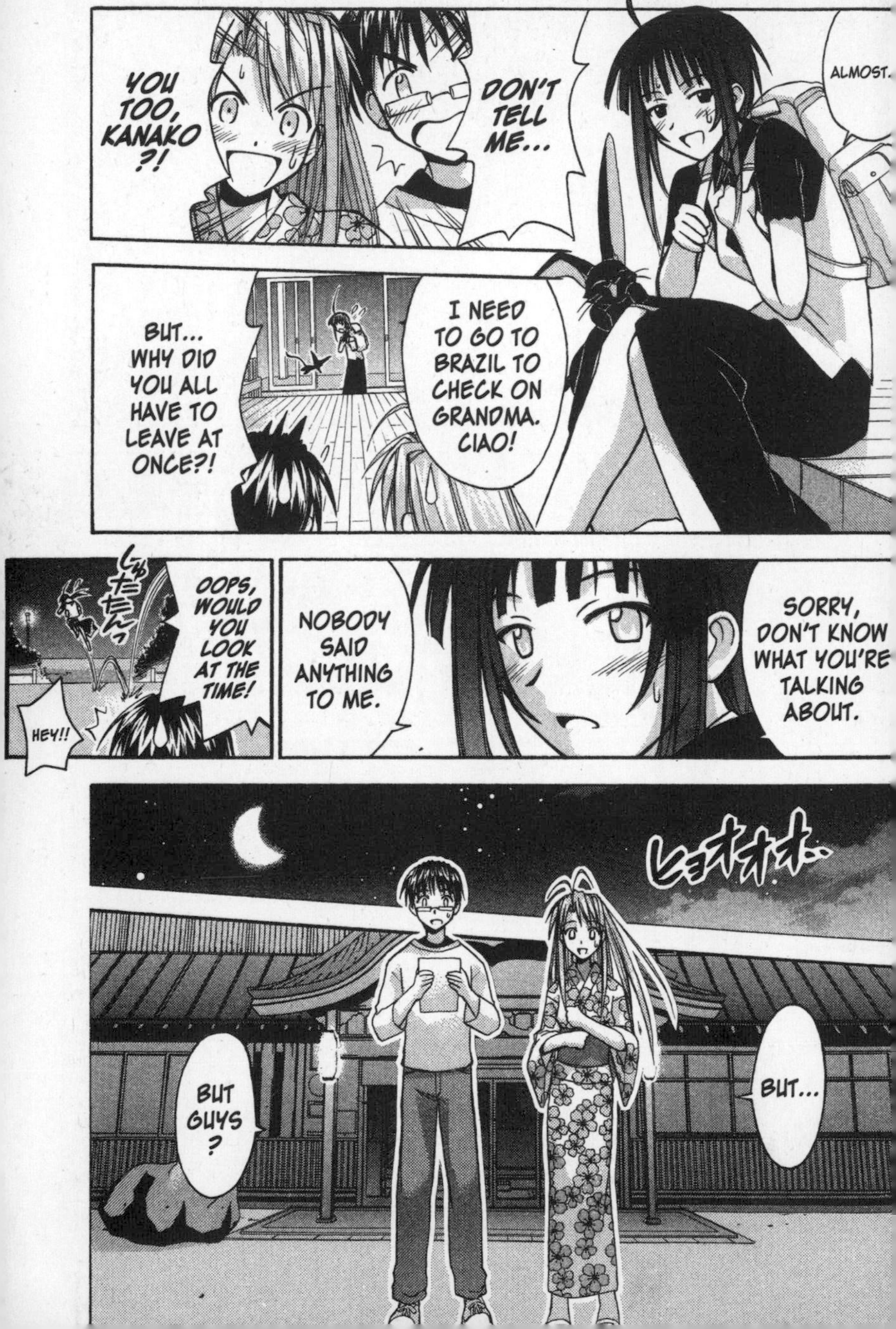
ALMOST.
DON'T TELL ME...
YOU TOO, KANAKO?!
I NEED TO GO TO BRAZIL TO CHECK ON GRANDMA. CIAO!
BUT... WHY DID YOU ALL HAVE TO LEAVE AT ONCE?!
SORRY, DON'T KNOW WHAT YOU'RE TALKING ABOUT.
NOBODY SAID ANYTHING TO ME.
OOPS, WOULD YOU LOOK AT THE TIME!
しゅたたんっ
HEY!!
ヒョオオオ
BUT...
BUT GUYS?

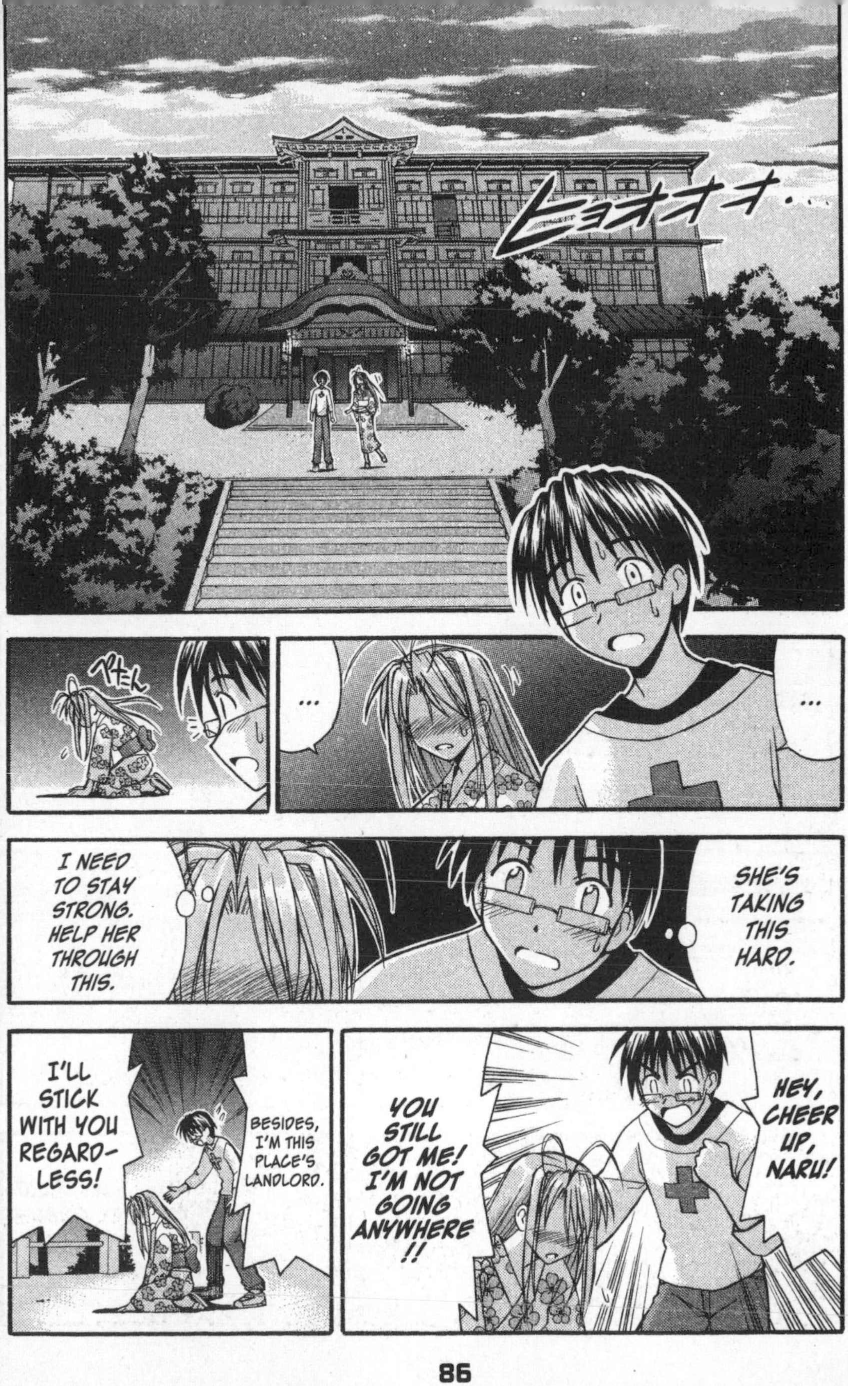
ヒョオオオ…
...
...
ぺたん
SHE'S TAKING THIS HARD.
I NEED TO STAY STRONG. HELP HER THROUGH THIS.
HEY, CHEER UP, NARU!
YOU STILL GOT ME! I'M NOT GOING ANYWHERE!!
BESIDES, I'M THIS PLACE'S LANDLORD.
I'LL STICK WITH YOU REGARDLESS!

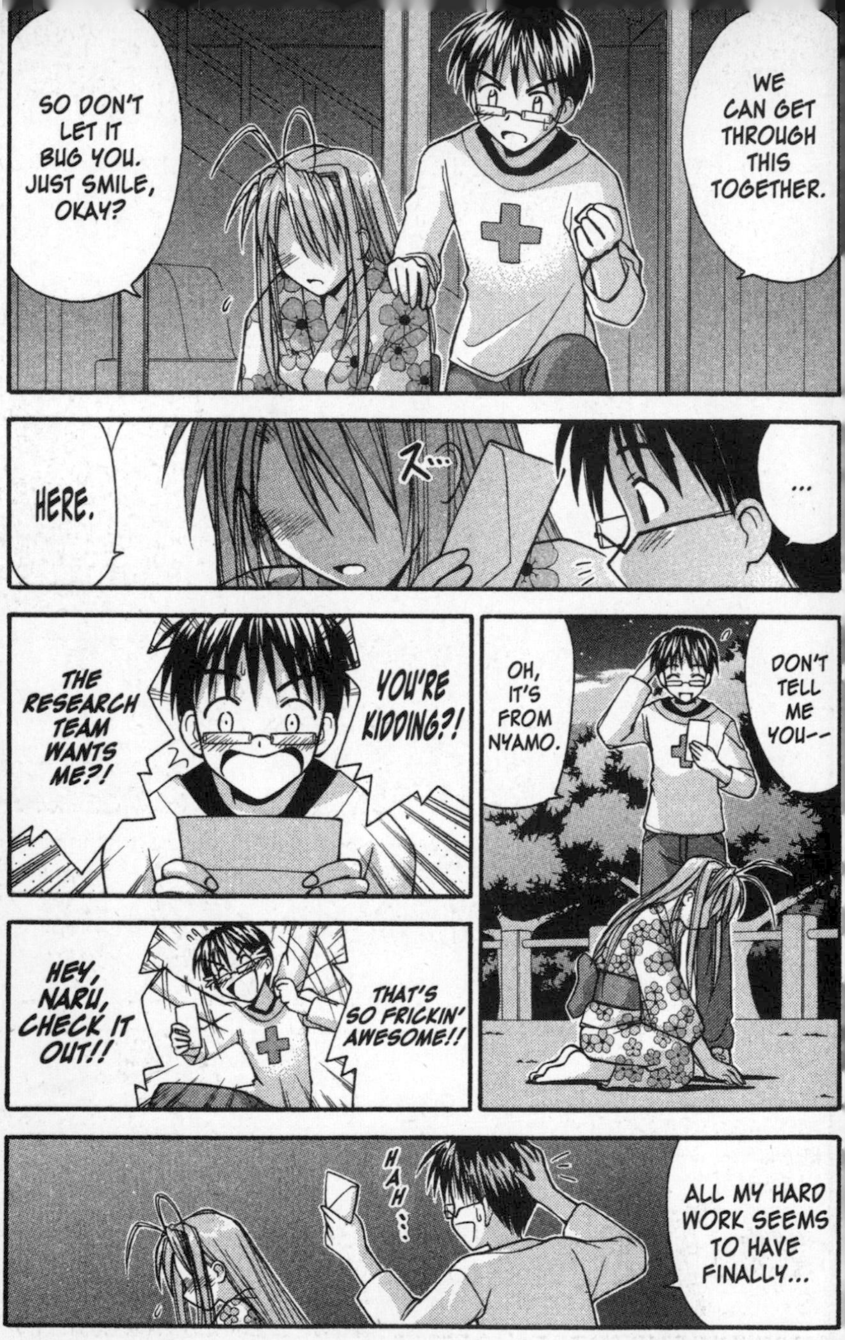
WE CAN GET THROUGH THIS TOGETHER.
SO DON'T LET IT BUG YOU. JUST SMILE, OKAY?
...
ス...
HERE.
DON'T TELL ME YOU--
OH, IT'S FROM NYAMO.
YOU'RE KIDDING?!
THE RESEARCH TEAM WANTS ME?!
THAT'S SO FRICKIN' AWESOME!!
HEY, NARU, CHECK IT OUT!!
ALL MY HARD WORK SEEMS TO HAVE FINALLY...
HAH...

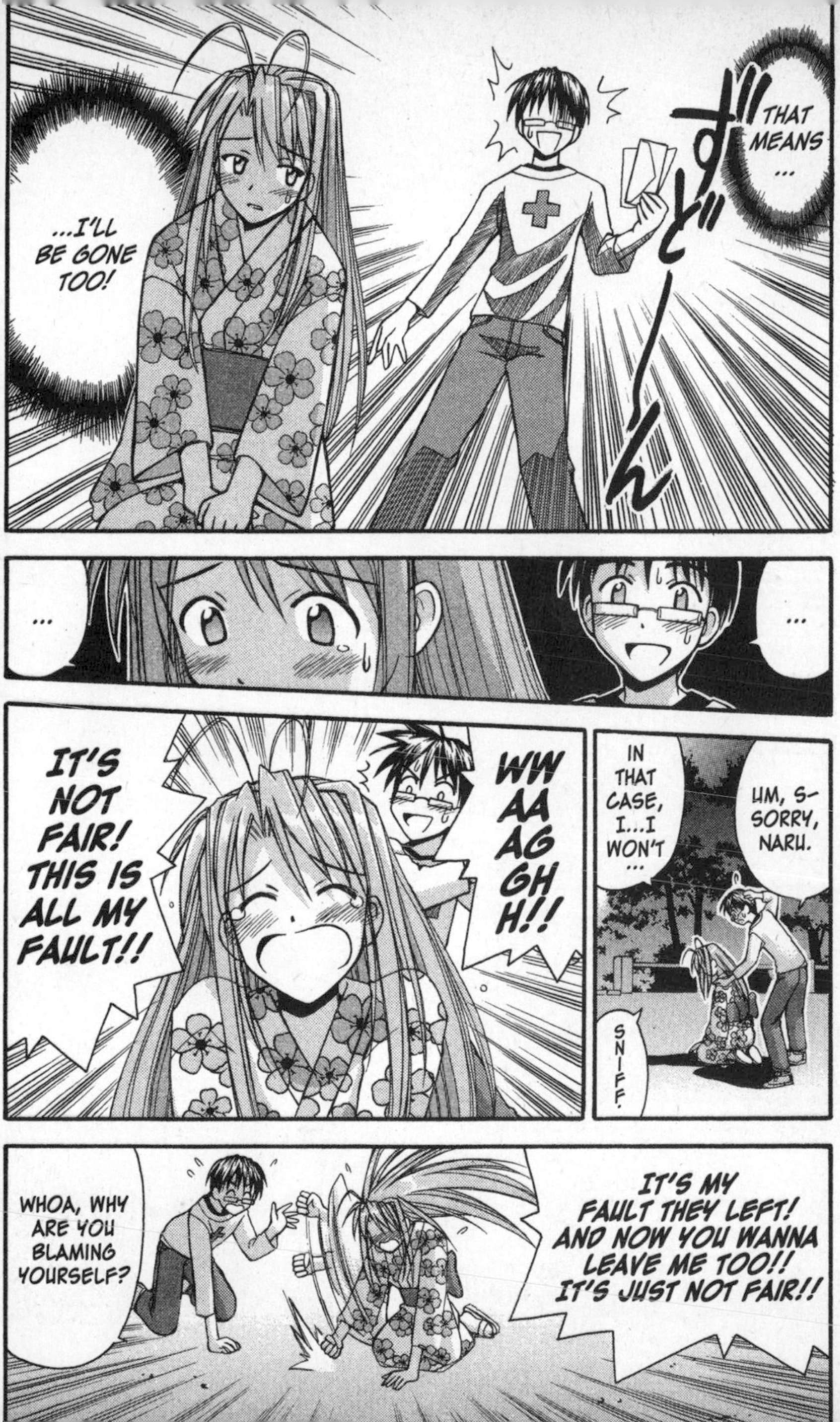
THAT MEANS ...
ずどーん
...I'LL BE GONE TOO!
...
...
UM, S-SORRY, NARU.
IN THAT CASE, I...I WON'T ...
SNIFF.
WWAAAGGHH!!
IT'S NOT FAIR! THIS IS ALL MY FAULT!!
IT'S MY FAULT THEY LEFT! AND NOW YOU WANNA LEAVE ME TOO!! IT'S JUST NOT FAIR!!
WHOA, WHY ARE YOU BLAMING YOURSELF?

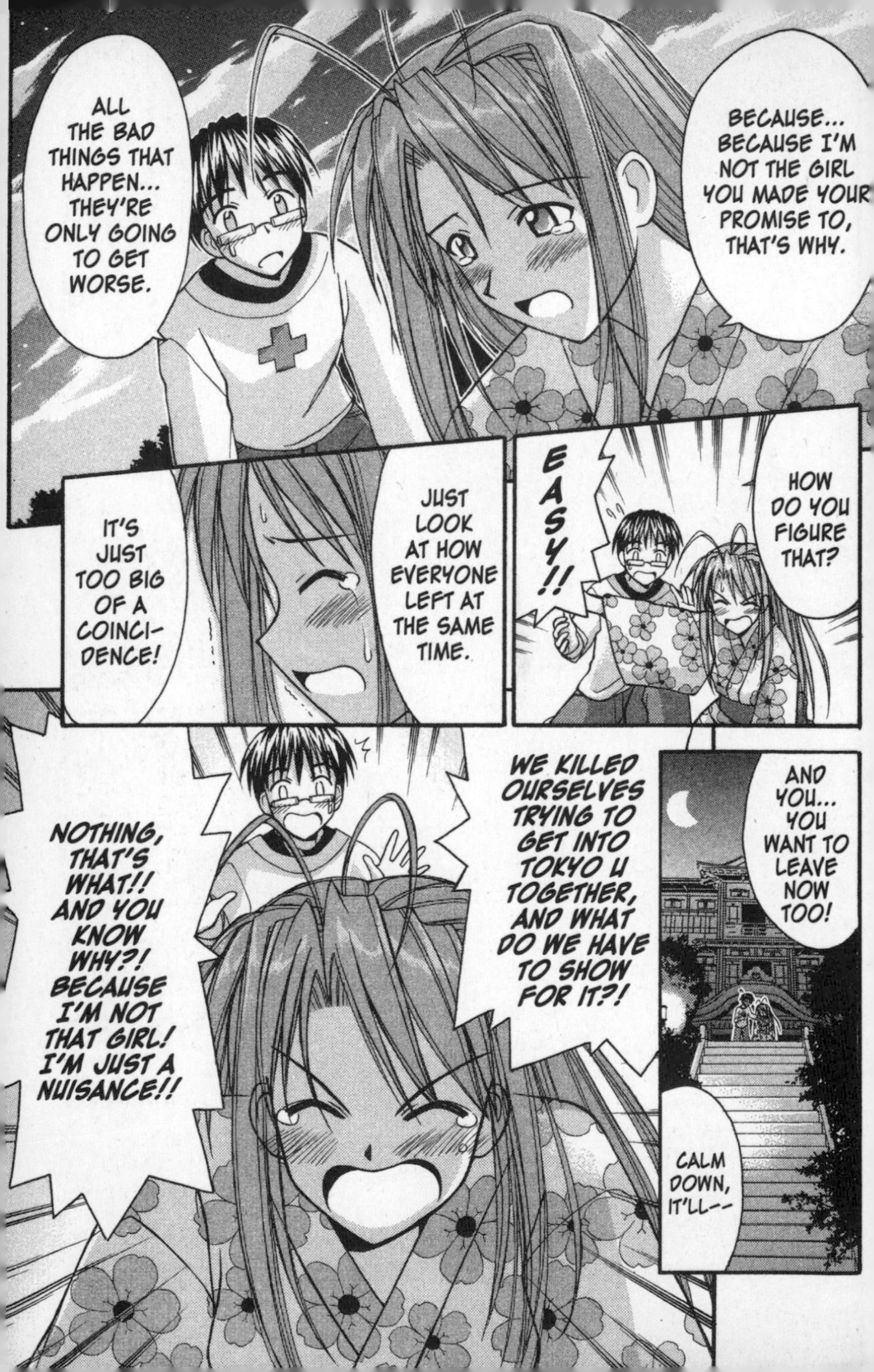
BECAUSE... BECAUSE I'M NOT THE GIRL YOU MADE YOUR PROMISE TO, THAT'S WHY.
ALL THE BAD THINGS THAT HAPPEN... THEY'RE ONLY GOING TO GET WORSE.
HOW DO YOU FIGURE THAT?
EASY!!
JUST LOOK AT HOW EVERYONE LEFT AT THE SAME TIME.
IT'S JUST TOO BIG OF A COINCIDENCE!
AND YOU... YOU WANT TO LEAVE NOW TOO!
CALM DOWN, IT'LL--
WE KILLED OURSELVES TRYING TO GET INTO TOKYO U TOGETHER, AND WHAT DO WE HAVE TO SHOW FOR IT?!
NOTHING, THAT'S WHAT!! AND YOU KNOW WHY?! BECAUSE I'M NOT THAT GIRL! I'M JUST A NUISANCE!!

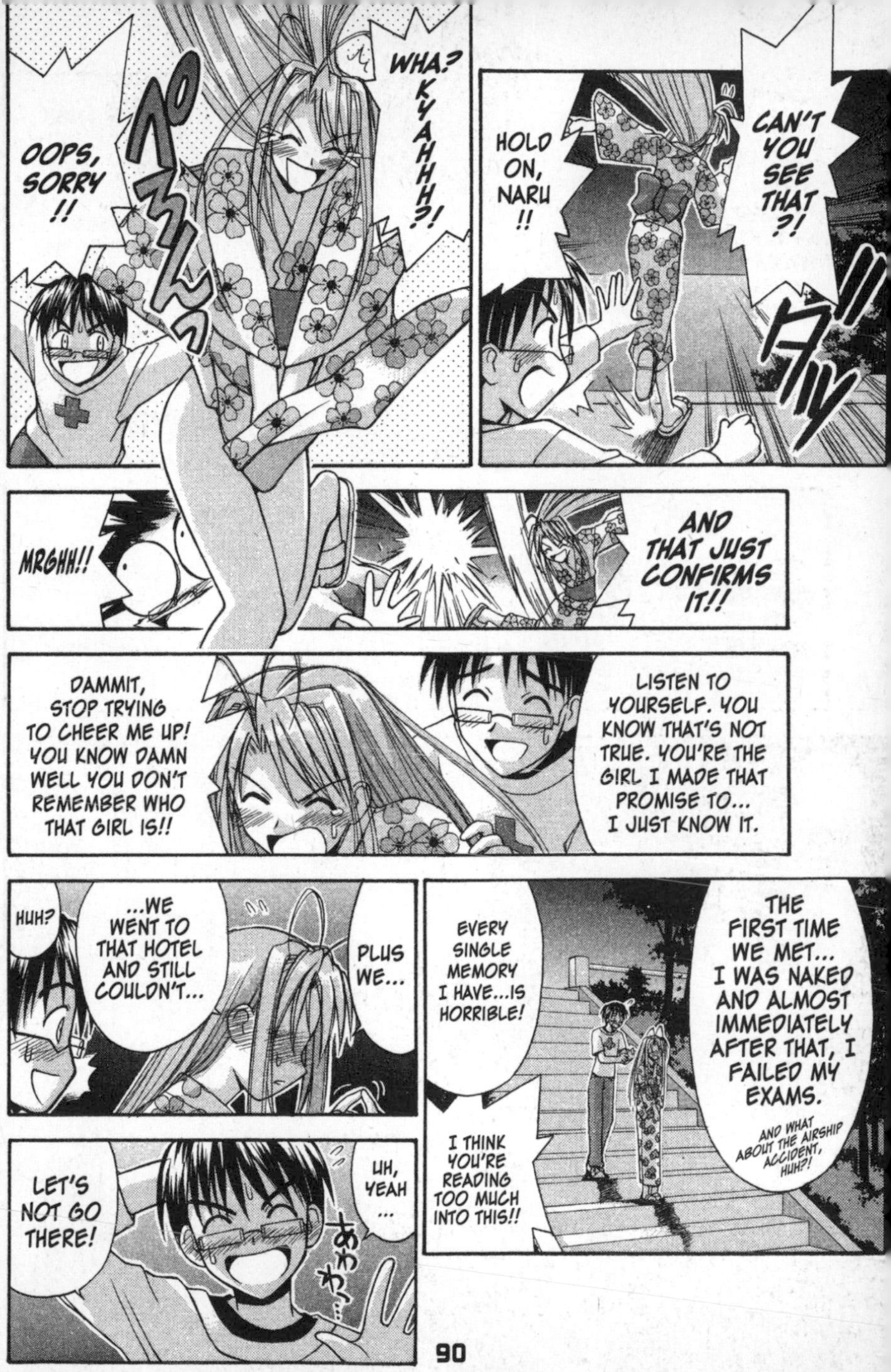
CAN'T YOU SEE THAT?!
HOLD ON, NARU!!
WHA? KYAHHHH?!
OOPS, SORRY!!
AND THAT JUST CONFIRMS IT!!
MRGHH!!
LISTEN TO YOURSELF. YOU KNOW THAT'S NOT TRUE. YOU'RE THE GIRL I MADE THAT PROMISE TO... I JUST KNOW IT.
DAMMIT, STOP TRYING TO CHEER ME UP! YOU KNOW DAMN WELL YOU DON'T REMEMBER WHO THAT GIRL IS!!
THE FIRST TIME WE MET... I WAS NAKED AND ALMOST IMMEDIATELY AFTER THAT, I FAILED MY EXAMS.
EVERY SINGLE MEMORY I HAVE...IS HORRIBLE!
AND WHAT ABOUT THE AIRSHIP ACCIDENT, HUH?!
I THINK YOU'RE READING TOO MUCH INTO THIS!!
PLUS WE...
...WE WENT TO THAT HOTEL AND STILL COULDN'T...
HUH?
UH, YEAH ...
LET'S NOT GO THERE!

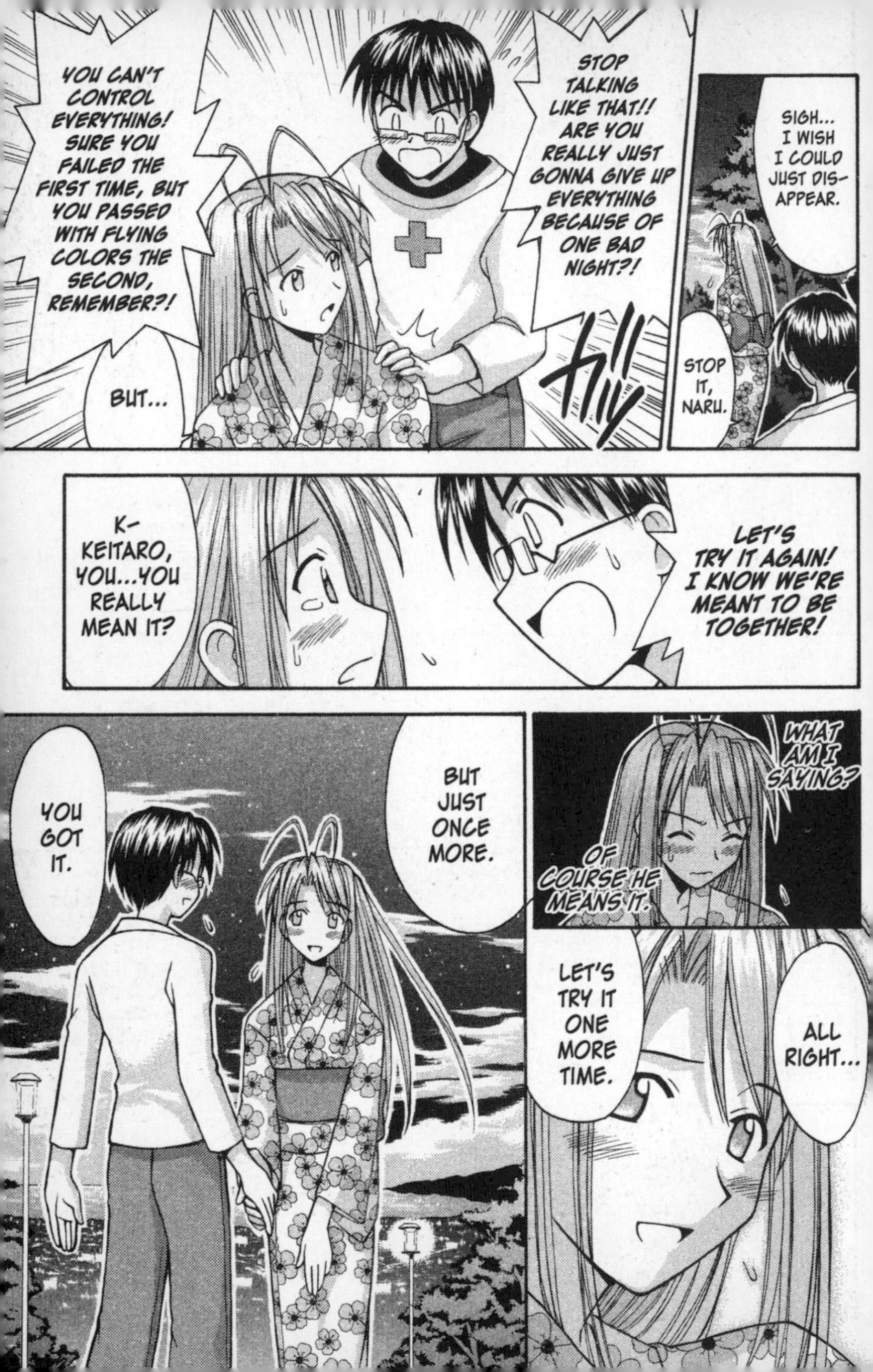
SIGH... I WISH I COULD JUST DIS-APPEAR.
STOP IT, NARU.
STOP TALKING LIKE THAT!! ARE YOU REALLY JUST GONNA GIVE UP EVERYTHING BECAUSE OF ONE BAD NIGHT?!
YOU CAN'T CONTROL EVERYTHING! SURE YOU FAILED THE FIRST TIME, BUT YOU PASSED WITH FLYING COLORS THE SECOND, REMEMBER?!
BUT...
LET'S TRY IT AGAIN! I KNOW WE'RE MEANT TO BE TOGETHER!
K-KEITARO, YOU...YOU REALLY MEAN IT?
WHAT AM I SAYING?
OF COURSE HE MEANS IT.
ALL RIGHT...
LET'S TRY IT ONE MORE TIME.
BUT JUST ONCE MORE.
YOU GOT IT.

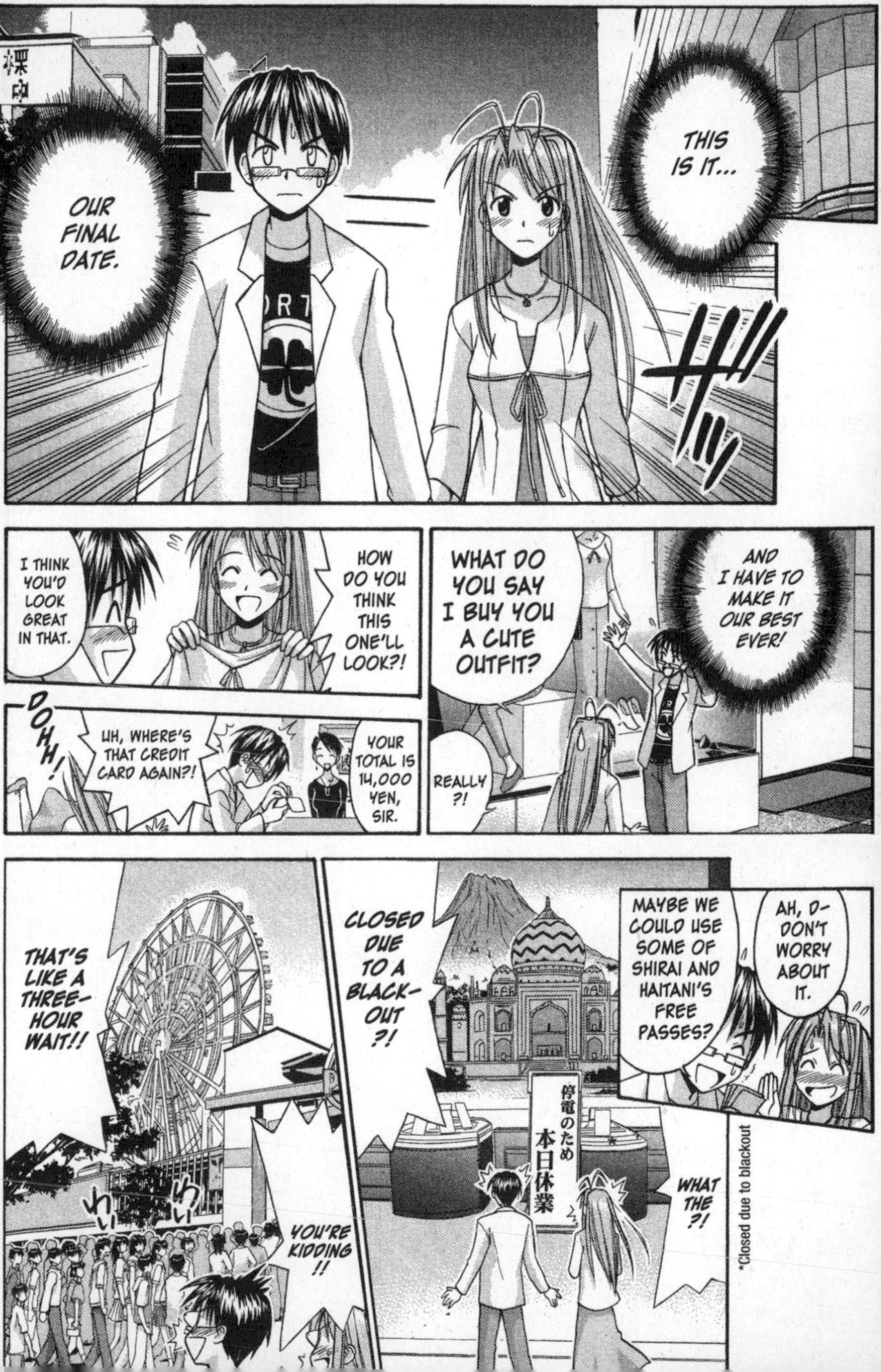
THIS IS IT...
OUR FINAL DATE.
ザッ
AND I HAVE TO MAKE IT OUR BEST EVER!
WHAT DO YOU SAY I BUY YOU A CUTE OUTFIT?
REALLY ?!
HOW DO YOU THINK THIS ONE'LL LOOK?!
I THINK YOU'D LOOK GREAT IN THAT.
YOUR TOTAL IS 14,000 YEN, SIR.
UH, WHERE'S THAT CREDIT CARD AGAIN?!
DOHH!
AH, D-DON'T WORRY ABOUT IT.
MAYBE WE COULD USE SOME OF SHIRAI AND HAITANI'S FREE PASSES?
停電のため 本日休業*
CLOSED DUE TO A BLACK-OUT ?!
WHAT THE ?!
THAT'S LIKE A THREE-HOUR WAIT!!
わいわい
YOU'RE KIDDING !!

*Closed due to blackout

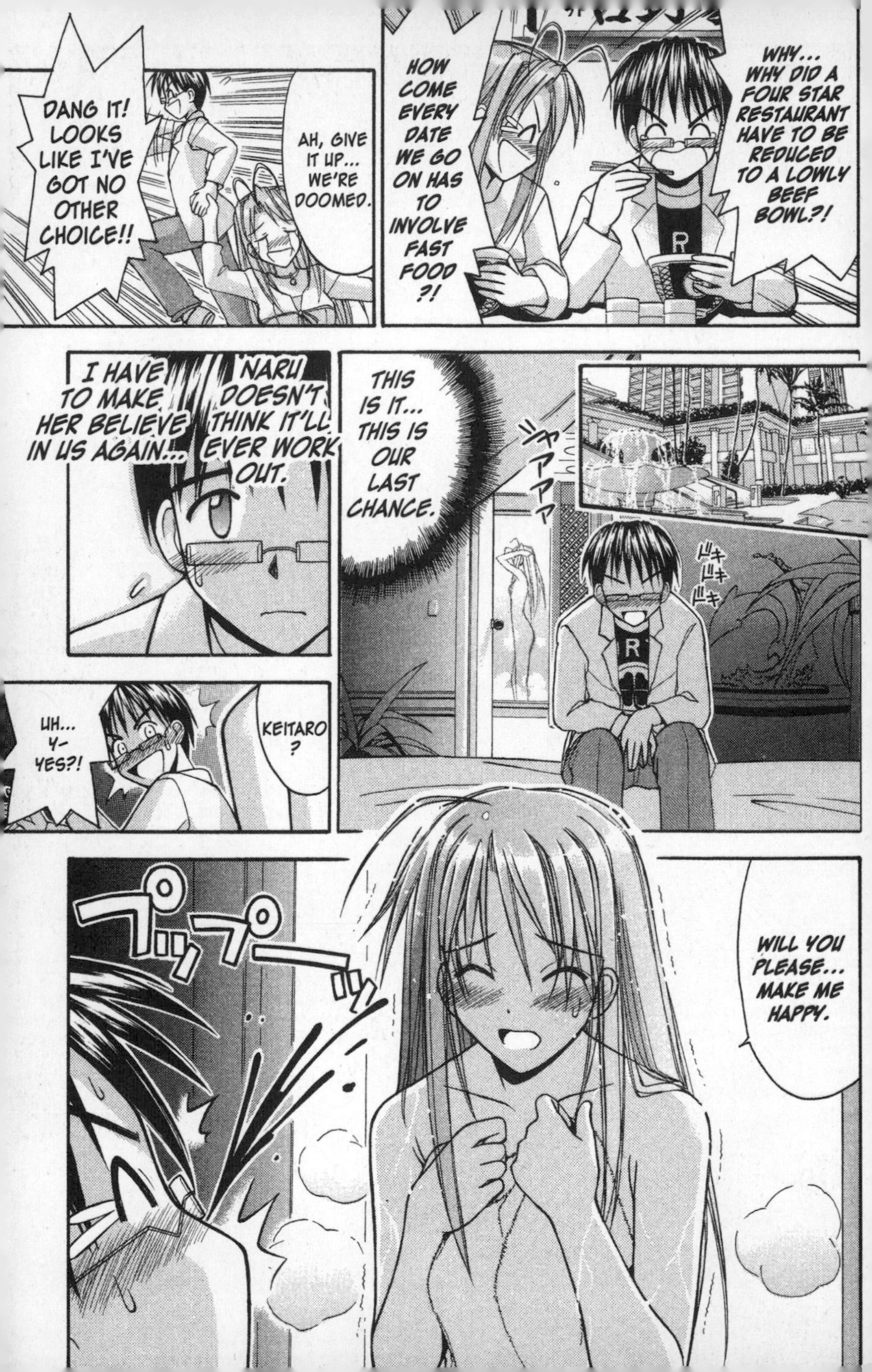
WHY... WHY DID A FOUR STAR RESTAURANT HAVE TO BE REDUCED TO A LOWLY BEEF BOWL?!
HOW COME EVERY DATE WE GO ON HAS TO INVOLVE FAST FOOD?!
AH, GIVE IT UP... WE'RE DOOMED.
DANG IT! LOOKS LIKE I'VE GOT NO OTHER CHOICE!!
シャアアア
ドキドキドキ
THIS IS IT... THIS IS OUR LAST CHANCE.
NARU DOESN'T THINK IT'LL EVER WORK OUT.
I HAVE TO MAKE HER BELIEVE IN US AGAIN...
KEITARO?
UH... Y-YES?!
WILL YOU PLEASE... MAKE ME HAPPY.
プップーッ

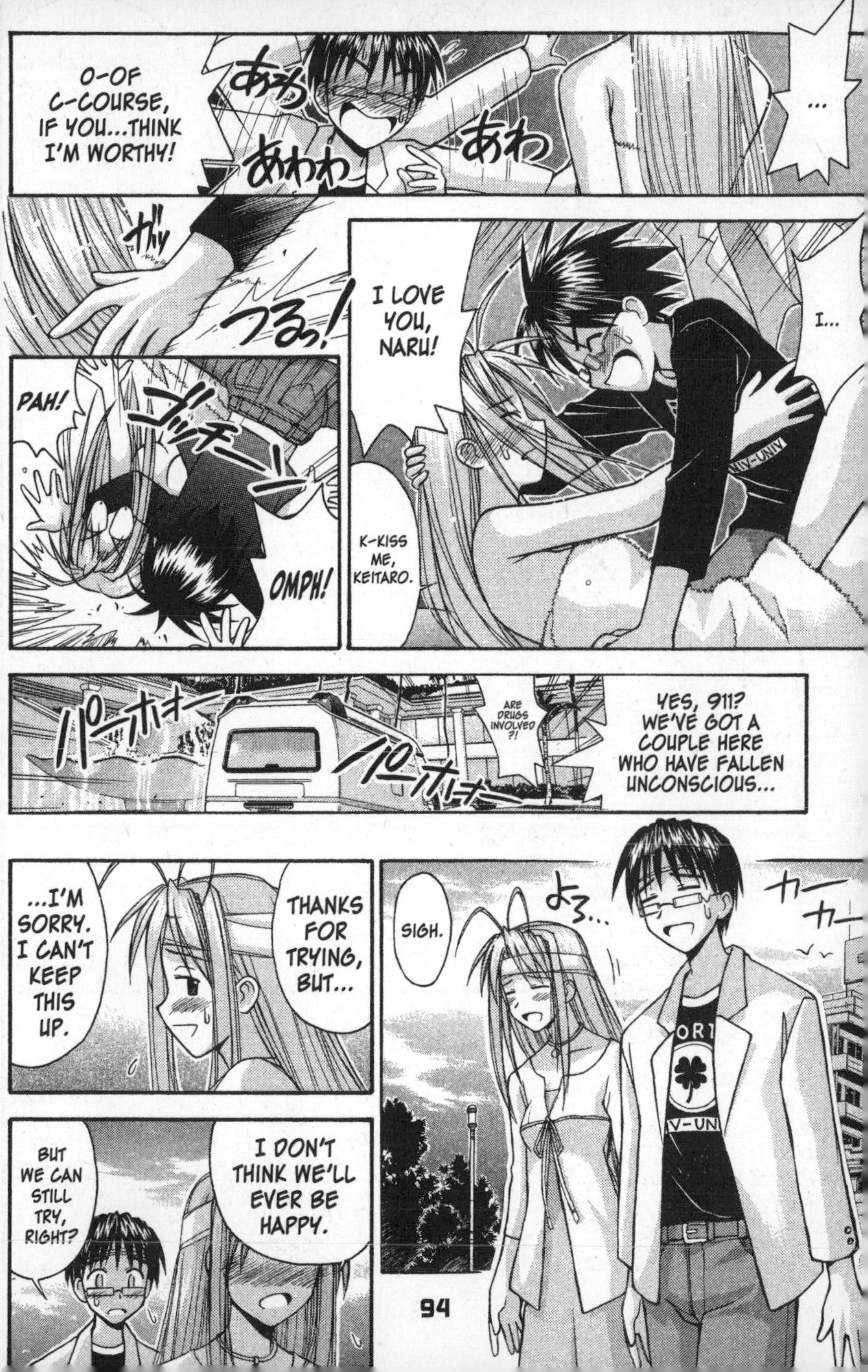
...
あわ
あわわ
あわ
O-OF C-COURSE, IF YOU...THINK I'M WORTHY!
I...
I LOVE YOU, NARU!
K-KISS ME, KEITARO.
つるっ!
PAH!
OMPH!
YES, 911? WE'VE GOT A COUPLE HERE WHO HAVE FALLEN UNCONSCIOUS...
ARE DRUGS INVOLVED ?!
SIGH.
よろ...
THANKS FOR TRYING, BUT...
...I'M SORRY. I CAN'T KEEP THIS UP.
I DON'T THINK WE'LL EVER BE HAPPY.
BUT WE CAN STILL TRY, RIGHT?

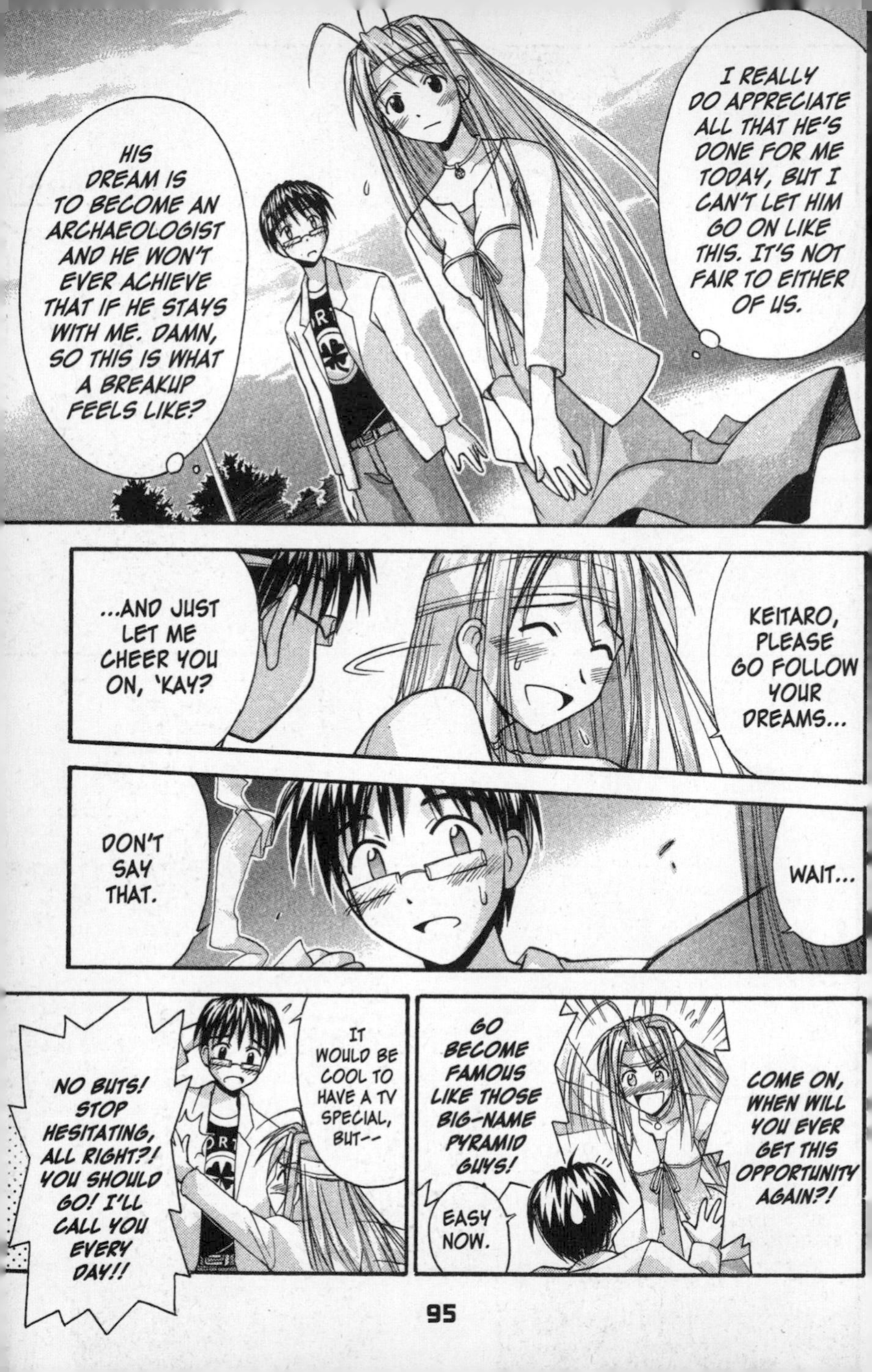
I REALLY DO APPRECIATE ALL THAT HE'S DONE FOR ME TODAY, BUT I CAN'T LET HIM GO ON LIKE THIS. IT'S NOT FAIR TO EITHER OF US.
HIS DREAM IS TO BECOME AN ARCHAEOLOGIST AND HE WON'T EVER ACHIEVE THAT IF HE STAYS WITH ME. DAMN, SO THIS IS WHAT A BREAKUP FEELS LIKE?
KEITARO, PLEASE GO FOLLOW YOUR DREAMS...
...AND JUST LET ME CHEER YOU ON, 'KAY?
WAIT...
DON'T SAY THAT.
COME ON, WHEN WILL YOU EVER GET THIS OPPORTUNITY AGAIN?!
GO BECOME FAMOUS LIKE THOSE BIG-NAME PYRAMID GUYS!
EASY NOW.
IT WOULD BE COOL TO HAVE A TV SPECIAL, BUT--
NO BUTS! STOP HESITATING, ALL RIGHT?! YOU SHOULD GO! I'LL CALL YOU EVERY DAY!!

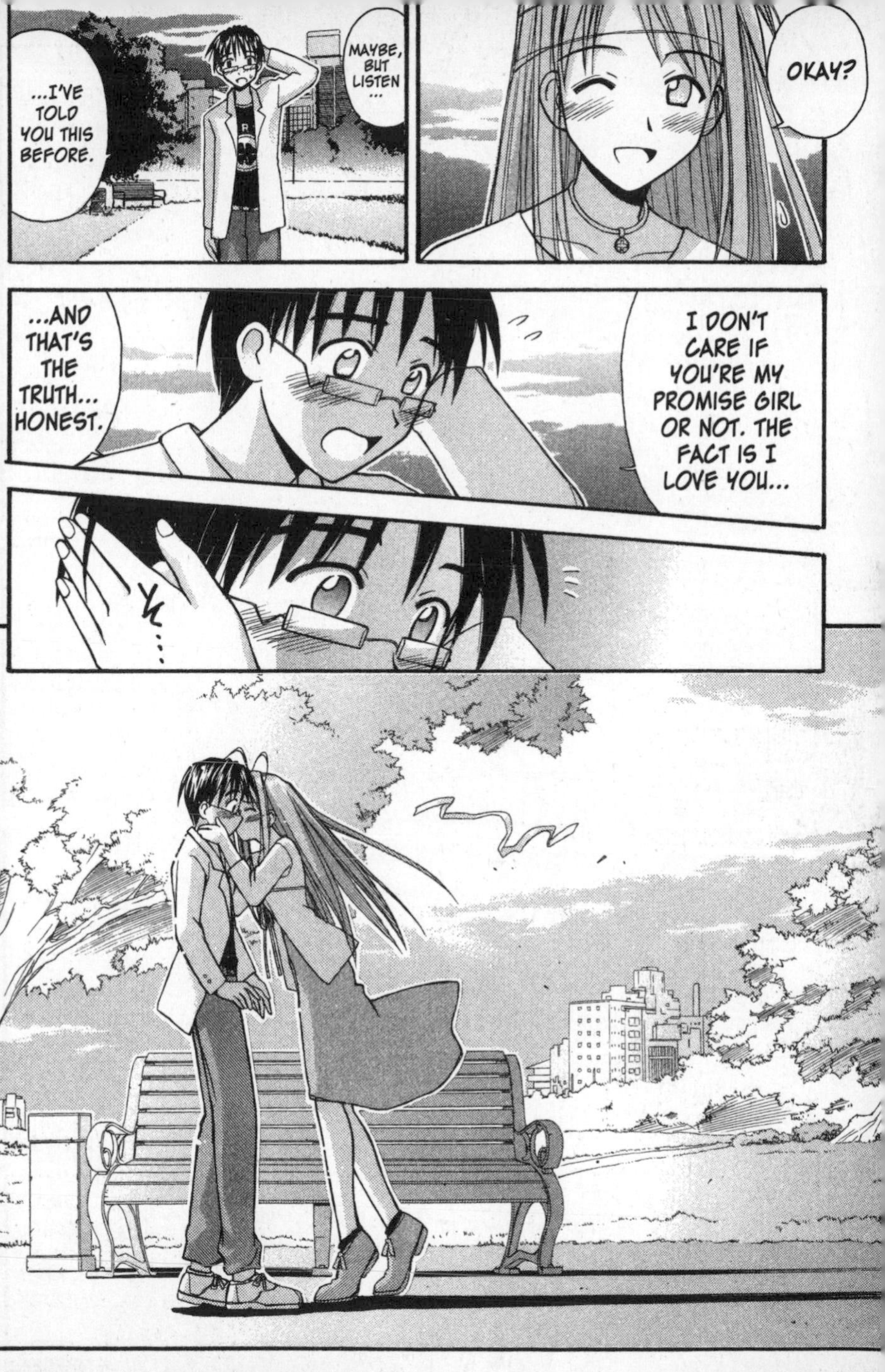
OKAY?
MAYBE, BUT LISTEN...
...I'VE TOLD YOU THIS BEFORE.
I DON'T CARE IF YOU'RE MY PROMISE GIRL OR NOT. THE FACT IS I LOVE YOU...
...AND THAT'S THE TRUTH... HONEST.

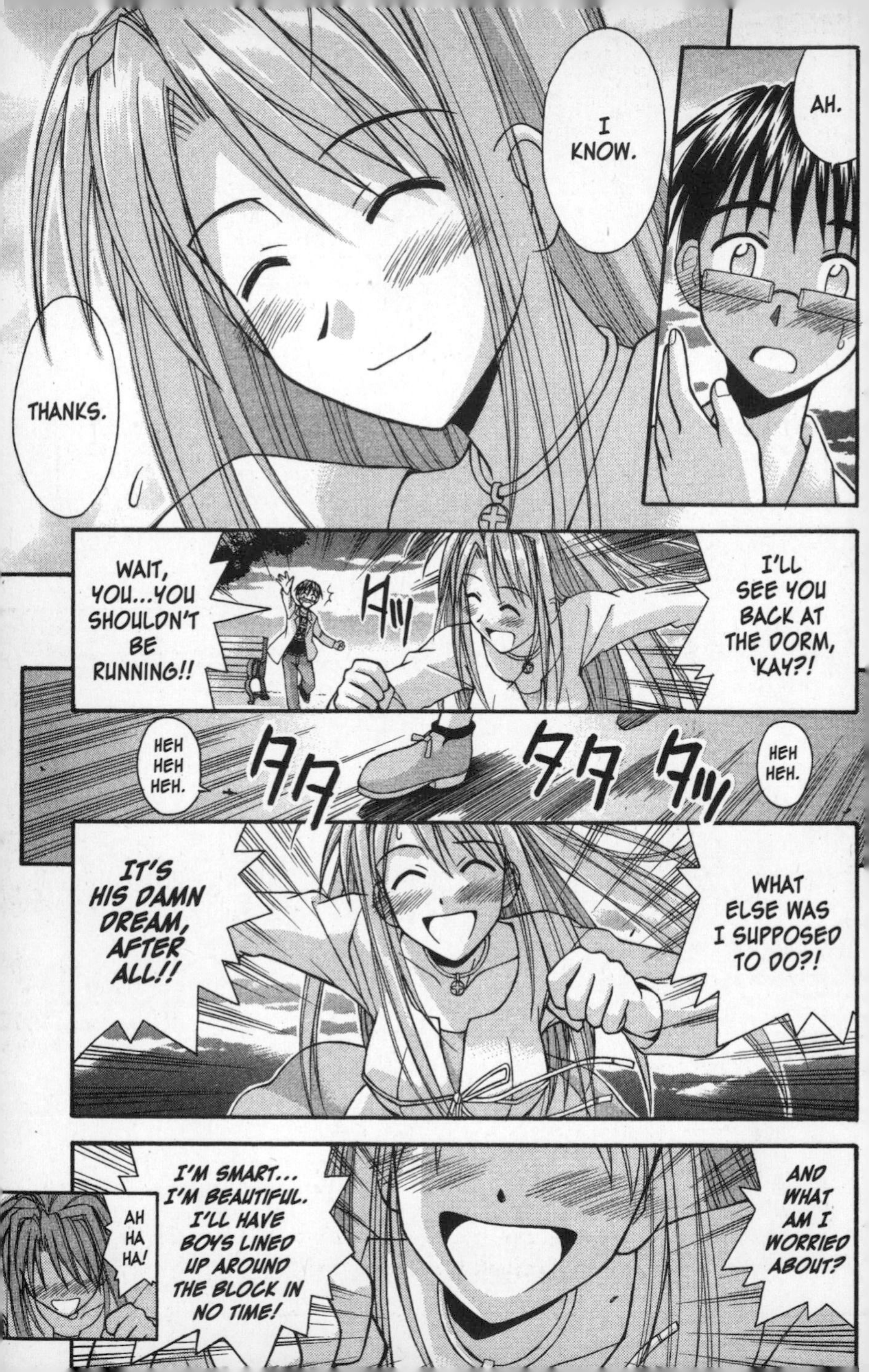
AH.
I KNOW.
THANKS.
I'LL SEE YOU BACK AT THE DORM, 'KAY?!
タッ
WAIT, YOU...YOU SHOULDN'T BE RUNNING!!
HEH HEH.
タッ
タタ
タタ
HEH HEH HEH.
WHAT ELSE WAS I SUPPOSED TO DO?!
IT'S HIS DAMN DREAM, AFTER ALL!!
AND WHAT AM I WORRIED ABOUT?
I'M SMART... I'M BEAUTIFUL. I'LL HAVE BOYS LINED UP AROUND THE BLOCK IN NO TIME!
AH HA HA!

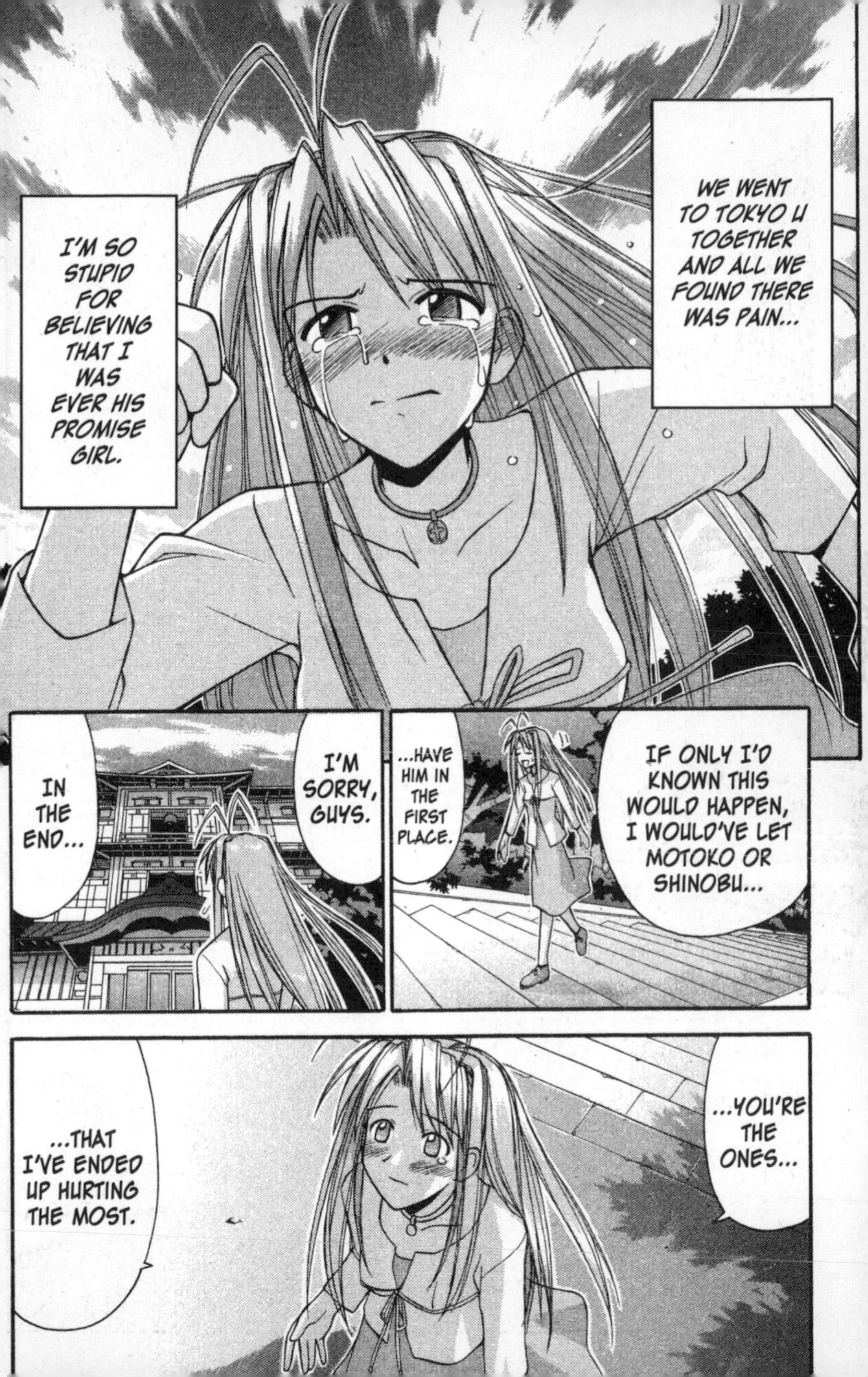
WE WENT TO TOKYO U TOGETHER AND ALL WE FOUND THERE WAS PAIN...
I'M SO STUPID FOR BELIEVING THAT I WAS EVER HIS PROMISE GIRL.
IF ONLY I'D KNOWN THIS WOULD HAPPEN, I WOULD'VE LET MOTOKO OR SHINOBU...
...HAVE HIM IN THE FIRST PLACE.
I'M SORRY, GUYS.
IN THE END...
...YOU'RE THE ONES...
...THAT I'VE ENDED UP HURTING THE MOST.

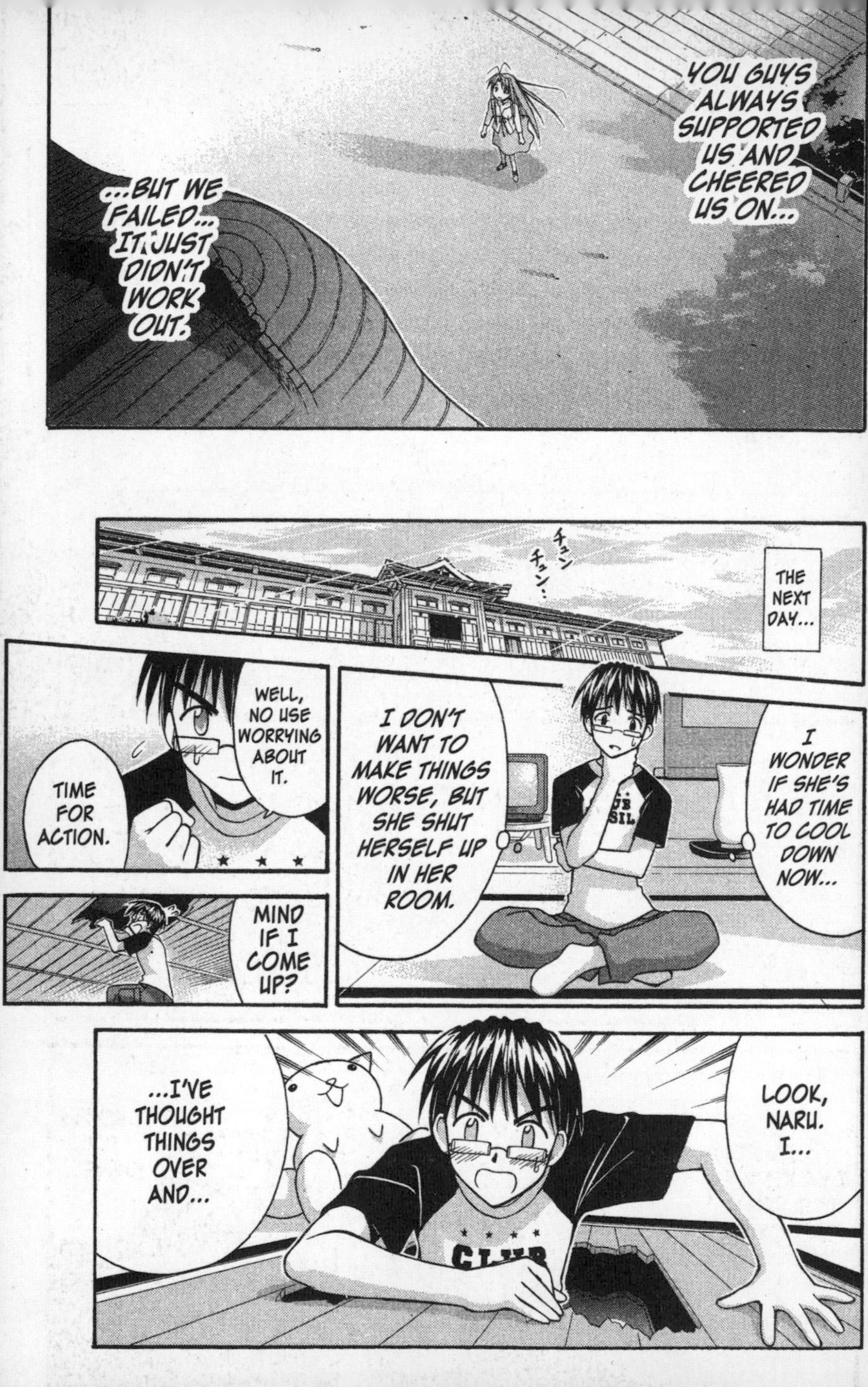
YOU GUYS ALWAYS SUPPORTED US AND CHEERED US ON...
...BUT WE FAILED... IT JUST DIDN'T WORK OUT.
THE NEXT DAY...
チュン チュン…
I WONDER IF SHE'S HAD TIME TO COOL DOWN NOW...
I DON'T WANT TO MAKE THINGS WORSE, BUT SHE SHUT HERSELF UP IN HER ROOM.
WELL, NO USE WORRYING ABOUT IT.
TIME FOR ACTION.
MIND IF I COME UP?
LOOK, NARU. I...
...I'VE THOUGHT THINGS OVER AND...

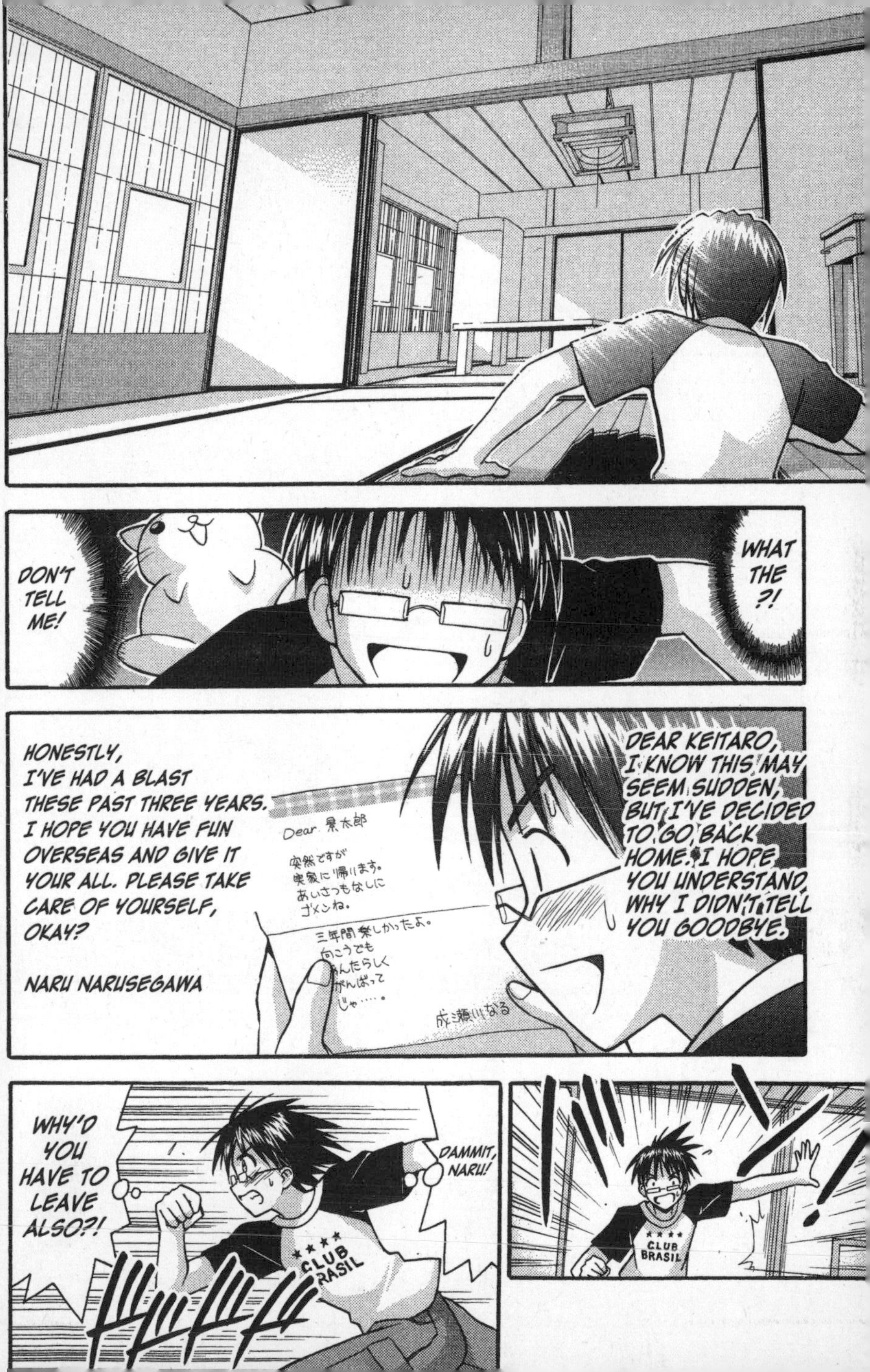
WHAT THE?!
DON'T TELL ME!
DEAR KEITARO, I KNOW THIS MAY SEEM SUDDEN, BUT I'VE DECIDED TO GO BACK HOME. I HOPE YOU UNDERSTAND WHY I DIDN'T TELL YOU GOODBYE.
Dear 景太郎
突然ですが
実家に帰ります。
あいさつもなしに
ゴメンね。
三年間楽しかったよ。
向こうでも
んたらしく
がんばって
じゃ……。
成瀬川なる
HONESTLY, I'VE HAD A BLAST THESE PAST THREE YEARS. I HOPE YOU HAVE FUN OVERSEAS AND GIVE IT YOUR ALL. PLEASE TAKE CARE OF YOURSELF, OKAY?
NARU NARUSEGAWA
CLUB BRASIL
DAMMIT, NARU!
WHY'D YOU HAVE TO LEAVE ALSO?!
CLUB BRASIL

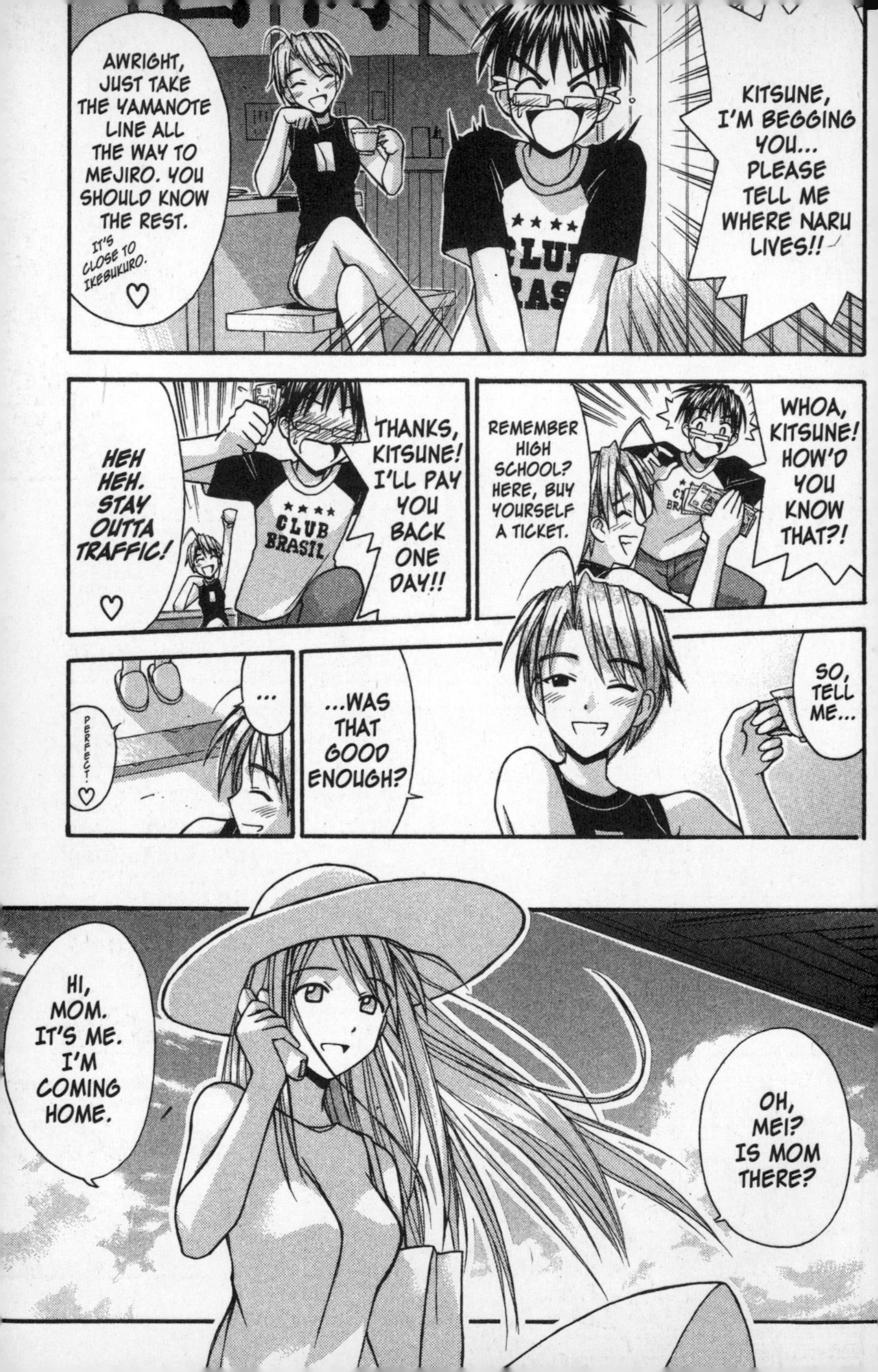
KITSUNE, I'M BEGGING YOU... PLEASE TELL ME WHERE NARU LIVES!!
AWRIGHT, JUST TAKE THE YAMANOTE LINE ALL THE WAY TO MEJIRO. YOU SHOULD KNOW THE REST.
IT'S CLOSE TO IKEBUKURO. ♡
WHOA, KITSUNE! HOW'D YOU KNOW THAT?!
REMEMBER HIGH SCHOOL? HERE, BUY YOURSELF A TICKET.
THANKS, KITSUNE! I'LL PAY YOU BACK ONE DAY!!
HEH HEH. STAY OUTTA TRAFFIC! ♡
SO, TELL ME...
...WAS THAT GOOD ENOUGH?
...
PERFECT. ♡
OH, MEI? IS MOM THERE?
HI, MOM. IT'S ME. I'M COMING HOME.

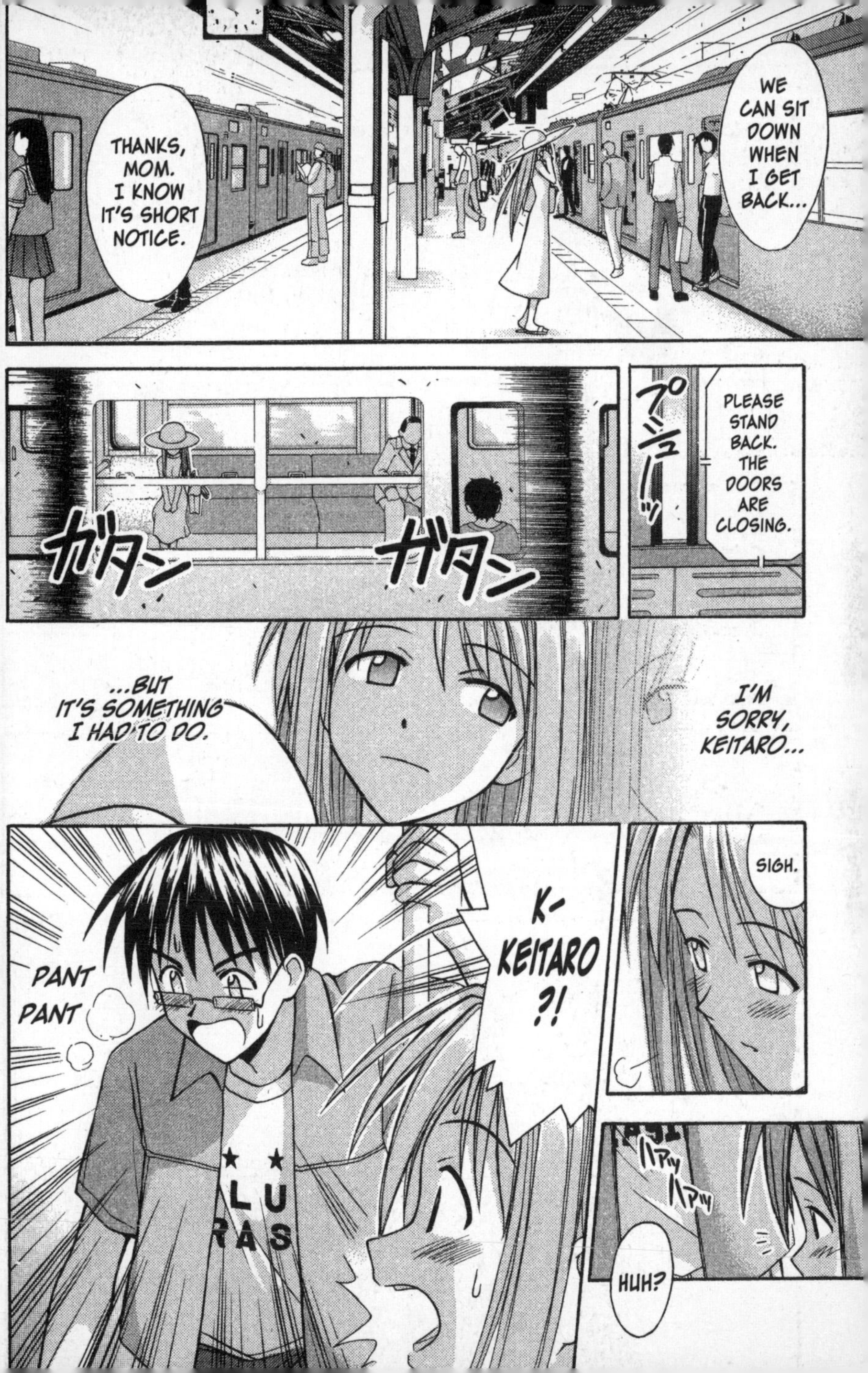
WE CAN SIT DOWN WHEN I GET BACK...
THANKS, MOM. I KNOW IT'S SHORT NOTICE.
プシューッ
PLEASE STAND BACK. THE DOORS ARE CLOSING.
ガタン
ガタン
I'M SORRY, KEITARO...
...BUT IT'S SOMETHING I HAD TO DO.
SIGH.
ハアッ
ハアッ
HUH?
K-KEITARO?!
PANT PANT

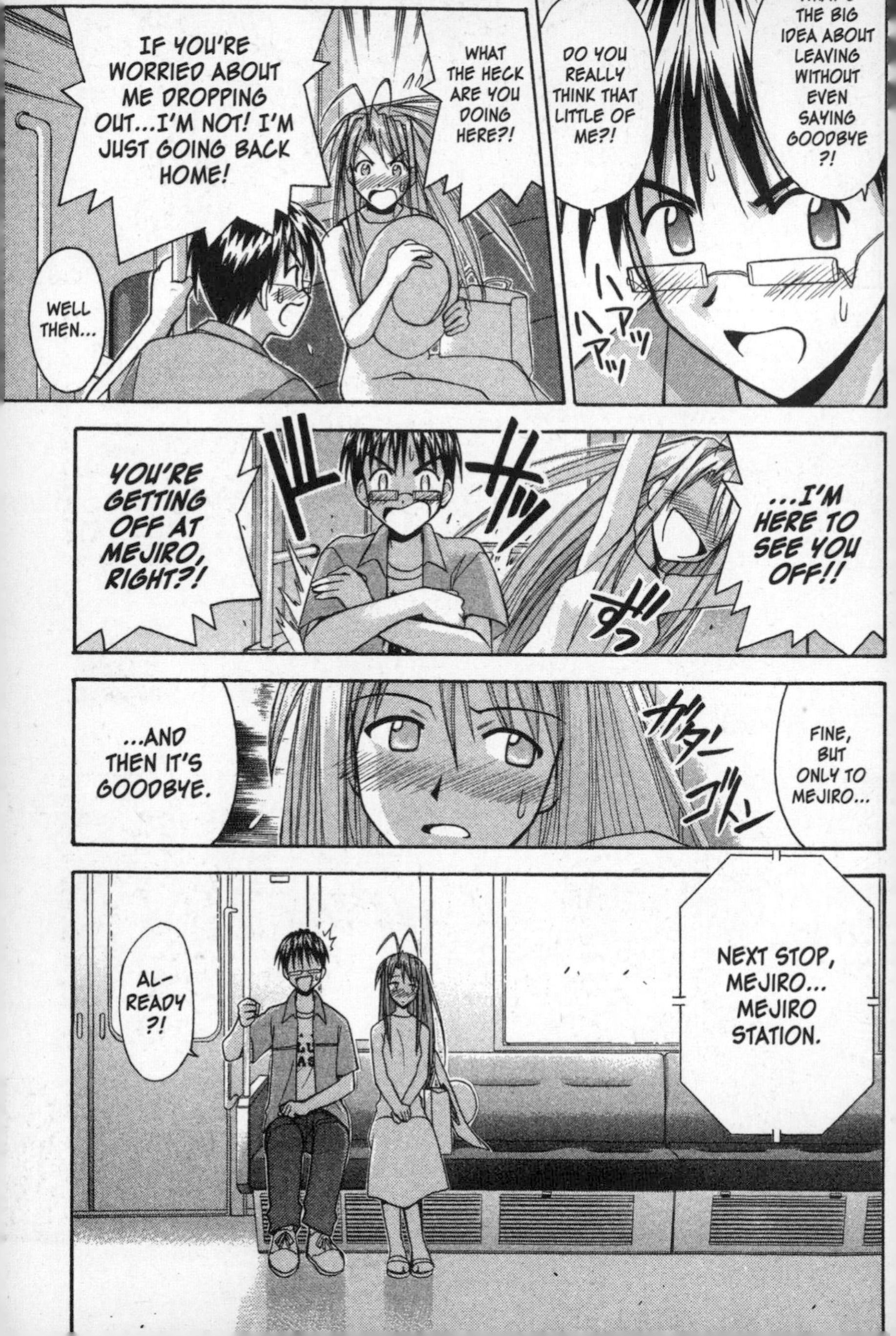
WHAT'S THE BIG IDEA ABOUT LEAVING WITHOUT EVEN SAYING GOODBYE ?!
DO YOU REALLY THINK THAT LITTLE OF ME?!
ハァッ ハァッ
WHAT THE HECK ARE YOU DOING HERE?!
IF YOU'RE WORRIED ABOUT ME DROPPING OUT...I'M NOT! I'M JUST GOING BACK HOME!
WELL THEN...
...I'M HERE TO SEE YOU OFF!!
YOU'RE GETTING OFF AT MEJIRO, RIGHT?!
FINE, BUT ONLY TO MEJIRO...
ガタン ゴトン
...AND THEN IT'S GOODBYE.
NEXT STOP, MEJIRO... MEJIRO STATION.
AL-READY ?!

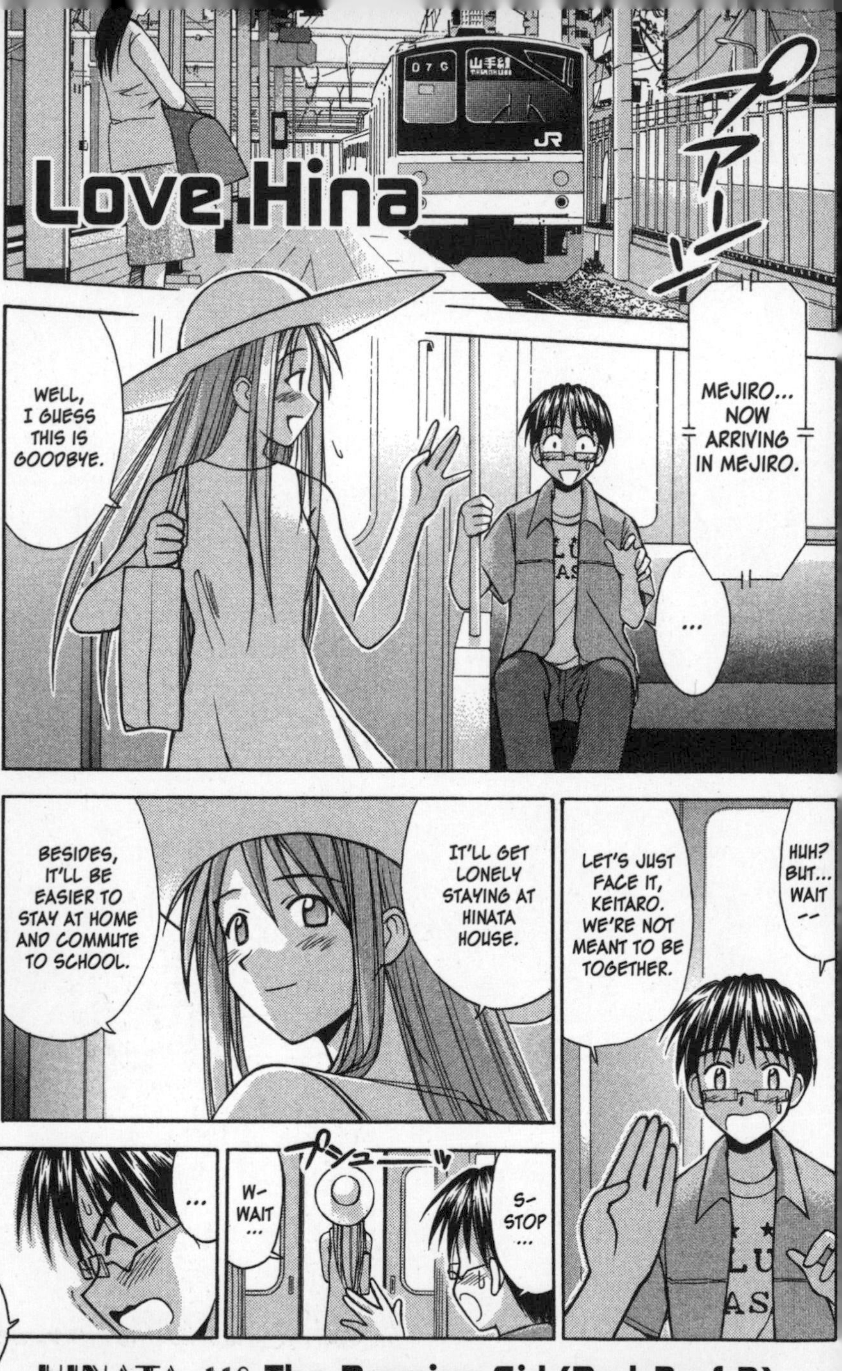
Love Hina
MEJIRO... NOW ARRIVING IN MEJIRO.
WELL, I GUESS THIS IS GOODBYE.
...
HUH? BUT... WAIT --
LET'S JUST FACE IT, KEITARO. WE'RE NOT MEANT TO BE TOGETHER.
IT'LL GET LONELY STAYING AT HINATA HOUSE.
BESIDES, IT'LL BE EASIER TO STAY AT HOME AND COMMUTE TO SCHOOL.
S-STOP ...
W-WAIT ...
...
AHH!

HINATA.118 The Promise Girl (Part 2 of 2)

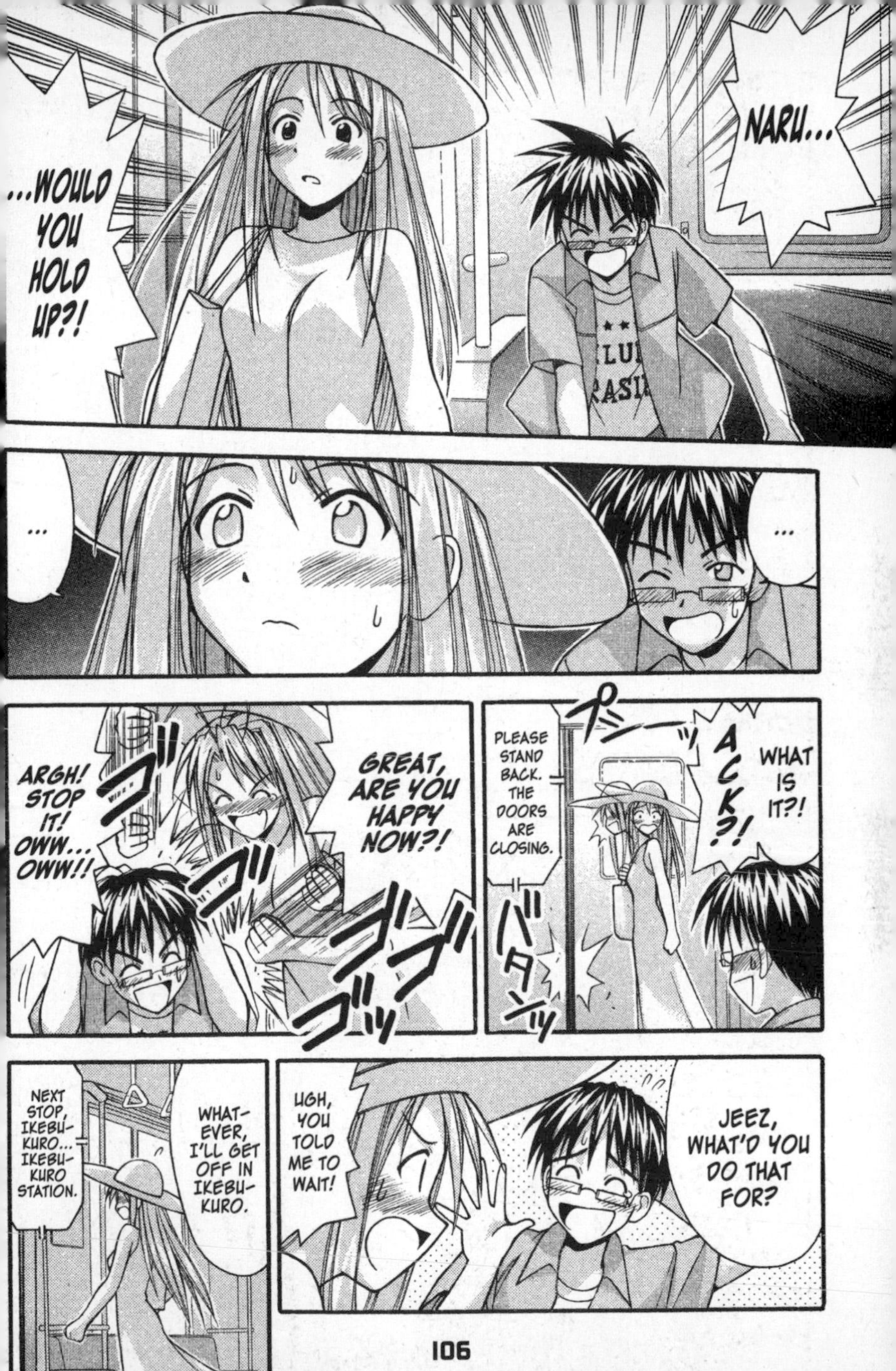
NARU...
...WOULD YOU HOLD UP?!
...
...
WHAT IS IT?!
ACK?!
プシーーッ
PLEASE STAND BACK. THE DOORS ARE CLOSING.
バタンッ
GREAT, ARE YOU HAPPY NOW?!
ARGH! STOP IT! OWW... OWW!!
JEEZ, WHAT'D YOU DO THAT FOR?
UGH, YOU TOLD ME TO WAIT!
WHAT-EVER, I'LL GET OFF IN IKEBU-KURO.
NEXT STOP, IKEBU-KURO... IKEBU-KURO STATION.

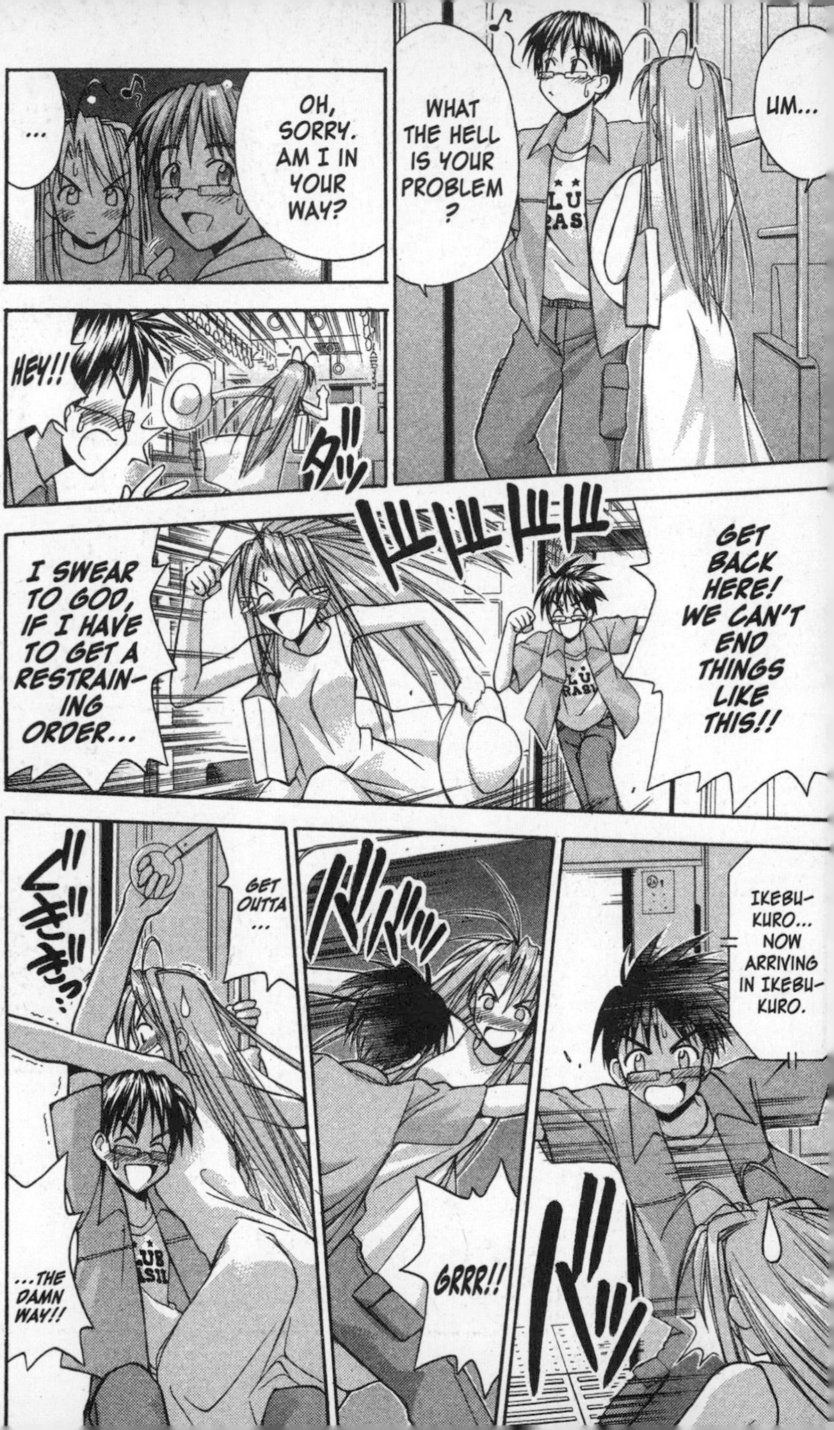
UM...
WHAT THE HELL IS YOUR PROBLEM?
OH, SORRY. AM I IN YOUR WAY?
...
HEY!!
GET BACK HERE! WE CAN'T END THINGS LIKE THIS!!
I SWEAR TO GOD, IF I HAVE TO GET A RESTRAINING ORDER...
IKEBUKURO... NOW ARRIVING IN IKEBUKURO.
GRRR!!
GET OUTTA...
...THE DAMN WAY!!

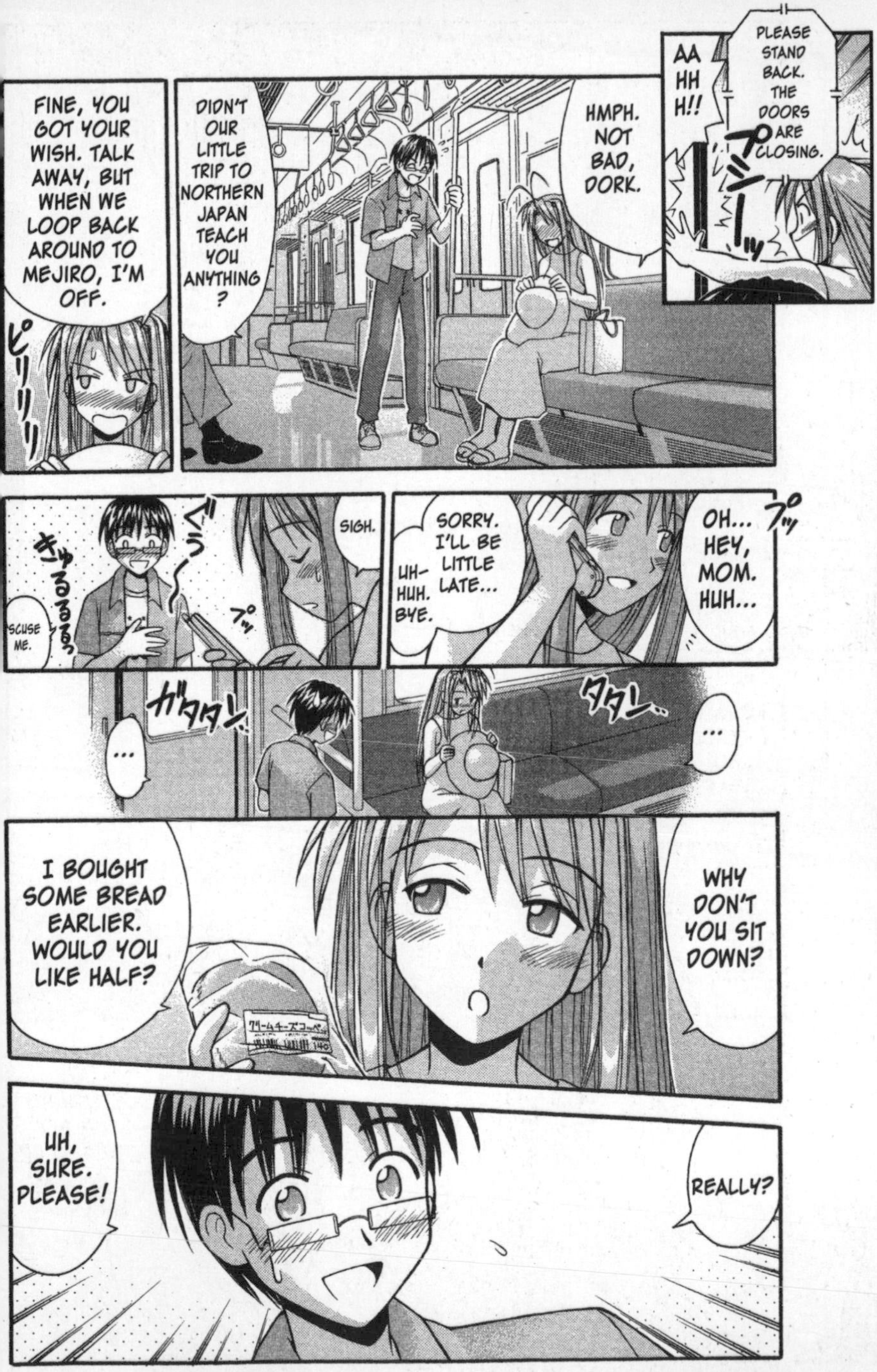
PLEASE STAND BACK. THE DOORS ARE CLOSING.
AA HH H!!
HMPH. NOT BAD, DORK.
DIDN'T OUR LITTLE TRIP TO NORTHERN JAPAN TEACH YOU ANYTHING?
FINE, YOU GOT YOUR WISH. TALK AWAY, BUT WHEN WE LOOP BACK AROUND TO MEJIRO, I'M OFF.
OH... HEY, MOM. HUH...
SORRY. I'LL BE LITTLE LATE...
UH-HUH. BYE.
SIGH.
'SCUSE ME.
...
...
WHY DON'T YOU SIT DOWN?
I BOUGHT SOME BREAD EARLIER. WOULD YOU LIKE HALF?
REALLY?
UH, SURE. PLEASE!

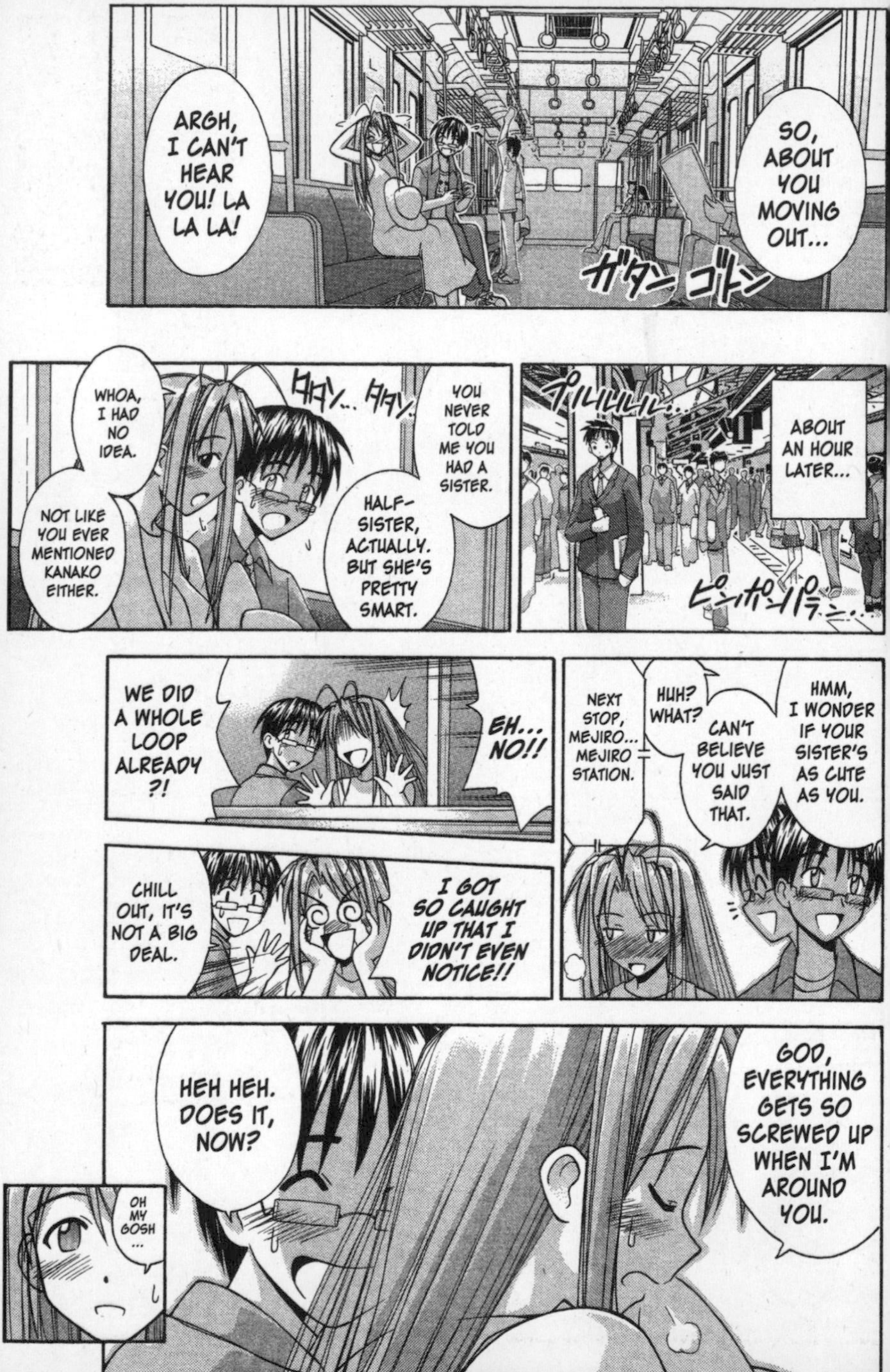
SO, ABOUT YOU MOVING OUT...
ARGH, I CAN'T HEAR YOU! LA LA LA!
ガタン ゴトン
ABOUT AN HOUR LATER...
プルルルル...
ピンポンパラン...
YOU NEVER TOLD ME YOU HAD A SISTER.
HALF-SISTER, ACTUALLY. BUT SHE'S PRETTY SMART.
タタン... タタン...
WHOA, I HAD NO IDEA.
NOT LIKE YOU EVER MENTIONED KANAKO EITHER.
HMM, I WONDER IF YOUR SISTER'S AS CUTE AS YOU.
HUH? WHAT?
CAN'T BELIEVE YOU JUST SAID THAT.
NEXT STOP, MEJIRO... MEJIRO STATION.
EH... NO!!
WE DID A WHOLE LOOP ALREADY?!
I GOT SO CAUGHT UP THAT I DIDN'T EVEN NOTICE!!
CHILL OUT, IT'S NOT A BIG DEAL.
GOD, EVERYTHING GETS SO SCREWED UP WHEN I'M AROUND YOU.
HEH HEH. DOES IT, NOW?
OH MY GOSH...

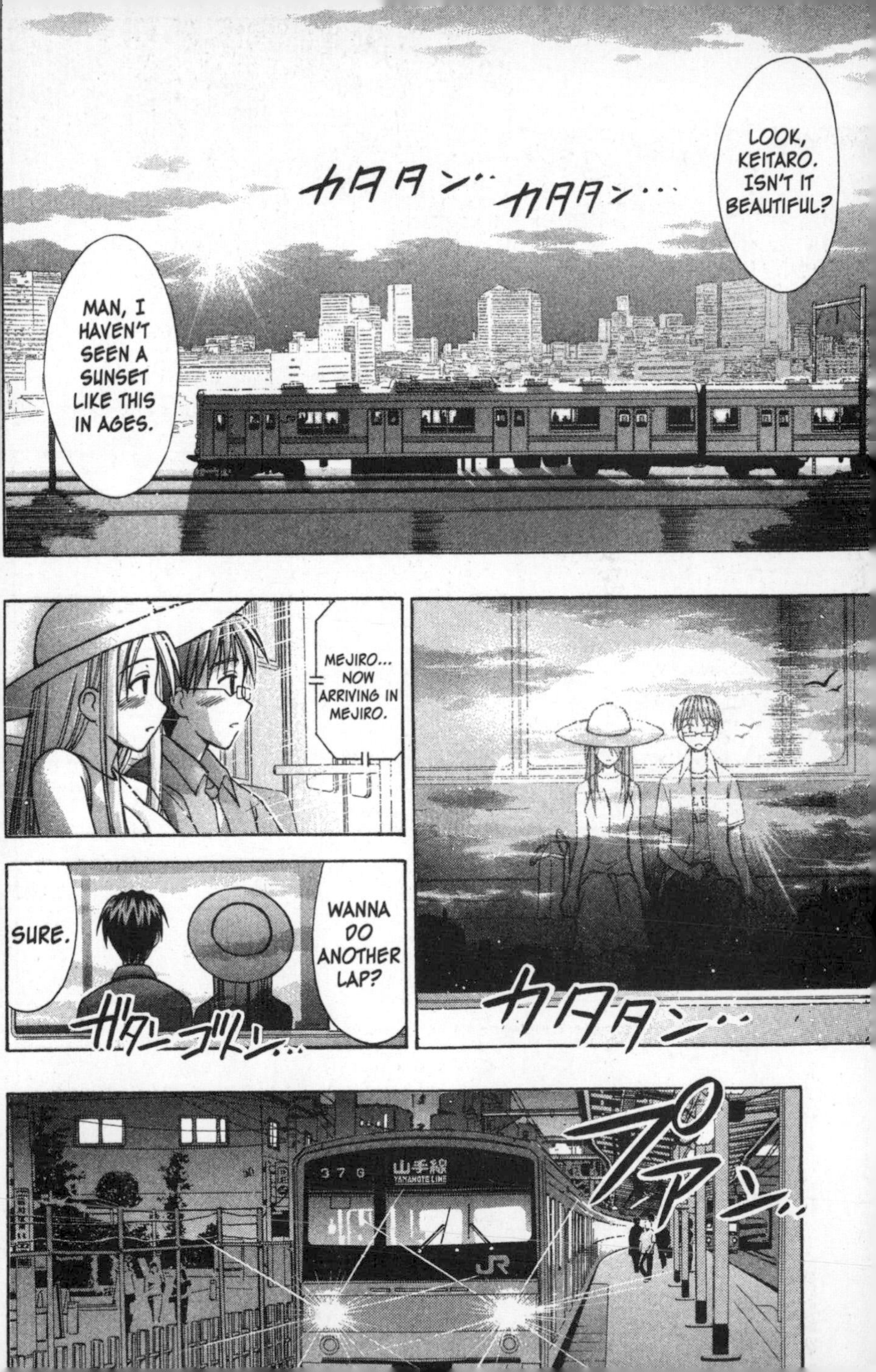
LOOK, KEITARO. ISN'T IT BEAUTIFUL?
カタタン‥ カタタン‥‥
MAN, I HAVEN'T SEEN A SUNSET LIKE THIS IN AGES.
カタタン‥
MEJIRO... NOW ARRIVING IN MEJIRO.
WANNA DO ANOTHER LAP?
SURE.
ガタンゴトン‥
プァン‥
37 G
山手線
YAMANOTE LINE
JR

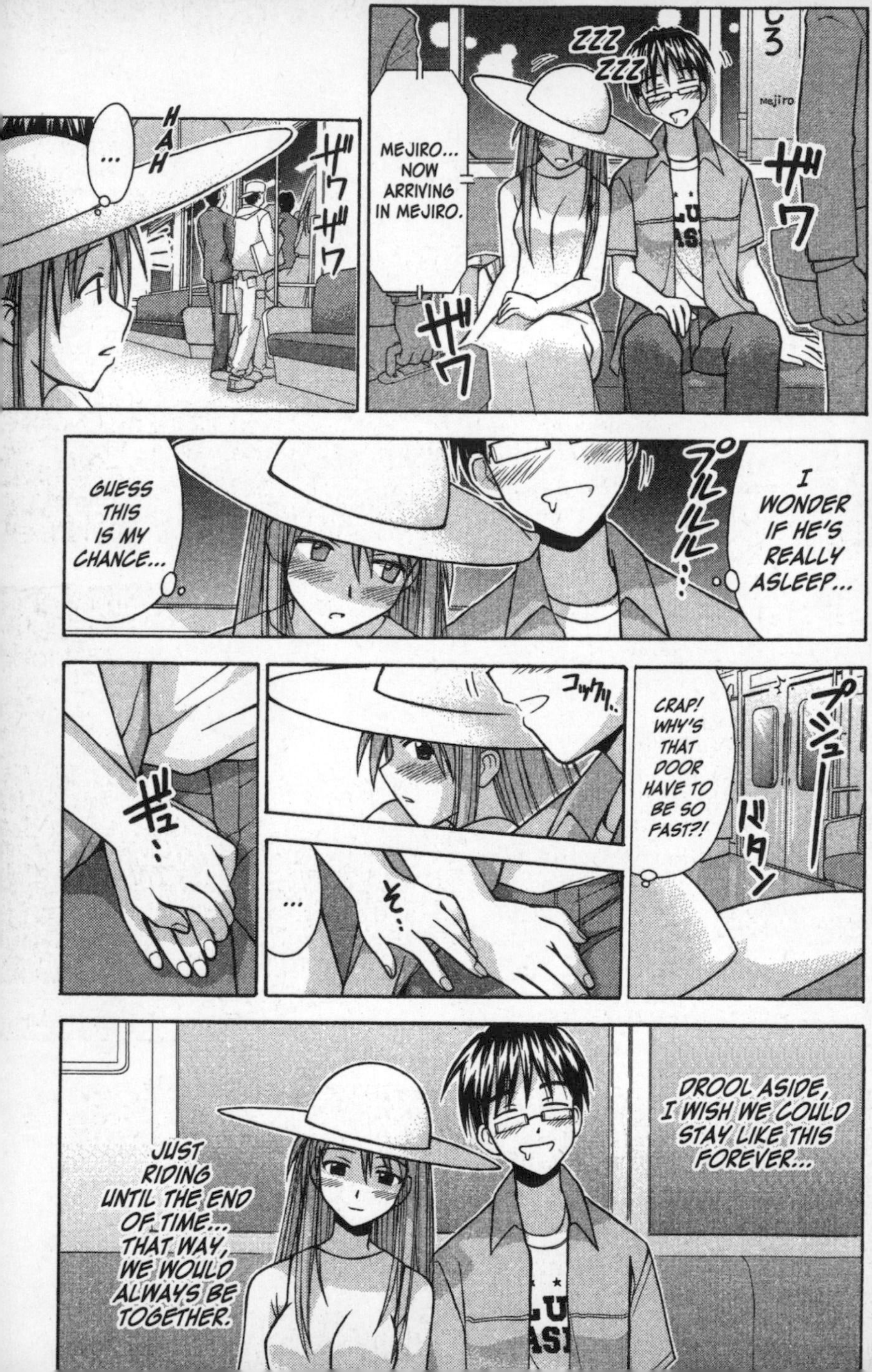
ZZZ
ZZZ
Mejiro
ザワ
MEJIRO... NOW ARRIVING IN MEJIRO.
ザワ
HAH
...
ザワザワ
I WONDER IF HE'S REALLY ASLEEP...
プルル...
GUESS THIS IS MY CHANCE...
プシュー
バタン
CRAP! WHY'S THAT DOOR HAVE TO BE SO FAST?!
コックリ..
...
そ..
ギュ..
DROOL ASIDE, I WISH WE COULD STAY LIKE THIS FOREVER...
JUST RIDING UNTIL THE END OF TIME... THAT WAY, WE WOULD ALWAYS BE TOGETHER.

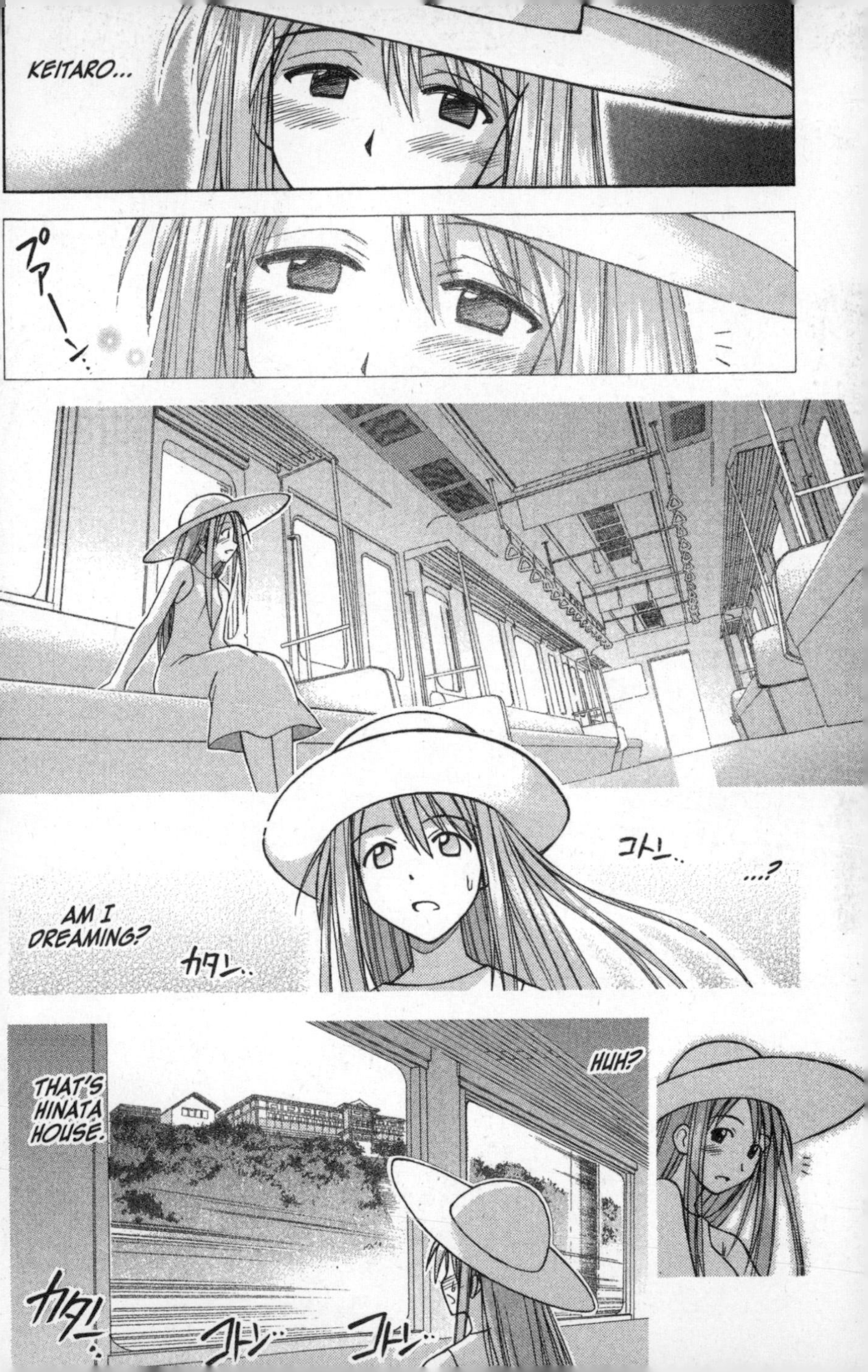
KEITARO...
プァーン…
コトン..
...?
AM I DREAMING?
カタン..
HUH?
THAT'S HINATA HOUSE.
コトン..
コトン..
カタン..

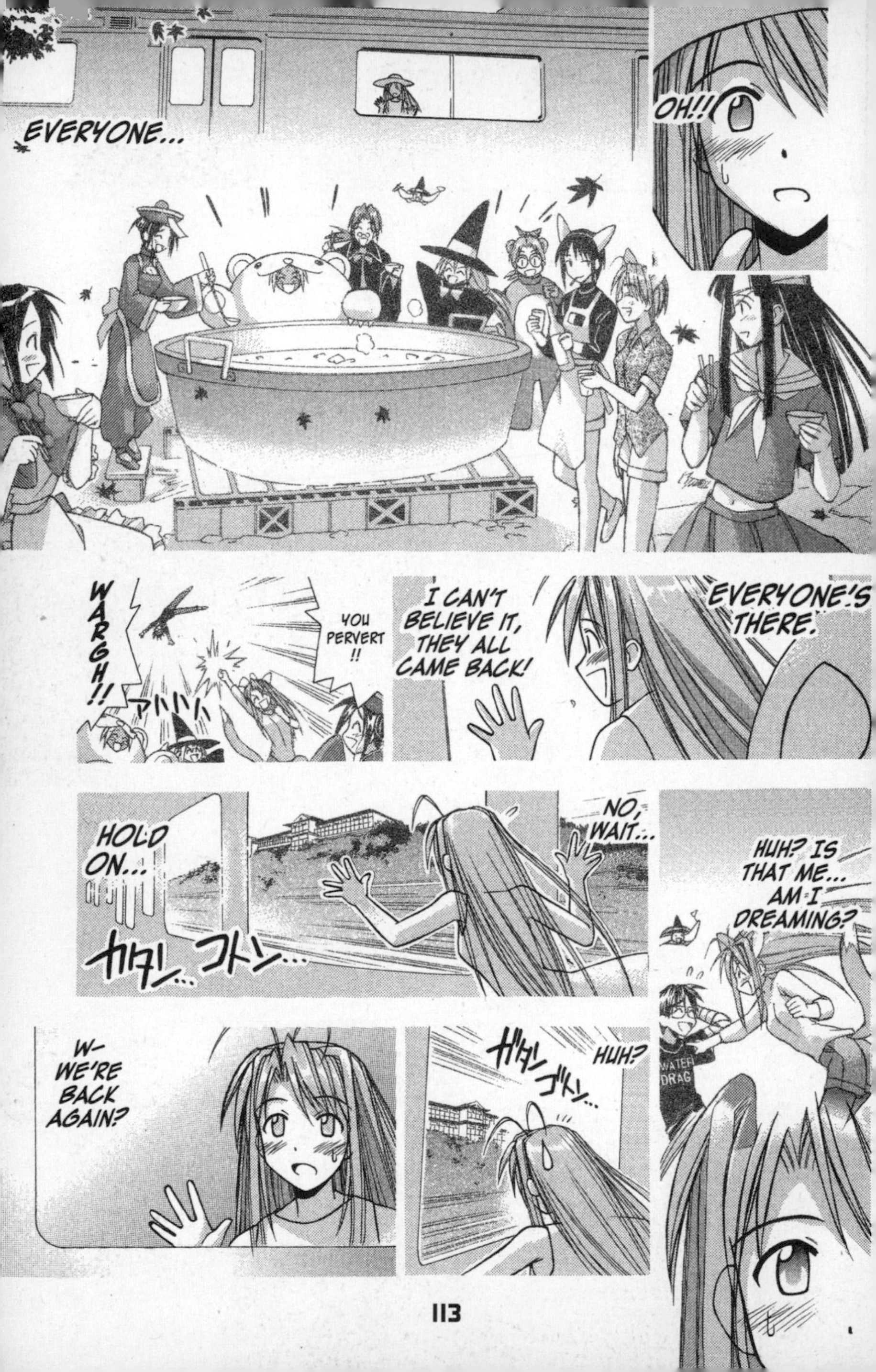
OH!!
EVERYONE...
EVERYONE'S THERE.
I CAN'T BELIEVE IT, THEY ALL CAME BACK!
YOU PERVERT !!
WARGH!!
アハハハ
HUH? IS THAT ME... AM I DREAMING?
WATER DRAG
NO, WAIT...
HOLD ON...
カタン... コトン...
HUH?
ガタン ゴトン...
W-WE'RE BACK AGAIN?

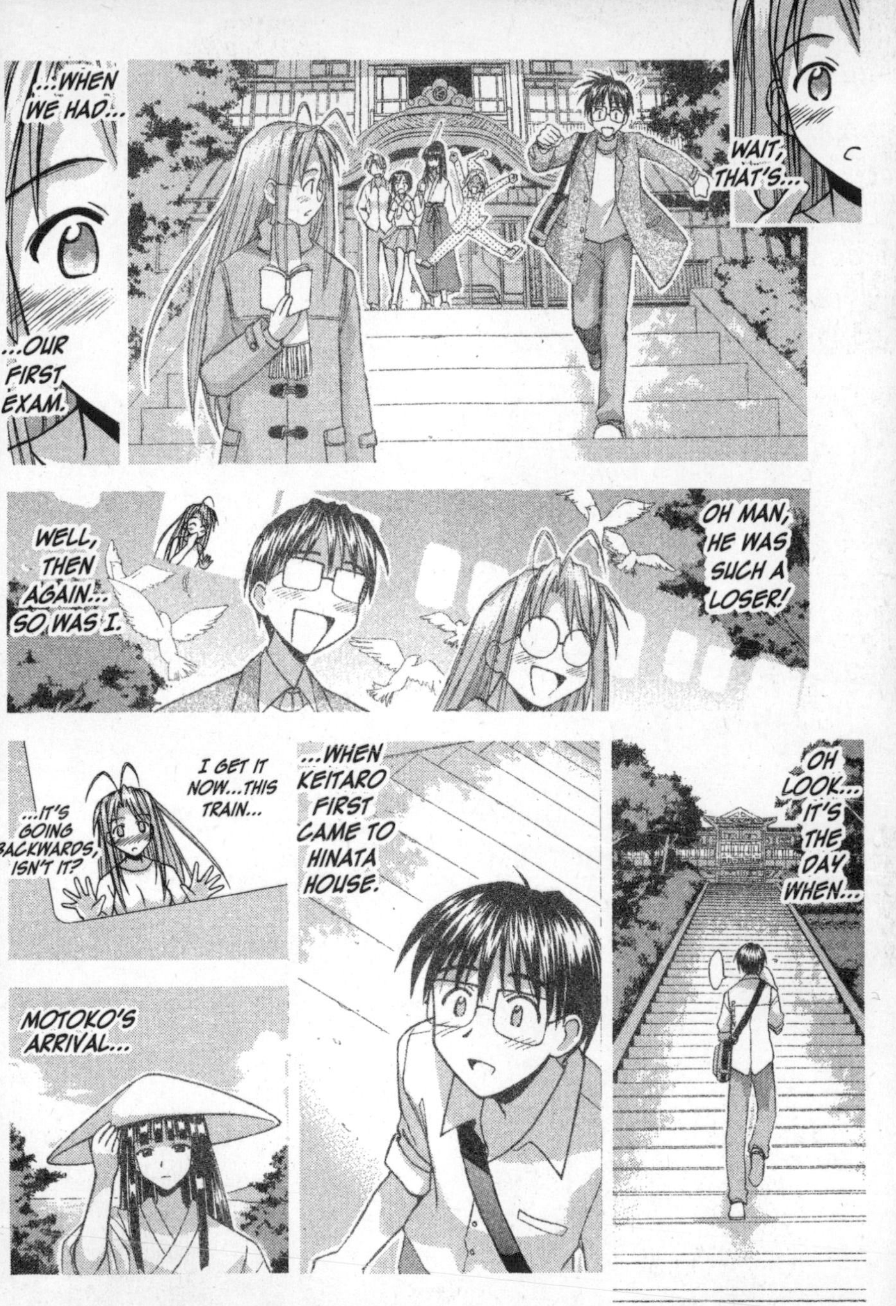
WAIT, THAT'S...
...WHEN WE HAD...
...OUR FIRST EXAM.
OH MAN, HE WAS SUCH A LOSER!
WELL, THEN AGAIN... SO WAS I.
OH LOOK... IT'S THE DAY WHEN...
...WHEN KEITARO FIRST CAME TO HINATA HOUSE.
I GET IT NOW...THIS TRAIN...
...IT'S GOING BACKWARDS, ISN'T IT?
MOTOKO'S ARRIVAL...

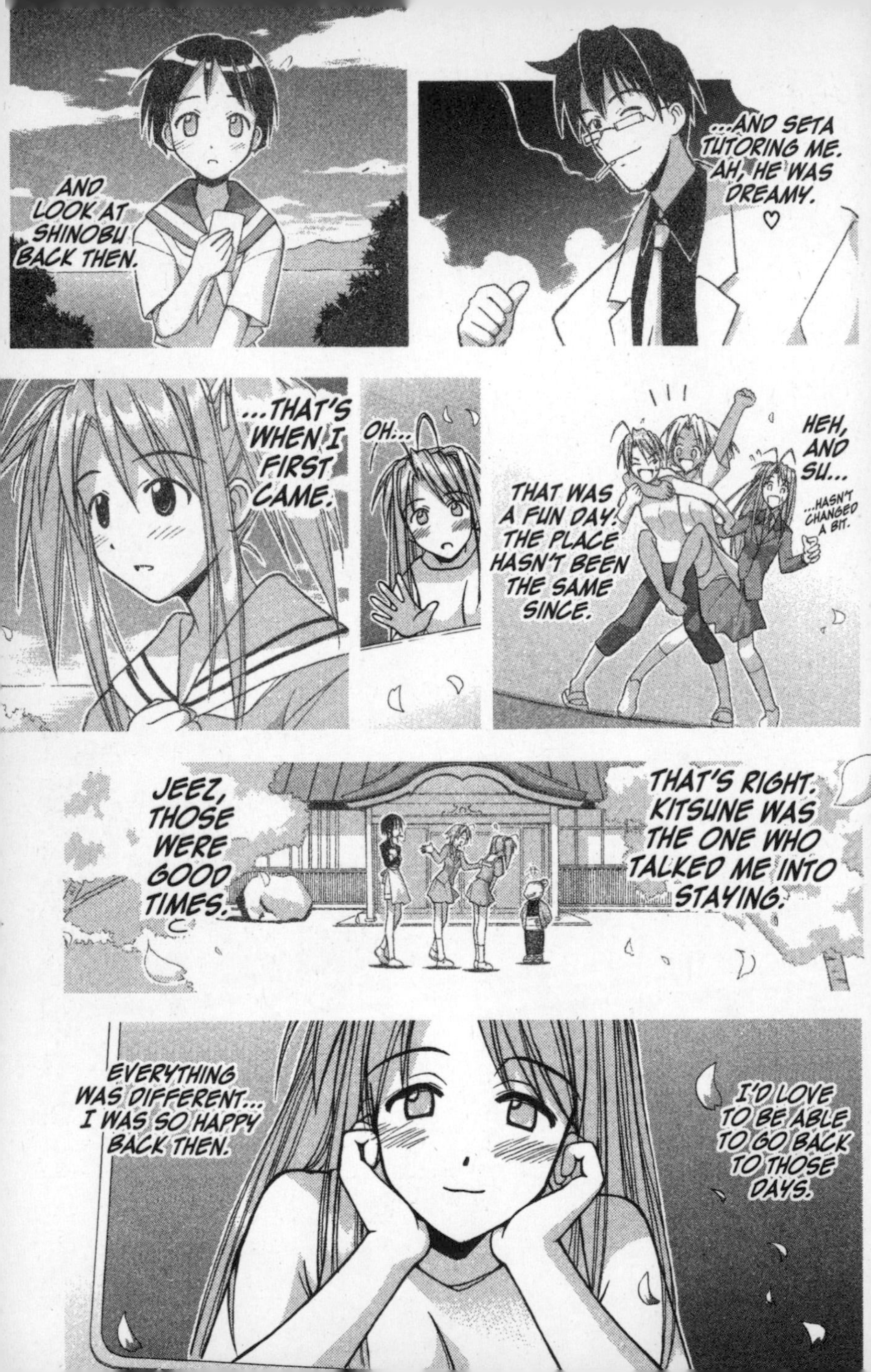
...AND SETA TUTORING ME. AH, HE WAS DREAMY. ♡
AND LOOK AT SHINOBU BACK THEN.
HEH, AND SU...
...HASN'T CHANGED A BIT.
THAT WAS A FUN DAY. THE PLACE HASN'T BEEN THE SAME SINCE.
OH...
...THAT'S WHEN I FIRST CAME.
THAT'S RIGHT. KITSUNE WAS THE ONE WHO TALKED ME INTO STAYING.
JEEZ, THOSE WERE GOOD TIMES.
I'D LOVE TO BE ABLE TO GO BACK TO THOSE DAYS.
EVERYTHING WAS DIFFERENT... I WAS SO HAPPY BACK THEN.

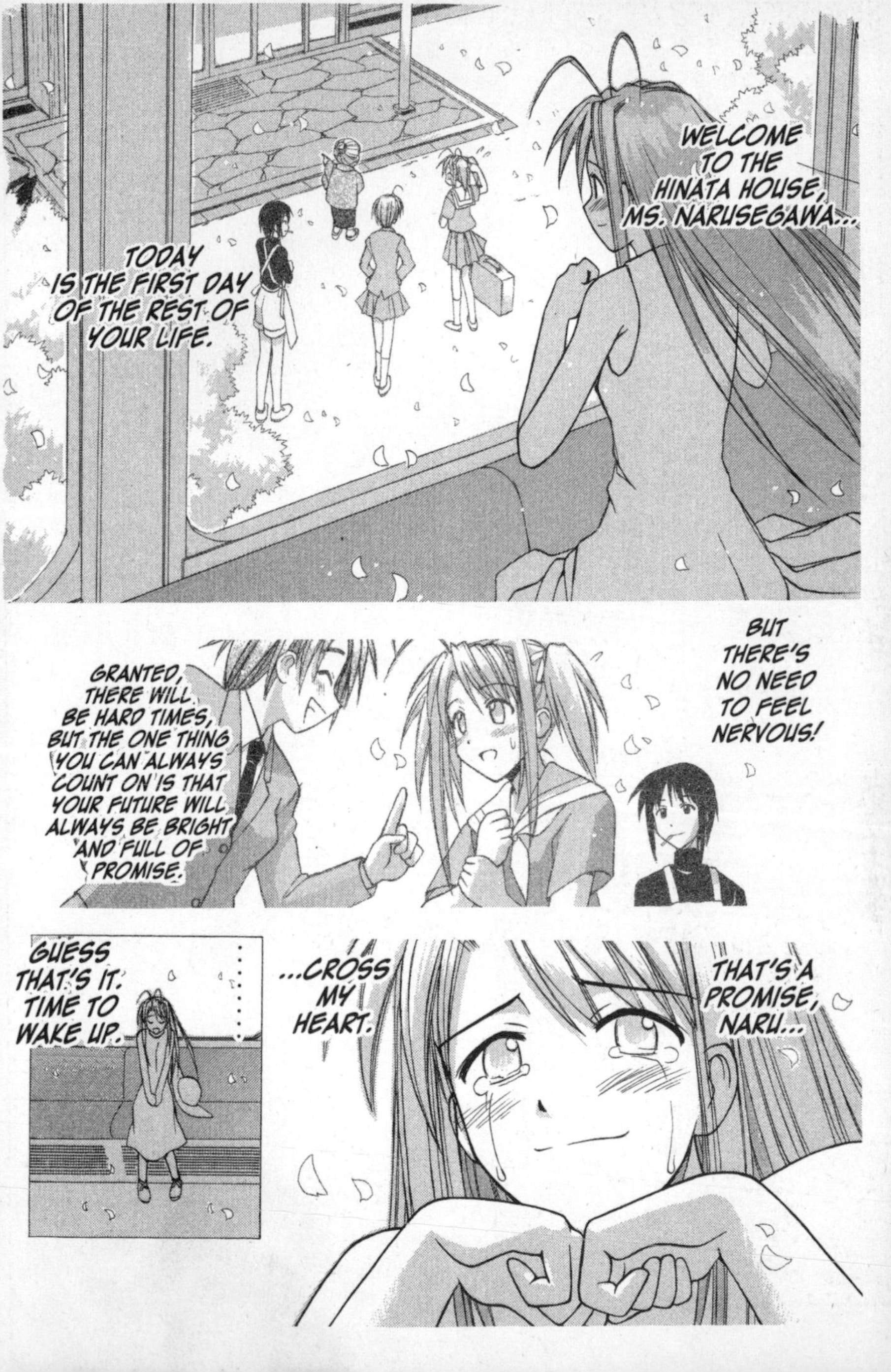
WELCOME TO THE HINATA HOUSE, MS. NARUSEGAWA...
TODAY IS THE FIRST DAY OF THE REST OF YOUR LIFE.
BUT THERE'S NO NEED TO FEEL NERVOUS!
GRANTED, THERE WILL BE HARD TIMES, BUT THE ONE THING YOU CAN ALWAYS COUNT ON IS THAT YOUR FUTURE WILL ALWAYS BE BRIGHT AND FULL OF PROMISE.
THAT'S A PROMISE, NARU...
...CROSS MY HEART.
....
GUESS THAT'S IT. TIME TO WAKE UP.

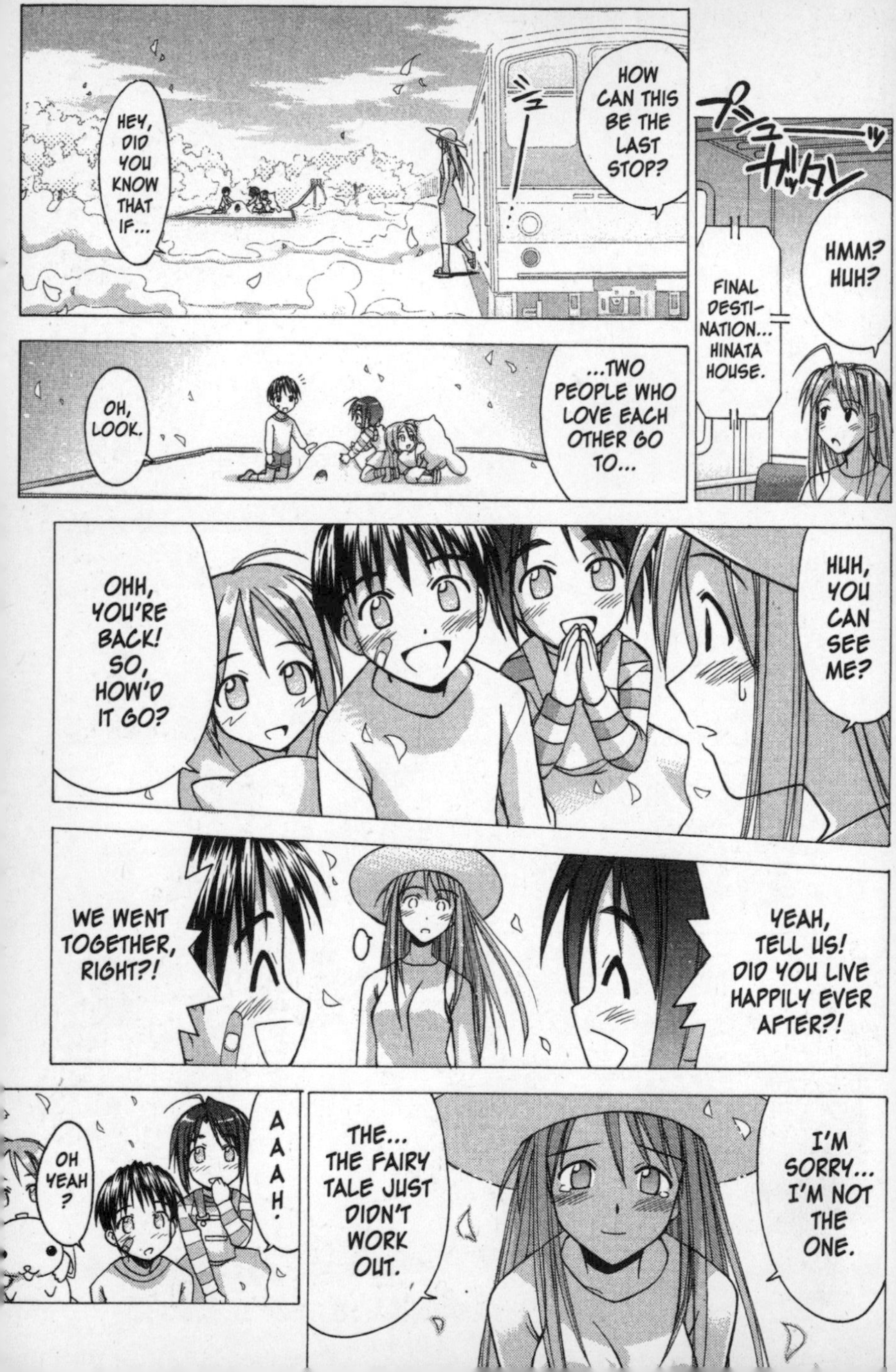
プシューッ
ガタン
HMM? HUH?
FINAL DESTI-NATION... HINATA HOUSE.
HOW CAN THIS BE THE LAST STOP?
HEY, DID YOU KNOW THAT IF...
...TWO PEOPLE WHO LOVE EACH OTHER GO TO...
OH, LOOK.
HUH, YOU CAN SEE ME?
OHH, YOU'RE BACK! SO, HOW'D IT GO?
YEAH, TELL US! DID YOU LIVE HAPPILY EVER AFTER?!
WE WENT TOGETHER, RIGHT?!
I'M SORRY... I'M NOT THE ONE.
THE... THE FAIRY TALE JUST DIDN'T WORK OUT.
AAAAH!
OH YEAH?

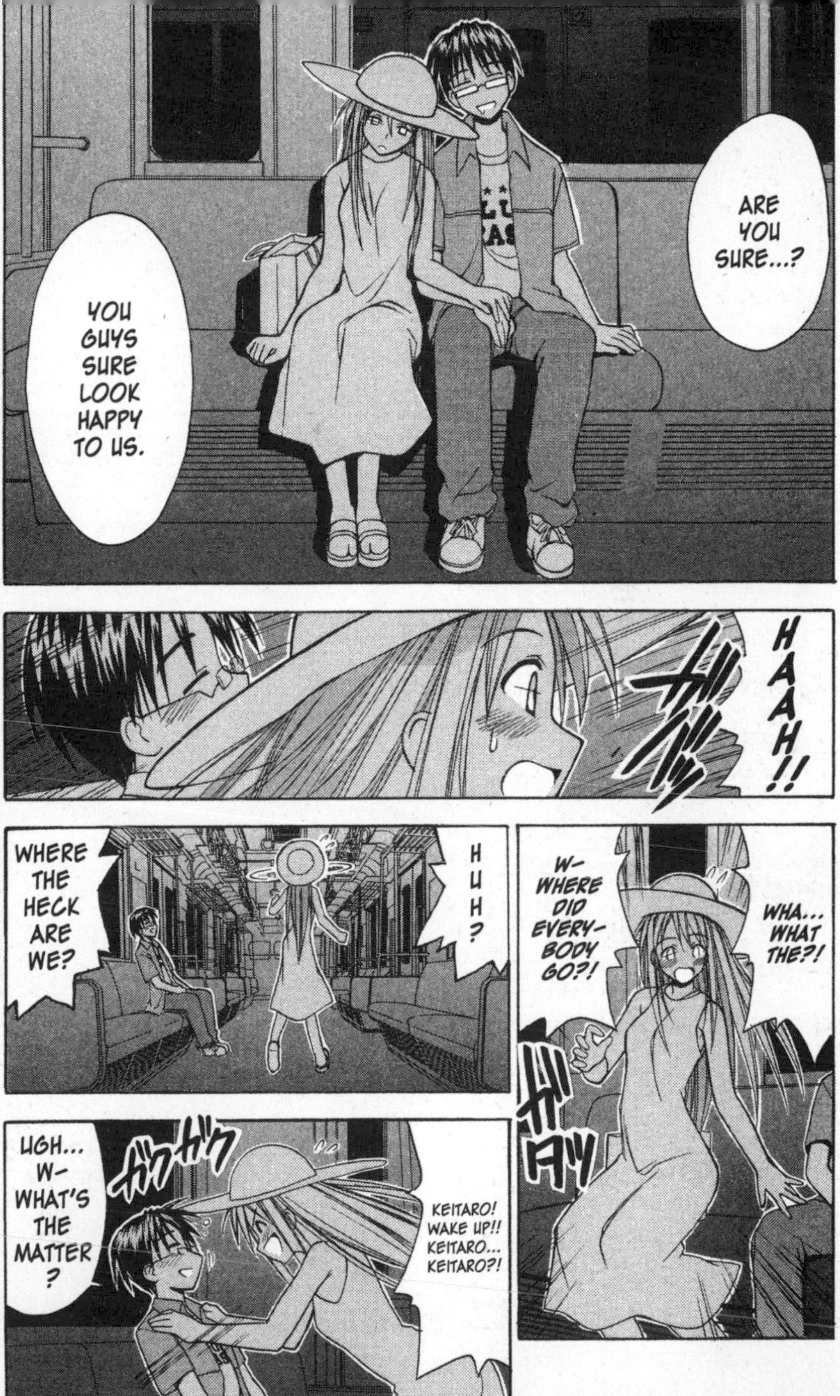

ARE YOU SURE...?
YOU GUYS SURE LOOK HAPPY TO US.
HAAAH!!
WHA... WHAT THE?!
W-WHERE DID EVERY-BODY GO?!
HUH?
WHERE THE HECK ARE WE?
KEITARO! WAKE UP!! KEITARO... KEITARO?!
ガクガク
UGH... W-WHAT'S THE MATTER?

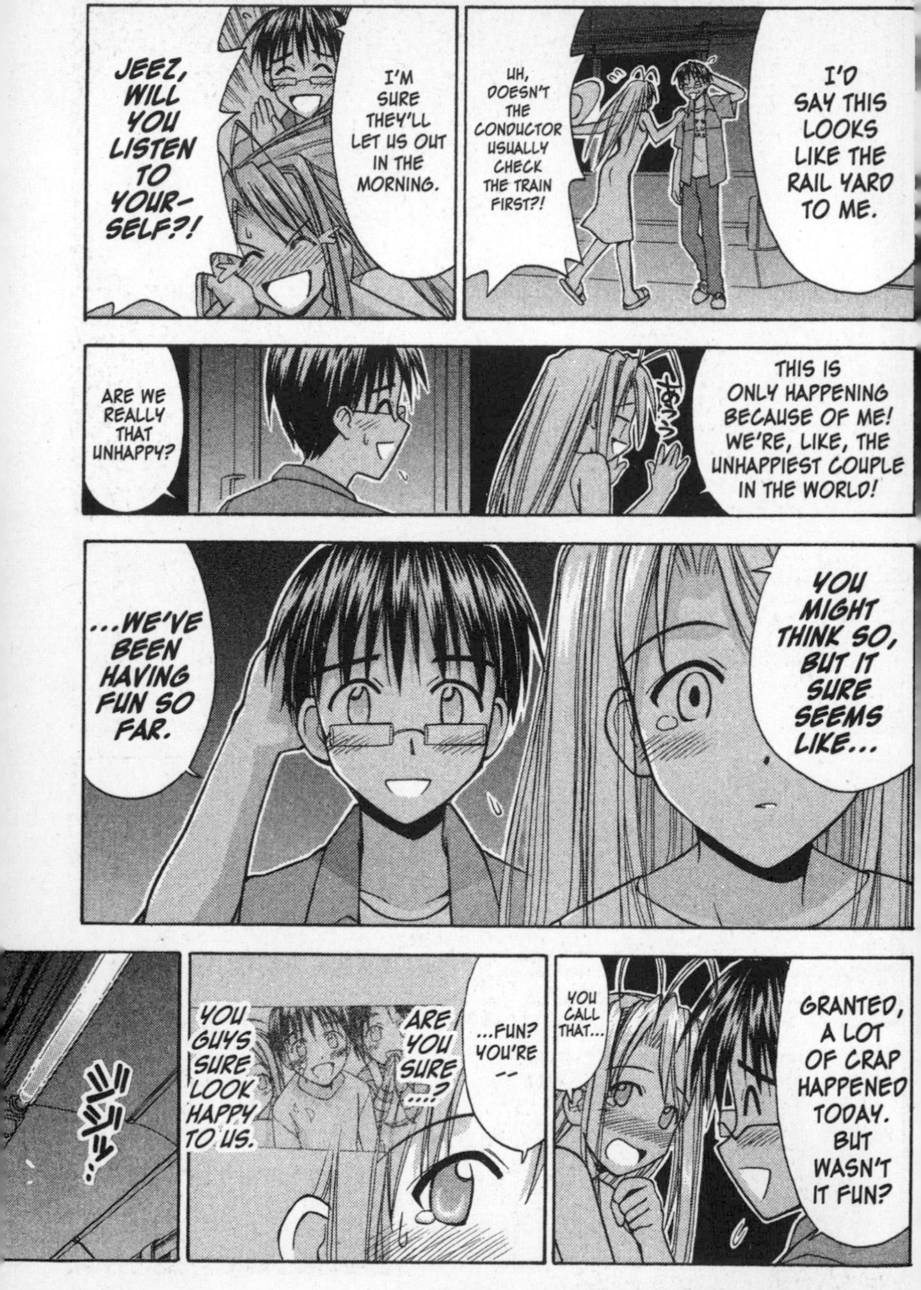
I'D SAY THIS LOOKS LIKE THE RAIL YARD TO ME.
UH, DOESN'T THE CONDUCTOR USUALLY CHECK THE TRAIN FIRST?!
I'M SURE THEY'LL LET US OUT IN THE MORNING.
JEEZ, WILL YOU LISTEN TO YOUR-SELF?!
THIS IS ONLY HAPPENING BECAUSE OF ME! WE'RE, LIKE, THE UNHAPPIEST COUPLE IN THE WORLD!
ARE WE REALLY THAT UNHAPPY?
YOU MIGHT THINK SO, BUT IT SURE SEEMS LIKE...
...WE'VE BEEN HAVING FUN SO FAR.
GRANTED, A LOT OF CRAP HAPPENED TODAY. BUT WASN'T IT FUN?
YOU CALL THAT...
...FUN? YOU'RE --
ARE YOU SURE...?
YOU GUYS SURE LOOK HAPPY TO US.

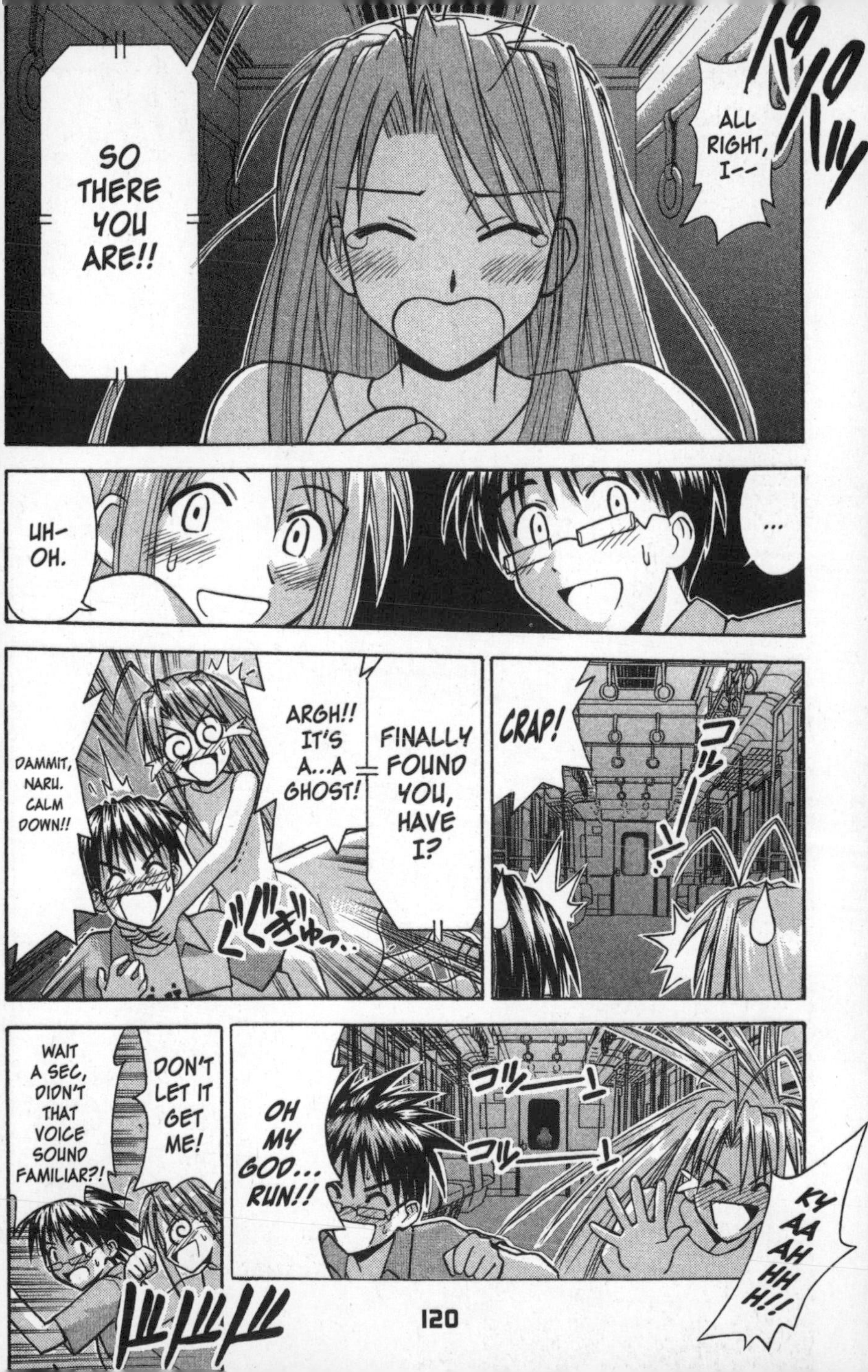
ALL RIGHT, I--
SO THERE YOU ARE!!
...
UH-OH.
CRAP!
FINALLY FOUND YOU, HAVE I?
ARGH!! IT'S A...A GHOST!
DAMMIT, NARU. CALM DOWN!!
KYAAAAHHHH!!
OH MY GOD... RUN!!
DON'T LET IT GET ME!
WAIT A SEC, DIDN'T THAT VOICE SOUND FAMILIAR?!

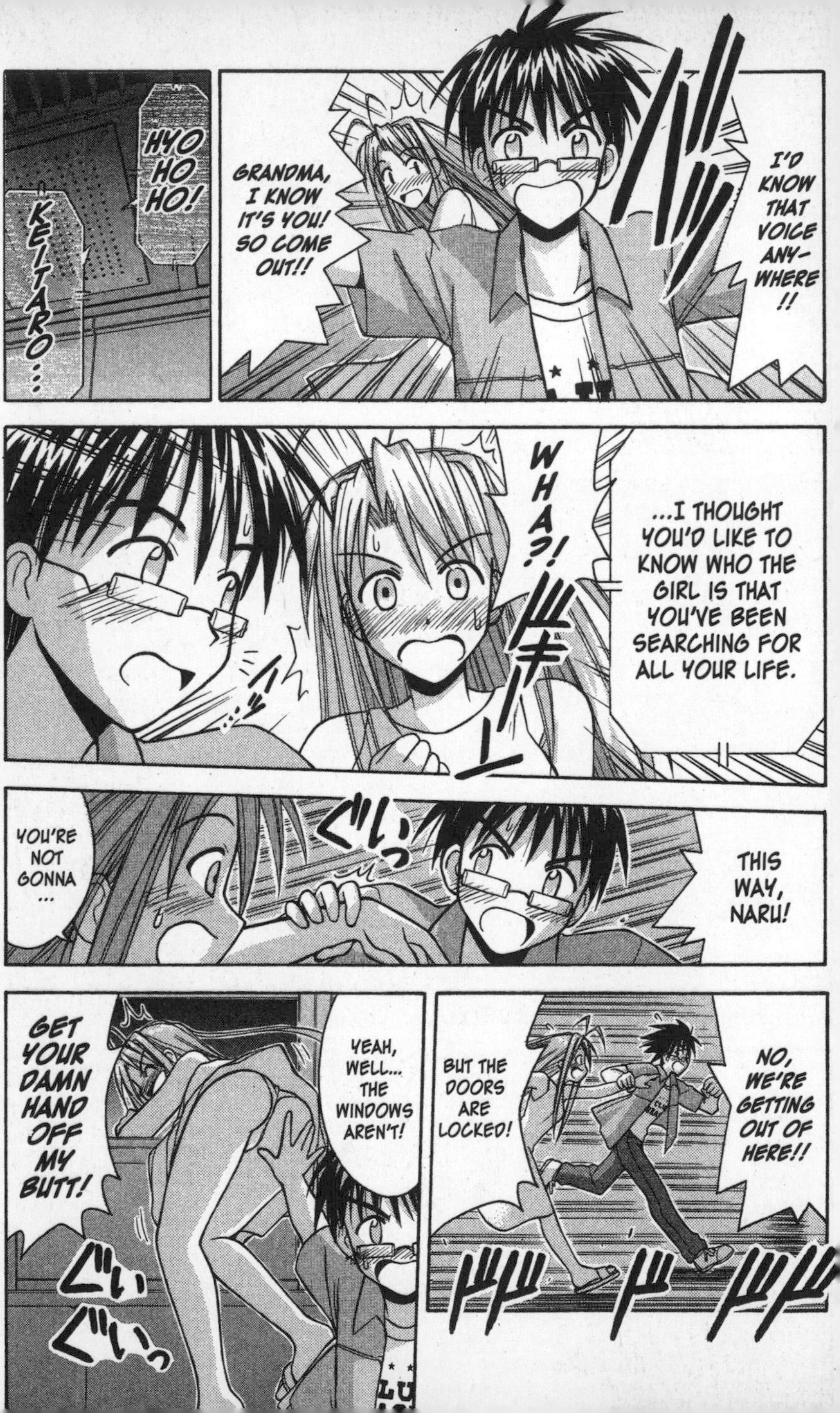
I'D KNOW THAT VOICE ANYWHERE!!
GRANDMA, I KNOW IT'S YOU! SO COME OUT!!
HYO HO HO!
KEITARO...
...I THOUGHT YOU'D LIKE TO KNOW WHO THE GIRL IS THAT YOU'VE BEEN SEARCHING FOR ALL YOUR LIFE.
WHA?!
THIS WAY, NARU!
YOU'RE NOT GONNA ...
NO, WE'RE GETTING OUT OF HERE!!
BUT THE DOORS ARE LOCKED!
YEAH, WELL... THE WINDOWS AREN'T!
GET YOUR DAMN HAND OFF MY BUTT!

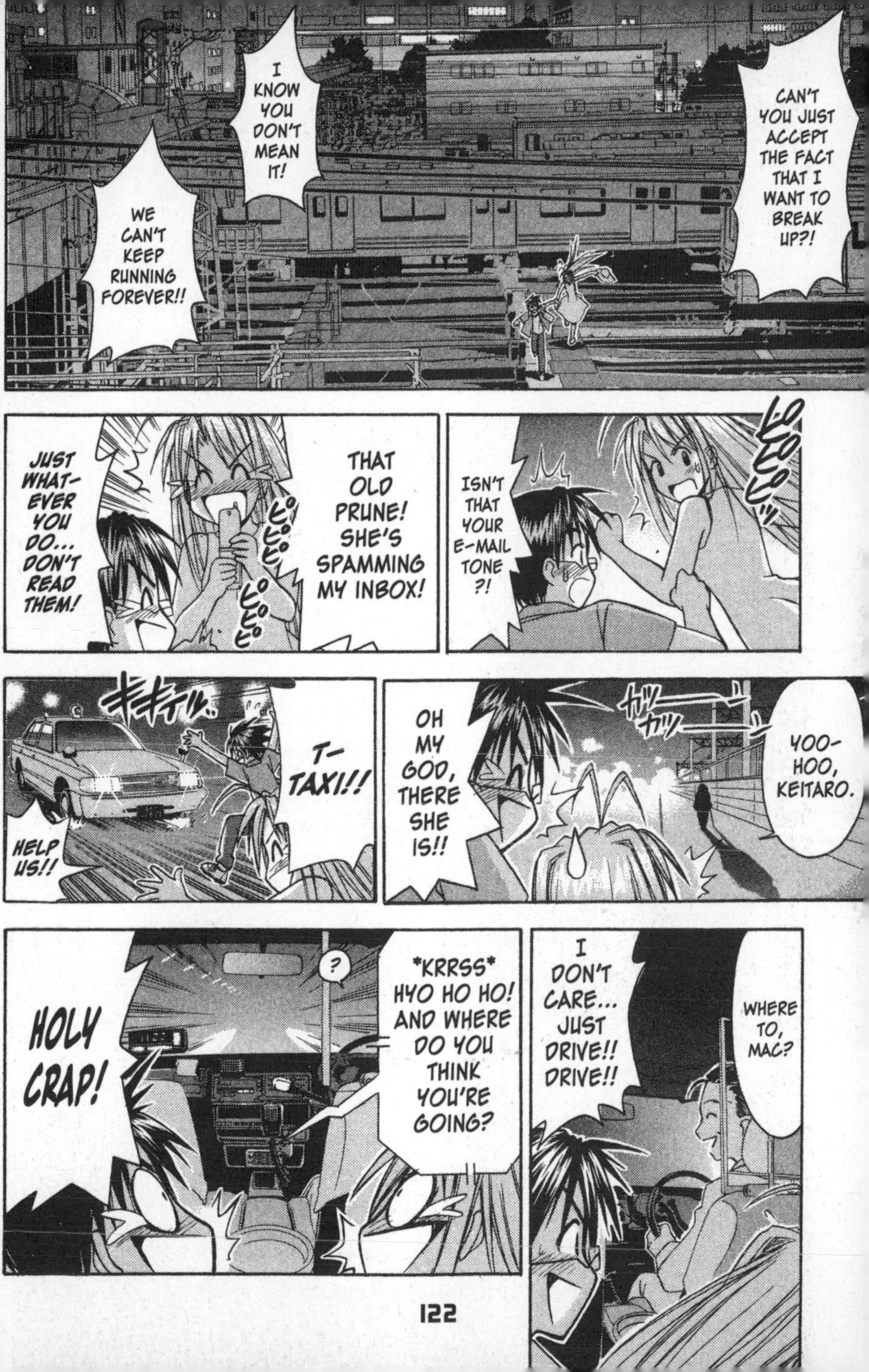
CAN'T YOU JUST ACCEPT THE FACT THAT I WANT TO BREAK UP?!
I KNOW YOU DON'T MEAN IT!
WE CAN'T KEEP RUNNING FOREVER!!
ISN'T THAT YOUR E-MAIL TONE?!
THAT OLD PRUNE! SHE'S SPAMMING MY INBOX!
JUST WHATEVER YOU DO... DON'T READ THEM!
YOO-HOO, KEITARO.
OH MY GOD, THERE SHE IS!!
T-TAXI!!
HELP US!!
WHERE TO, MAC?
I DON'T CARE... JUST DRIVE!! DRIVE!!
?
KRRSS HYO HO HO! AND WHERE DO YOU THINK YOU'RE GOING?
HOLY CRAP!

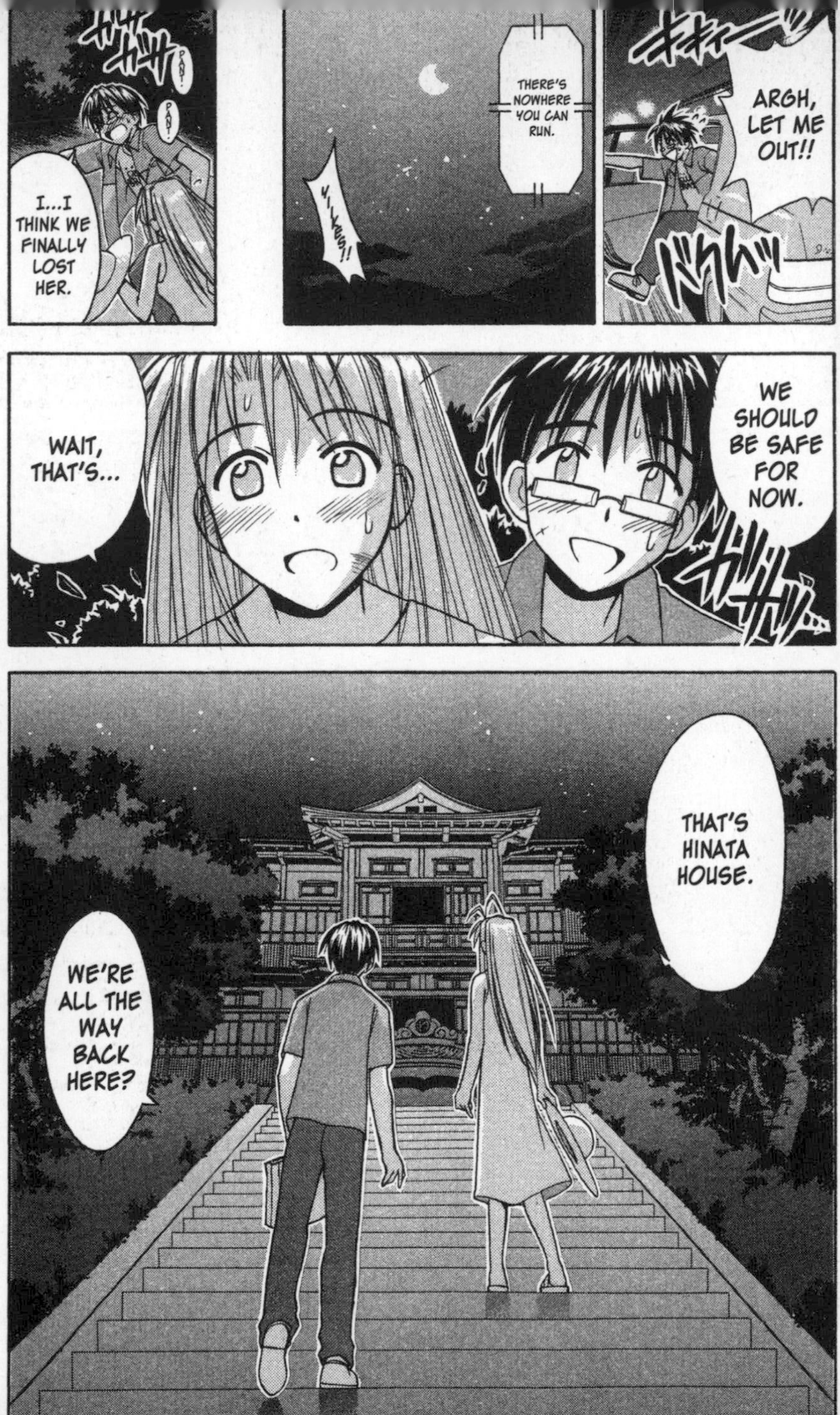
ARGH, LET ME OUT!!
THERE'S NOWHERE YOU CAN RUN.
YIKES!!
PANT!
PANT!
I...I THINK WE FINALLY LOST HER.
WE SHOULD BE SAFE FOR NOW.
WAIT, THAT'S...
THAT'S HINATA HOUSE.
WE'RE ALL THE WAY BACK HERE?

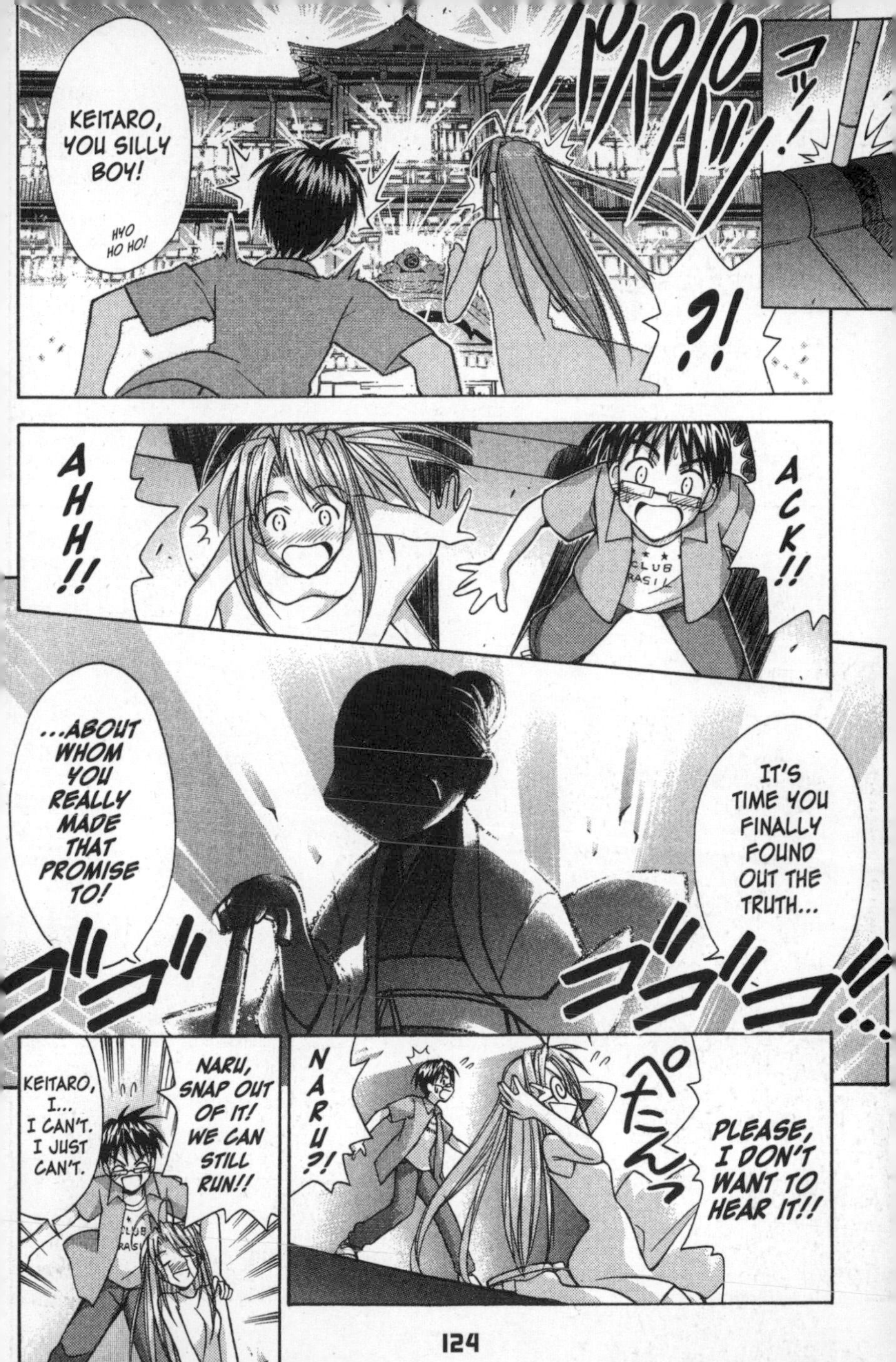
コッ!
?!
KEITARO, YOU SILLY BOY!
HYO HO HO!
ACK!!
AHH!!
IT'S TIME YOU FINALLY FOUND OUT THE TRUTH...
...ABOUT WHOM YOU REALLY MADE THAT PROMISE TO!
PLEASE, I DON'T WANT TO HEAR IT!!
ぺたんっ
NARU?!
NARU, SNAP OUT OF IT! WE CAN STILL RUN!!
KEITARO, I... I CAN'T. I JUST CAN'T.

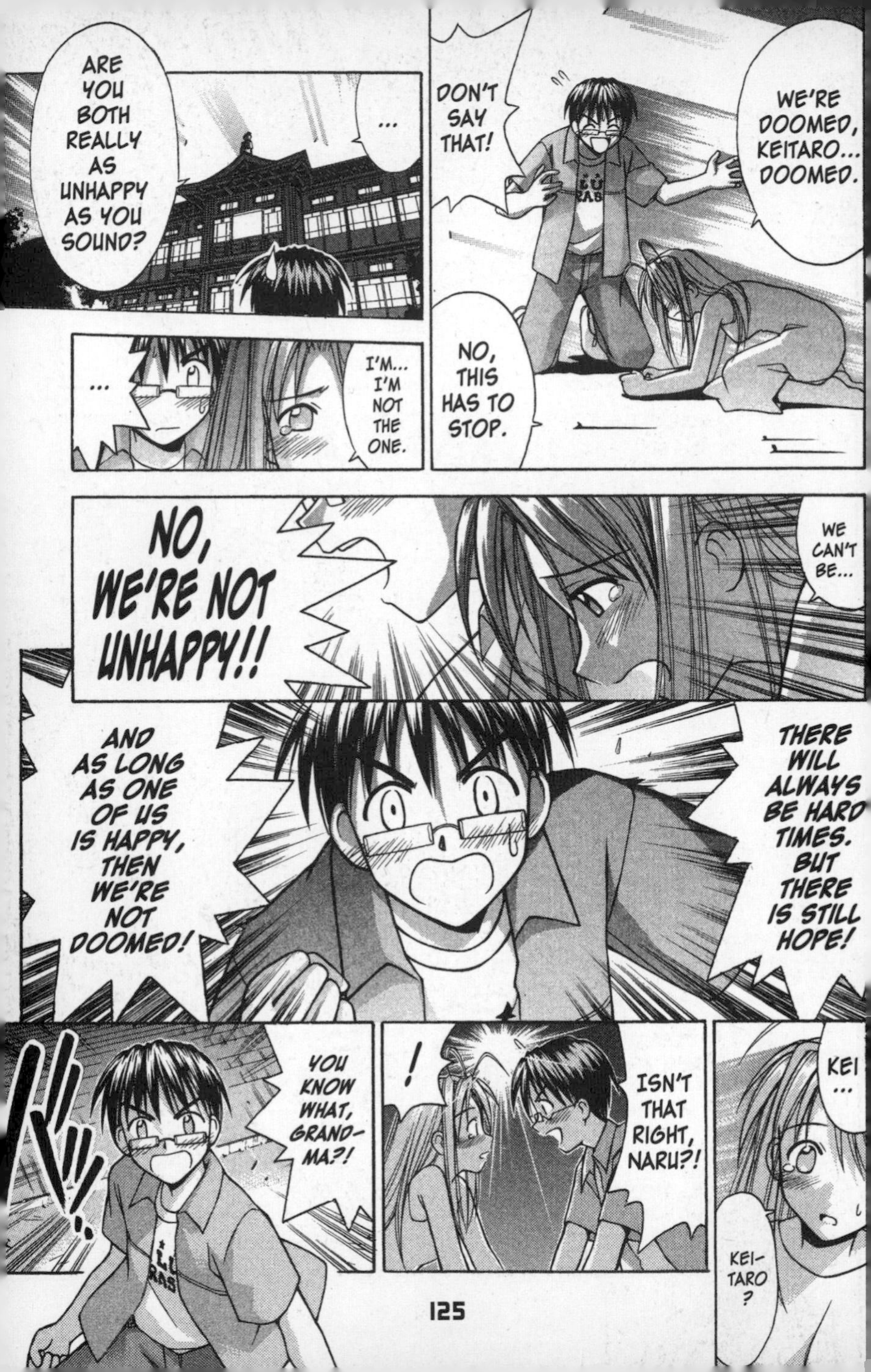
WE'RE DOOMED, KEITARO... DOOMED.
DON'T SAY THAT!
NO, THIS HAS TO STOP.
ARE YOU BOTH REALLY AS UNHAPPY AS YOU SOUND?
...
I'M... I'M NOT THE ONE.
...
WE CAN'T BE...
NO, WE'RE NOT UNHAPPY!!
THERE WILL ALWAYS BE HARD TIMES. BUT THERE IS STILL HOPE!
AND AS LONG AS ONE OF US IS HAPPY, THEN WE'RE NOT DOOMED!
KEI...
KEI-TARO?
ISN'T THAT RIGHT, NARU?!
!
YOU KNOW WHAT, GRAND-MA?!

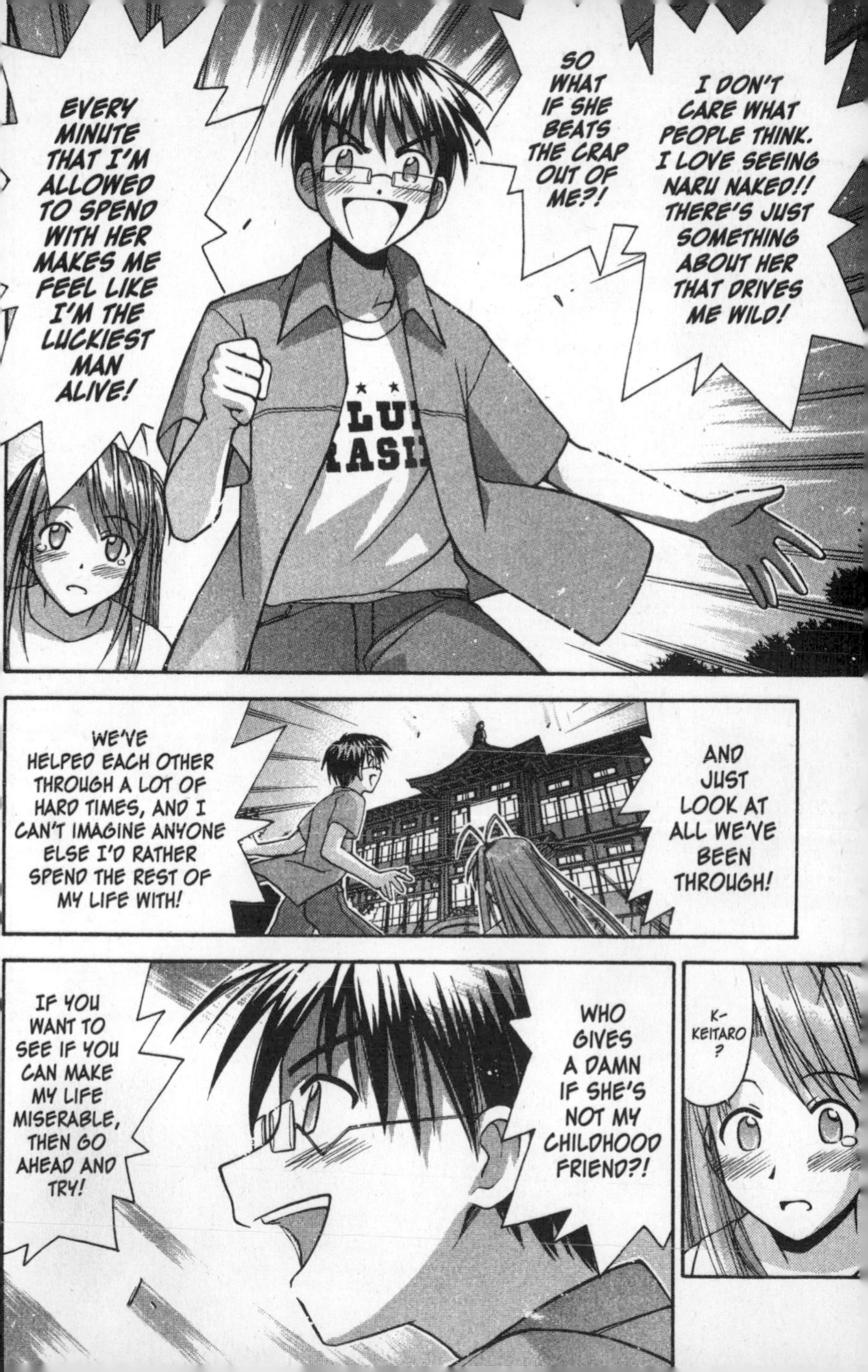
I DON'T CARE WHAT PEOPLE THINK. I LOVE SEEING NARU NAKED!! THERE'S JUST SOMETHING ABOUT HER THAT DRIVES ME WILD!
SO WHAT IF SHE BEATS THE CRAP OUT OF ME?!
EVERY MINUTE THAT I'M ALLOWED TO SPEND WITH HER MAKES ME FEEL LIKE I'M THE LUCKIEST MAN ALIVE!
AND JUST LOOK AT ALL WE'VE BEEN THROUGH!
WE'VE HELPED EACH OTHER THROUGH A LOT OF HARD TIMES, AND I CAN'T IMAGINE ANYONE ELSE I'D RATHER SPEND THE REST OF MY LIFE WITH!
K-KEITARO?
WHO GIVES A DAMN IF SHE'S NOT MY CHILDHOOD FRIEND?!
IF YOU WANT TO SEE IF YOU CAN MAKE MY LIFE MISERABLE, THEN GO AHEAD AND TRY!

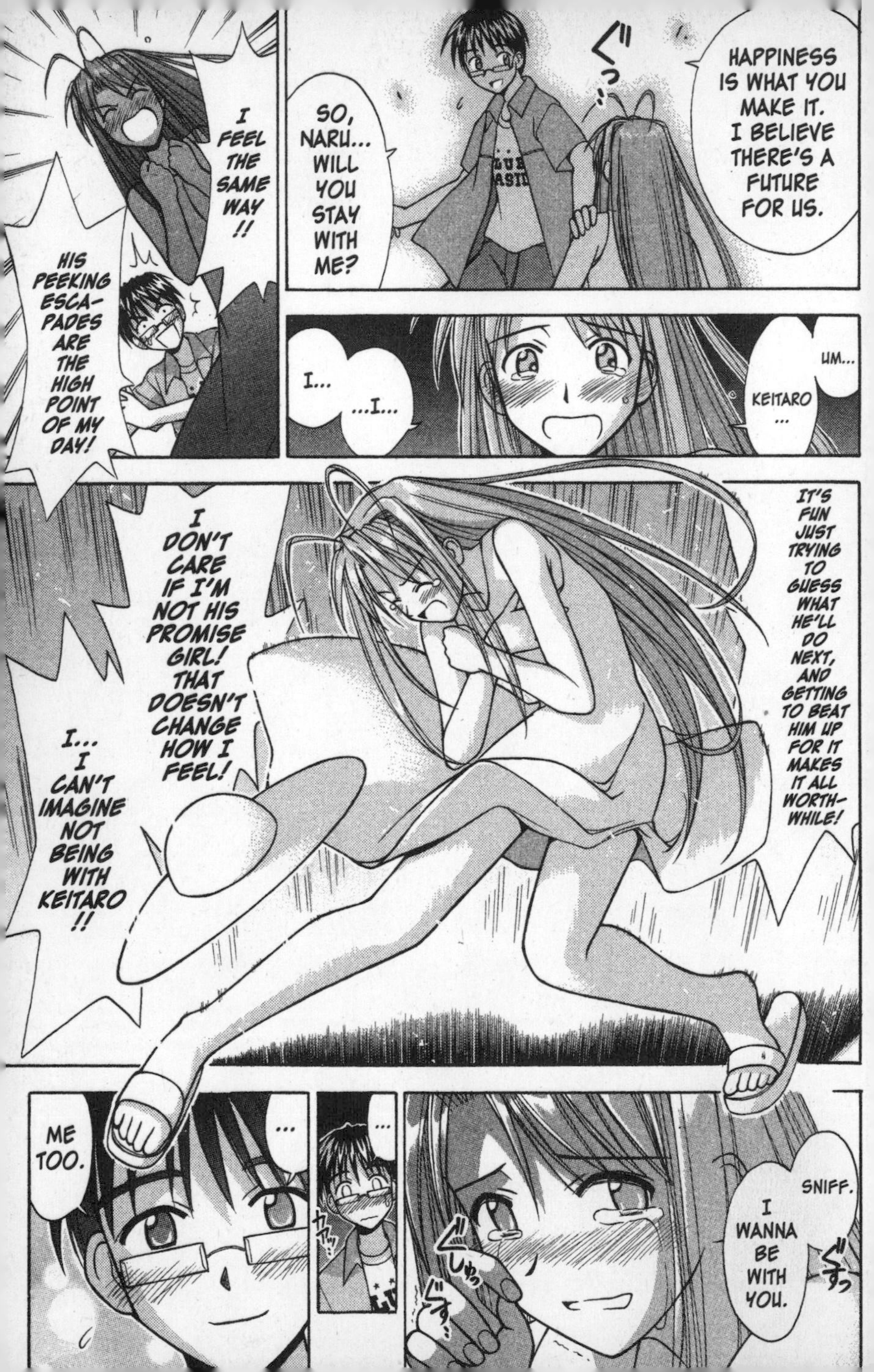
HAPPINESS IS WHAT YOU MAKE IT. I BELIEVE THERE'S A FUTURE FOR US.
ぐっ
SO, NARU... WILL YOU STAY WITH ME?
UM... KEITARO...
I... ...I...
I FEEL THE SAME WAY!!
HIS PEEKING ESCAPADES ARE THE HIGH POINT OF MY DAY!
IT'S FUN JUST TRYING TO GUESS WHAT HE'LL DO NEXT, AND GETTING TO BEAT HIM UP FOR IT MAKES IT ALL WORTHWHILE!
I DON'T CARE IF I'M NOT HIS PROMISE GIRL! THAT DOESN'T CHANGE HOW I FEEL!
I... I CAN'T IMAGINE NOT BEING WITH KEITARO!!
SNIFF. I WANNA BE WITH YOU.
...
...
ME TOO.

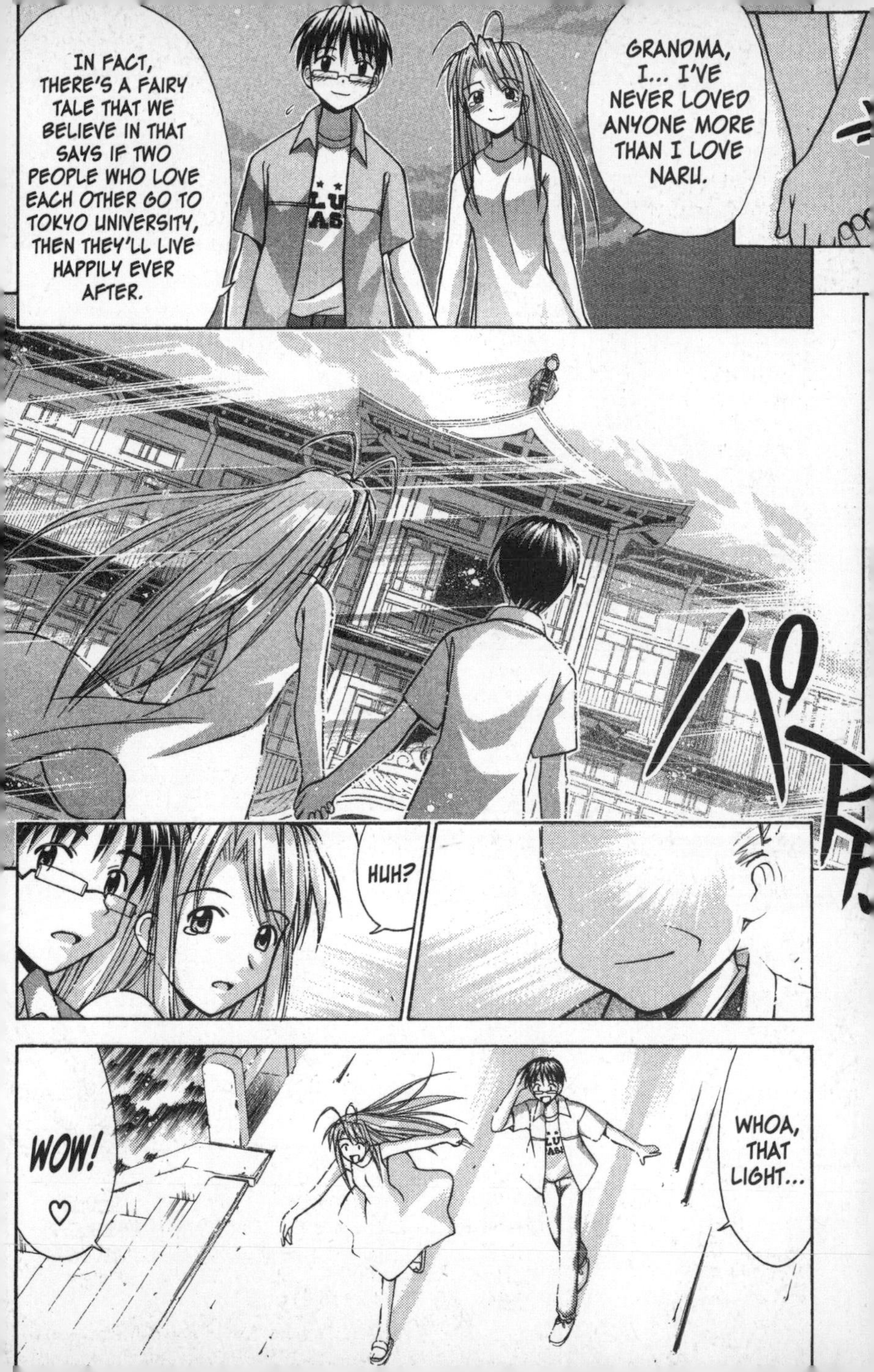

GRANDMA, I... I'VE NEVER LOVED ANYONE MORE THAN I LOVE NARU.
IN FACT, THERE'S A FAIRY TALE THAT WE BELIEVE IN THAT SAYS IF TWO PEOPLE WHO LOVE EACH OTHER GO TO TOKYO UNIVERSITY, THEN THEY'LL LIVE HAPPILY EVER AFTER.
HUH?
WHOA, THAT LIGHT...
WOW! ♡

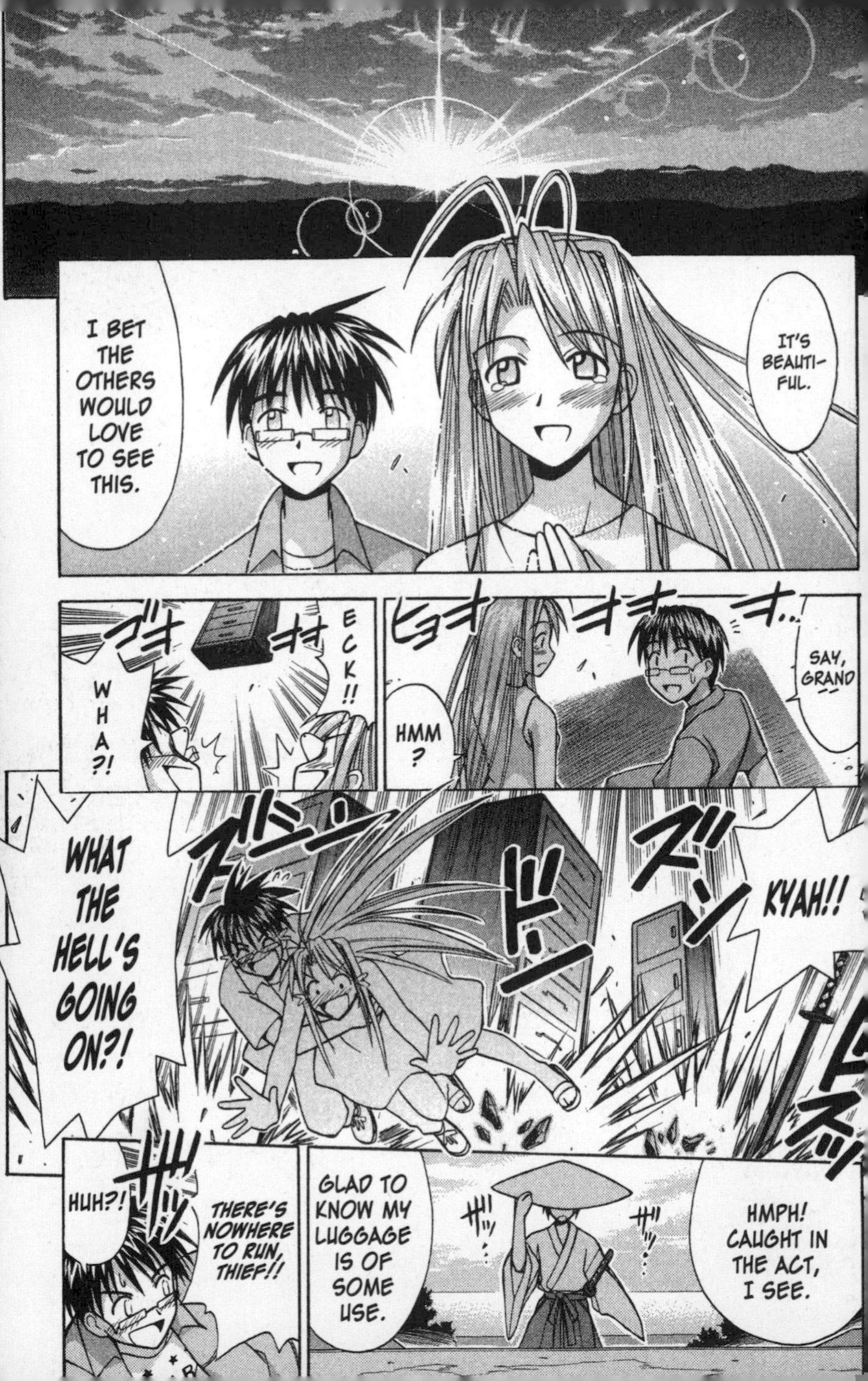
IT'S BEAUTIFUL.
I BET THE OTHERS WOULD LOVE TO SEE THIS.
SAY, GRAND—
HMM?
ECK!!
WHA?!
KYAH!!
WHAT THE HELL'S GOING ON?!
HMPH! CAUGHT IN THE ACT, I SEE.
GLAD TO KNOW MY LUGGAGE IS OF SOME USE.
THERE'S NOWHERE TO RUN, THIEF!!
HUH?!

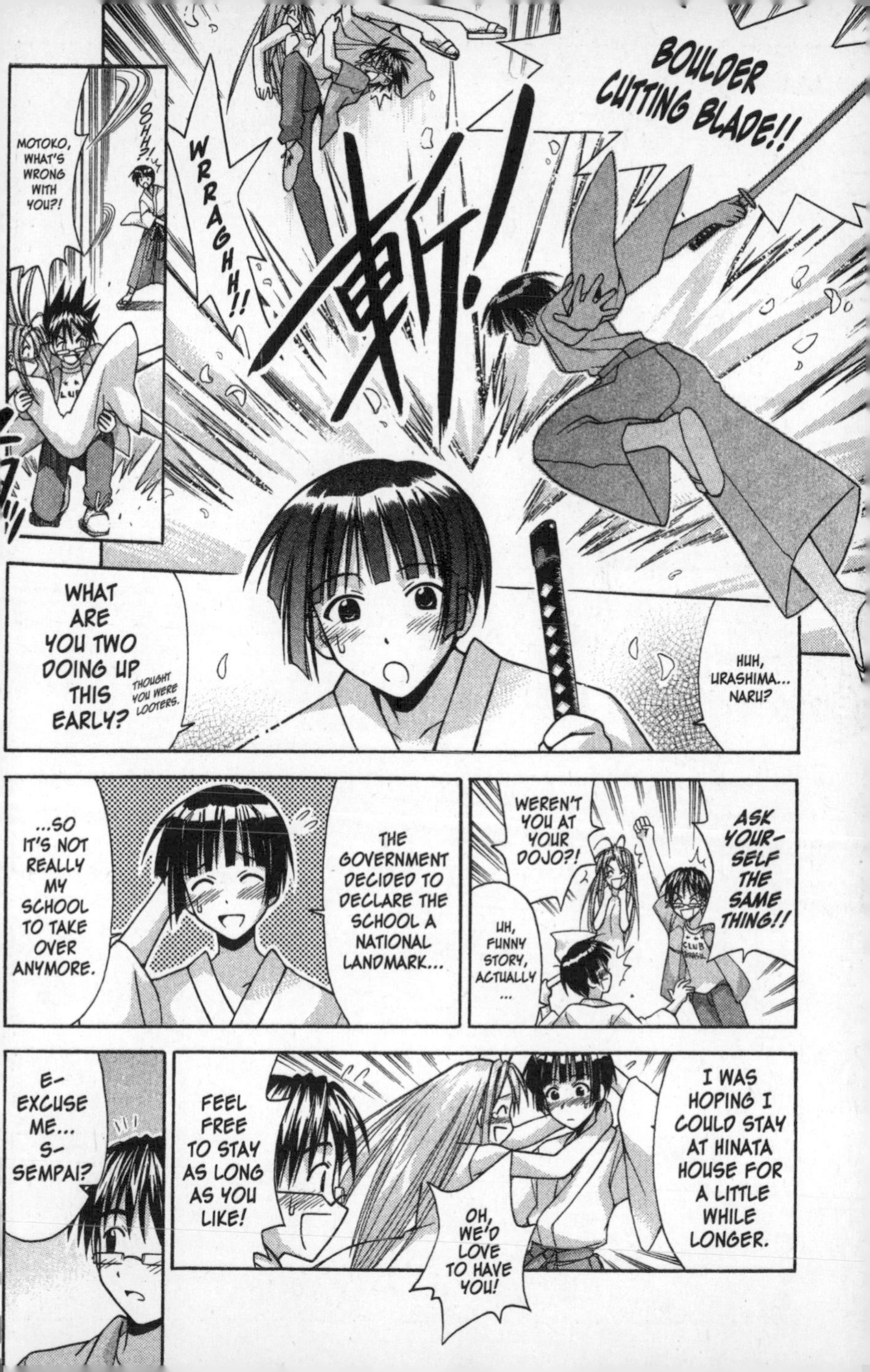
BOULDER CUTTING BLADE!!
斬!
WRRAGHH!!
OOHH?!
MOTOKO, WHAT'S WRONG WITH YOU?!
HUH, URASHIMA... NARU?
WHAT ARE YOU TWO DOING UP THIS EARLY?
THOUGHT YOU WERE LOOTERS.
ASK YOURSELF THE SAME THING!!
WEREN'T YOU AT YOUR DOJO?!
UH, FUNNY STORY, ACTUALLY...
THE GOVERNMENT DECIDED TO DECLARE THE SCHOOL A NATIONAL LANDMARK...
...SO IT'S NOT REALLY MY SCHOOL TO TAKE OVER ANYMORE.
I WAS HOPING I COULD STAY AT HINATA HOUSE FOR A LITTLE WHILE LONGER.
OH, WE'D LOVE TO HAVE YOU!
FEEL FREE TO STAY AS LONG AS YOU LIKE!
E-EXCUSE ME... S-SEMPAI?

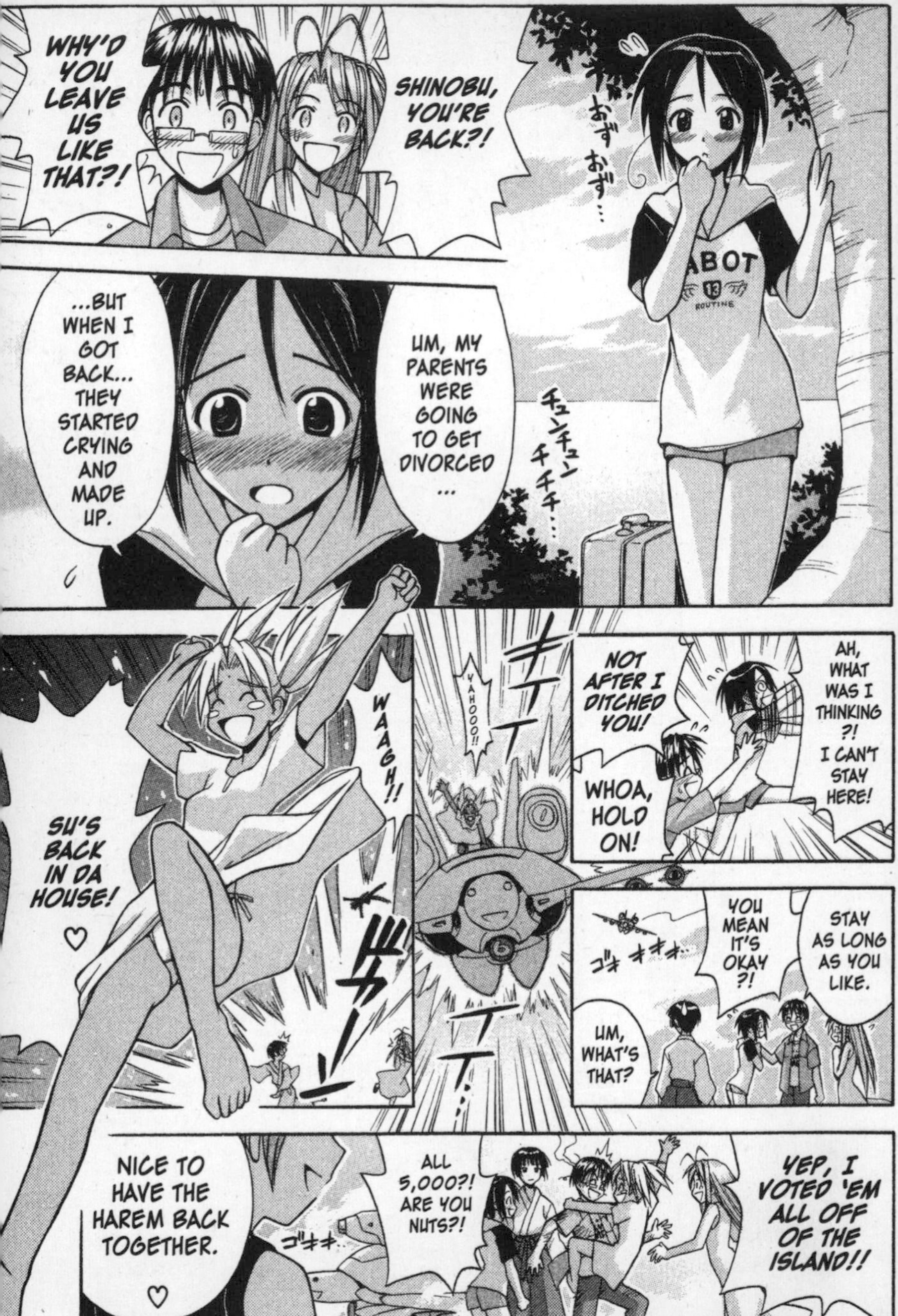

おず おず…
チュンチュン チチチ…
SHINOBU, YOU'RE BACK?!
WHY'D YOU LEAVE US LIKE THAT?!
UM, MY PARENTS WERE GOING TO GET DIVORCED ...
...BUT WHEN I GOT BACK... THEY STARTED CRYING AND MADE UP.
AH, WHAT WAS I THINKING?! I CAN'T STAY HERE!
NOT AFTER I DITCHED YOU!
WHOA, HOLD ON!
STAY AS LONG AS YOU LIKE.
YOU MEAN IT'S OKAY?!
ゴォ オオオ…
UM, WHAT'S THAT?
YAHOOOO!!
WAAAGH!!
SU'S BACK IN DA HOUSE! ♡
YEP, I VOTED 'EM ALL OFF OF THE ISLAND!!
ALL 5,000?! ARE YOU NUTS?!
NICE TO HAVE THE HAREM BACK TOGETHER. ♡

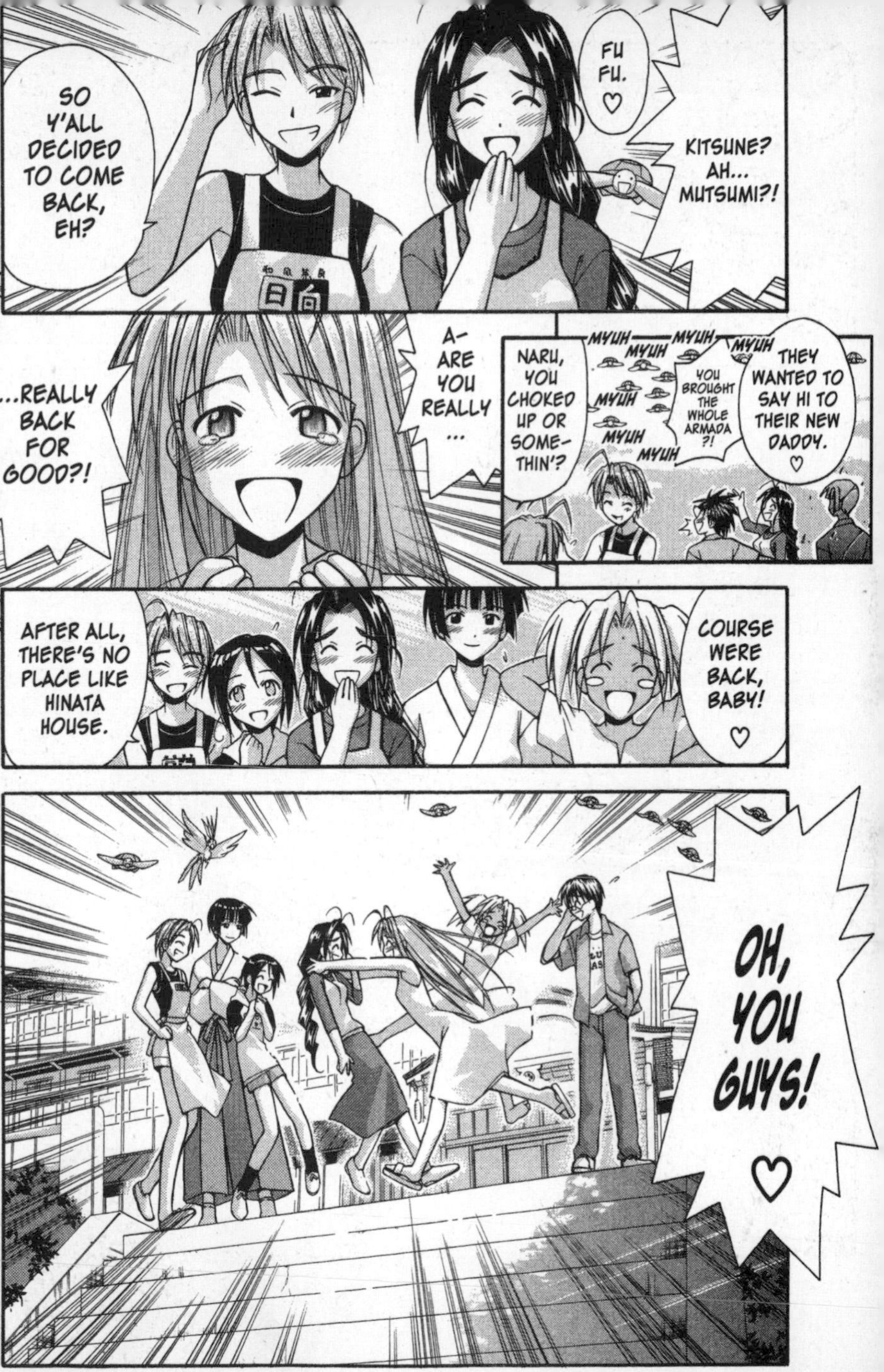
KITSUNE? AH... MUTSUMI?!
FU FU. ♡
SO Y'ALL DECIDED TO COME BACK, EH?
MYUH MYUH MYUH MYUH MYUH MYUH MYUH
THEY WANTED TO SAY HI TO THEIR NEW DADDY. ♡
YOU BROUGHT THE WHOLE ARMADA ?!
NARU, YOU CHOKED UP OR SOME-THIN'?
A- ARE YOU REALLY ...
...REALLY BACK FOR GOOD?!
COURSE WERE BACK, BABY! ♡
AFTER ALL, THERE'S NO PLACE LIKE HINATA HOUSE.
OH, YOU GUYS! ♡

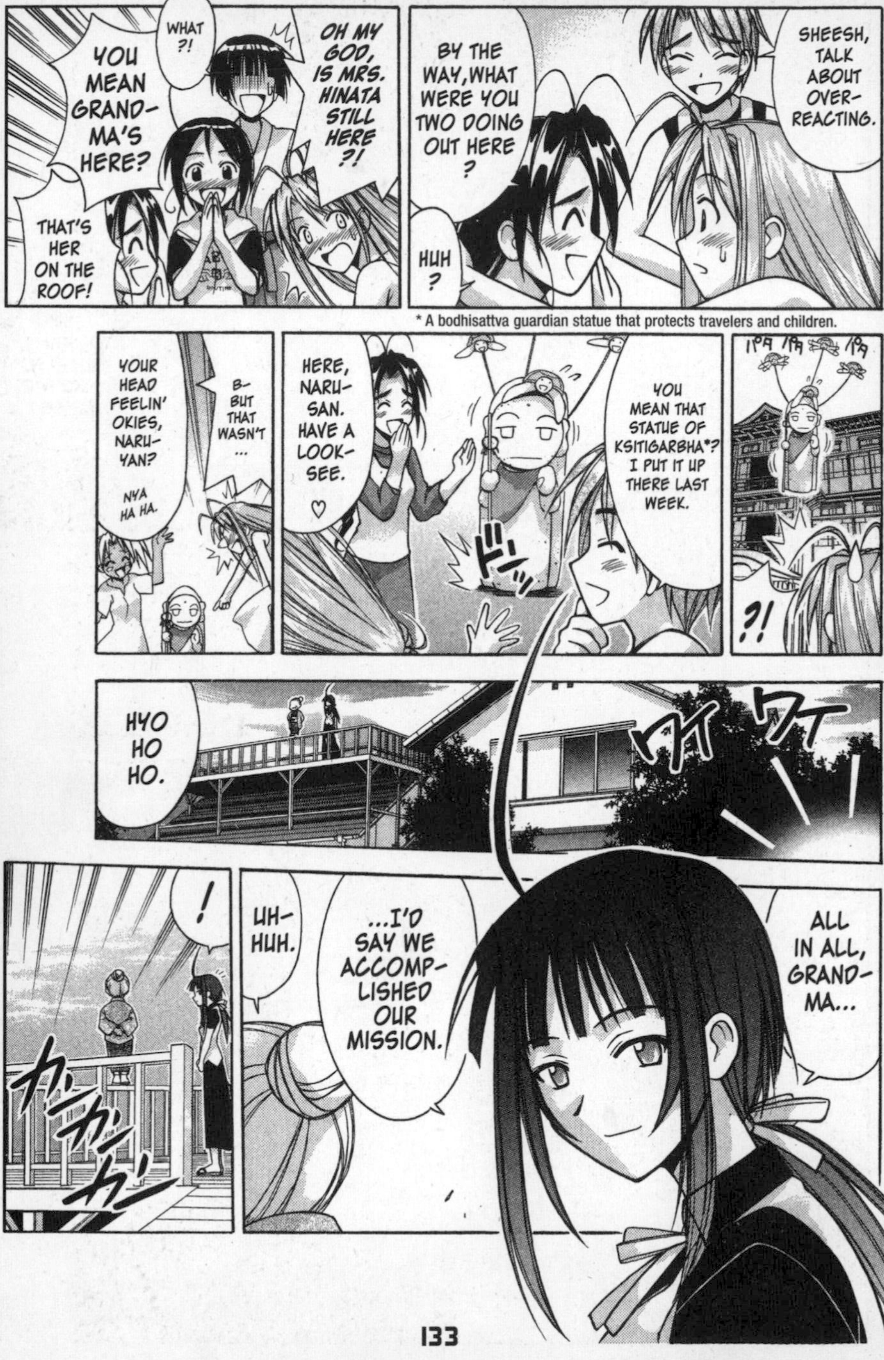
SHEESH, TALK ABOUT OVER-REACTING.
BY THE WAY, WHAT WERE YOU TWO DOING OUT HERE?
HUH?
OH MY GOD, IS MRS. HINATA STILL HERE?!
WHAT?!
YOU MEAN GRANDMA'S HERE?
THAT'S HER ON THE ROOF!
?!
YOU MEAN THAT STATUE OF KSITIGARBHA*? I PUT IT UP THERE LAST WEEK.
HERE, NARU-SAN. HAVE A LOOK-SEE. ♡
B-BUT THAT WASN'T ...
YOUR HEAD FEELIN' OKIES, NARU-YAN?
NYA HA HA.
HYO HO HO.
ALL IN ALL, GRANDMA...
...I'D SAY WE ACCOMPLISHED OUR MISSION.
UH-HUH.
!

* A bodhisattva guardian statue that protects travelers and children.

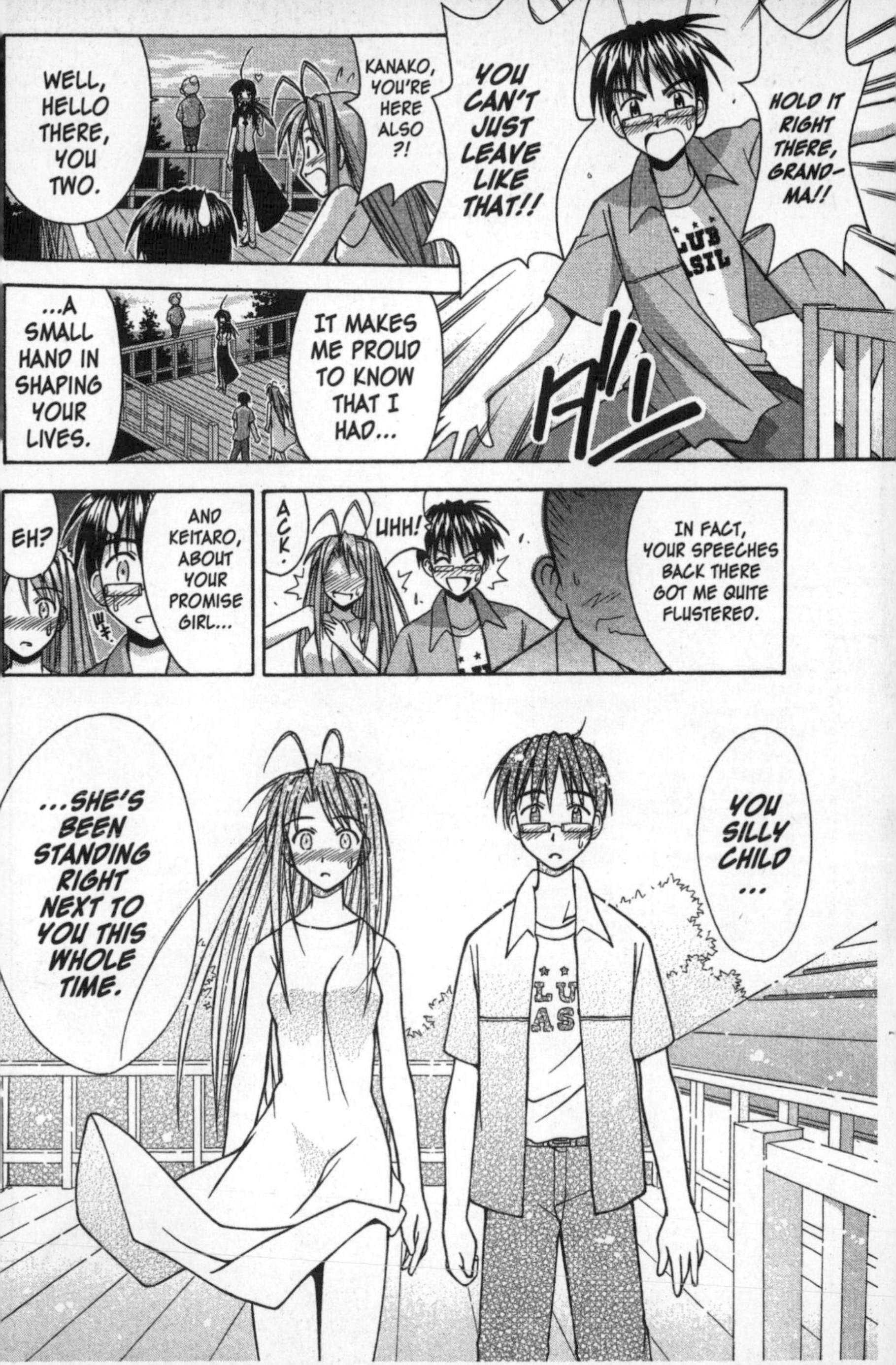
HOLD IT RIGHT THERE, GRAND-MA!!
YOU CAN'T JUST LEAVE LIKE THAT!!
KANAKO, YOU'RE HERE ALSO ?!
WELL, HELLO THERE, YOU TWO.
IT MAKES ME PROUD TO KNOW THAT I HAD...
...A SMALL HAND IN SHAPING YOUR LIVES.
IN FACT, YOUR SPEECHES BACK THERE GOT ME QUITE FLUSTERED.
UHH!
ACK.
AND KEITARO, ABOUT YOUR PROMISE GIRL...
EH?
YOU SILLY CHILD...
...SHE'S BEEN STANDING RIGHT NEXT TO YOU THIS WHOLE TIME.

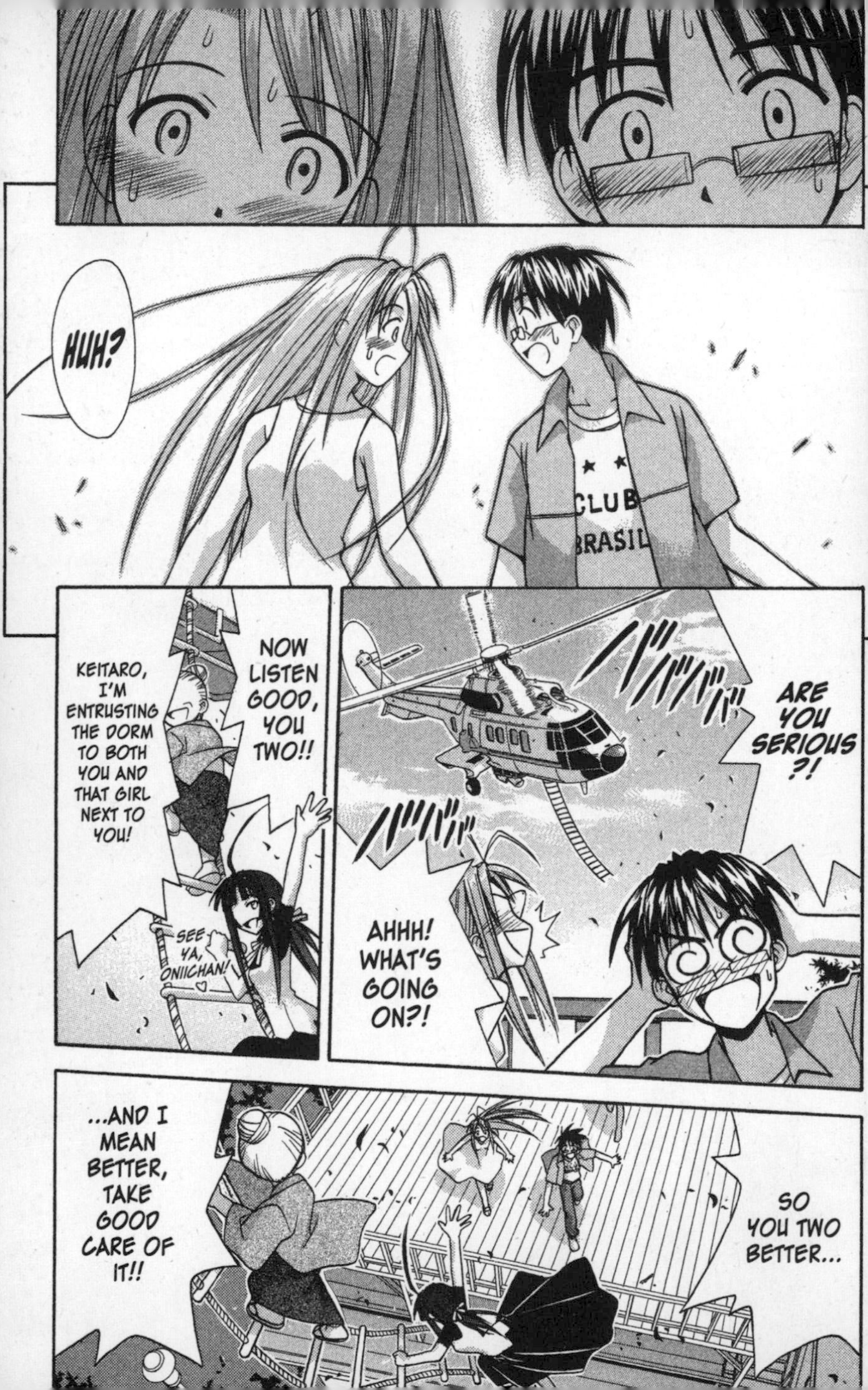
HUH?
ARE YOU SERIOUS?!
AHHH! WHAT'S GOING ON?!
NOW LISTEN GOOD, YOU TWO!!
KEITARO, I'M ENTRUSTING THE DORM TO BOTH YOU AND THAT GIRL NEXT TO YOU!
SEE YA, ONIICHAN! ♡
SO YOU TWO BETTER...
...AND I MEAN BETTER, TAKE GOOD CARE OF IT!!

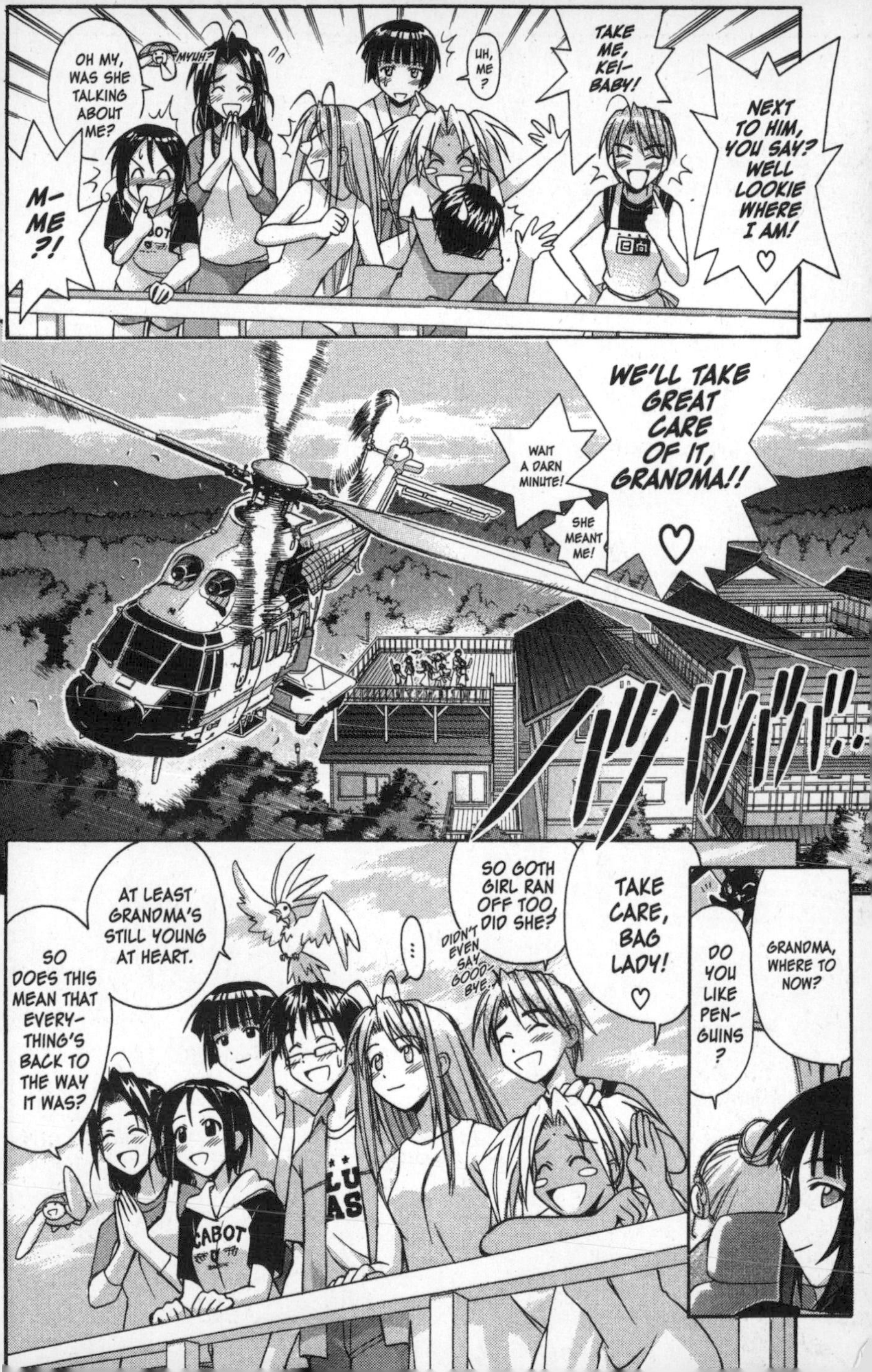
NEXT TO HIM, YOU SAY? WELL LOOKIE WHERE I AM! ♡
TAKE ME, KEI-BABY!
UH, ME?
MYUH?
OH MY, WAS SHE TALKING ABOUT ME?
M-ME?!
WE'LL TAKE GREAT CARE OF IT, GRANDMA!! ♡
WAIT A DARN MINUTE!
SHE MEANT ME!
GRANDMA, WHERE TO NOW?
DO YOU LIKE PEN-GUINS?
TAKE CARE, BAG LADY! ♡
SO GOTH GIRL RAN OFF TOO, DID SHE?
DIDN'T EVEN SAY GOOD-BYE...
...
AT LEAST GRANDMA'S STILL YOUNG AT HEART.
SO DOES THIS MEAN THAT EVERY-THING'S BACK TO THE WAY IT WAS?

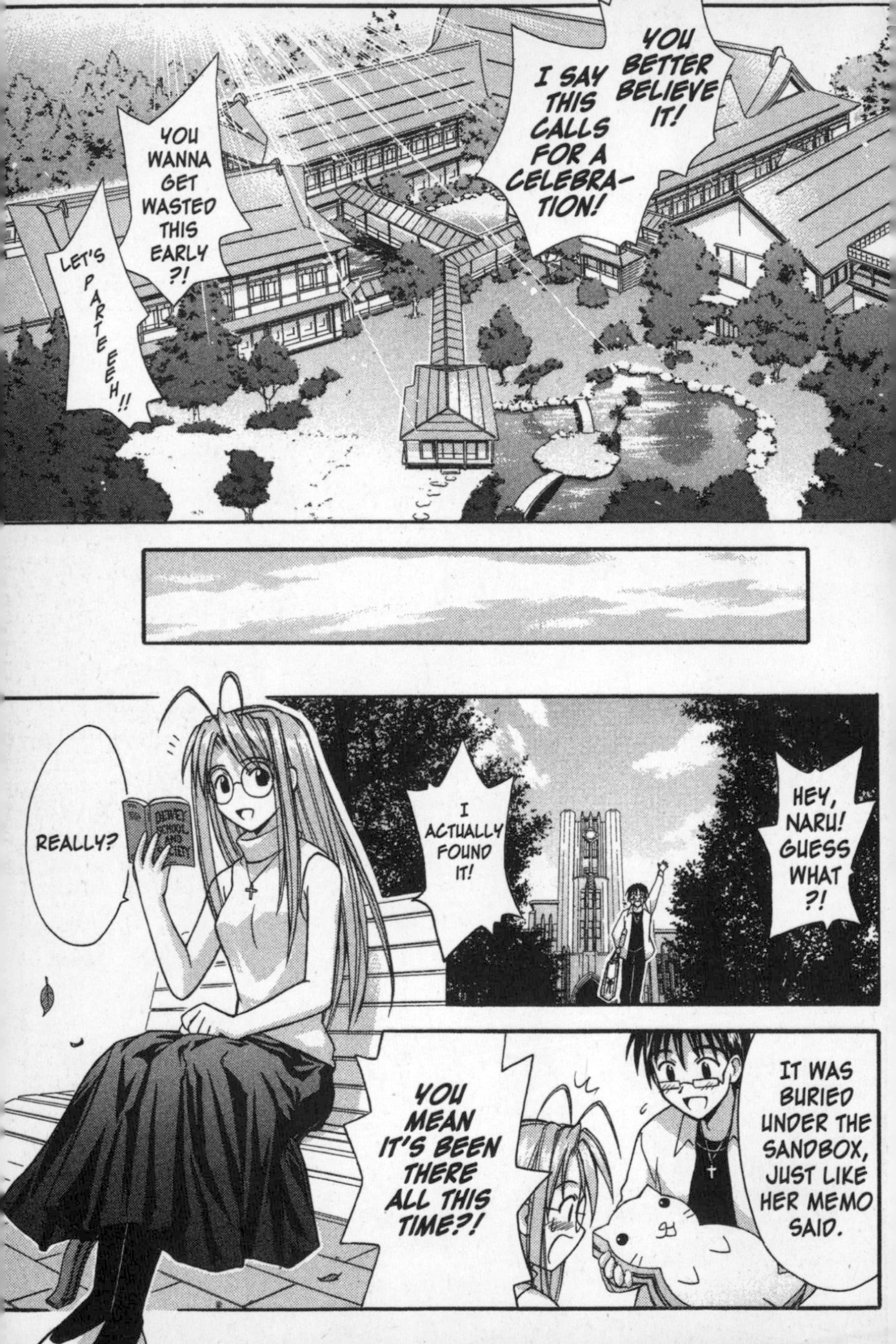
YOU BETTER BELIEVE IT!
I SAY THIS CALLS FOR A CELEBRATION!
YOU WANNA GET WASTED THIS EARLY?!
LET'S PARTEEEH!!
HEY, NARU! GUESS WHAT?!
I ACTUALLY FOUND IT!
IT WAS BURIED UNDER THE SANDBOX, JUST LIKE HER MEMO SAID.
YOU MEAN IT'S BEEN THERE ALL THIS TIME?!
REALLY?

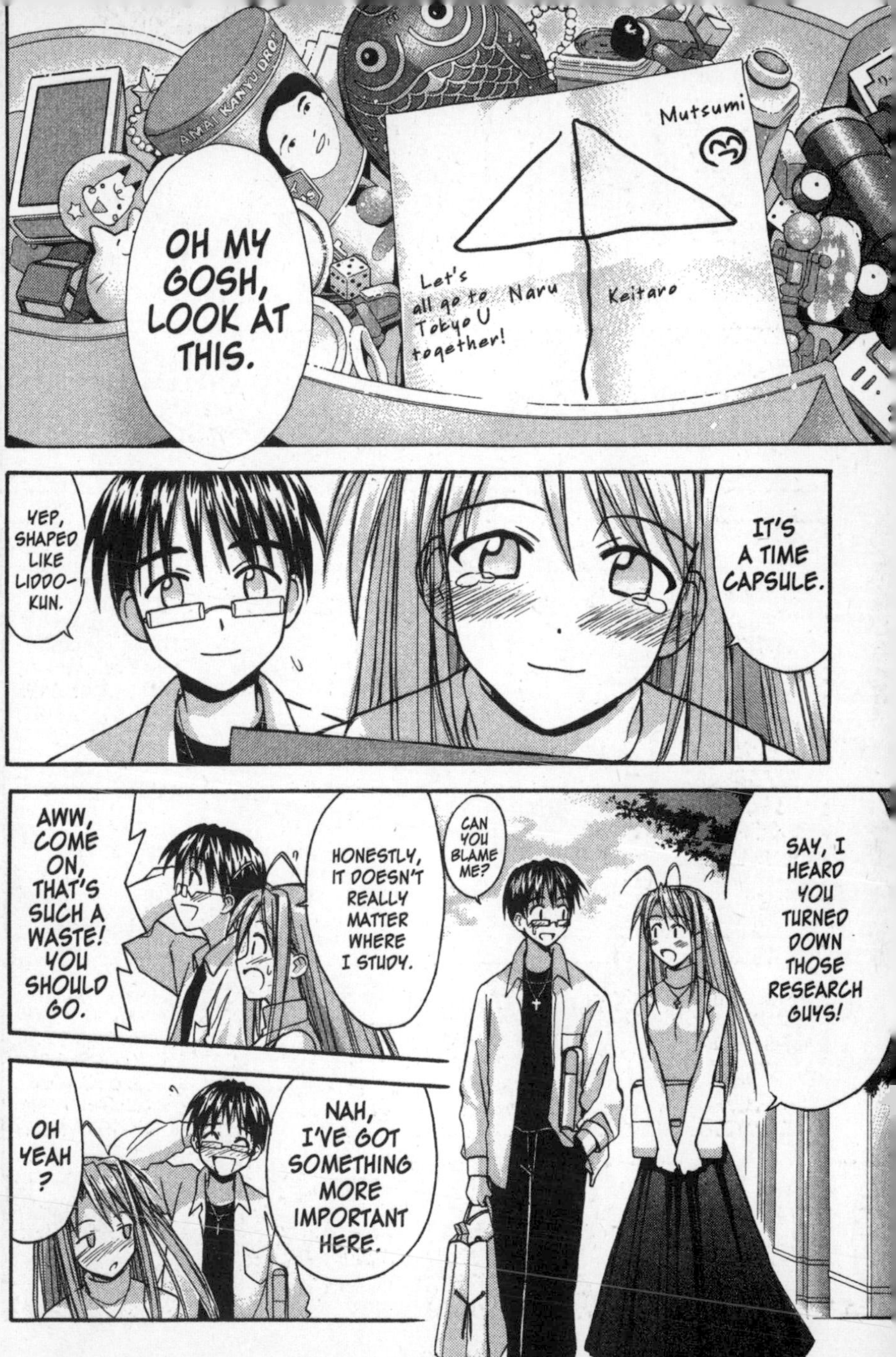
Mutsumi
Let's all go to Tokyo U together!
Naru
Keitaro
OH MY GOSH, LOOK AT THIS.
IT'S A TIME CAPSULE.
YEP, SHAPED LIKE LIDDO-KUN.
SAY, I HEARD YOU TURNED DOWN THOSE RESEARCH GUYS!
CAN YOU BLAME ME?
HONESTLY, IT DOESN'T REALLY MATTER WHERE I STUDY.
AWW, COME ON, THAT'S SUCH A WASTE! YOU SHOULD GO.
NAH, I'VE GOT SOMETHING MORE IMPORTANT HERE.
OH YEAH?

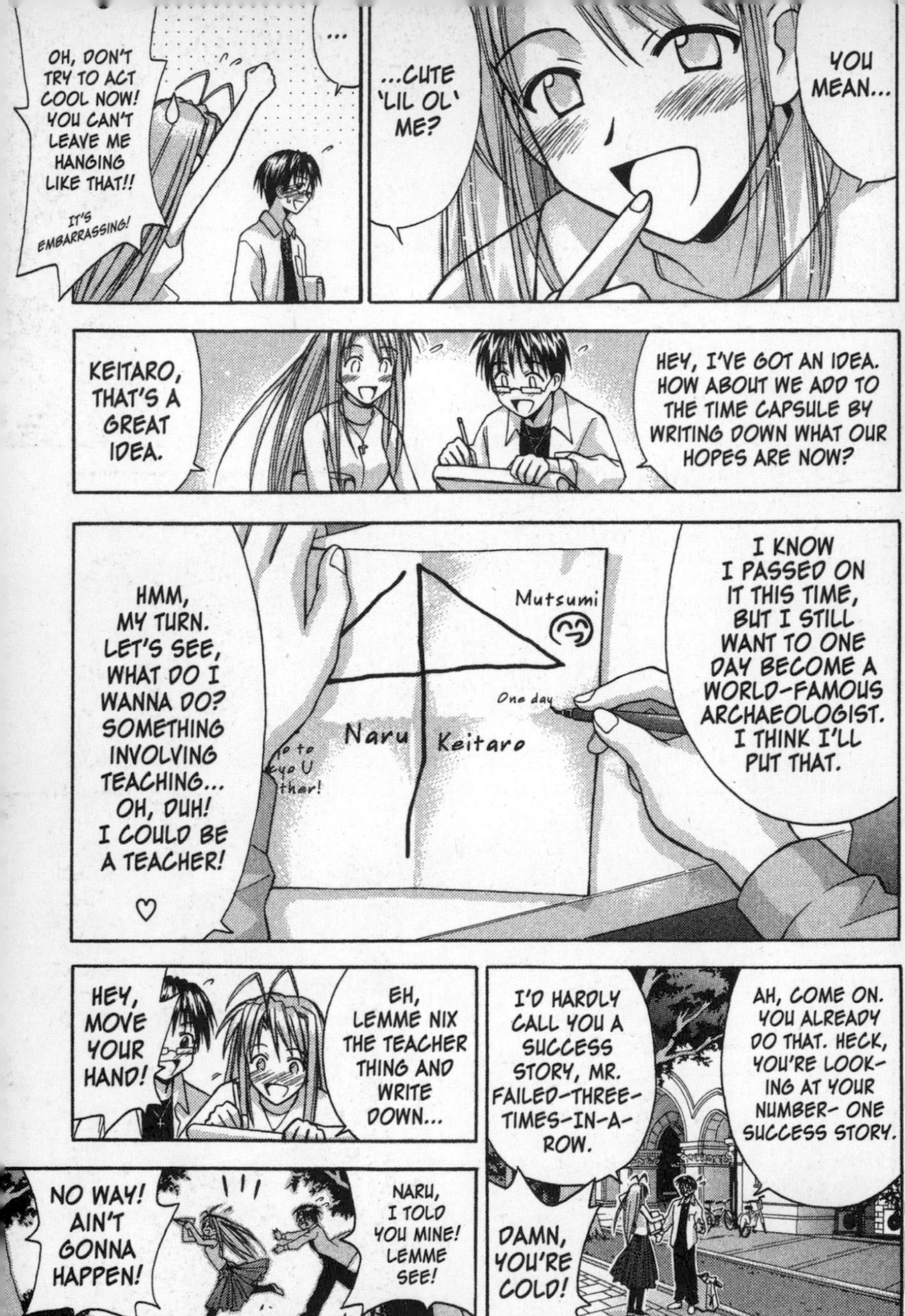
YOU MEAN...
...CUTE 'LIL OL' ME?
...
OH, DON'T TRY TO ACT COOL NOW! YOU CAN'T LEAVE ME HANGING LIKE THAT!!
IT'S EMBARRASSING!
HEY, I'VE GOT AN IDEA. HOW ABOUT WE ADD TO THE TIME CAPSULE BY WRITING DOWN WHAT OUR HOPES ARE NOW?
KEITARO, THAT'S A GREAT IDEA.
I KNOW I PASSED ON IT THIS TIME, BUT I STILL WANT TO ONE DAY BECOME A WORLD-FAMOUS ARCHAEOLOGIST. I THINK I'LL PUT THAT.
Mutsumi
One day
Keitaro
Naru
HMM, MY TURN. LET'S SEE, WHAT DO I WANNA DO? SOMETHING INVOLVING TEACHING... OH, DUH! I COULD BE A TEACHER!
♡
AH, COME ON. YOU ALREADY DO THAT. HECK, YOU'RE LOOKING AT YOUR NUMBER- ONE SUCCESS STORY.
I'D HARDLY CALL YOU A SUCCESS STORY, MR. FAILED-THREE-TIMES-IN-A-ROW.
DAMN, YOU'RE COLD!
EH, LEMME NIX THE TEACHER THING AND WRITE DOWN...
HEY, MOVE YOUR HAND!
NARU, I TOLD YOU MINE! LEMME SEE!
NO WAY! AIN'T GONNA HAPPEN!

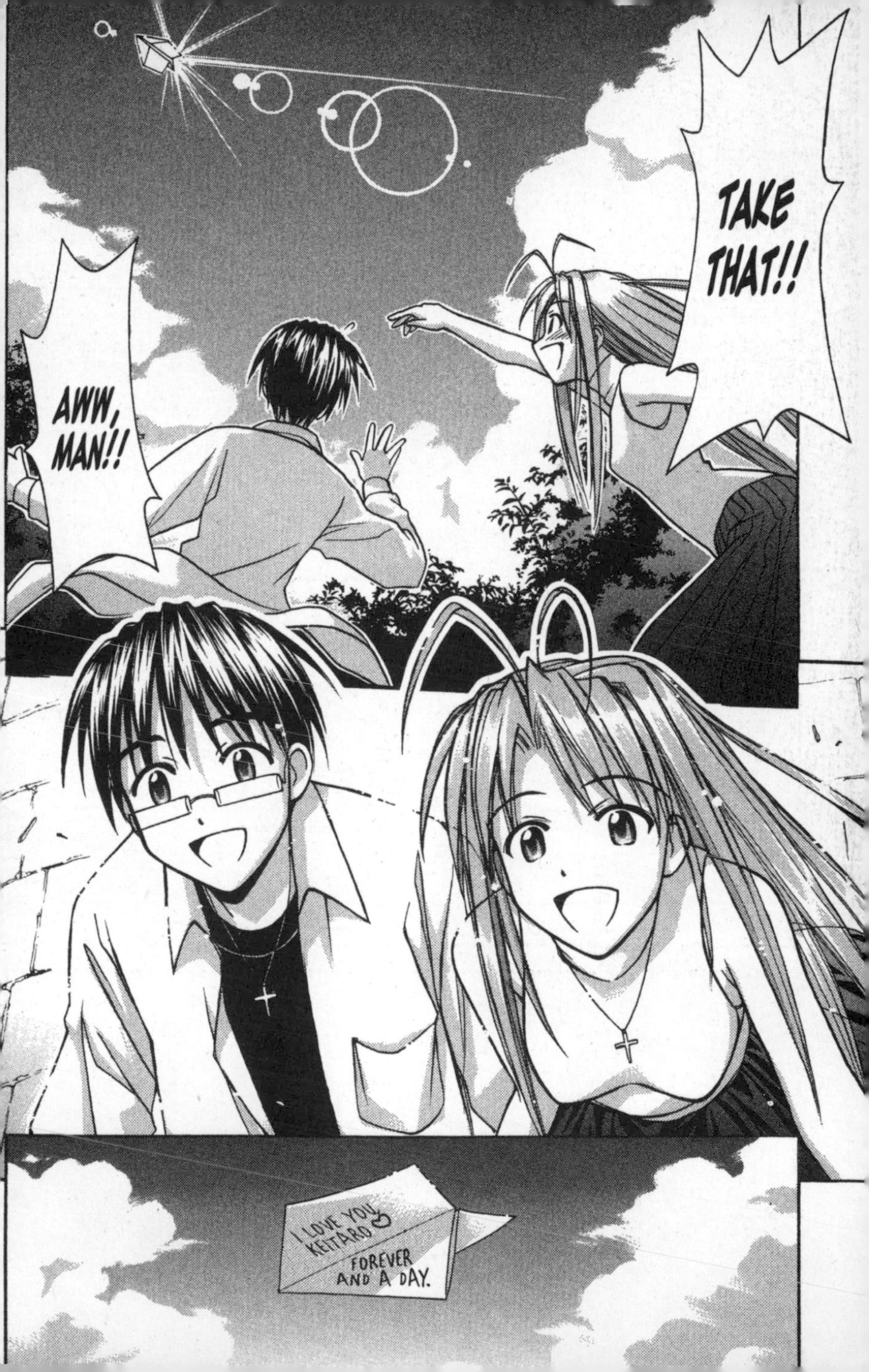
TAKE THAT!!
AWW, MAN!!
I LOVE YOU KEITARO
FOREVER AND A DAY.

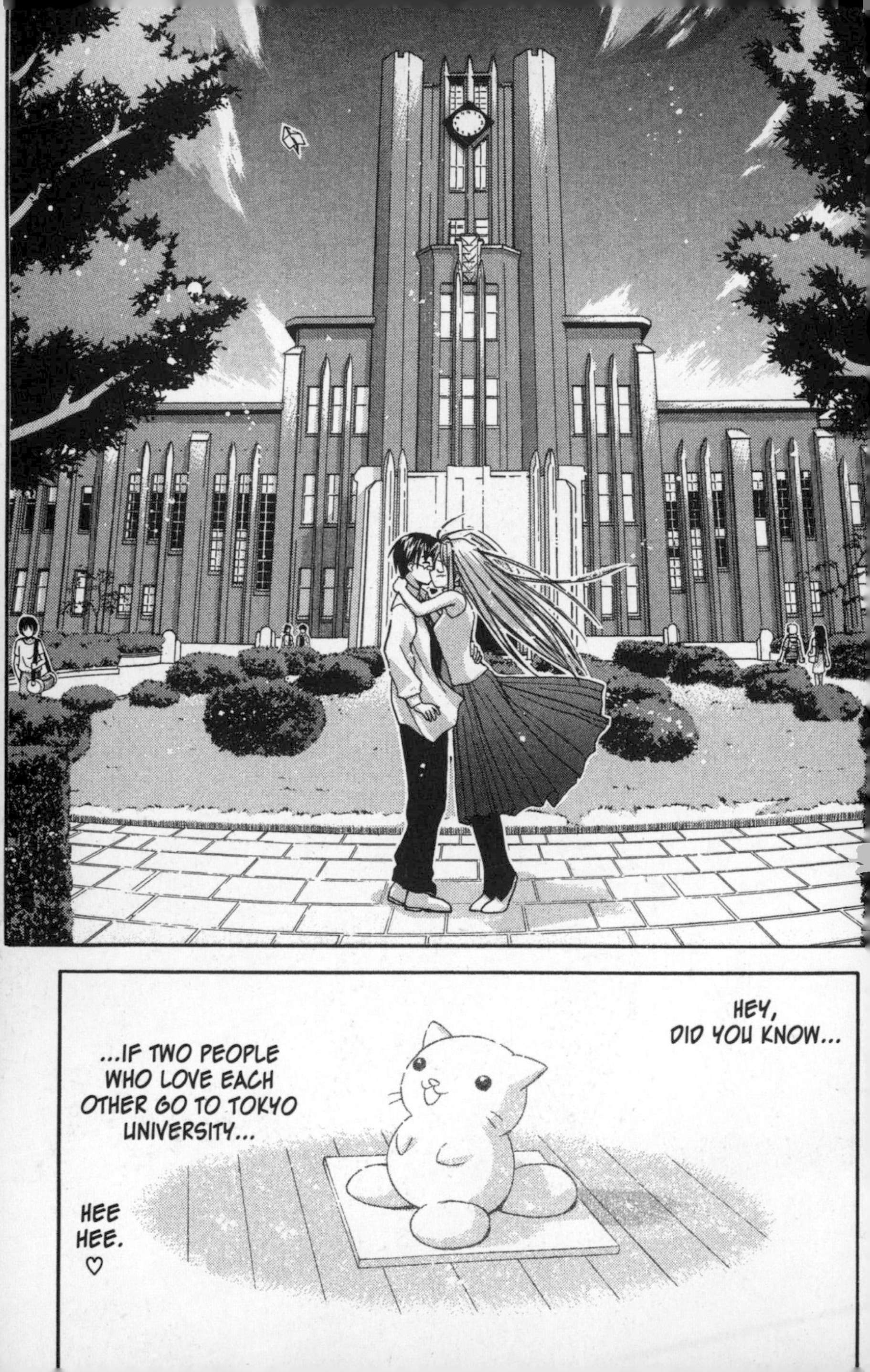
HEY, DID YOU KNOW...
...IF TWO PEOPLE WHO LOVE EACH OTHER GO TO TOKYO UNIVERSITY...
HEE HEE. ♡

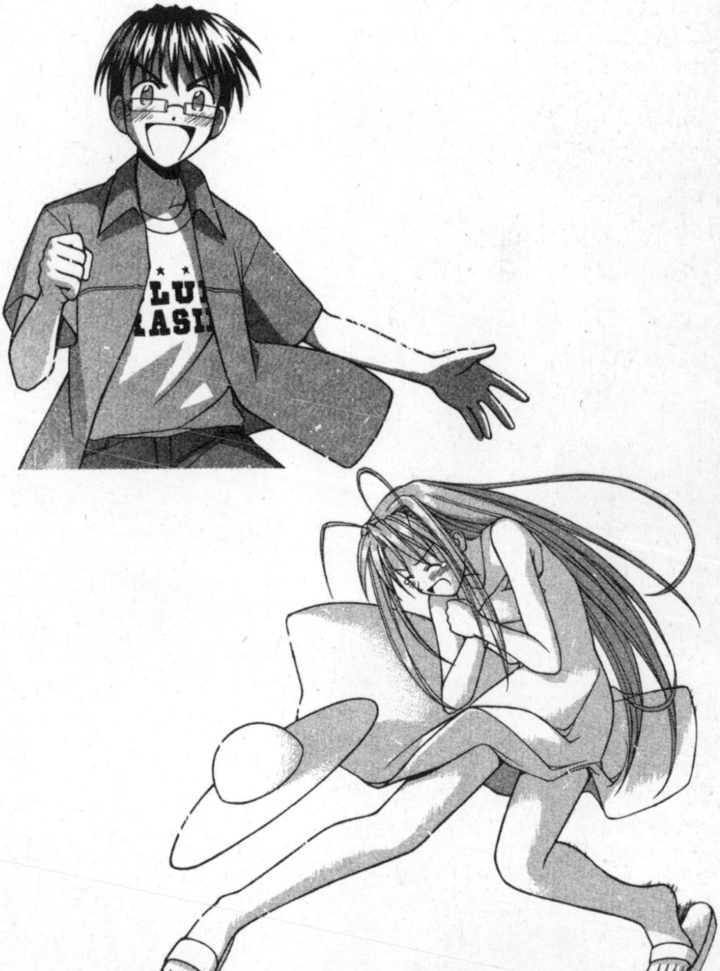

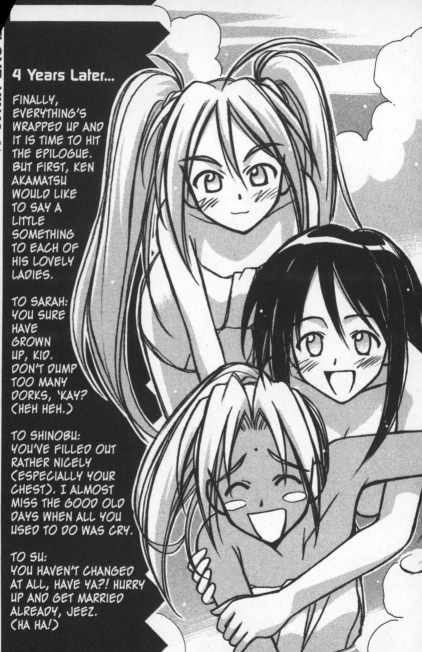

4 Years Later...

FINALLY, EVERYTHING'S WRAPPED UP AND IT IS TIME TO HIT THE EPILOGUE. BUT FIRST, KEN AKAMATSU WOULD LIKE TO SAY A LITTLE SOMETHING TO EACH OF HIS LOVELY LADIES.

TO SARAH: YOU SURE HAVE GROWN UP, KID. DON'T DUMP TOO MANY DORKS, 'KAY? (HEH HEH.)

TO SHINOBU: YOU'VE FILLED OUT RATHER NICELY (ESPECIALLY YOUR CHEST). I ALMOST MISS THE GOOD OLD DAYS WHEN ALL YOU USED TO DO WAS CRY.

TO SU: YOU HAVEN'T CHANGED AT ALL, HAVE YA?! HURRY UP AND GET MARRIED ALREADY, JEEZ. (HA HA!)

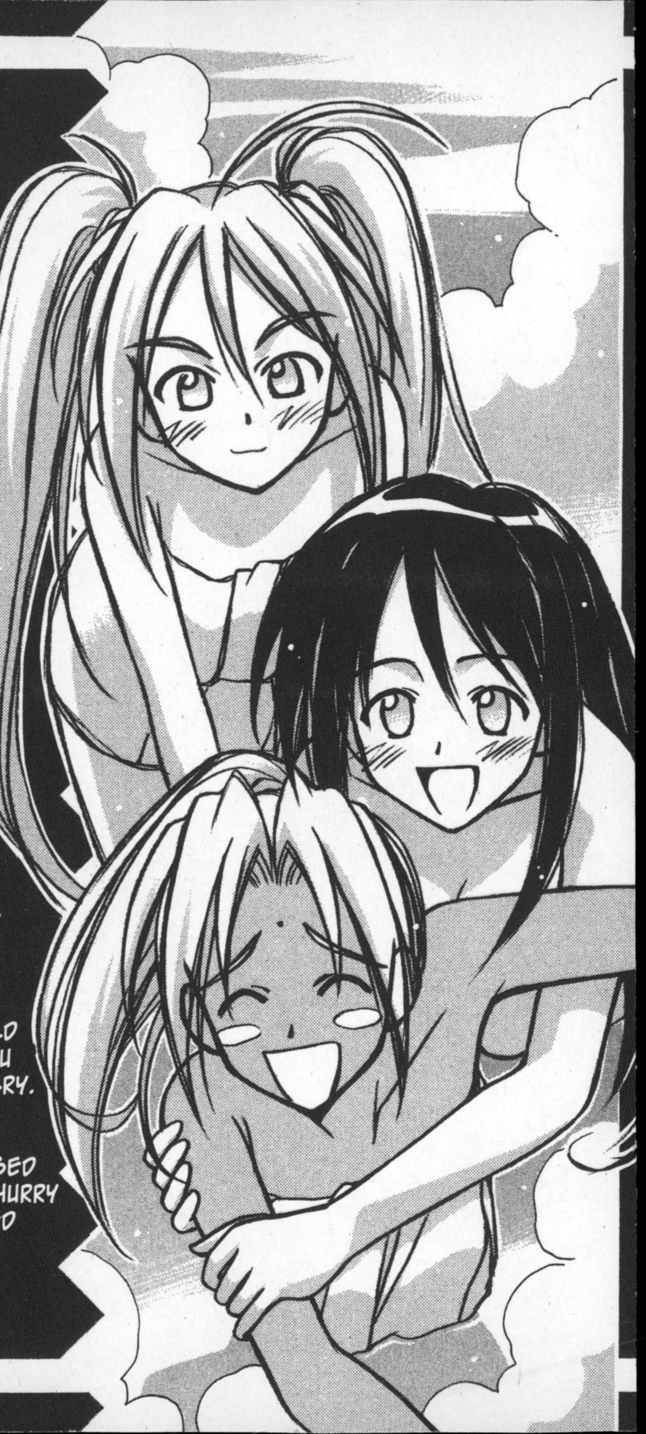

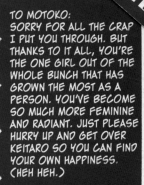

TO MOTOKO:
SORRY FOR ALL THE CRAP
I PUT YOU THROUGH. BUT
THANKS TO IT ALL, YOU'RE
THE ONE GIRL OUT OF THE
WHOLE BUNCH THAT HAS
GROWN THE MOST AS A
PERSON. YOU'VE BECOME
SO MUCH MORE FEMININE
AND RADIANT. JUST PLEASE
HURRY UP AND GET OVER
KEITARO SO YOU CAN FIND
YOUR OWN HAPPINESS.
(HEH HEH.)

TO KITSUNE:
THANK YOU FOR ALL OF
YOUR HELP KEEPING THE
STORYLINE MOVING ALONG
SMOOTHLY. I COULDN'T
HAVE DONE IT WITHOUT
YOU. I JUST FEEL BAD
THAT I DIDN'T/COULDN'T
EVER DRAW ANY REALLY
JUICY PARTS FOR YOU.
SORRY, BABE!!

TO NARU:
CONGRATULATIONS AND
SORRY FOR ALWAYS
DRAWING YOU
NAKED!! BUT AT
LEAST THAT'S ALL
OVER NOW. YEP,
YOU'RE FREE AT
LAST (MAYBE)!!
JUST REMEMBER,
KEITARO LOVES
YOU MORE THAN
ANYTHING IN THE
WORLD. SO JUST
BELIEVE IN HIS LOVE
AND LIVE HAPPILY EVER
AFTER.

[LOVE HINA] Characters

2001/12 – KEN AKAMATSU

Concept Gallery

Reference Collection

Love Hina:
Final Version

THIS IS IT! TIME TO TAKE A BRIEF LOOK AT THE DESIGN PROCESS THAT GOES INTO IMAGINING THE WORLD OF *LOVE HINA*. STARTING US OFF IS THE DORM'S NEWEST RESIDENT, MS. EMA MAEDA.

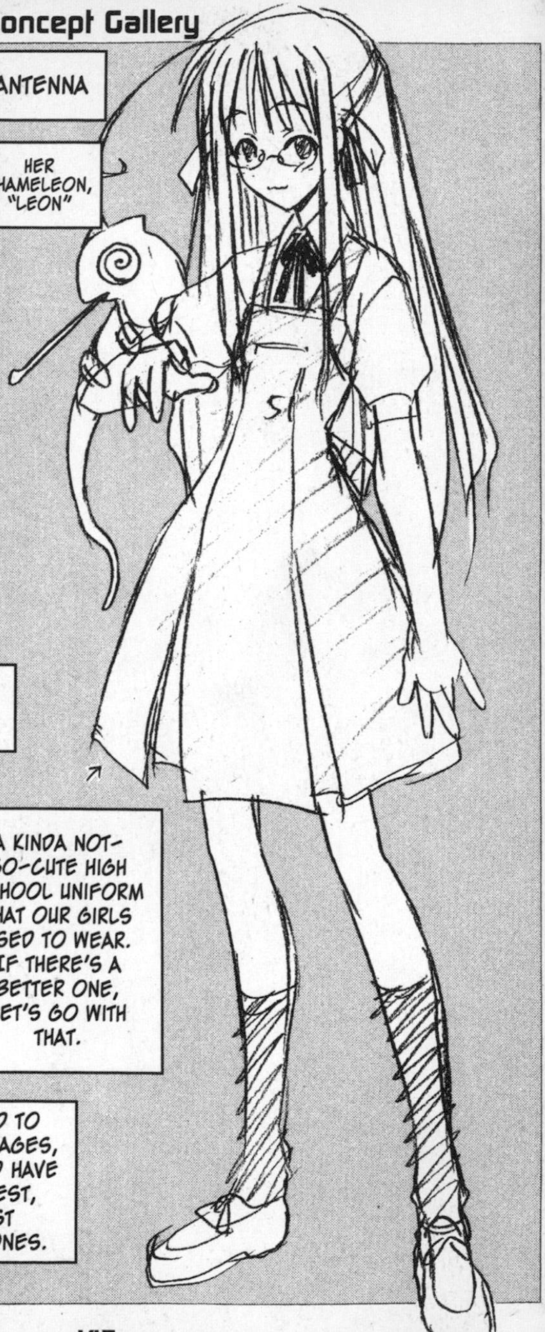
ANTENNA
HER CHAMELEON, "LEON"
EMA MAEDA - 15 YEARS OLD
A KINDA NOT-SO-CUTE HIGH SCHOOL UNIFORM THAT OUR GIRLS USED TO WEAR. IF THERE'S A BETTER ONE, LET'S GO WITH THAT.
IN REGARD TO HER APPENDAGES, SHE SHOULD HAVE THE THINNEST, WEAKEST LOOKING ONES.

EMA'S IMAGE IS REALLY THAT OF A NO FRILLS "SKINNY GIRL WITH GLASSES." HER HAIR STARTS OUT STRAIGHT AND ENDS IN A BIT OF A CURL. SHE EVEN HAS THE MAKINGS OF AN ANTENNA IN THE FRONT (HEH HEH).
AS FOR HER UNIFORM, I WANTED IT TO BE RATHER DRAB AND NOT TERRIBLY FASHIONABLE. THE KEY WORD I WANTED TO HEAR FROM PEOPLE WHEN THEY LOOKED AT HER WAS, "ORDINARY." (I DIDN'T BASE HER DESIGN ON ANYONE, EITHER.)

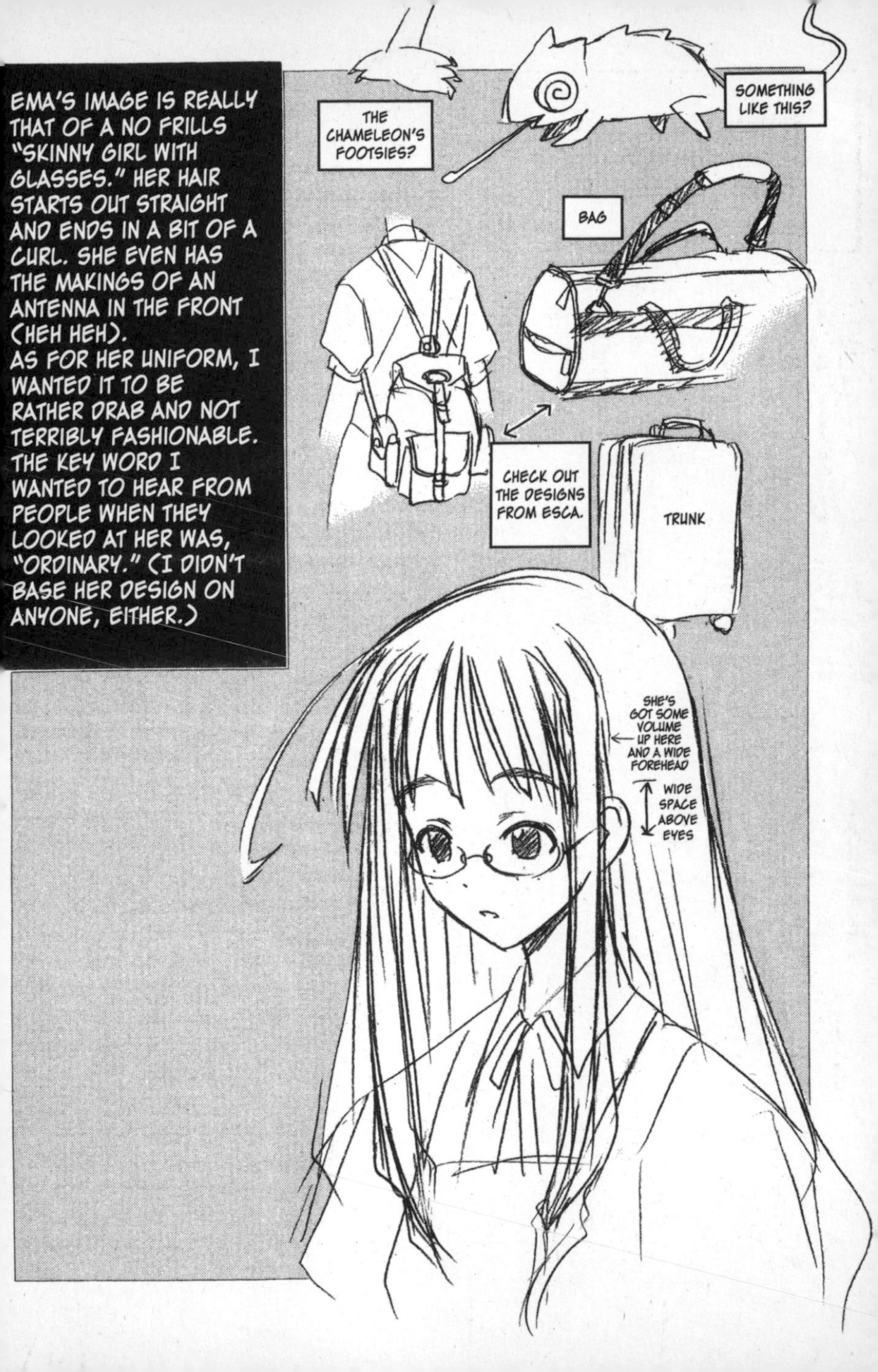
SOMETHING LIKE THIS?
THE CHAMELEON'S FOOTSIES?
BAG
CHECK OUT THE DESIGNS FROM ESCA.
TRUNK
SHE'S GOT SOME VOLUME UP HERE AND A WIDE FOREHEAD
WIDE SPACE ABOVE EYES

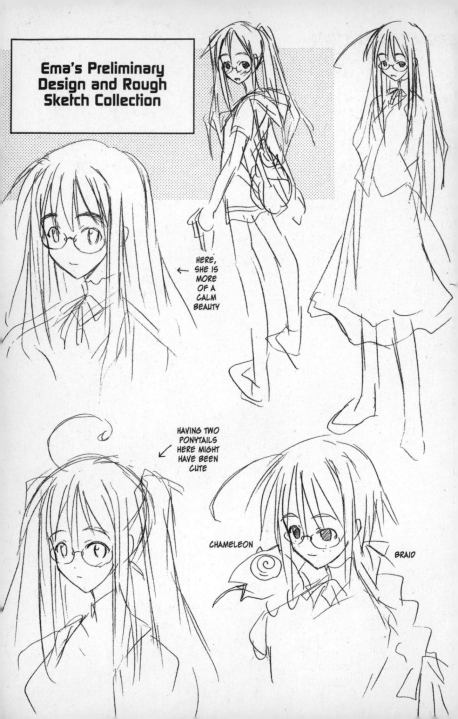

Ema's Preliminary Design and Rough Sketch Collection

← HERE, SHE IS MORE OF A CALM BEAUTY

HAVING TWO PONYTAILS HERE MIGHT HAVE BEEN CUTE

CHAMELEON

BRAID

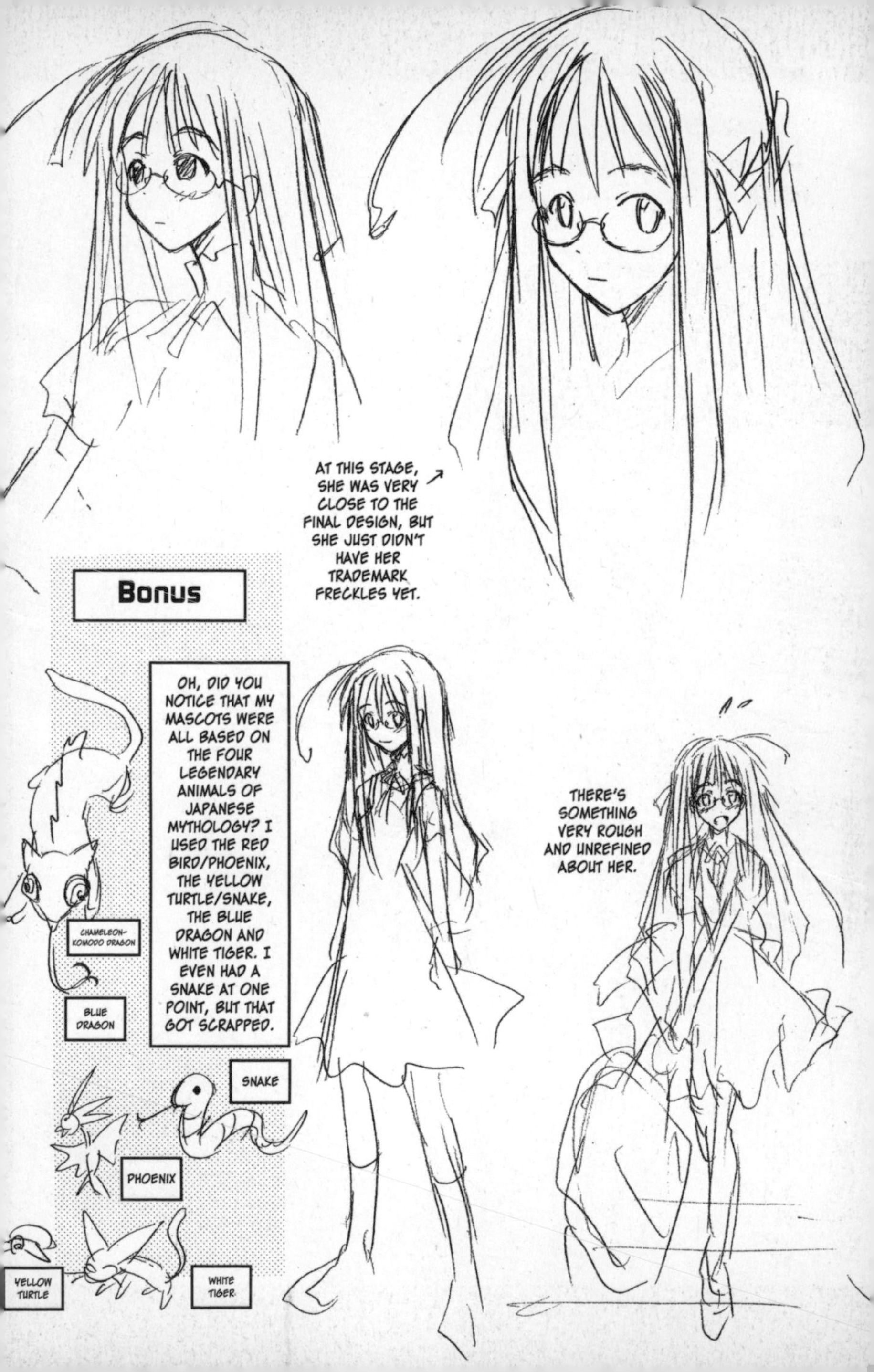
AT THIS STAGE, SHE WAS VERY CLOSE TO THE FINAL DESIGN, BUT SHE JUST DIDN'T HAVE HER TRADEMARK FRECKLES YET.
THERE'S SOMETHING VERY ROUGH AND UNREFINED ABOUT HER.
Bonus
OH, DID YOU NOTICE THAT MY MASCOTS WERE ALL BASED ON THE FOUR LEGENDARY ANIMALS OF JAPANESE MYTHOLOGY? I USED THE RED BIRD/PHOENIX, THE YELLOW TURTLE/SNAKE, THE BLUE DRAGON AND WHITE TIGER. I EVEN HAD A SNAKE AT ONE POINT, BUT THAT GOT SCRAPPED.
CHAMELEON-KOMODO DRAGON
BLUE DRAGON
SNAKE
PHOENIX
WHITE TIGER
YELLOW TURTLE

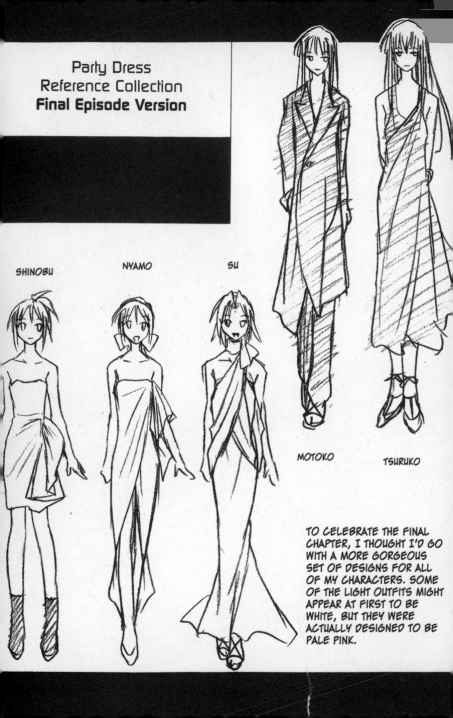

Party Dress Reference Collection
Final Episode Version

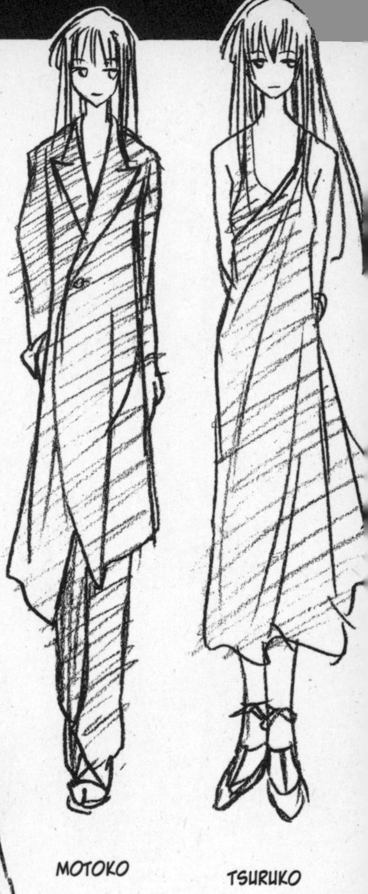
MOTOKO
TSURUKO

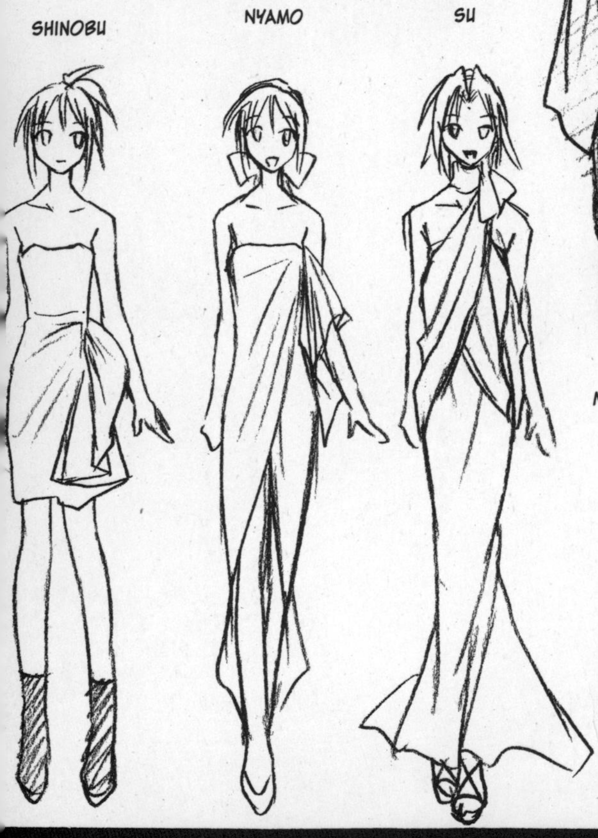
SHINOBU
NYAMO
SU

TO CELEBRATE THE FINAL CHAPTER, I THOUGHT I'D GO WITH A MORE GORGEOUS SET OF DESIGNS FOR ALL OF MY CHARACTERS. SOME OF THE LIGHT OUTFITS MIGHT APPEAR AT FIRST TO BE WHITE, BUT THEY WERE ACTUALLY DESIGNED TO BE PALE PINK.

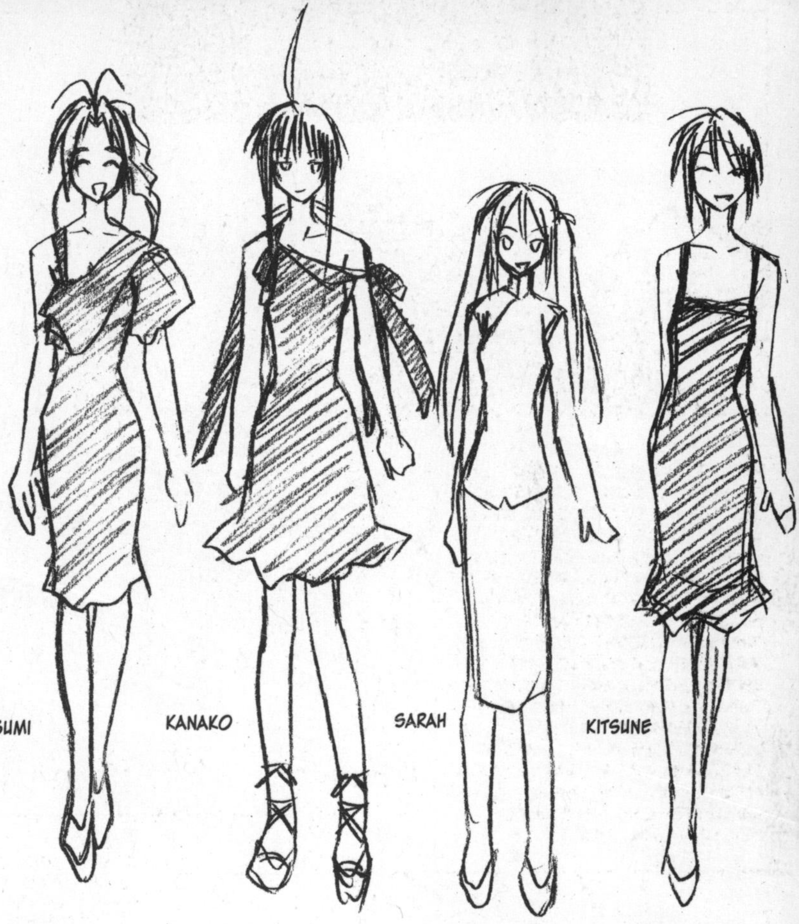
MUTSUMI
KANAKO
SARAH
KITSUNE

SINCE THERE ARE SO MANY CHARACTERS, IT WAS ACTUALLY REALLY HARD TO COME UP WITH UNIQUE DRESSES FOR ALL OF THEM.

HARUKA WILL BE WEARING THE DRESS SHE WORE IN THE MIDDLE OF THE HONEYMOON STORYLINE BACK IN VOL. 13.

The Scenery of Love Hina

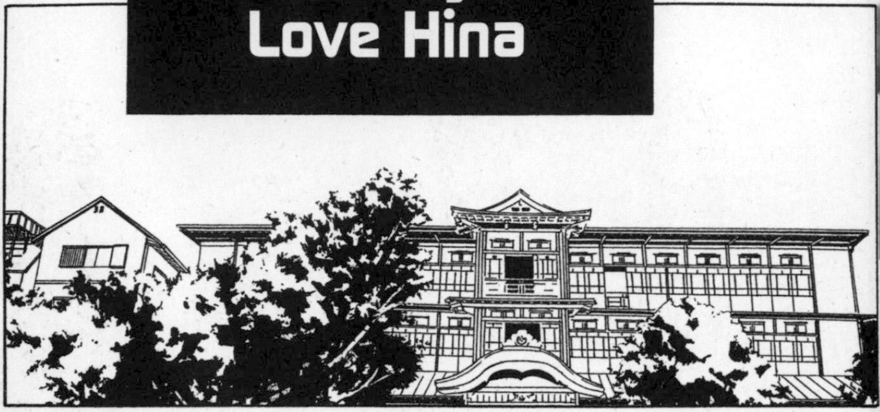

↑ NOT THAT I HAVE TO NOTE IT, BUT YES, THIS IS HINATA HOUSE--THE PLACE WHERE EVERYTHING STARTED.

ONLY THE MOST ASTUTE READERS MAY HAVE NOTICED, BUT IN *LOVE HINA*, ONE METHOD WE UTILIZED TO CUT DOWN ON PRODUCTION TIME IS CALLED "BANKING IMAGES" (AT LEAST THAT'S WHAT MY STAFF CALLS IT). THIS IS A PROCESS IN WHICH WE HAVE A BANK OF BARE-BONE LINE DRAWINGS FOR EACH AREA THAT WE USE OVER AND OVER AGAIN WITH MINOR ADJUSTMENTS. THESE "BANKED IMAGES" APPEAR QUITE FREQUENTLY THROUGHOUT THE MANGA'S RUN, AND A FUN LITTLE SIDE QUEST MIGHT BE TO GO BACK THROUGH THE SERIES AND COUNT HOW MANY TIMES WE USED THE SAME BACKGROUND OR LOCATION. [EDITOR'S NOTE: THIS ALSO EXPLAINS WHY THE CHARACTERS ALWAYS HAVE WHITE OUTLINES AROUND THEM.]

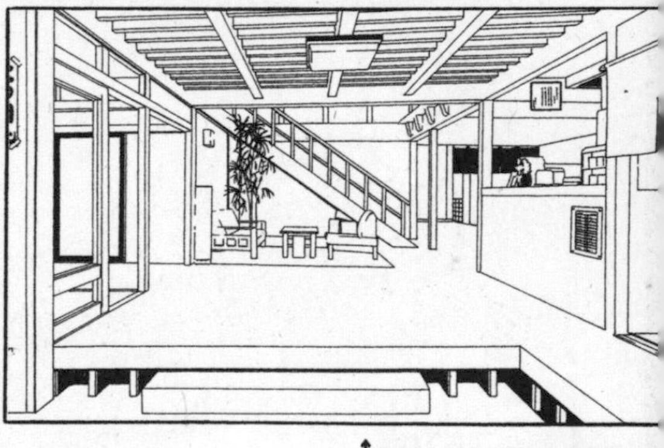

↑ THE FIRST FLOOR OF HINATA HOUSE'S LOBBY. THE RESIDENTS OF THE DORM CAN BE FOUND CAMPING OUT HERE QUITE A LOT. I'VE SEEN AND REVISITED THIS SCENE SO MANY TIMES IN THE MANGA THAT SOMETIMES I'M NOT SURE IF I WAS JUST SEEING IT, OR ACTUALLY LYING ON THE COUCH!! (HEH HEH.)

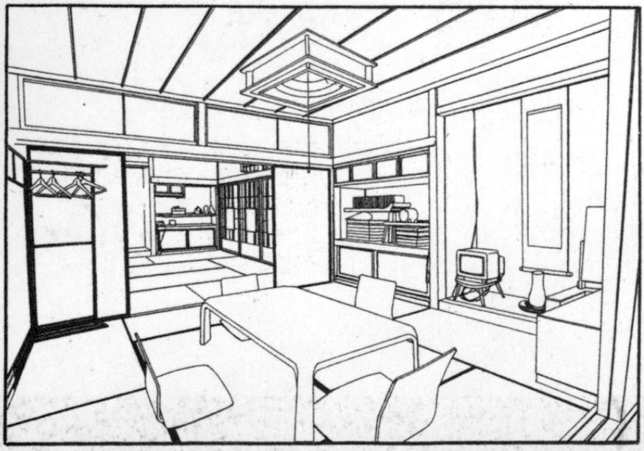

← AND HERE'S THE LANDLORD'S ROOM (A.K.A. KEITARO'S ROOM). I'M SURE YOU'RE ALL FAMILIAR WITH THIS CUT.

THE CAFÉ → IS BY FAR THE ONE PLACE OUT OF ALL THE LOCATIONS IN THE *LOVE HINA* UNIVERSE THAT REALLY, REALLY MAKES *LOVE HINA* UNIQUELY *LOVE HINA* FOR ME.

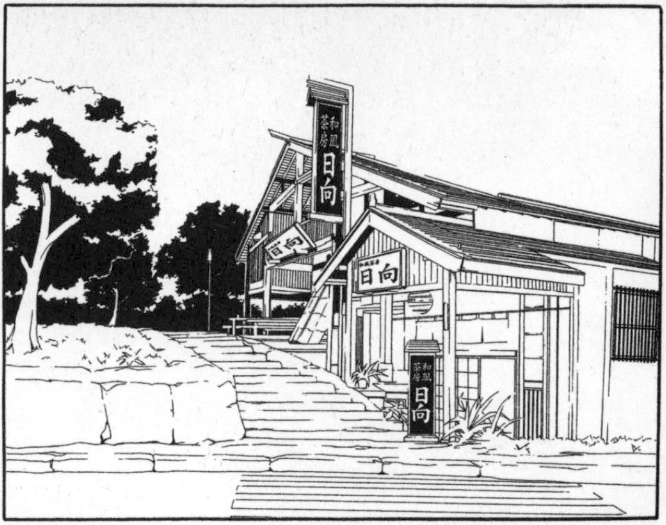
和風
茶房
日向

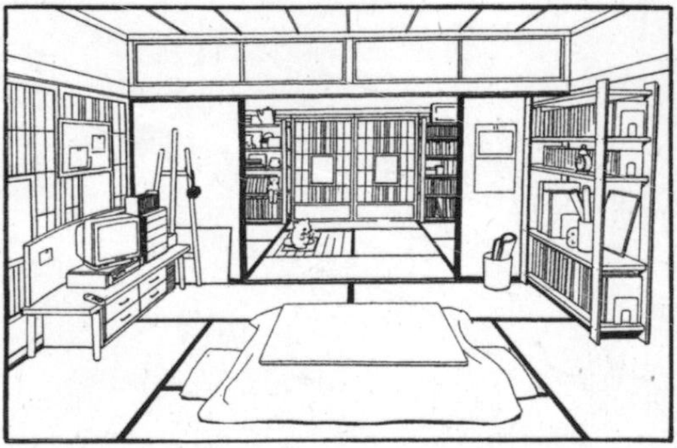

← AND HERE'S NARU'S ROOM WHERE SHE SPENT SO MUCH OF HER TIME TUTORING KEITARO. THERE'S JUST SOMETHING ABOUT SEEING A COMPLETELY EMPTY HINATA HOUSE THAT'S A LITTLE WEIRD. EVEN THOUGH IT'S EMPTY, IT STILL LOOKS HOMEY.

LAST BUT NOT LEAST, WE HAVE SETA'S INFAMOUS VAN. EVEN THOUGH IT'S NOT AN ACTUAL PLACE, IT'S STILL AN INTEGRAL PART OF THE SERIES. I BET IF ANYONE HAPPENED TO JOIN THE HINATA CREW ON A ROAD TRIP, THEY'D END UP EITHER TRAUMATIZED FOR LIFE OR HAVING ONE AMAZING THRILL RIDE.
↓

WELL, I HOPE YOU ENJOYED THIS LAST PEEK INTO THE WORLD OF *LOVE HINA*. IT MIGHT BE FUN TO GO BACK THROUGH THE OLDER VOLUMES AND CHECK OUT ALL THE THINGS I JUST MENTIONED. MIGHT GIVE YOU A BRAND NEW PERSPECTIVE ON THE SERIES. WELL, IT'S FAREWELL FOR NOW. UNTIL WE MEET AGAIN.

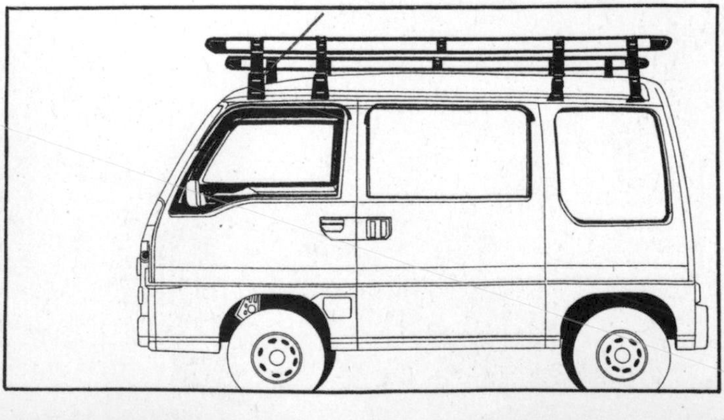

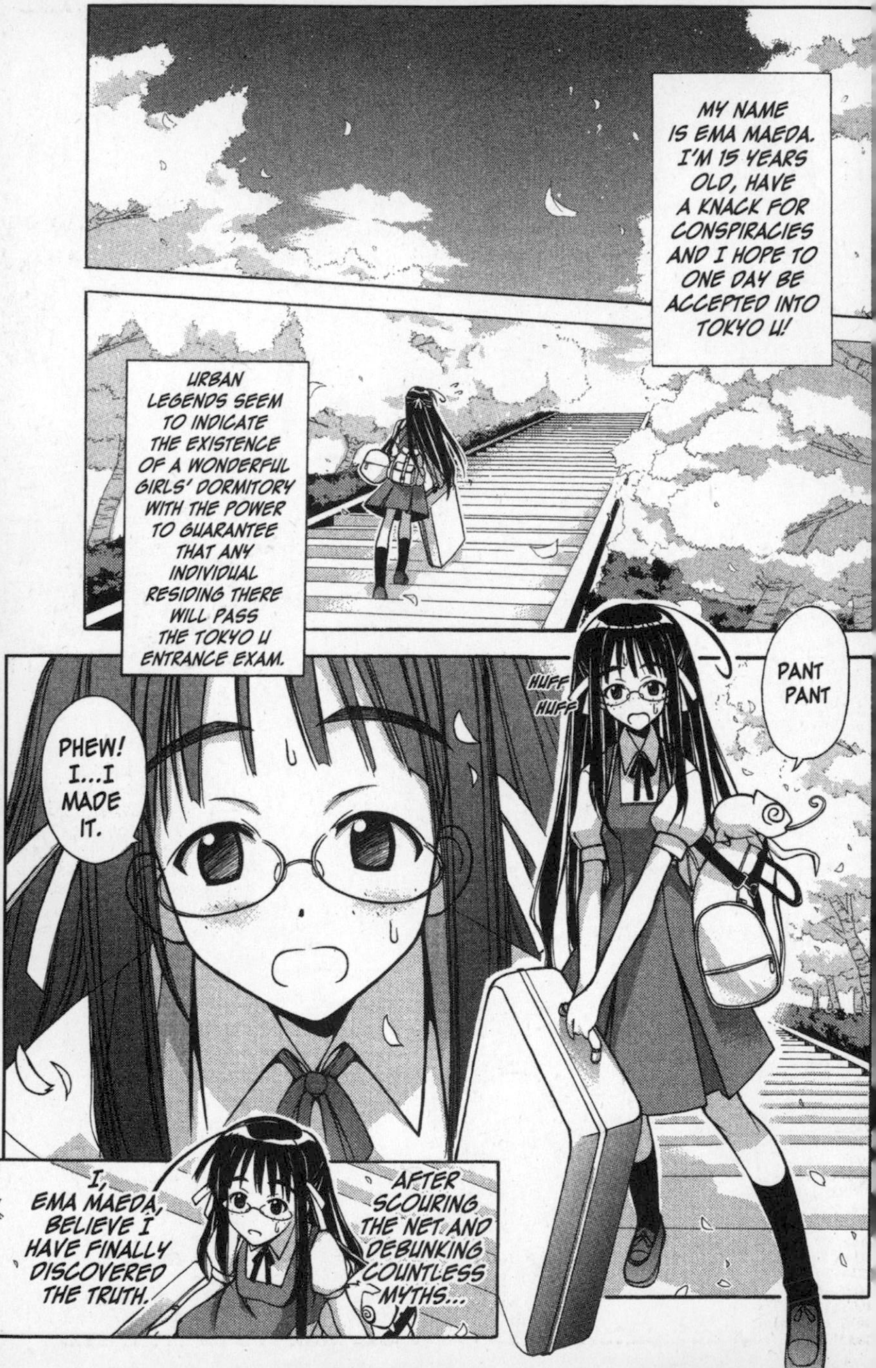
MY NAME IS EMA MAEDA. I'M 15 YEARS OLD, HAVE A KNACK FOR CONSPIRACIES AND I HOPE TO ONE DAY BE ACCEPTED INTO TOKYO U!
URBAN LEGENDS SEEM TO INDICATE THE EXISTENCE OF A WONDERFUL GIRLS' DORMITORY WITH THE POWER TO GUARANTEE THAT ANY INDIVIDUAL RESIDING THERE WILL PASS THE TOKYO U ENTRANCE EXAM.
PANT PANT
HUFF HUFF
PHEW! I...I MADE IT.
AFTER SCOURING THE NET AND DEBUNKING COUNTLESS MYTHS...
I, EMA MAEDA, BELIEVE I HAVE FINALLY DISCOVERED THE TRUTH.

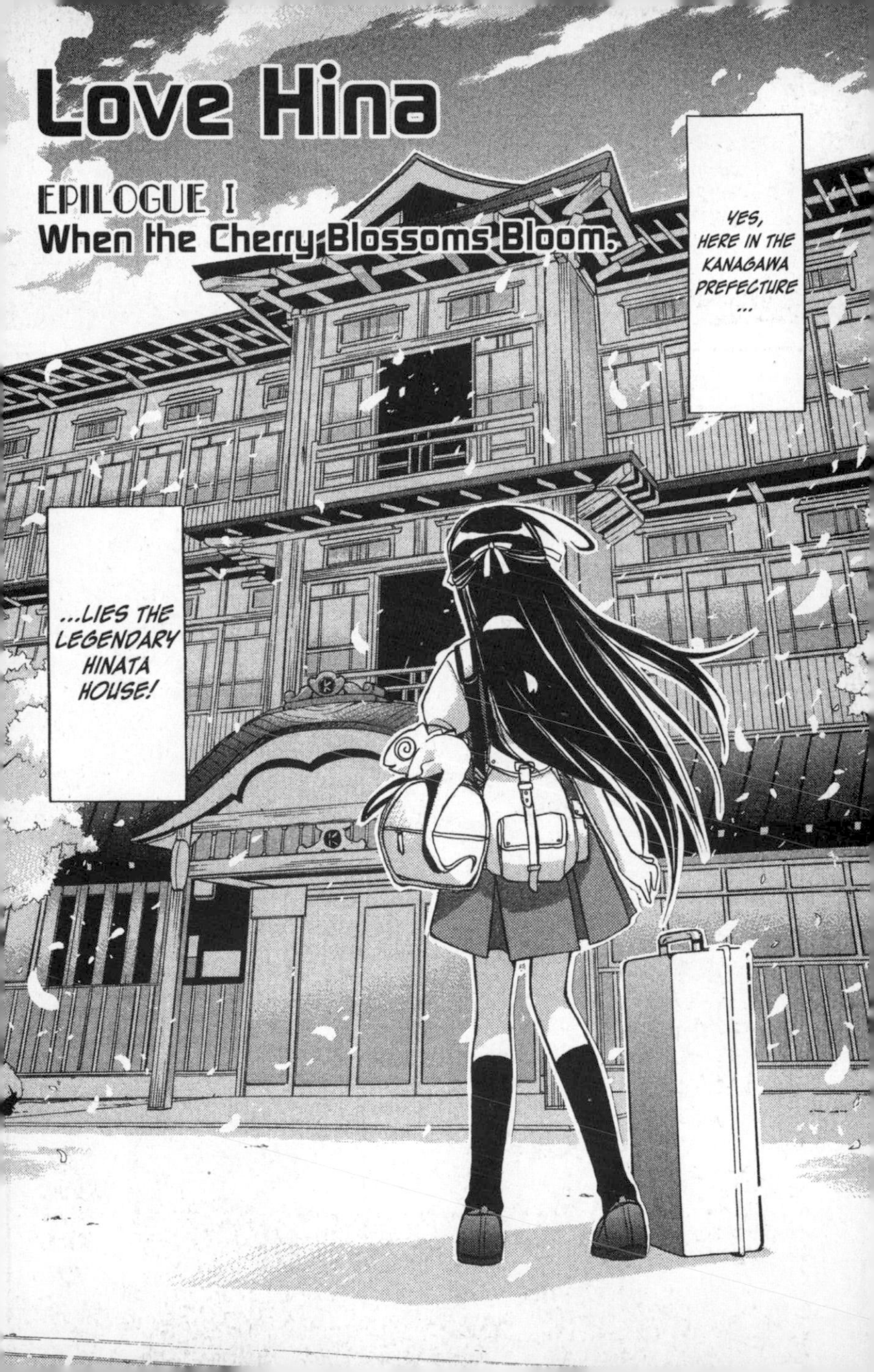
Love Hina
EPILOGUE I
When the Cherry Blossoms Bloom.
YES, HERE IN THE KANAGAWA PREFECTURE ...
...LIES THE LEGENDARY HINATA HOUSE!

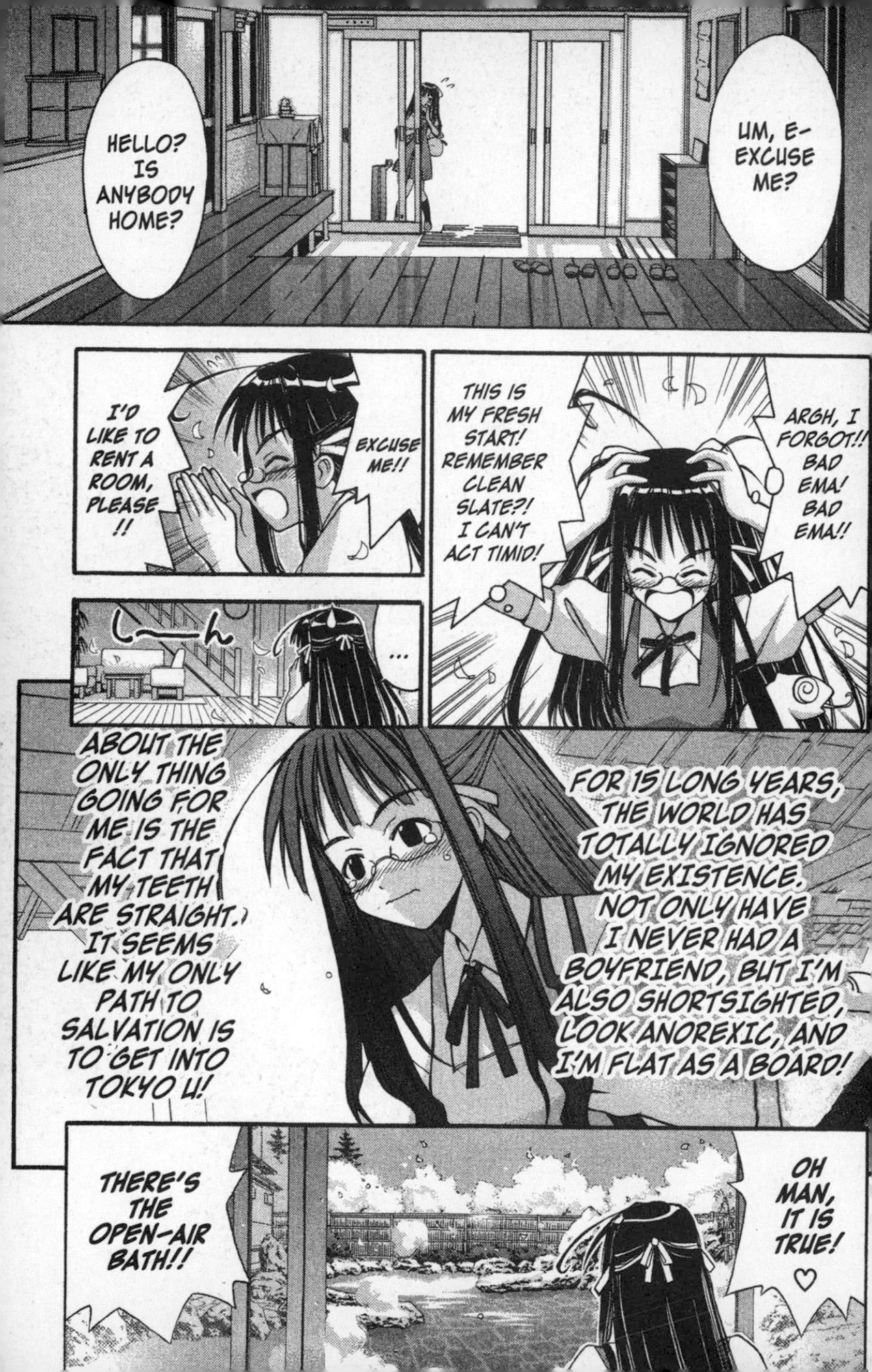
UM, E-EXCUSE ME?
HELLO? IS ANYBODY HOME?
ARGH, I FORGOT!! BAD EMA! BAD EMA!!
THIS IS MY FRESH START! REMEMBER CLEAN SLATE?! I CAN'T ACT TIMID!
EXCUSE ME!!
I'D LIKE TO RENT A ROOM, PLEASE!!
しーん
...
FOR 15 LONG YEARS, THE WORLD HAS TOTALLY IGNORED MY EXISTENCE. NOT ONLY HAVE I NEVER HAD A BOYFRIEND, BUT I'M ALSO SHORTSIGHTED, LOOK ANOREXIC, AND I'M FLAT AS A BOARD!
ABOUT THE ONLY THING GOING FOR ME IS THE FACT THAT MY TEETH ARE STRAIGHT. IT SEEMS LIKE MY ONLY PATH TO SALVATION IS TO GET INTO TOKYO U!
OH MAN, IT IS TRUE! ♡
THERE'S THE OPEN-AIR BATH!!

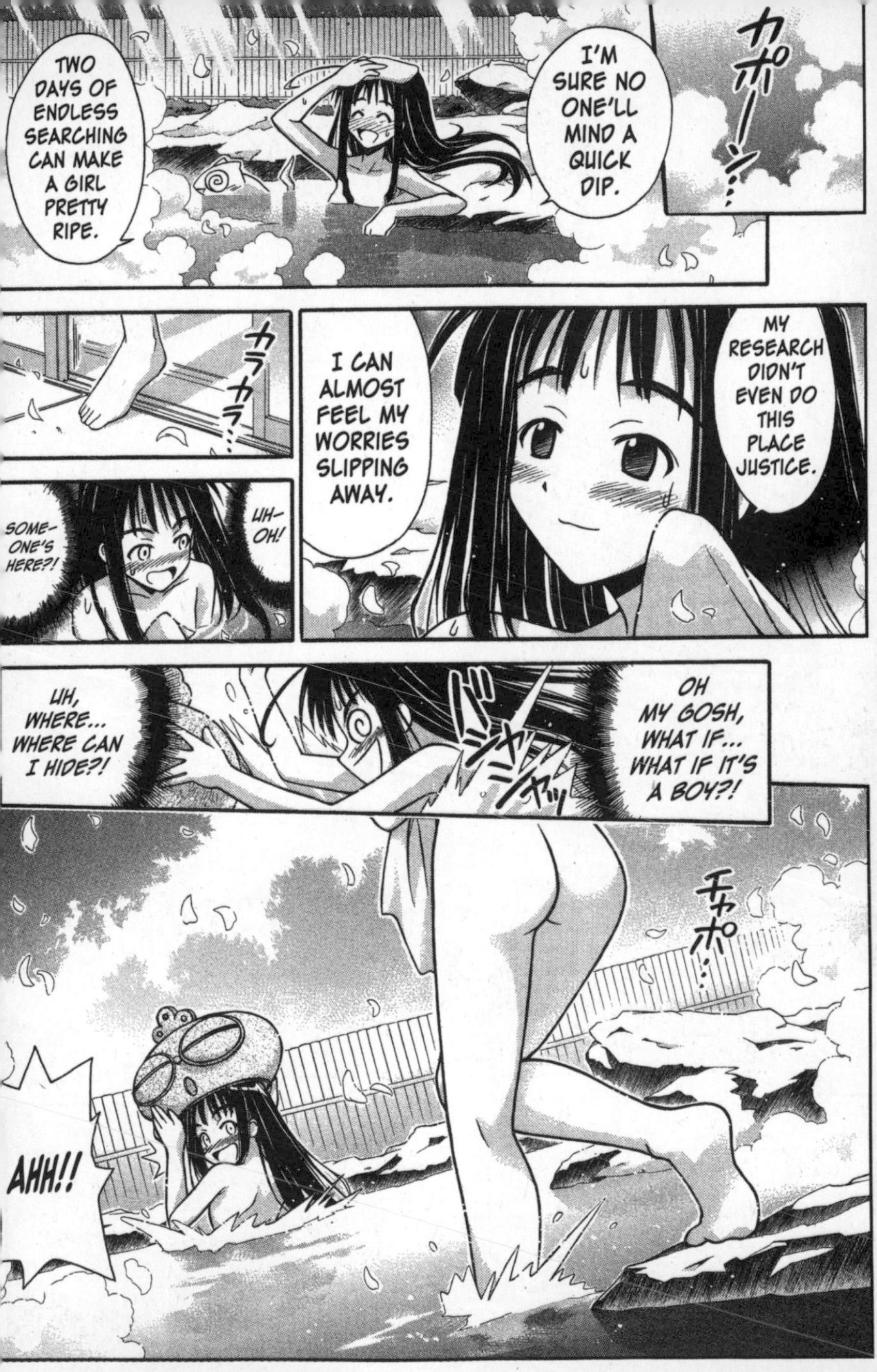
カポーン…
I'M SURE NO ONE'LL MIND A QUICK DIP.
TWO DAYS OF ENDLESS SEARCHING CAN MAKE A GIRL PRETTY RIPE.
MY RESEARCH DIDN'T EVEN DO THIS PLACE JUSTICE.
I CAN ALMOST FEEL MY WORRIES SLIPPING AWAY.
カラカラ…
UH-OH!
SOME-ONE'S HERE?!
OH MY GOSH, WHAT IF... WHAT IF IT'S A BOY?!
UH, WHERE... WHERE CAN I HIDE?!
チャポ…
AHH!!

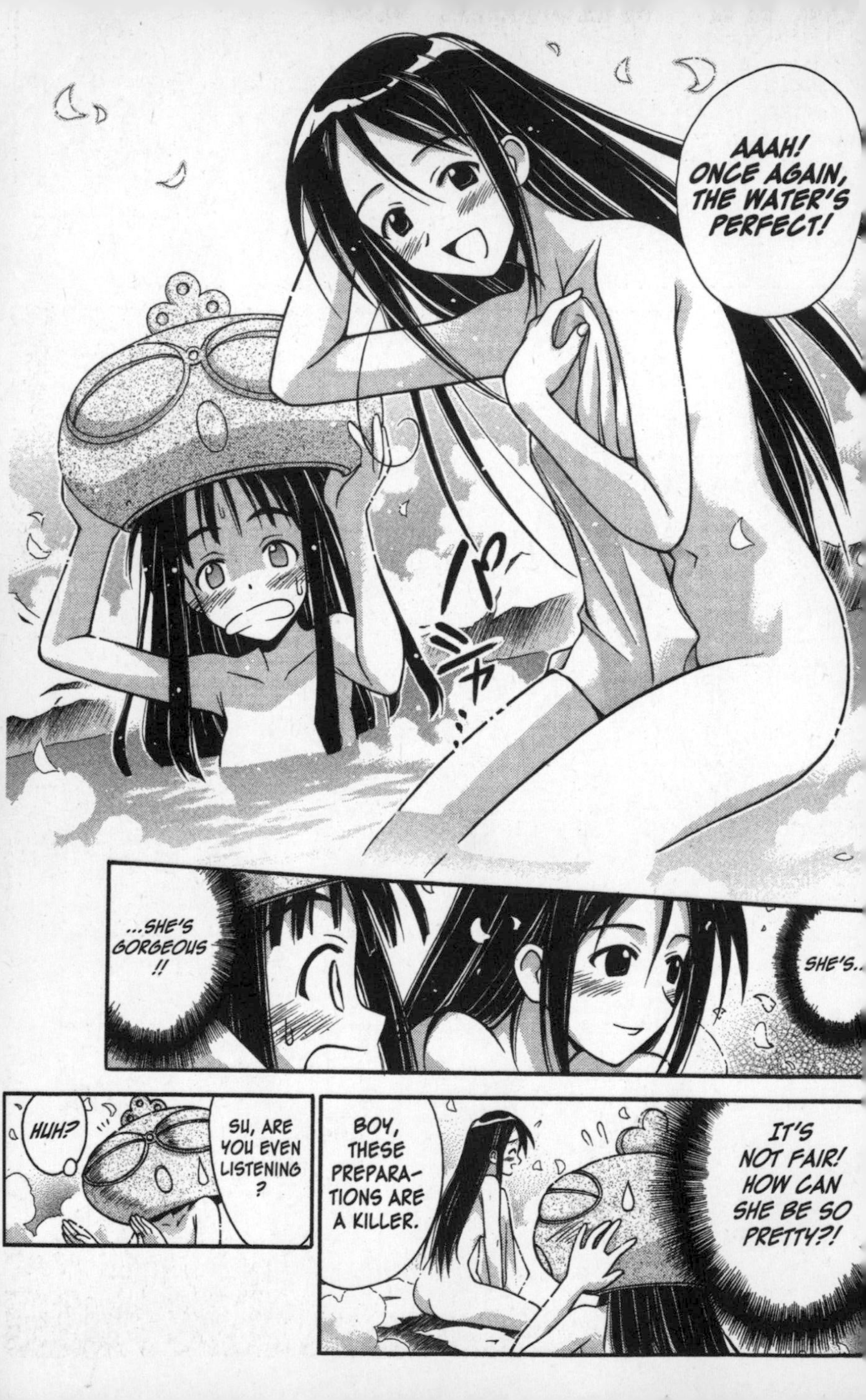
AAAH! ONCE AGAIN, THE WATER'S PERFECT!
SHE'S...
...SHE'S GORGEOUS !!
IT'S NOT FAIR! HOW CAN SHE BE SO PRETTY?!
BOY, THESE PREPARA-TIONS ARE A KILLER.
SU, ARE YOU EVEN LISTENING ?
HUH?

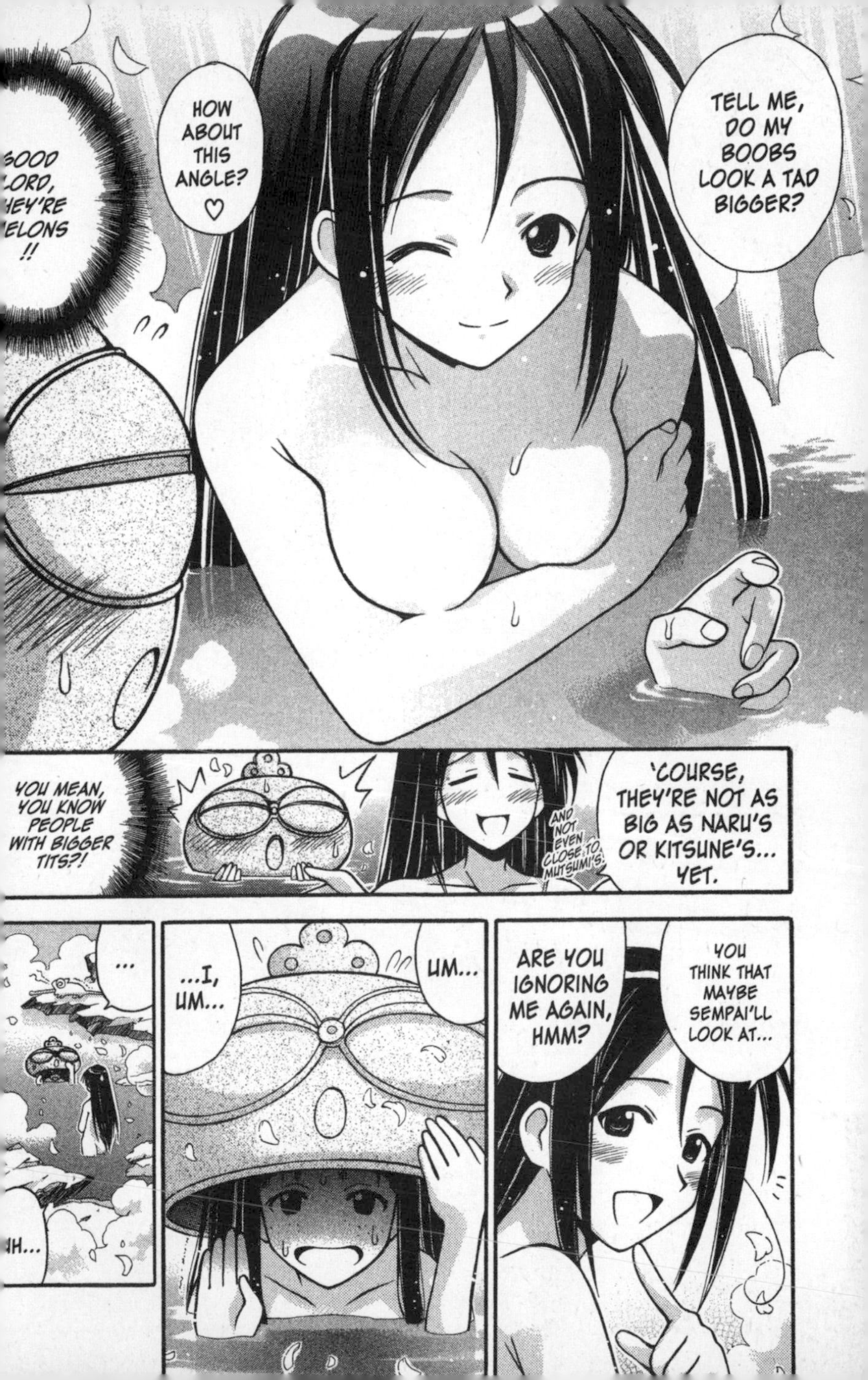
TELL ME, DO MY BOOBS LOOK A TAD BIGGER?
HOW ABOUT THIS ANGLE? ♡
GOOD LORD, THEY'RE MELONS !!
'COURSE, THEY'RE NOT AS BIG AS NARU'S OR KITSUNE'S... YET.
AND NOT EVEN CLOSE TO MUTSUMI'S.
YOU MEAN, YOU KNOW PEOPLE WITH BIGGER TITS?!
YOU THINK THAT MAYBE SEMPAI'LL LOOK AT...
ARE YOU IGNORING ME AGAIN, HMM?
UM...
...I, UM...
...
HH...

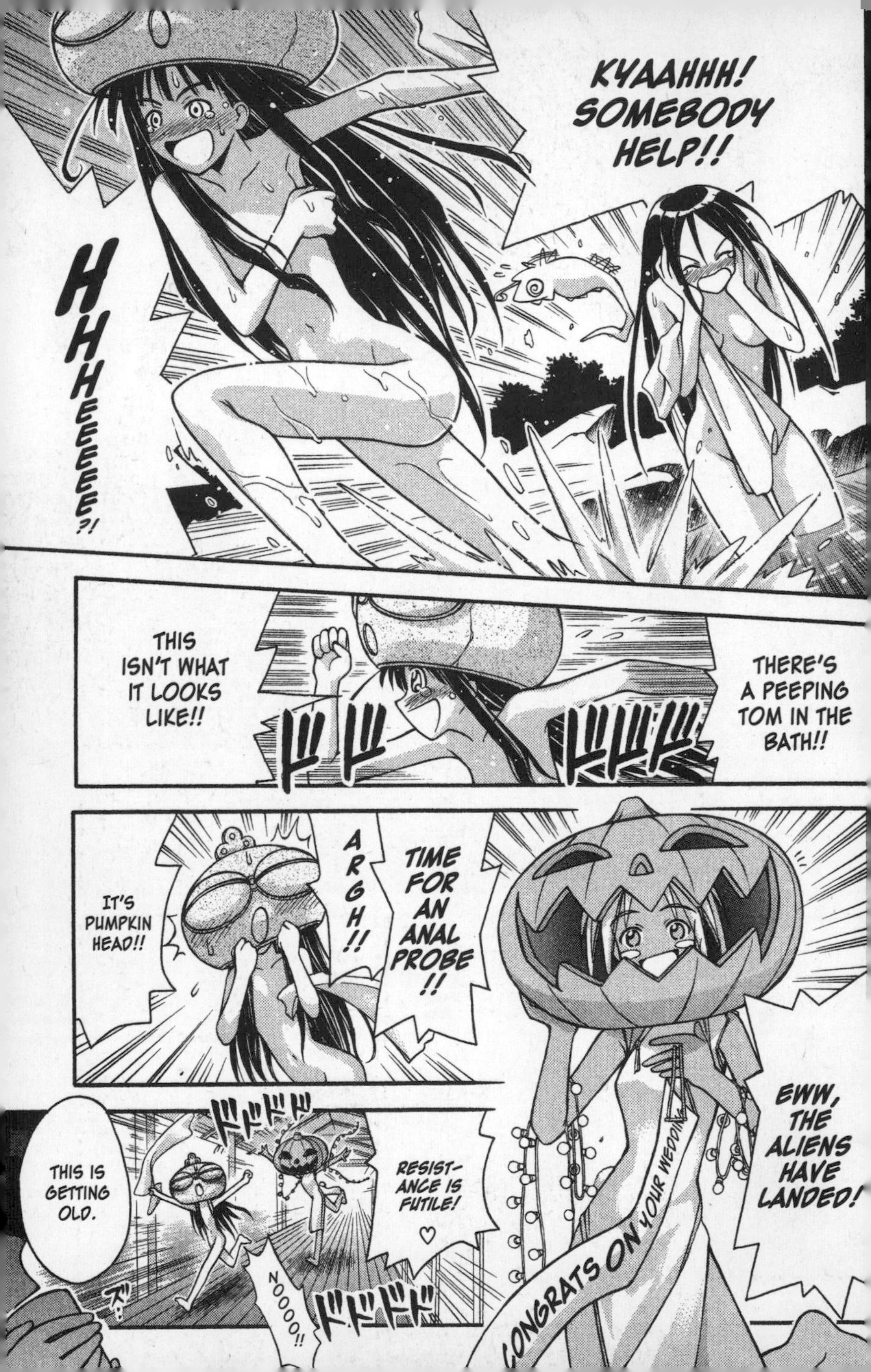
KYAAHHH! SOMEBODY HELP!!
HHHEEEEEEE?!
THERE'S A PEEPING TOM IN THE BATH!!
ドドドド
ドド
THIS ISN'T WHAT IT LOOKS LIKE!!
EWW, THE ALIENS HAVE LANDED!
CONGRATS ON YOUR WEDDING
TIME FOR AN ANAL PROBE!!
ARGH!!
IT'S PUMPKIN HEAD!!
ドドドド
RESIST-ANCE IS FUTILE! ♡
NOOOO!!
ドドドド
ズ
THIS IS GETTING OLD.

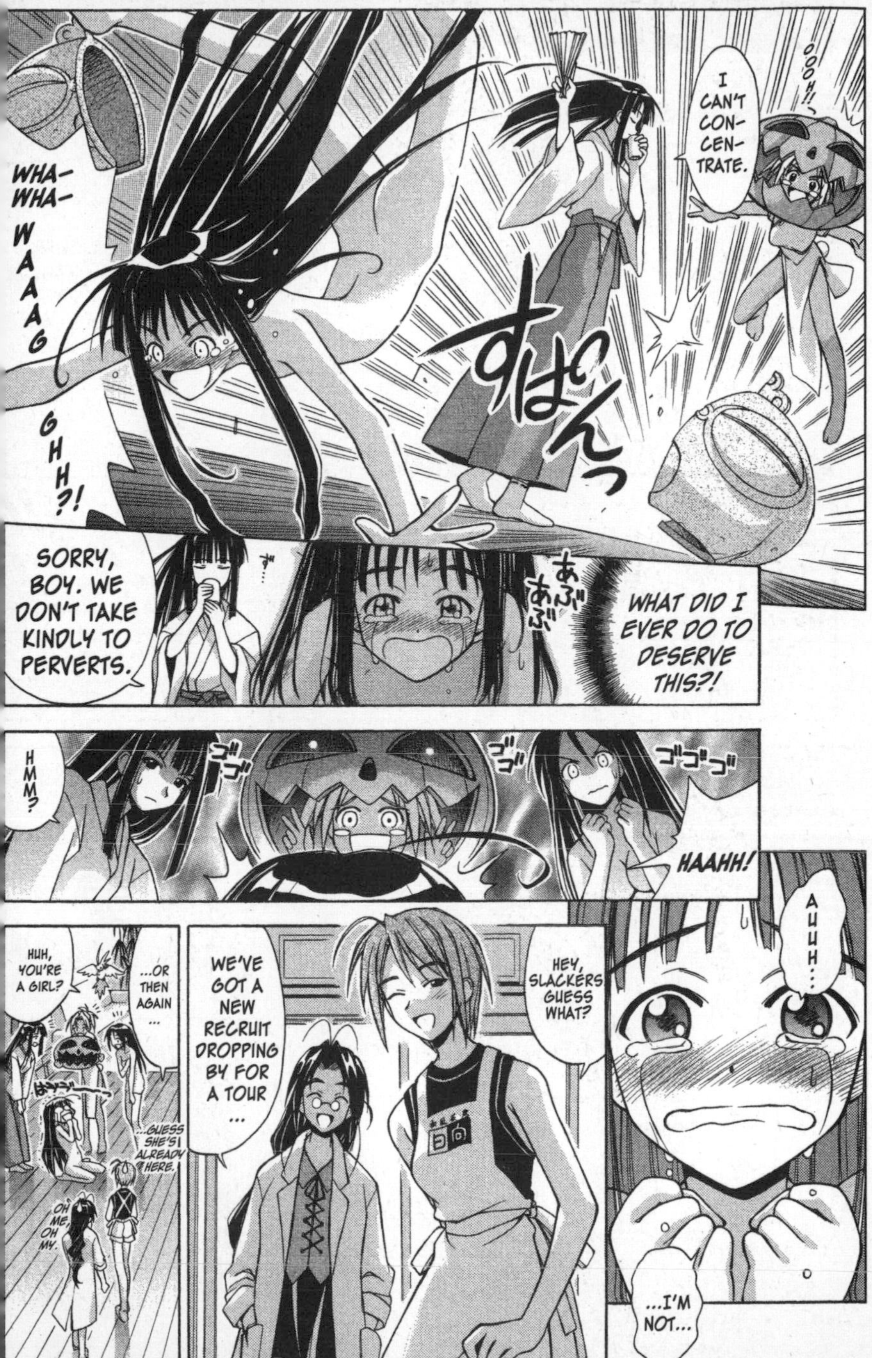
OOOH!!
I CAN'T CONCENTRATE.
すぱんっ
WHA-WHA-WAAAAGGHH?!
WHAT DID I EVER DO TO DESERVE THIS?!
あぶあぶ
ず
SORRY, BOY. WE DON'T TAKE KINDLY TO PERVERTS.
ゴゴゴ
HAAHH!
ゴゴ
ゴゴ
HMM?
AUUH...
...I'M NOT...
HEY, SLACKERS GUESS WHAT?
WE'VE GOT A NEW RECRUIT DROPPING BY FOR A TOUR ...
...OR THEN AGAIN ...
HUH, YOU'RE A GIRL?
...GUESS SHE'S ALREADY HERE.
OH ME, OH MY.

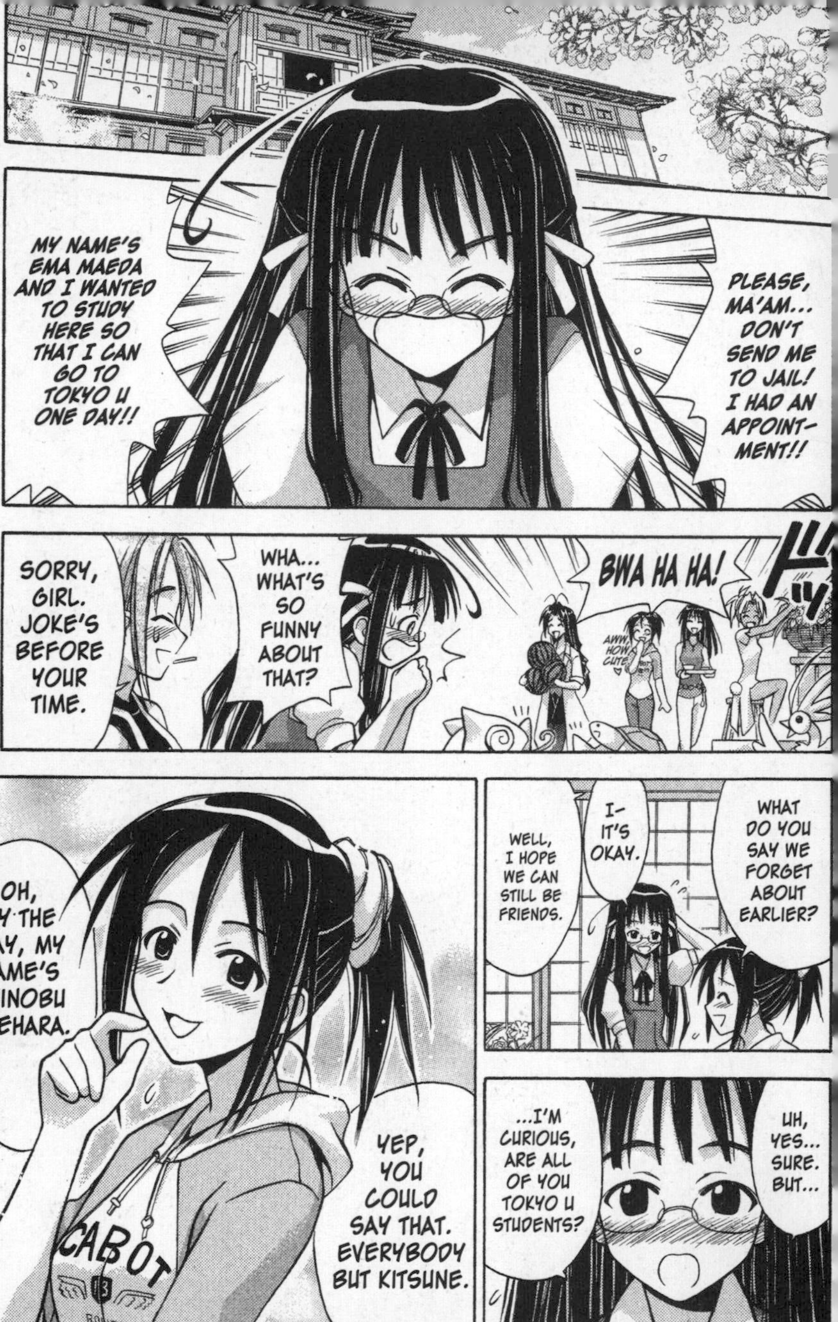
PLEASE, MA'AM... DON'T SEND ME TO JAIL! I HAD AN APPOINTMENT!!
MY NAME'S EMA MAEDA AND I WANTED TO STUDY HERE SO THAT I CAN GO TO TOKYO U ONE DAY!!
BWA HA HA!
AWW, HOW CUTE.
WHA... WHAT'S SO FUNNY ABOUT THAT?
SORRY, GIRL. JOKE'S BEFORE YOUR TIME.
WHAT DO YOU SAY WE FORGET ABOUT EARLIER?
I- IT'S OKAY.
WELL, I HOPE WE CAN STILL BE FRIENDS.
UH, YES... SURE. BUT...
...I'M CURIOUS, ARE ALL OF YOU TOKYO U STUDENTS?
OH, BY THE WAY, MY NAME'S SHINOBU MAEHARA.
YEP, YOU COULD SAY THAT. EVERYBODY BUT KITSUNE.
CABOT
13
ROUTINE

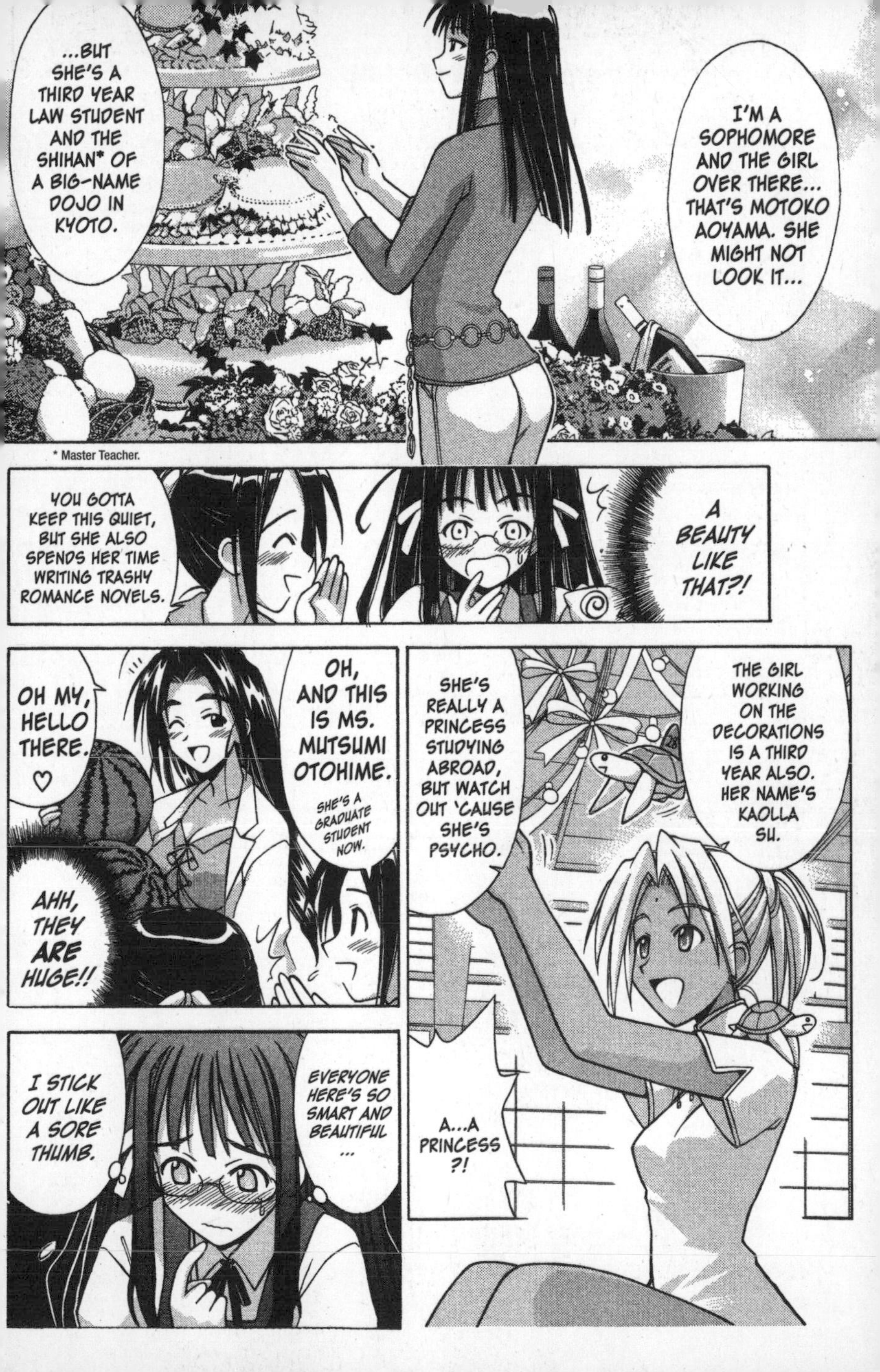
I'M A SOPHOMORE AND THE GIRL OVER THERE... THAT'S MOTOKO AOYAMA. SHE MIGHT NOT LOOK IT...
...BUT SHE'S A THIRD YEAR LAW STUDENT AND THE SHIHAN* OF A BIG-NAME DOJO IN KYOTO.
* Master Teacher.
A BEAUTY LIKE THAT?!
YOU GOTTA KEEP THIS QUIET, BUT SHE ALSO SPENDS HER TIME WRITING TRASHY ROMANCE NOVELS.
THE GIRL WORKING ON THE DECORATIONS IS A THIRD YEAR ALSO. HER NAME'S KAOLLA SU.
SHE'S REALLY A PRINCESS STUDYING ABROAD, BUT WATCH OUT 'CAUSE SHE'S PSYCHO.
A...A PRINCESS ?!
OH, AND THIS IS MS. MUTSUMI OTOHIME.
SHE'S A GRADUATE STUDENT NOW.
OH MY, HELLO THERE. ♡
AHH, THEY ARE HUGE!!
EVERYONE HERE'S SO SMART AND BEAUTIFUL ...
I STICK OUT LIKE A SORE THUMB.

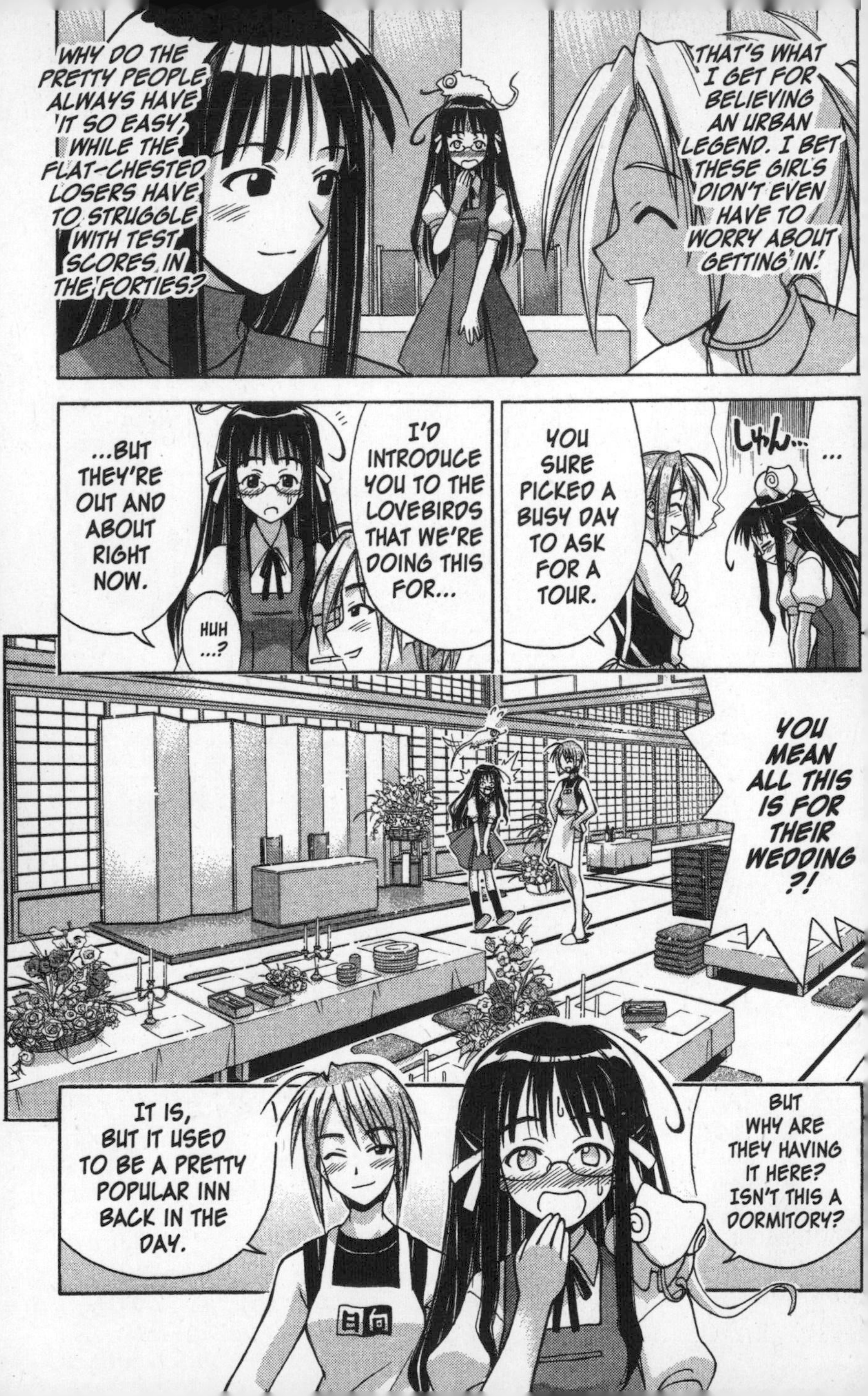
THAT'S WHAT I GET FOR BELIEVING AN URBAN LEGEND. I BET THESE GIRLS DIDN'T EVEN HAVE TO WORRY ABOUT GETTING IN.
WHY DO THE PRETTY PEOPLE ALWAYS HAVE IT SO EASY, WHILE THE FLAT-CHESTED LOSERS HAVE TO STRUGGLE WITH TEST SCORES IN THE FORTIES?
しゅん...
...
YOU SURE PICKED A BUSY DAY TO ASK FOR A TOUR.
I'D INTRODUCE YOU TO THE LOVEBIRDS THAT WE'RE DOING THIS FOR...
...BUT THEY'RE OUT AND ABOUT RIGHT NOW.
HUH ...?
YOU MEAN ALL THIS IS FOR THEIR WEDDING?!
BUT WHY ARE THEY HAVING IT HERE? ISN'T THIS A DORMITORY?
IT IS, BUT IT USED TO BE A PRETTY POPULAR INN BACK IN THE DAY.
日向

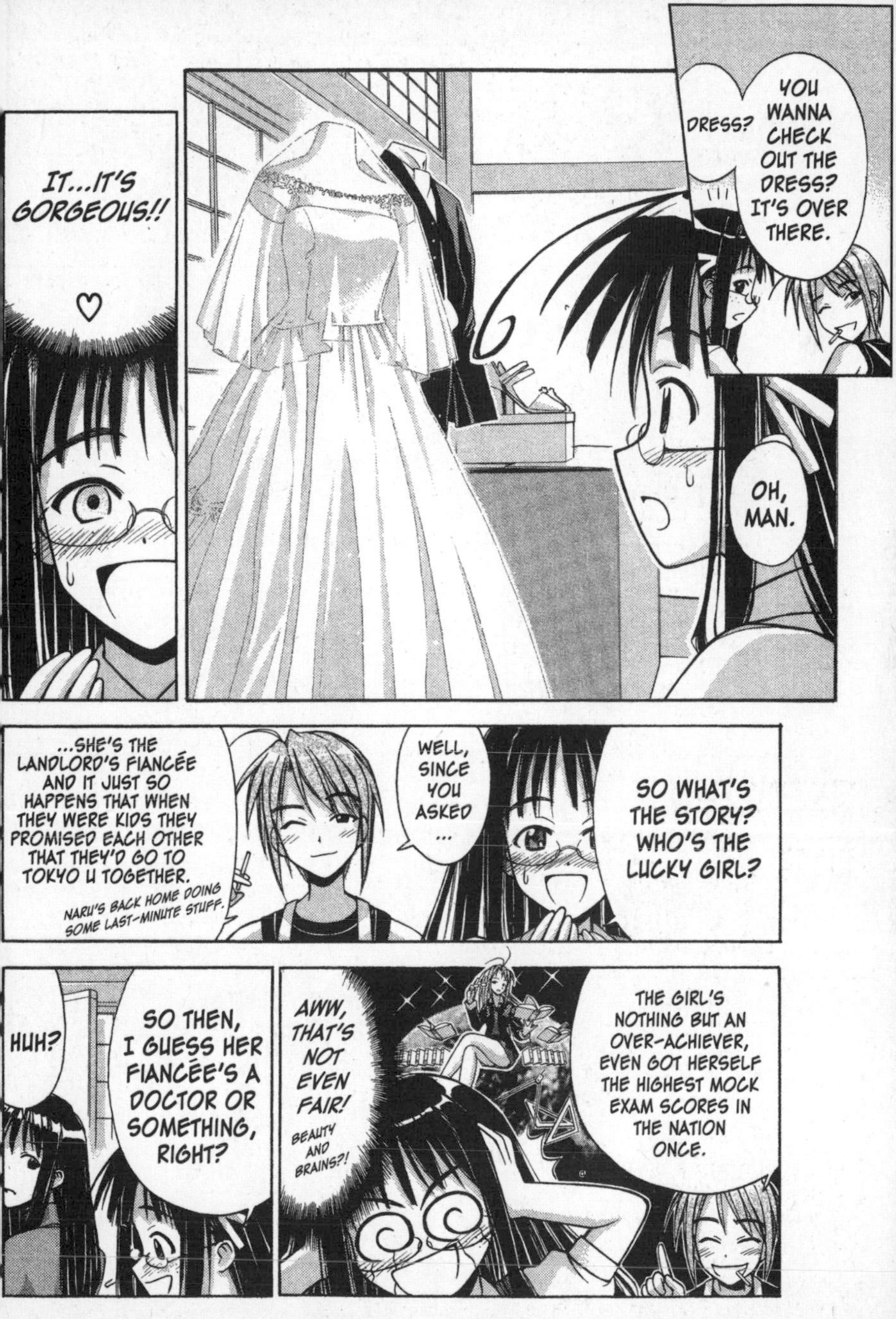
YOU WANNA CHECK OUT THE DRESS? IT'S OVER THERE.
DRESS?
OH, MAN.
IT...IT'S GORGEOUS!!
SO WHAT'S THE STORY? WHO'S THE LUCKY GIRL?
WELL, SINCE YOU ASKED ...
...SHE'S THE LANDLORD'S FIANCÉE AND IT JUST SO HAPPENS THAT WHEN THEY WERE KIDS THEY PROMISED EACH OTHER THAT THEY'D GO TO TOKYO U TOGETHER.
NARU'S BACK HOME DOING SOME LAST-MINUTE STUFF.
THE GIRL'S NOTHING BUT AN OVER-ACHIEVER, EVEN GOT HERSELF THE HIGHEST MOCK EXAM SCORES IN THE NATION ONCE.
AWW, THAT'S NOT EVEN FAIR!
BEAUTY AND BRAINS?!
SO THEN, I GUESS HER FIANCÉE'S A DOCTOR OR SOMETHING, RIGHT?
HUH?

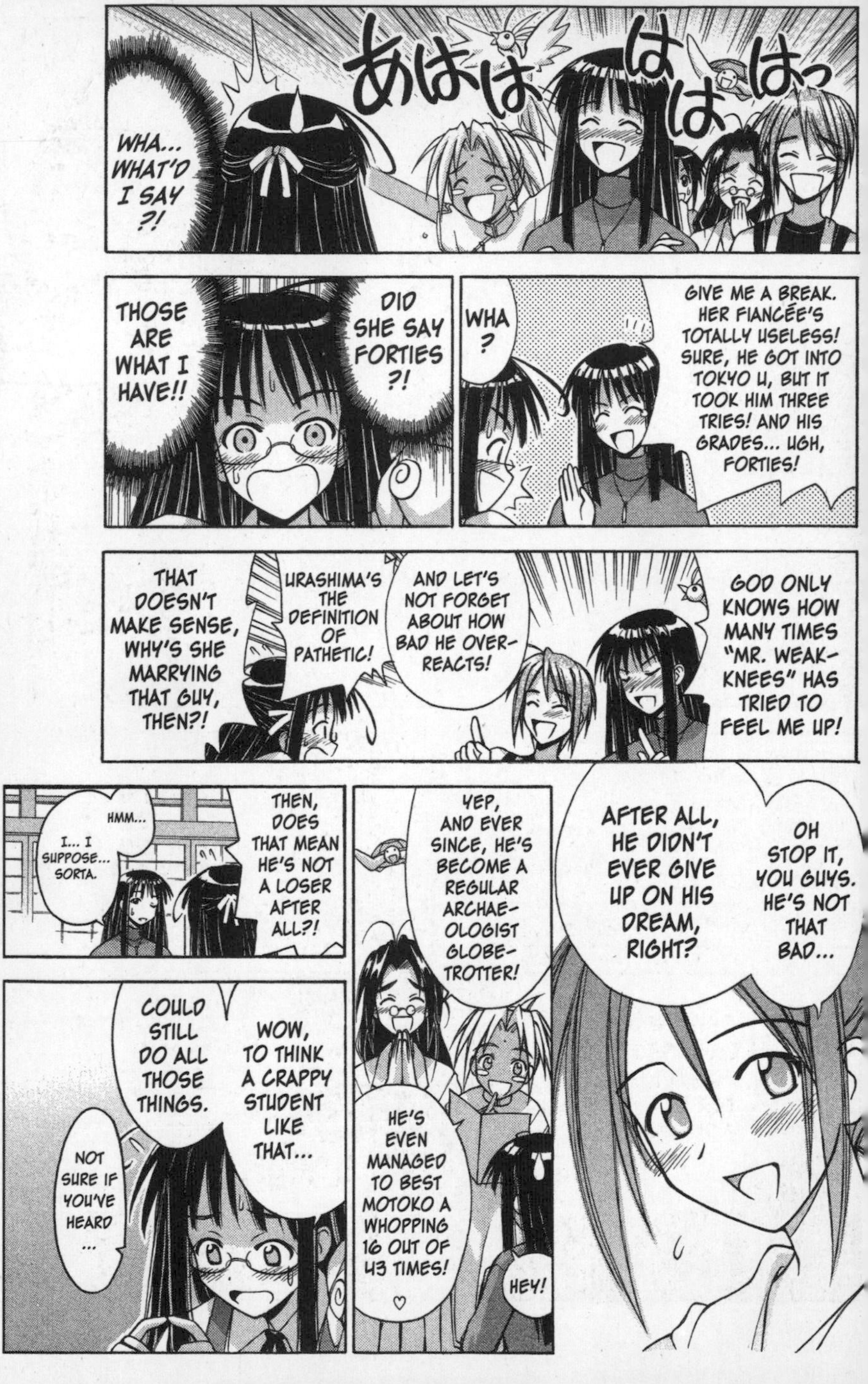
あはははははっ
WHA... WHAT'D I SAY ?!
GIVE ME A BREAK. HER FIANCÉE'S TOTALLY USELESS! SURE, HE GOT INTO TOKYO U, BUT IT TOOK HIM THREE TRIES! AND HIS GRADES... UGH, FORTIES!
WHA ?
DID SHE SAY FORTIES ?!
THOSE ARE WHAT I HAVE!!
GOD ONLY KNOWS HOW MANY TIMES "MR. WEAK-KNEES" HAS TRIED TO FEEL ME UP!
AND LET'S NOT FORGET ABOUT HOW BAD HE OVER-REACTS!
URASHIMA'S THE DEFINITION OF PATHETIC!
THAT DOESN'T MAKE SENSE, WHY'S SHE MARRYING THAT GUY, THEN?!
OH STOP IT, YOU GUYS. HE'S NOT THAT BAD...
AFTER ALL, HE DIDN'T EVER GIVE UP ON HIS DREAM, RIGHT?
YEP, AND EVER SINCE, HE'S BECOME A REGULAR ARCHAE-OLOGIST GLOBE-TROTTER!
HE'S EVEN MANAGED TO BEST MOTOKO A WHOPPING 16 OUT OF 43 TIMES! ♡
HEY!
THEN, DOES THAT MEAN HE'S NOT A LOSER AFTER ALL?!
HMM...
I... I SUPPOSE... SORTA.
WOW, TO THINK A CRAPPY STUDENT LIKE THAT...
COULD STILL DO ALL THOSE THINGS.
NOT SURE IF YOU'VE HEARD ...

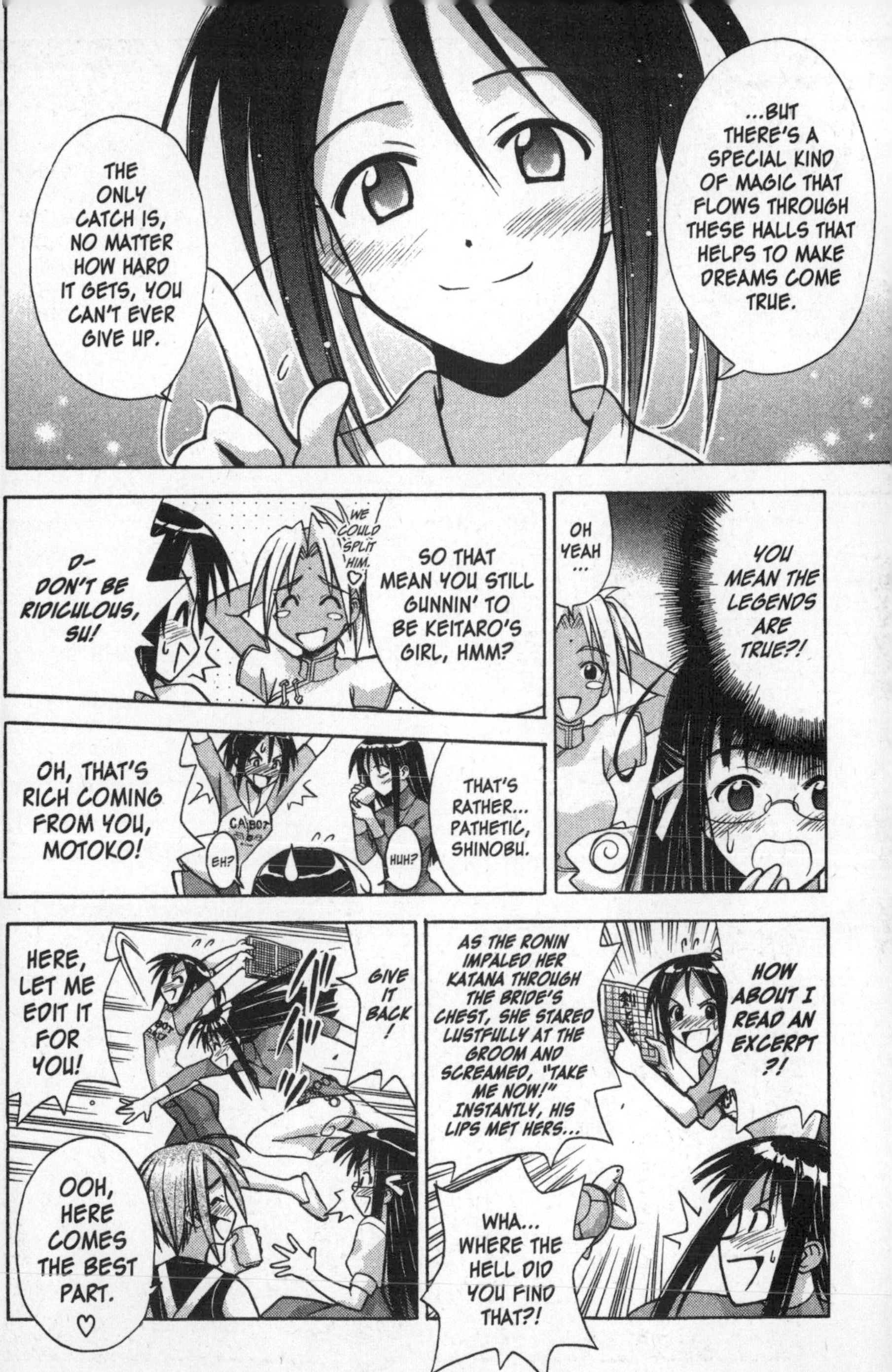
...BUT THERE'S A SPECIAL KIND OF MAGIC THAT FLOWS THROUGH THESE HALLS THAT HELPS TO MAKE DREAMS COME TRUE.
THE ONLY CATCH IS, NO MATTER HOW HARD IT GETS, YOU CAN'T EVER GIVE UP.
YOU MEAN THE LEGENDS ARE TRUE?!
OH YEAH ...
SO THAT MEAN YOU STILL GUNNIN' TO BE KEITARO'S GIRL, HMM?
WE COULD SPLIT HIM. ♡
D-DON'T BE RIDICULOUS, SU!
THAT'S RATHER... PATHETIC, SHINOBU.
HUH?
EH?
OH, THAT'S RICH COMING FROM YOU, MOTOKO!
HOW ABOUT I READ AN EXCERPT ?!
AS THE RONIN IMPALED HER KATANA THROUGH THE BRIDE'S CHEST, SHE STARED LUSTFULLY AT THE GROOM AND SCREAMED, "TAKE ME NOW!" INSTANTLY, HIS LIPS MET HERS...
WHA... WHERE THE HELL DID YOU FIND THAT?!
GIVE IT BACK!
HERE, LET ME EDIT IT FOR YOU!
OOH, HERE COMES THE BEST PART. ♡

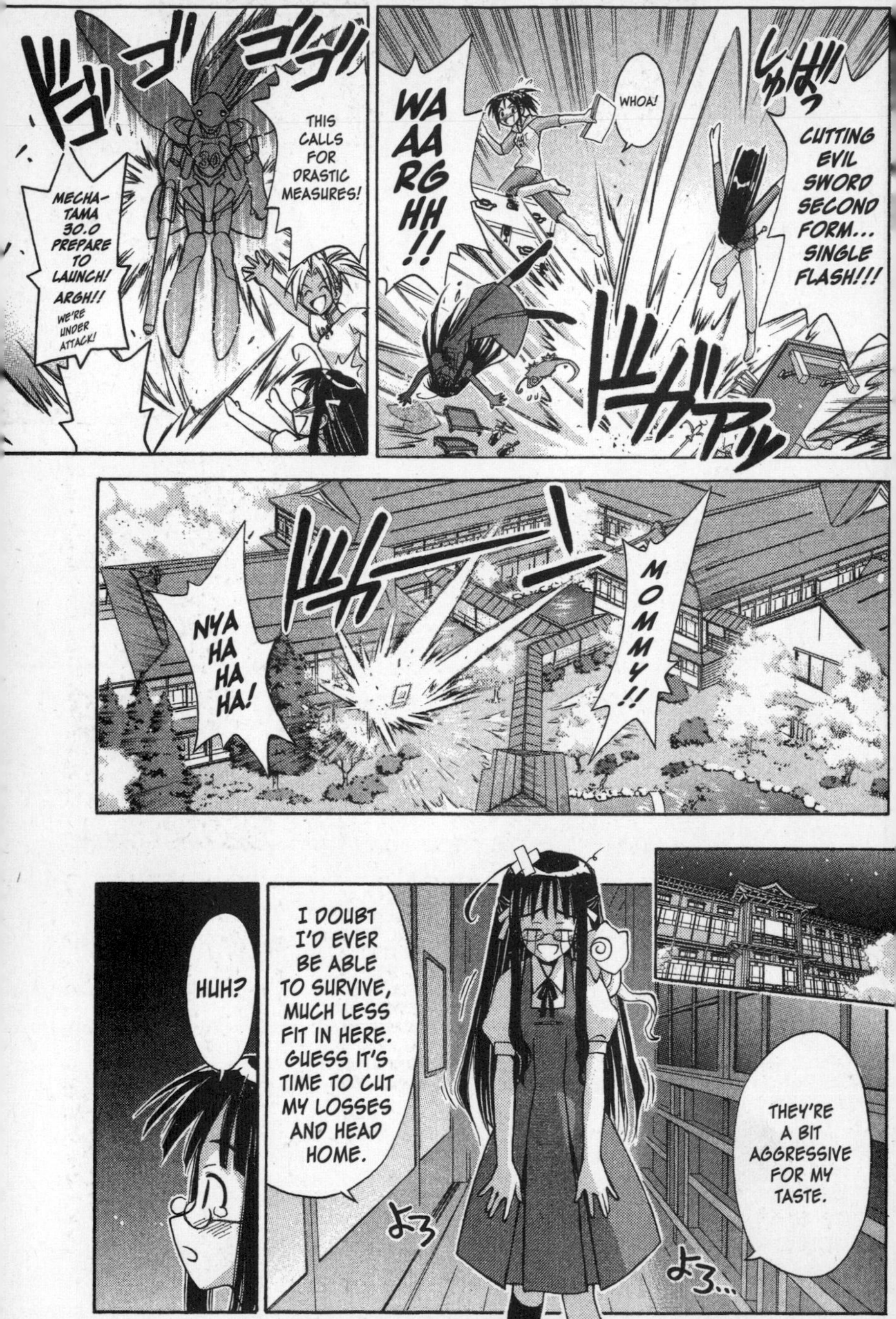
しゅばっ
CUTTING EVIL SWORD SECOND FORM... SINGLE FLASH!!!
WHOA!
WAAARGHH!!
THIS CALLS FOR DRASTIC MEASURES!
MECHATAMA 30.0 PREPARE TO LAUNCH!
ARGH!! WE'RE UNDER ATTACK!
MOMMY!!
NYA HA HA HA HA!
THEY'RE A BIT AGGRESSIVE FOR MY TASTE.
I DOUBT I'D EVER BE ABLE TO SURVIVE, MUCH LESS FIT IN HERE. GUESS IT'S TIME TO CUT MY LOSSES AND HEAD HOME.
よろ
よろ...
HUH?

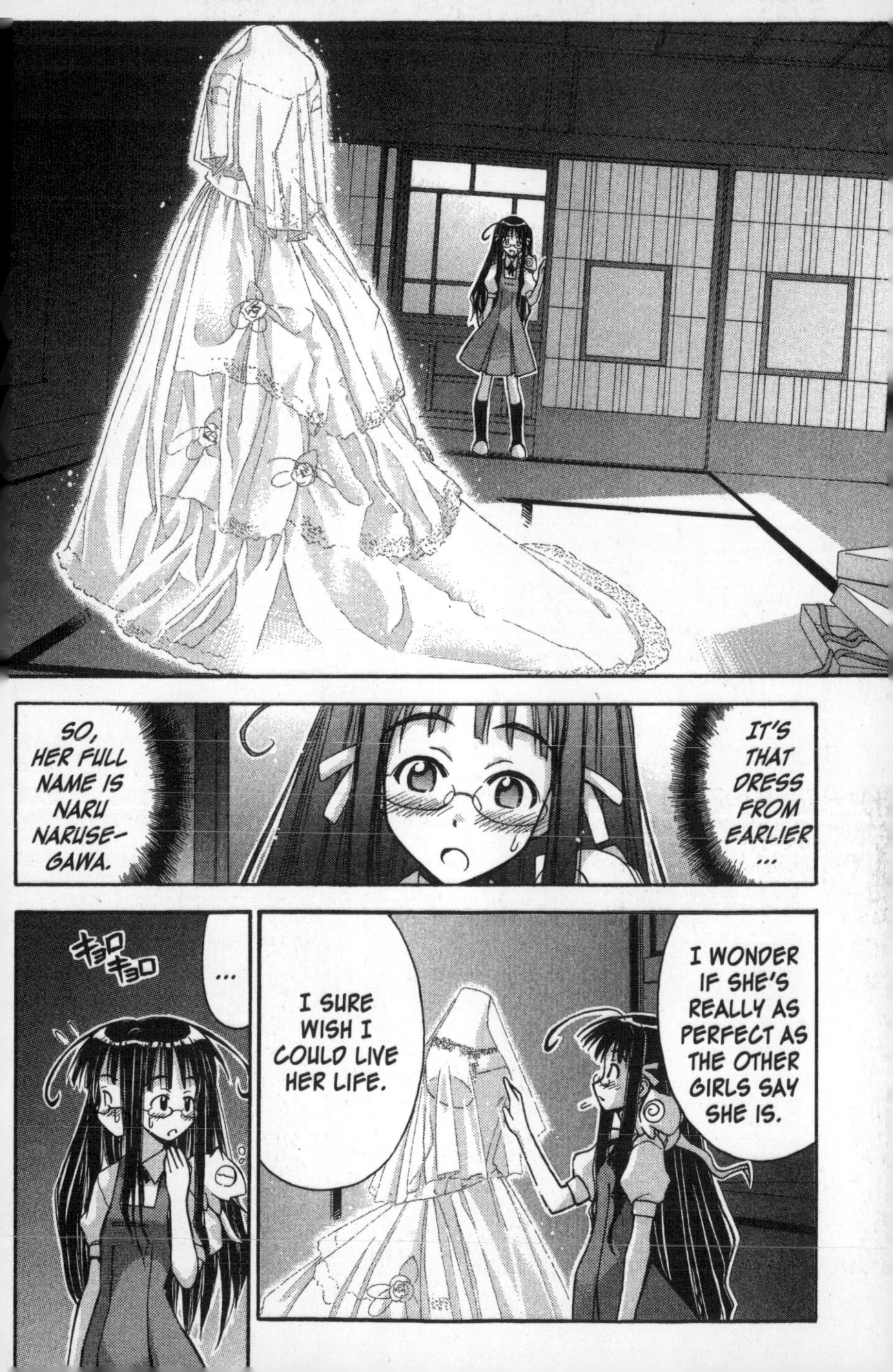
IT'S THAT DRESS FROM EARLIER...
SO, HER FULL NAME IS NARU NARUSE-GAWA.
I WONDER IF SHE'S REALLY AS PERFECT AS THE OTHER GIRLS SAY SHE IS.
I SURE WISH I COULD LIVE HER LIFE.
...
キョロキョロ

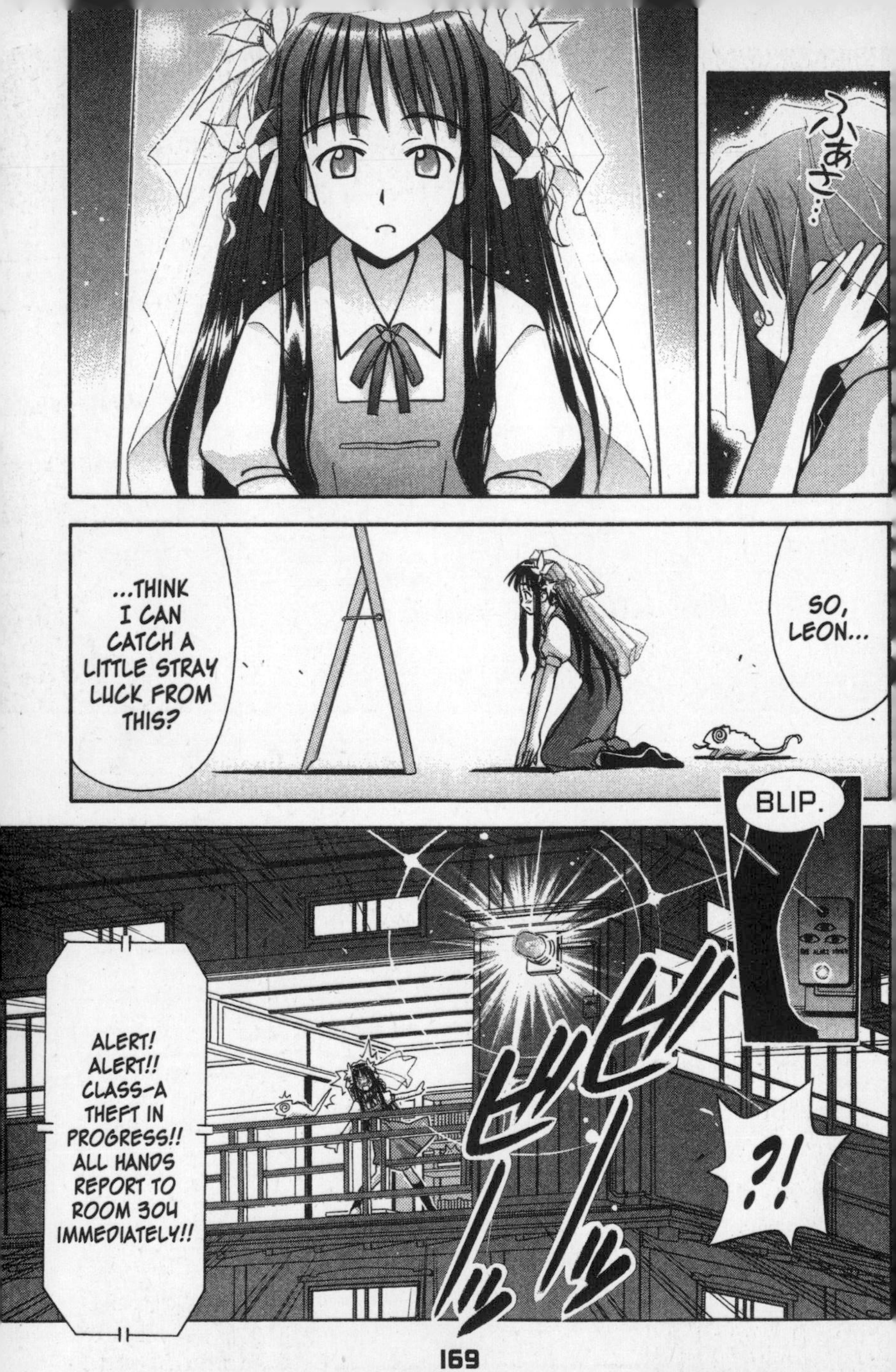
ふあさ…
SO, LEON...
...THINK I CAN CATCH A LITTLE STRAY LUCK FROM THIS?
BLIP.
?!
ALERT! ALERT!! CLASS-A THEFT IN PROGRESS!! ALL HANDS REPORT TO ROOM 304 IMMEDIATELY!!

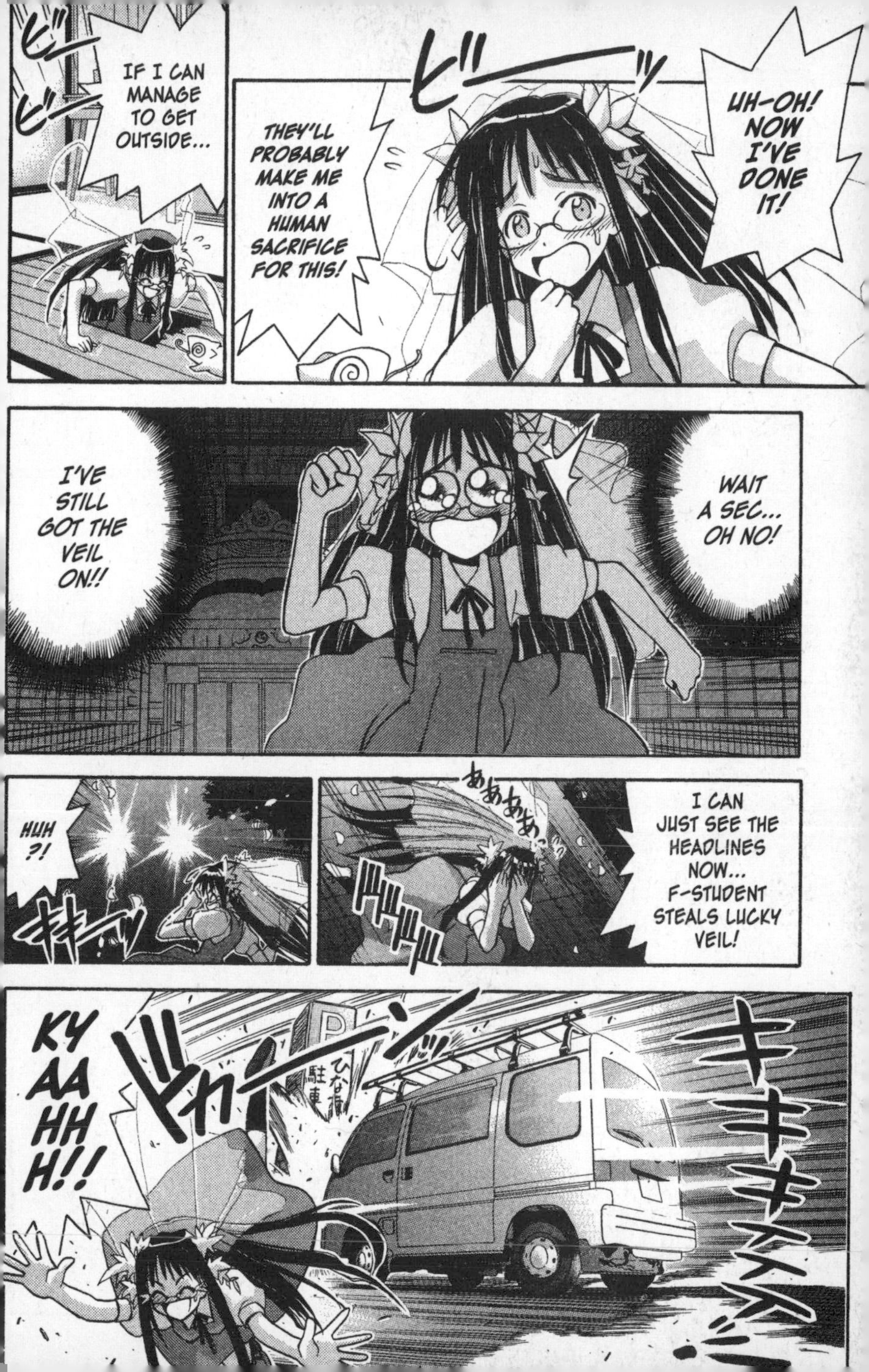
UH-OH! NOW I'VE DONE IT!
THEY'LL PROBABLY MAKE ME INTO A HUMAN SACRIFICE FOR THIS!
IF I CAN MANAGE TO GET OUTSIDE...
WAIT A SEC... OH NO!
I'VE STILL GOT THE VEIL ON!!
I CAN JUST SEE THE HEADLINES NOW... F-STUDENT STEALS LUCKY VEIL!
HUH ?!
KYAAHHHH!!

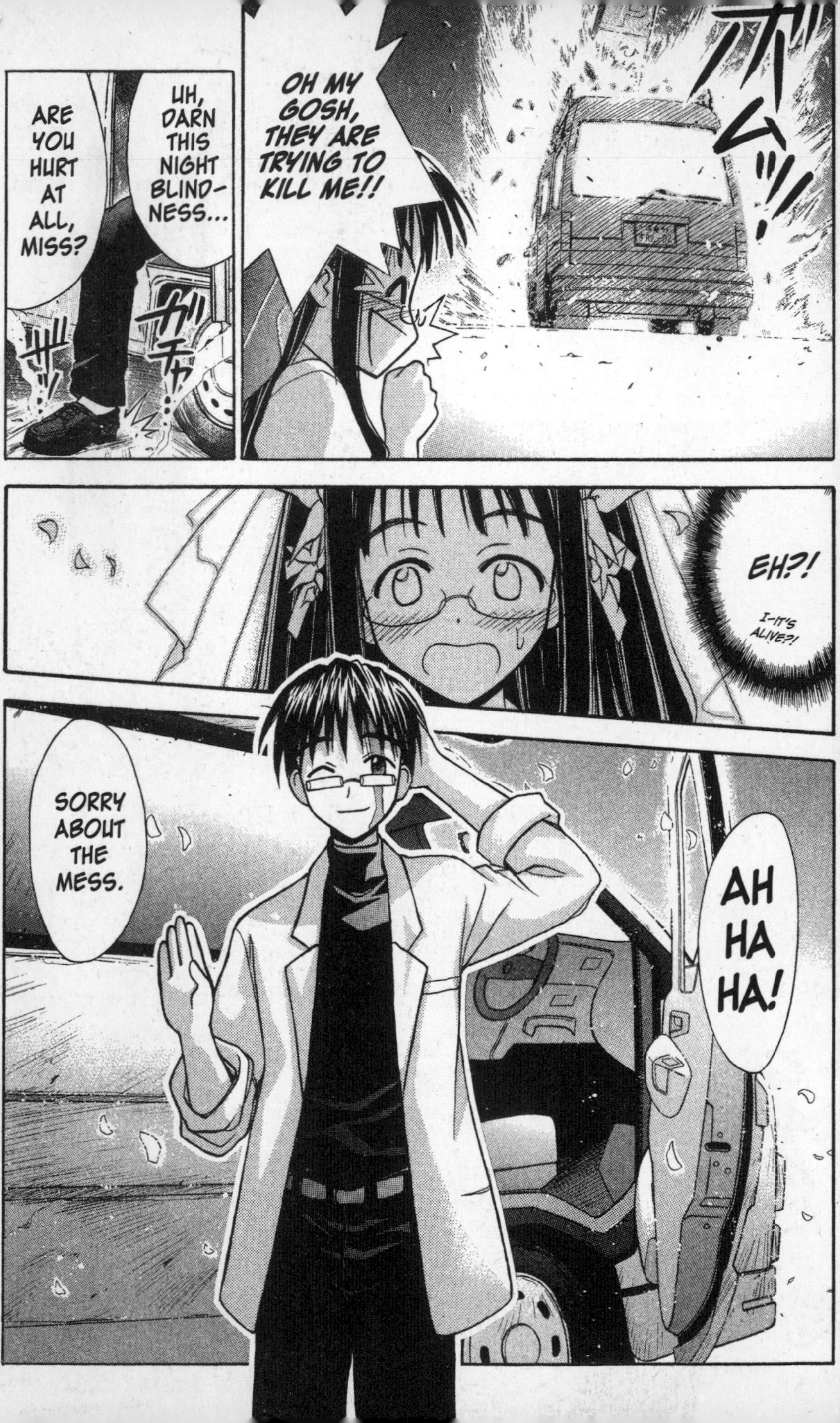
OH MY GOSH, THEY ARE TRYING TO KILL ME!!
UH, DARN THIS NIGHT BLIND-NESS...
ARE YOU HURT AT ALL, MISS?
EH?!
I-IT'S ALIVE?!
AH HA HA!
SORRY ABOUT THE MESS.

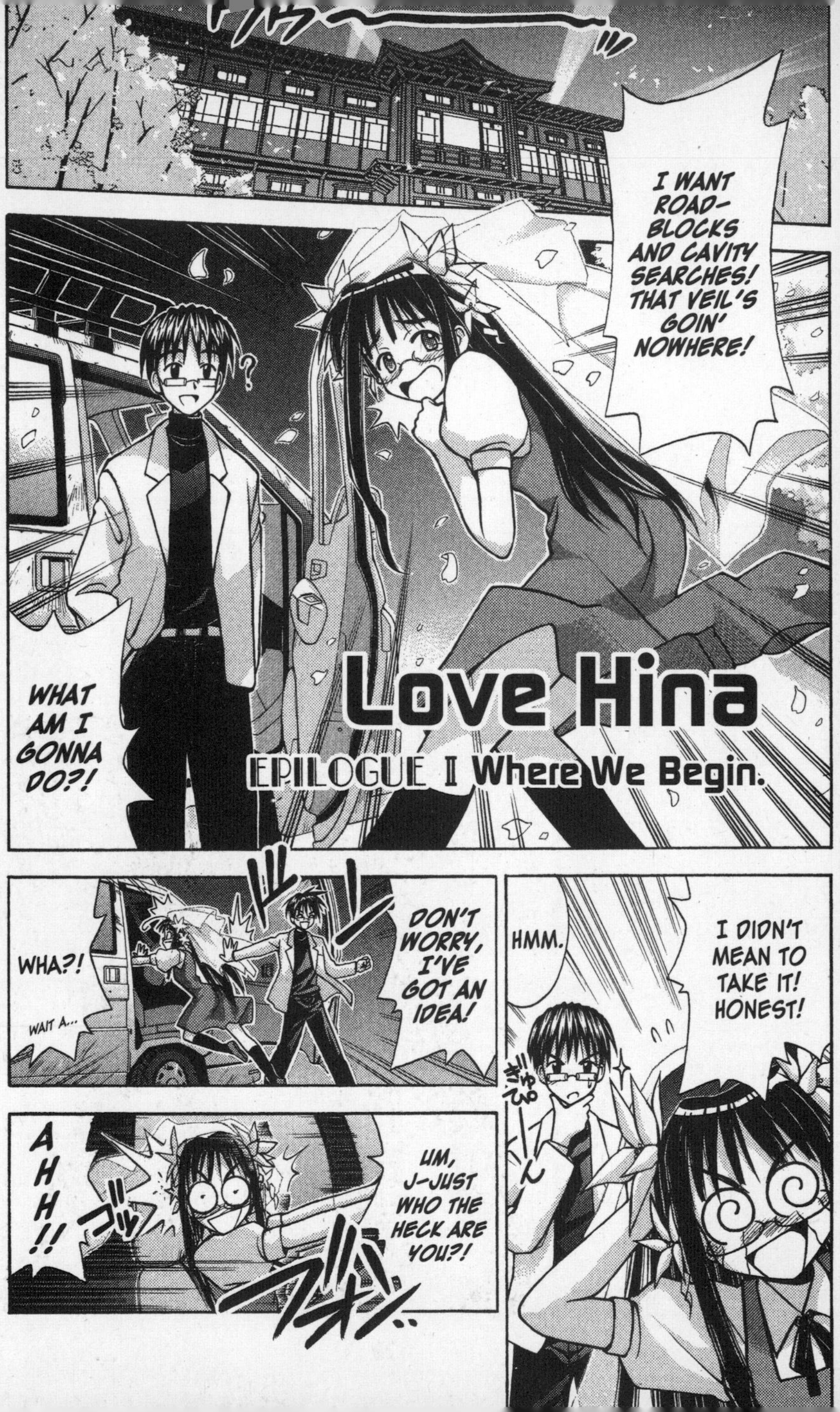
I WANT ROAD-BLOCKS AND CAVITY SEARCHES! THAT VEIL'S GOIN' NOWHERE!
Love Hina
EPILOGUE I Where We Begin.
WHAT AM I GONNA DO?!
I DIDN'T MEAN TO TAKE IT! HONEST!
HMM.
DON'T WORRY, I'VE GOT AN IDEA!
WHA?!
WAIT A...
UM, J-JUST WHO THE HECK ARE YOU?!
AHH!!

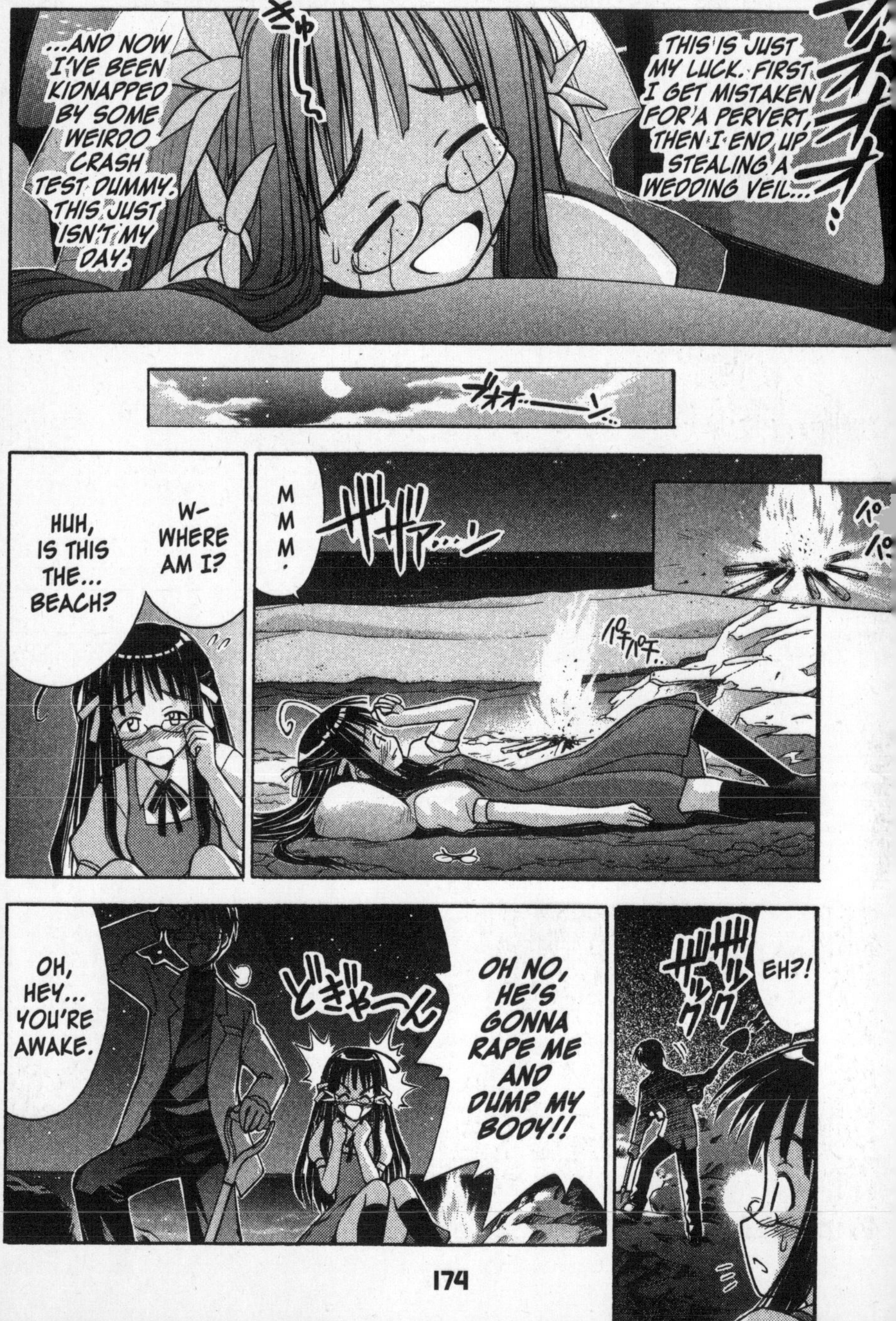
THIS IS JUST MY LUCK. FIRST I GET MISTAKEN FOR A PERVERT, THEN I END UP STEALING A WEDDING VEIL...
...AND NOW I'VE BEEN KIDNAPPED BY SOME WEIRDO CRASH TEST DUMMY. THIS JUST ISN'T MY DAY.
MMM.
W-WHERE AM I?
HUH, IS THIS THE... BEACH?
EH?!
OH, HEY... YOU'RE AWAKE.
OH NO, HE'S GONNA RAPE ME AND DUMP MY BODY!!

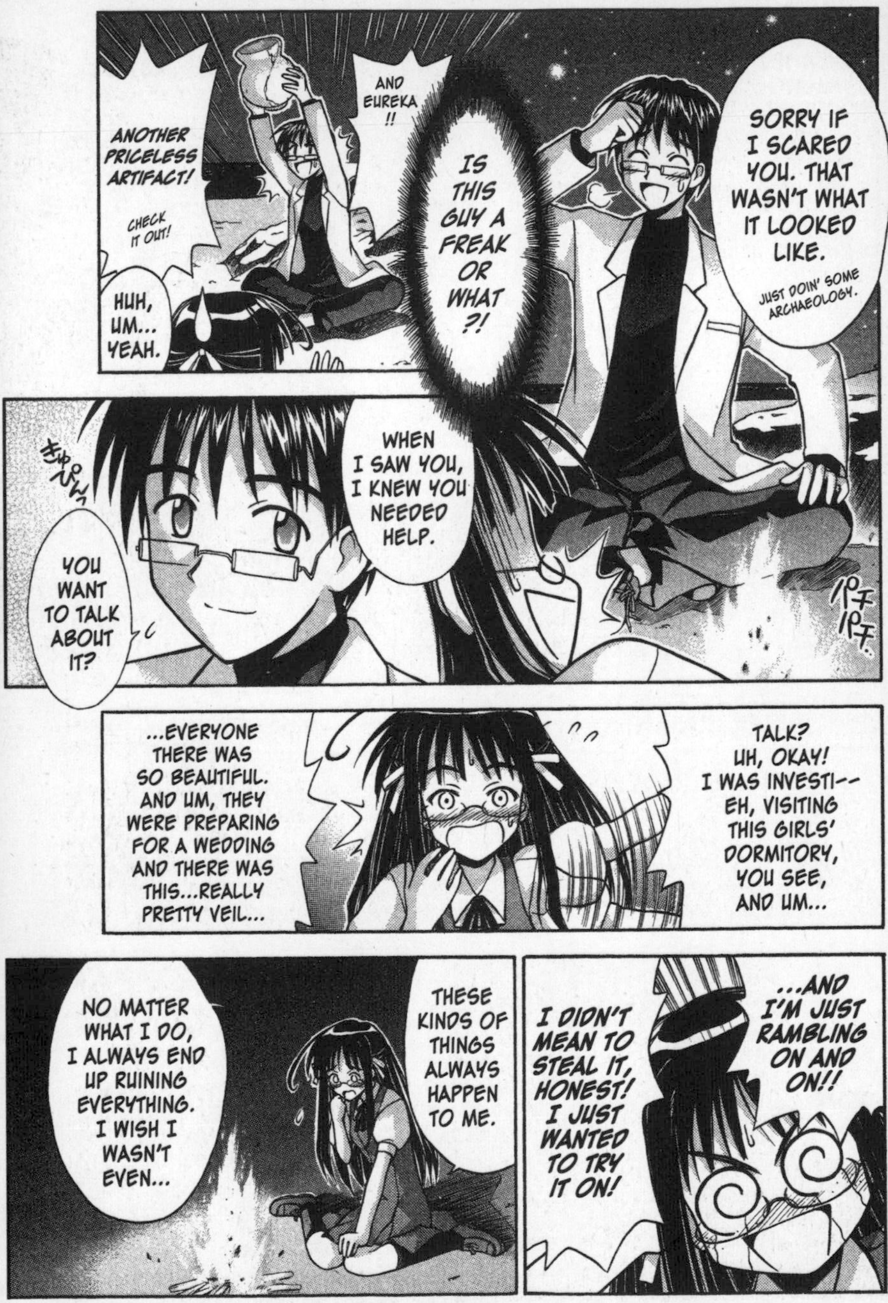
SORRY IF I SCARED YOU. THAT WASN'T WHAT IT LOOKED LIKE.
JUST DOIN' SOME ARCHAEOLOGY.
IS THIS GUY A FREAK OR WHAT?!
AND EUREKA!!
ANOTHER PRICELESS ARTIFACT!
CHECK IT OUT!
HUH, UM... YEAH.
パチパチ
WHEN I SAW YOU, I KNEW YOU NEEDED HELP.
YOU WANT TO TALK ABOUT IT?
TALK? UH, OKAY! I WAS INVESTI-- EH, VISITING THIS GIRLS' DORMITORY, YOU SEE, AND UM...
...EVERYONE THERE WAS SO BEAUTIFUL. AND UM, THEY WERE PREPARING FOR A WEDDING AND THERE WAS THIS...REALLY PRETTY VEIL...
...AND I'M JUST RAMBLING ON AND ON!!
I DIDN'T MEAN TO STEAL IT, HONEST! I JUST WANTED TO TRY IT ON!
THESE KINDS OF THINGS ALWAYS HAPPEN TO ME.
NO MATTER WHAT I DO, I ALWAYS END UP RUINING EVERYTHING. I WISH I WASN'T EVEN...

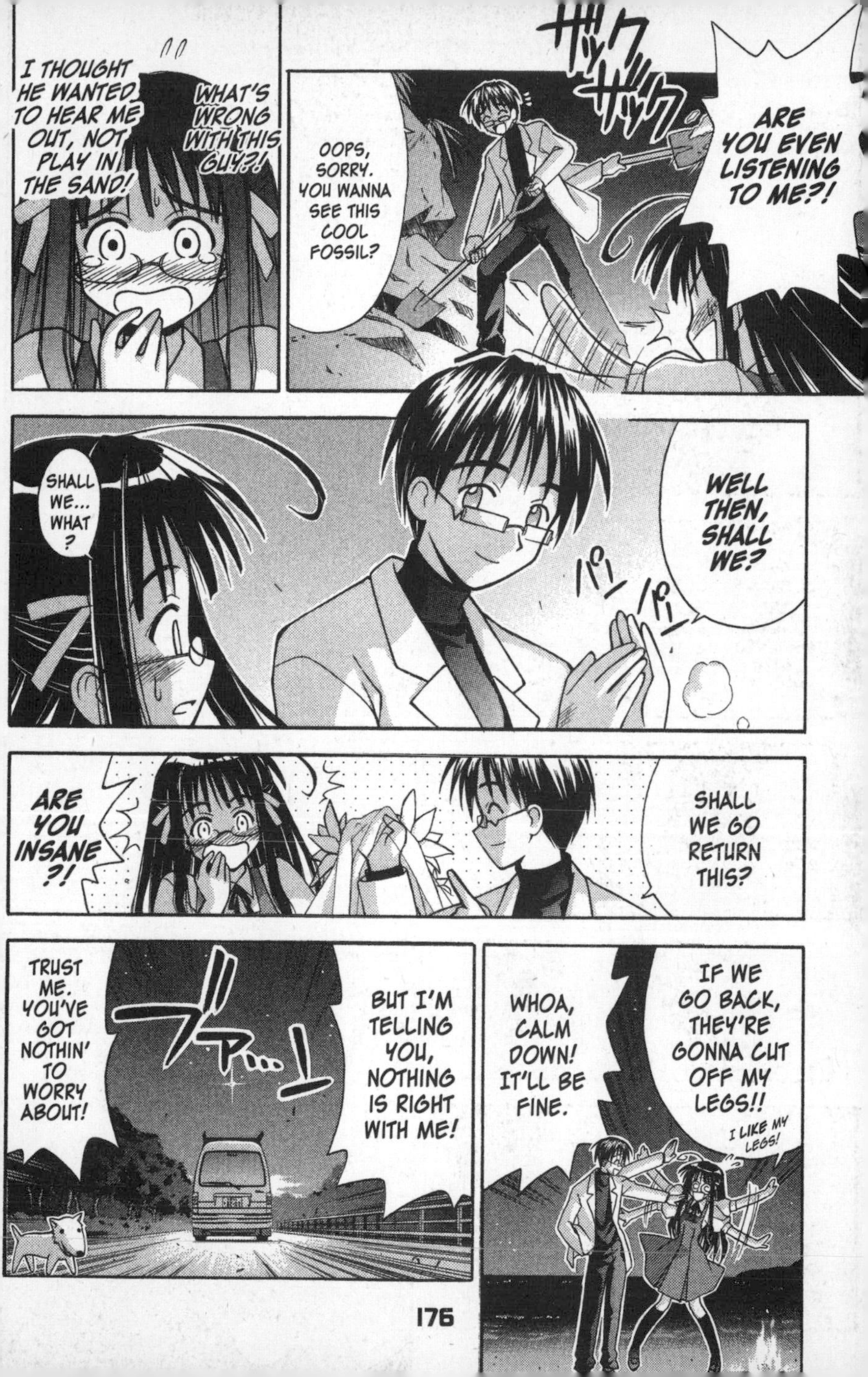
ARE YOU EVEN LISTENING TO ME?!
OOPS, SORRY. YOU WANNA SEE THIS COOL FOSSIL?
WHAT'S WRONG WITH THIS GUY?!
I THOUGHT HE WANTED TO HEAR ME OUT, NOT PLAY IN THE SAND!
WELL THEN, SHALL WE?
SHALL WE... WHAT?
SHALL WE GO RETURN THIS?
ARE YOU INSANE?!
IF WE GO BACK, THEY'RE GONNA CUT OFF MY LEGS!!
I LIKE MY LEGS!
WHOA, CALM DOWN! IT'LL BE FINE.
BUT I'M TELLING YOU, NOTHING IS RIGHT WITH ME!
TRUST ME. YOU'VE GOT NOTHIN' TO WORRY ABOUT!

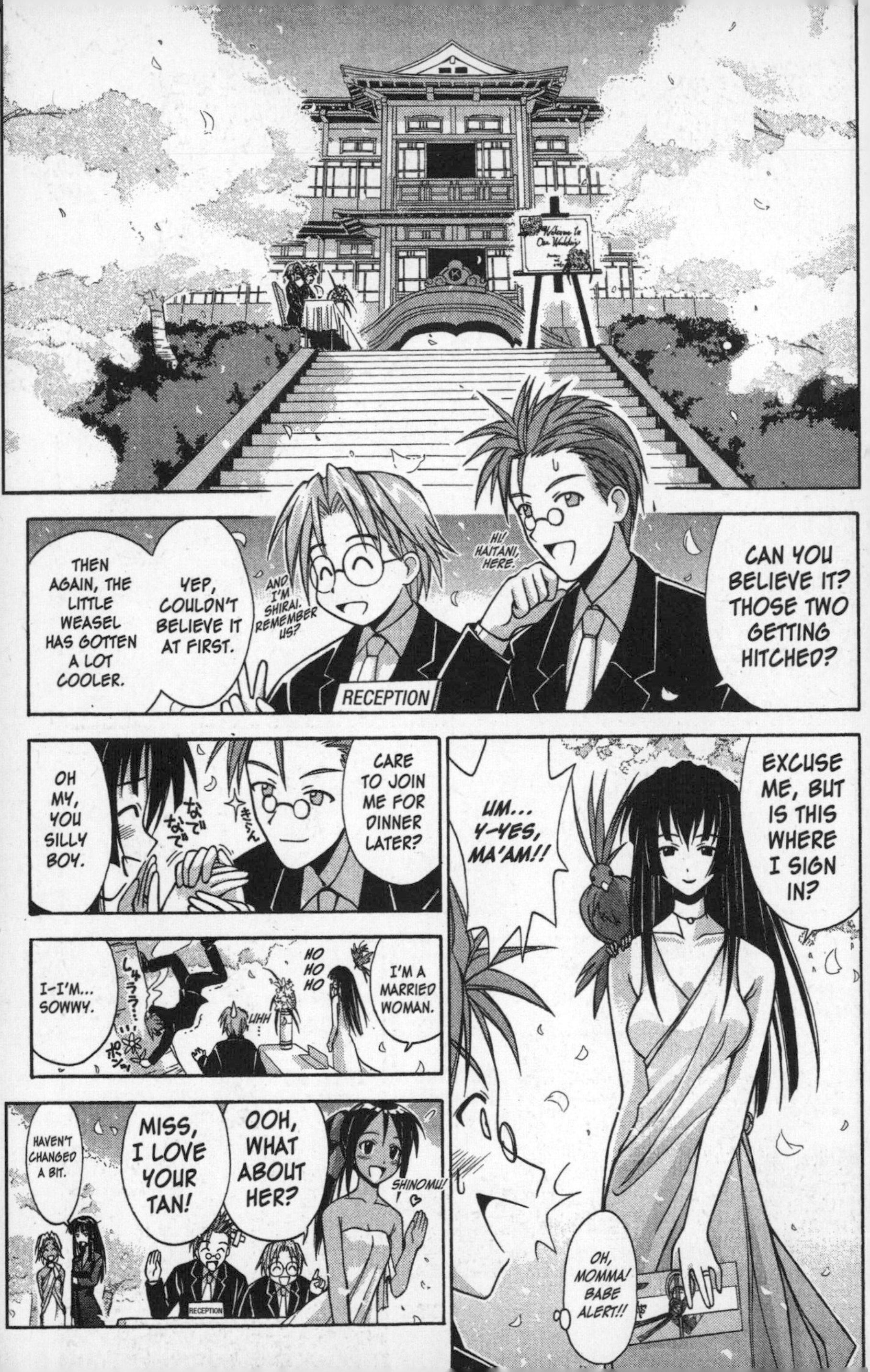

CAN YOU BELIEVE IT? THOSE TWO GETTING HITCHED?
HI! HAITANI, HERE.
AND I'M SHIRAI. REMEMBER US?
YEP, COULDN'T BELIEVE IT AT FIRST.
THEN AGAIN, THE LITTLE WEASEL HAS GOTTEN A LOT COOLER.
RECEPTION
EXCUSE ME, BUT IS THIS WHERE I SIGN IN?
UM... Y-YES, MA'AM!!
OH, MOMMA! BABE ALERT!!
CARE TO JOIN ME FOR DINNER LATER?
きらん
なでなで
OH MY, YOU SILLY BOY.
I'M A MARRIED WOMAN.
HO HO HO
UHH...
しゅらら…
ポンッ
I-I'M... SOWWY.
SHINOMU!
OOH, WHAT ABOUT HER?
MISS, I LOVE YOUR TAN!
HAVEN'T CHANGED A BIT.
RECEPTION

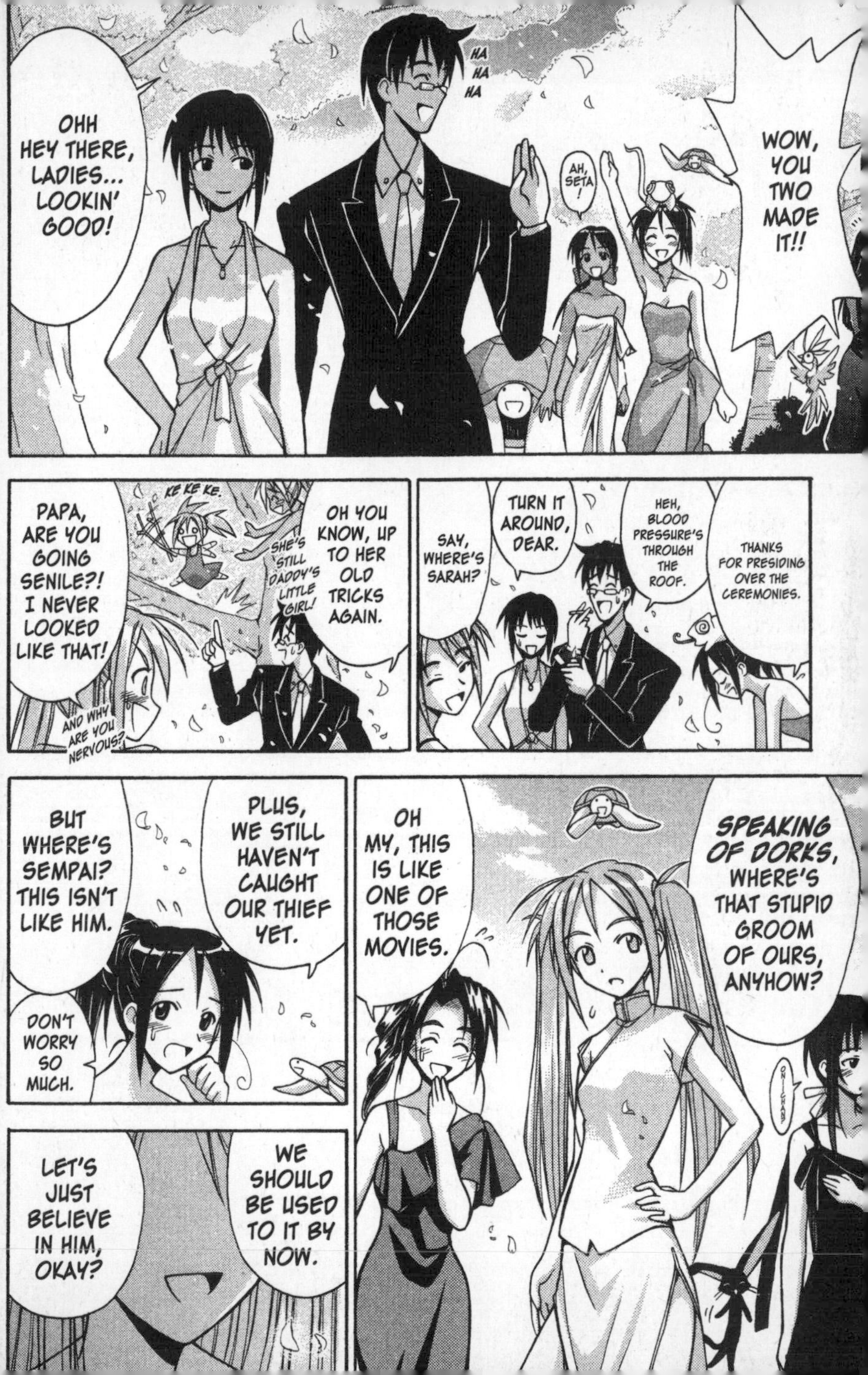
WOW, YOU TWO MADE IT!!
AH, SETA!
HA HA HA
OHH HEY THERE, LADIES... LOOKIN' GOOD!
THANKS FOR PRESIDING OVER THE CEREMONIES.
HEH, BLOOD PRESSURE'S THROUGH THE ROOF.
TURN IT AROUND, DEAR.
SAY, WHERE'S SARAH?
OH YOU KNOW, UP TO HER OLD TRICKS AGAIN.
SHE'S STILL DADDY'S LITTLE GIRL!
KE KE KE.
PAPA, ARE YOU GOING SENILE?! I NEVER LOOKED LIKE THAT!
AND WHY ARE YOU NERVOUS?
SPEAKING OF DORKS, WHERE'S THAT STUPID GROOM OF OURS, ANYHOW?
ONICHAN?
OH MY, THIS IS LIKE ONE OF THOSE MOVIES.
PLUS, WE STILL HAVEN'T CAUGHT OUR THIEF YET.
BUT WHERE'S SEMPAI? THIS ISN'T LIKE HIM.
DON'T WORRY SO MUCH.
WE SHOULD BE USED TO IT BY NOW.
LET'S JUST BELIEVE IN HIM, OKAY?

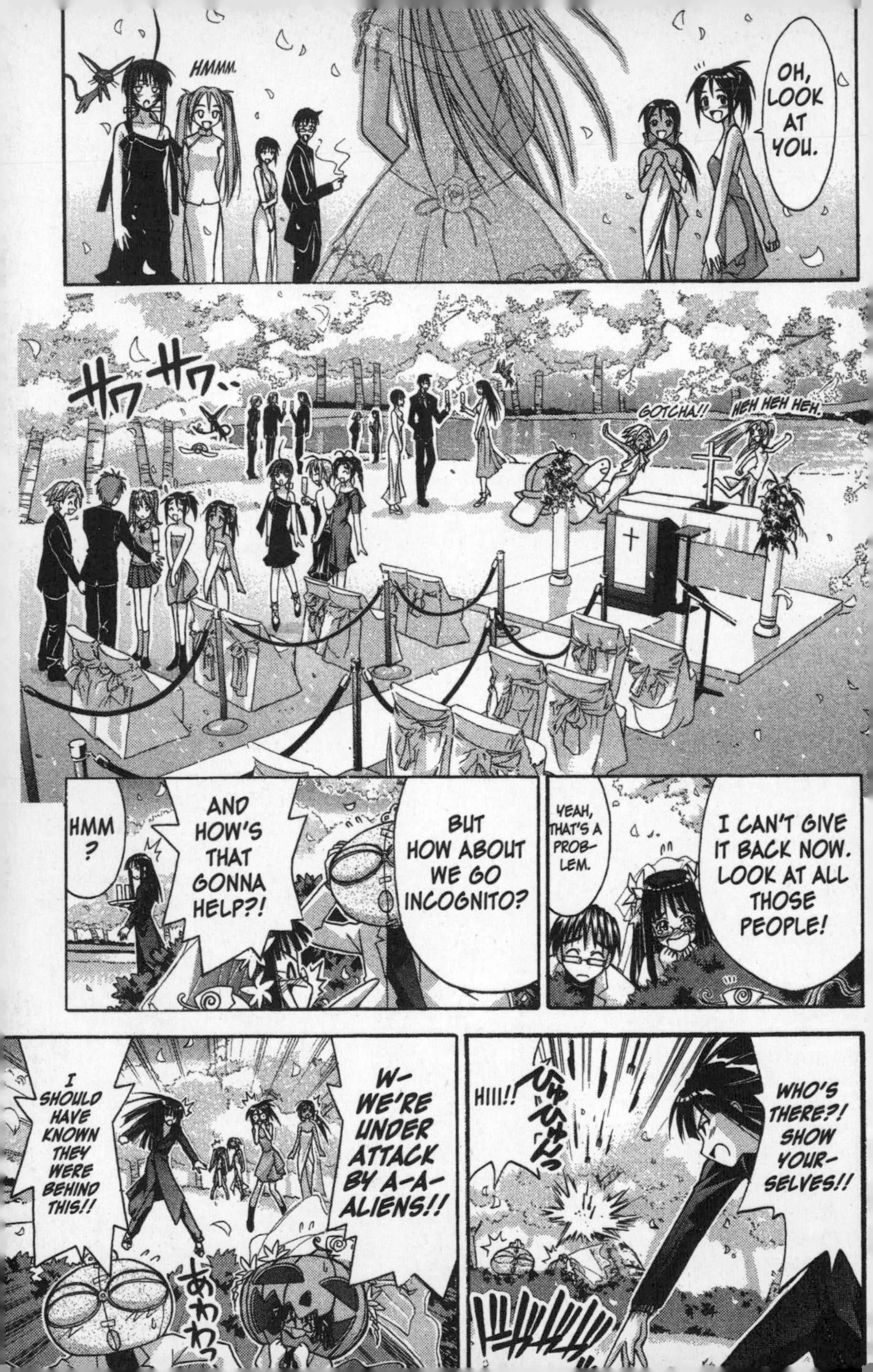
OH, LOOK AT YOU.
HMMM.
HEH HEH HEH.
GOTCHA!!
サワサワ…
I CAN'T GIVE IT BACK NOW. LOOK AT ALL THOSE PEOPLE!
YEAH, THAT'S A PROBLEM.
BUT HOW ABOUT WE GO INCOGNITO?
AND HOW'S THAT GONNA HELP?!
HMM?
WHO'S THERE?! SHOW YOURSELVES!!
ひゅひゅんっ
HIII!!
W-WE'RE UNDER ATTACK BY A-A-ALIENS!!
あわわっ
I SHOULD HAVE KNOWN THEY WERE BEHIND THIS!!

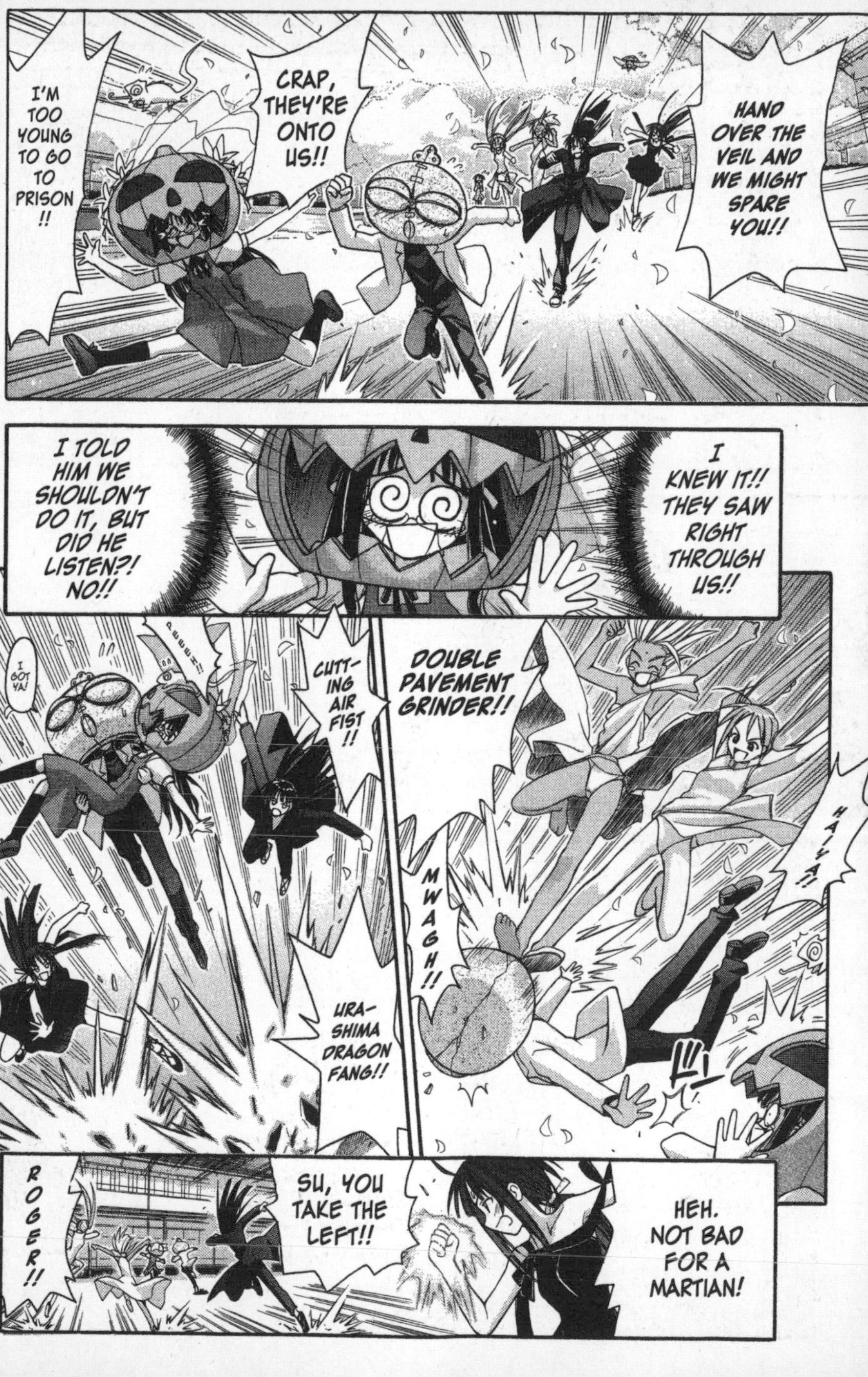
HAND OVER THE VEIL AND WE MIGHT SPARE YOU!!
CRAP, THEY'RE ONTO US!!
I'M TOO YOUNG TO GO TO PRISON!!
I KNEW IT!! THEY SAW RIGHT THROUGH US!!
I TOLD HIM WE SHOULDN'T DO IT, BUT DID HE LISTEN?! NO!!
HAIYA!!
DOUBLE PAVEMENT GRINDER!!
MWAGH!!
CUTTING-AIR FIST!!
I GOT YA!
URA-SHIMA DRAGON FANG!!
HEH. NOT BAD FOR A MARTIAN!
SU, YOU TAKE THE LEFT!!
ROGER!!

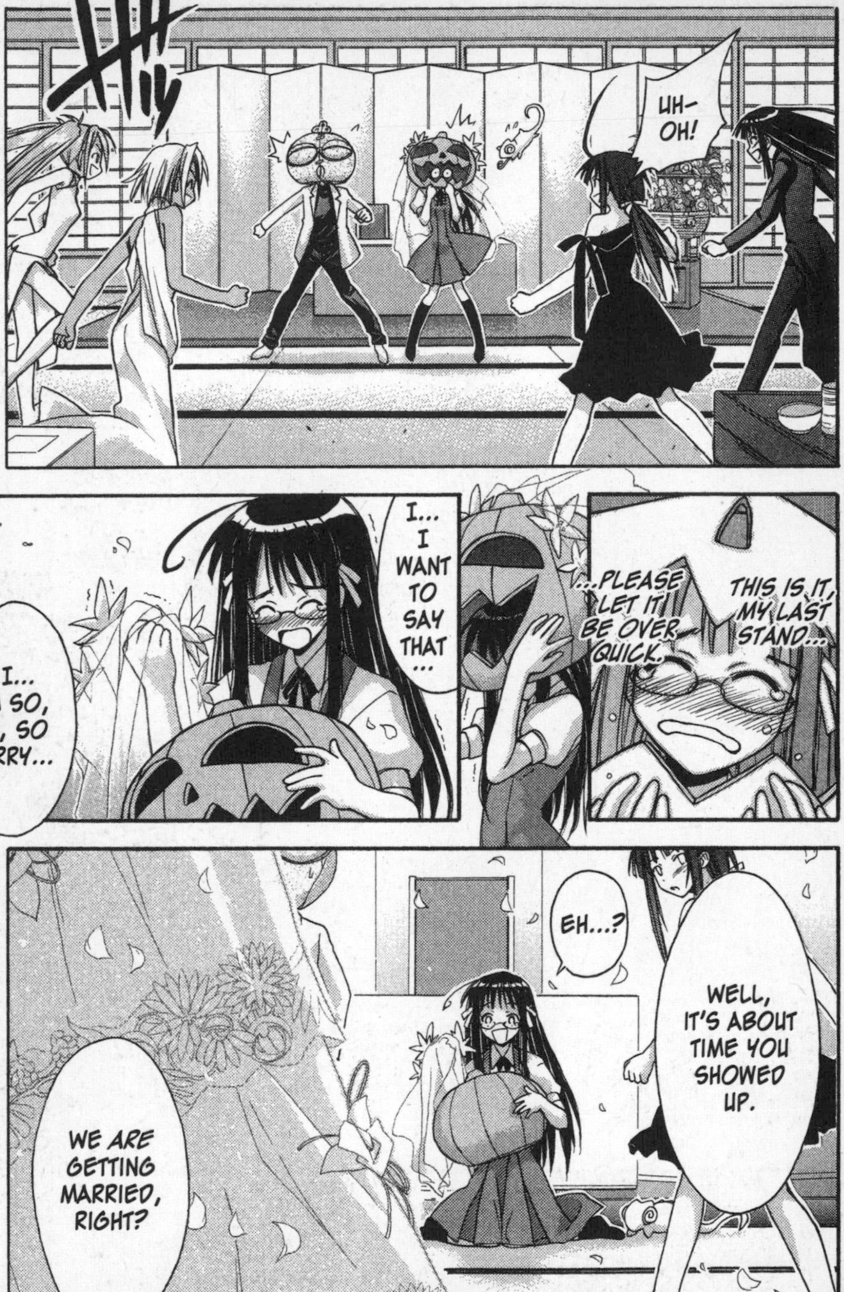
UH-OH!
THIS IS IT, MY LAST STAND...
...PLEASE LET IT BE OVER QUICK.
I... I WANT TO SAY THAT ...
...I... I'M SO, SO, SO SORRY...
WELL, IT'S ABOUT TIME YOU SHOWED UP.
EH...?
WE ARE GETTING MARRIED, RIGHT?

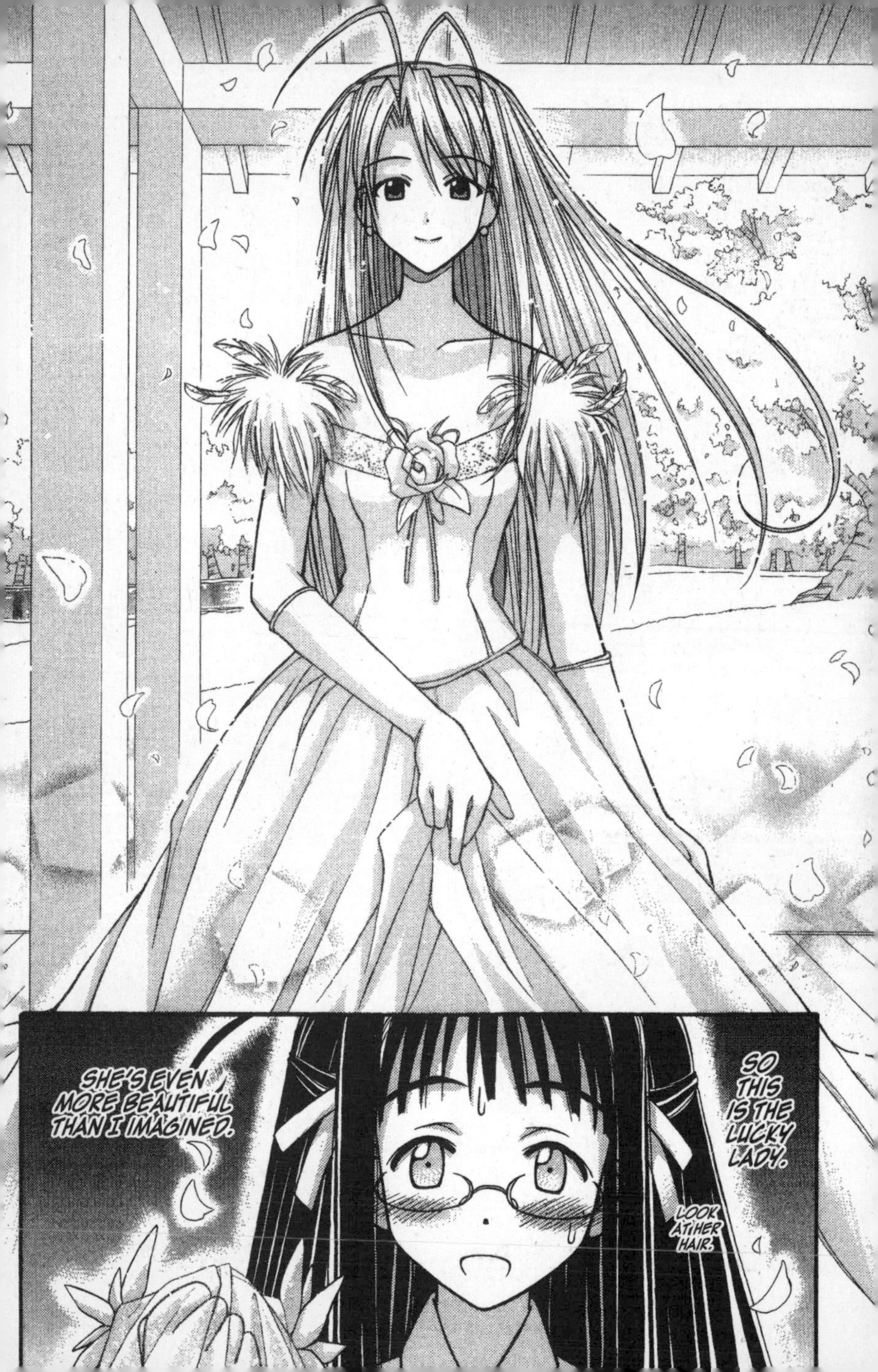
SO THIS IS THE LUCKY LADY.
SHE'S EVEN MORE BEAUTIFUL THAN I IMAGINED.
LOOK AT HER HAIR.

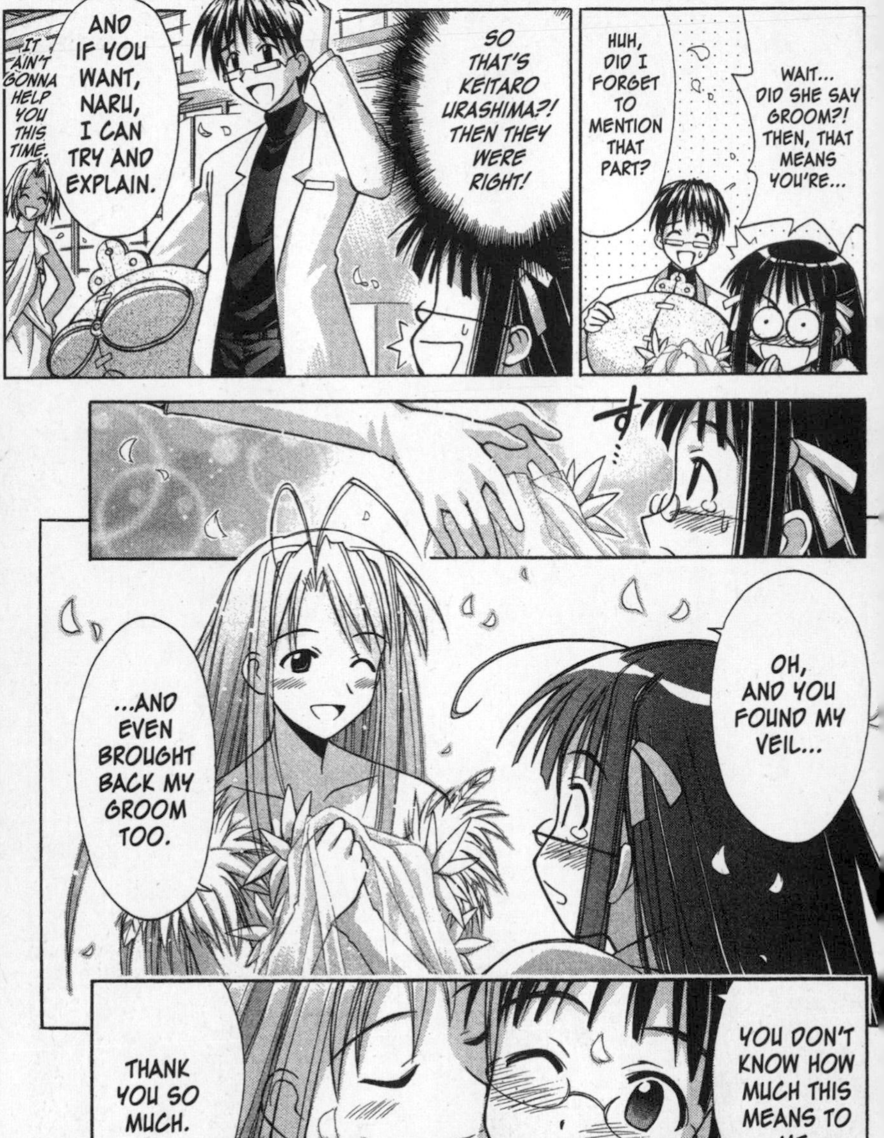
WAIT... DID SHE SAY GROOM?! THEN, THAT MEANS YOU'RE...
HUH, DID I FORGET TO MENTION THAT PART?
SO THAT'S KEITARO URASHIMA?! THEN THEY WERE RIGHT!
AND IF YOU WANT, NARU, I CAN TRY AND EXPLAIN.
IT AIN'T GONNA HELP YOU THIS TIME.
OH, AND YOU FOUND MY VEIL...
...AND EVEN BROUGHT BACK MY GROOM TOO.
YOU DON'T KNOW HOW MUCH THIS MEANS TO ME.
THANK YOU SO MUCH. ♡

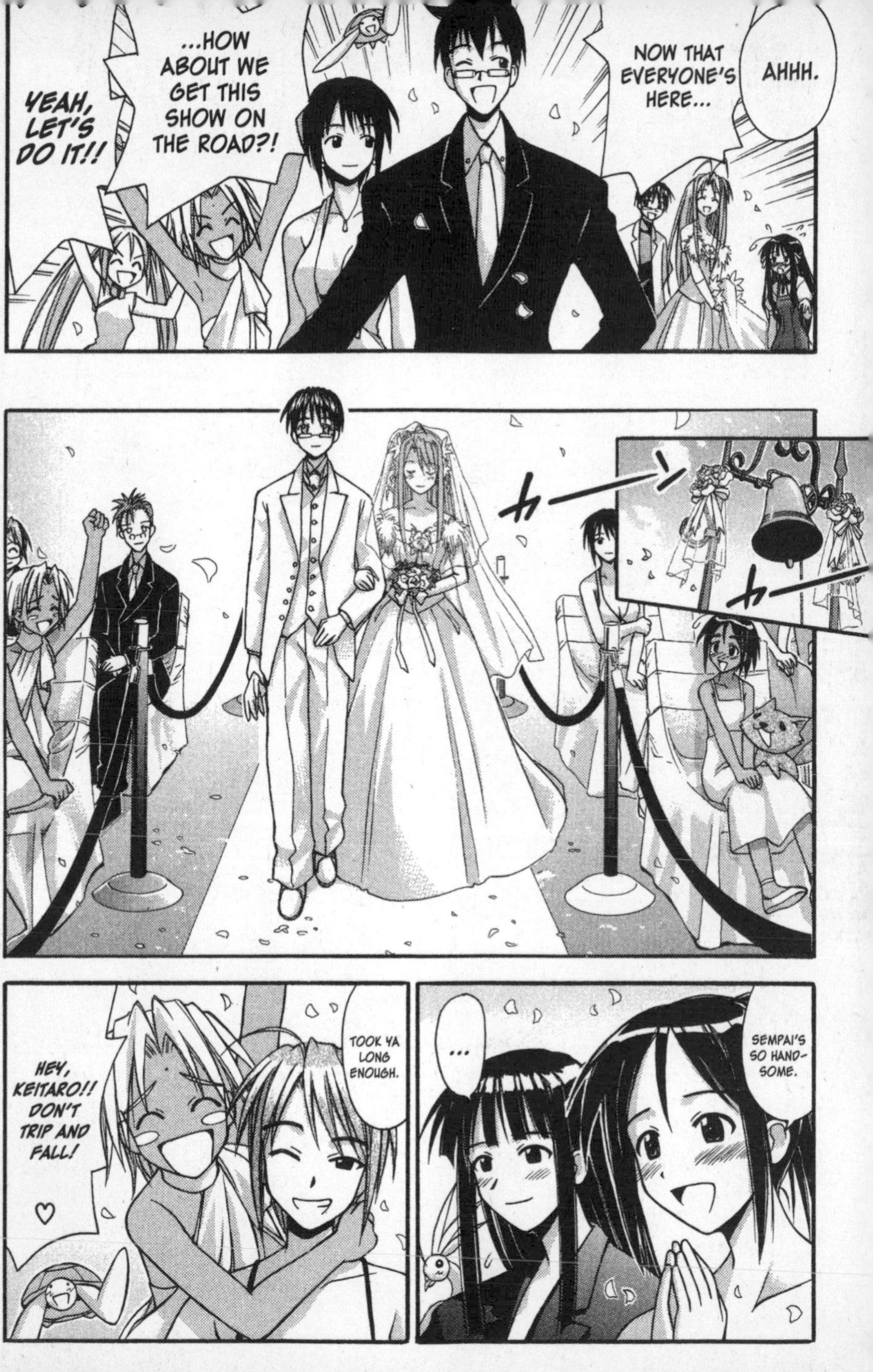
AHHH.
NOW THAT EVERYONE'S HERE...
...HOW ABOUT WE GET THIS SHOW ON THE ROAD?!
YEAH, LET'S DO IT!!
カーン
カー
SEMPAI'S SO HAND-SOME.
...
TOOK YA LONG ENOUGH.
HEY, KEITARO!! DON'T TRIP AND FALL!

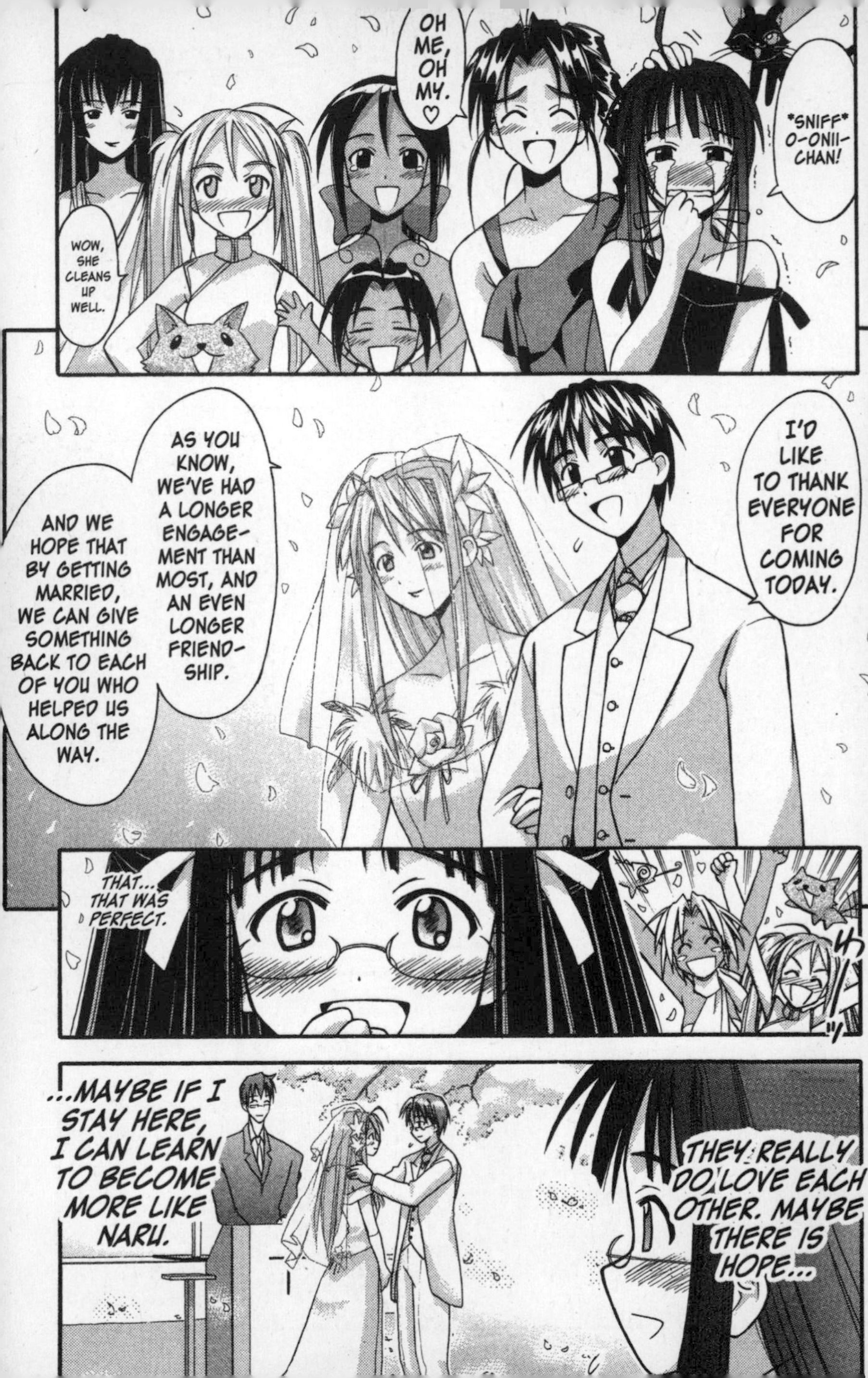
SNIFF O-ONII-CHAN!
OH ME, OH MY. ♡
WOW, SHE CLEANS UP WELL.
I'D LIKE TO THANK EVERYONE FOR COMING TODAY.
AS YOU KNOW, WE'VE HAD A LONGER ENGAGEMENT THAN MOST, AND AN EVEN LONGER FRIENDSHIP.
AND WE HOPE THAT BY GETTING MARRIED, WE CAN GIVE SOMETHING BACK TO EACH OF YOU WHO HELPED US ALONG THE WAY.
THAT... THAT WAS PERFECT.
THEY REALLY DO LOVE EACH OTHER. MAYBE THERE IS HOPE...
...MAYBE IF I STAY HERE, I CAN LEARN TO BECOME MORE LIKE NARU.

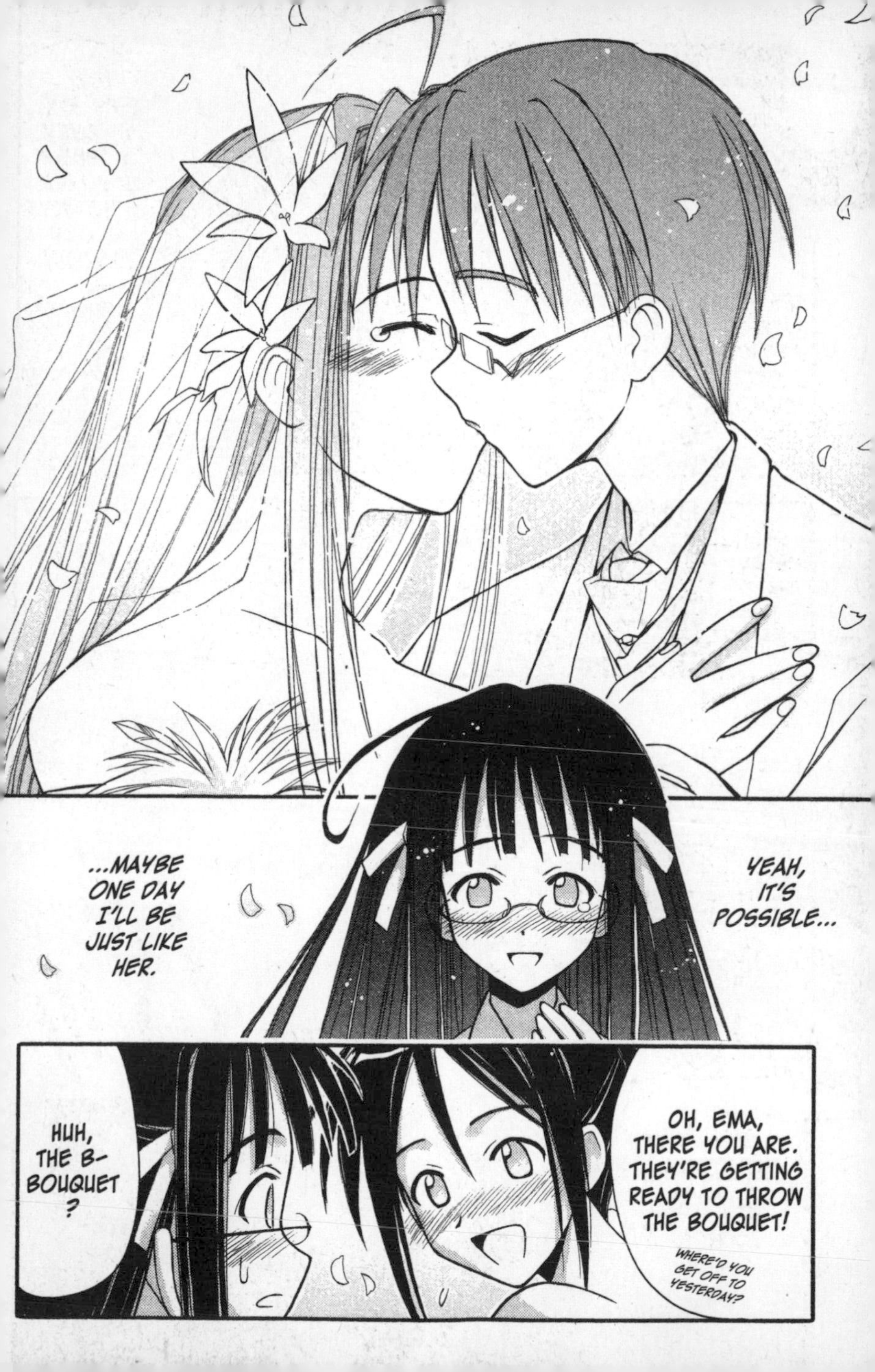
YEAH, IT'S POSSIBLE...
...MAYBE ONE DAY I'LL BE JUST LIKE HER.
OH, EMA, THERE YOU ARE. THEY'RE GETTING READY TO THROW THE BOUQUET!
WHERE'D YOU GET OFF TO YESTERDAY?
HUH, THE B-BOUQUET ?

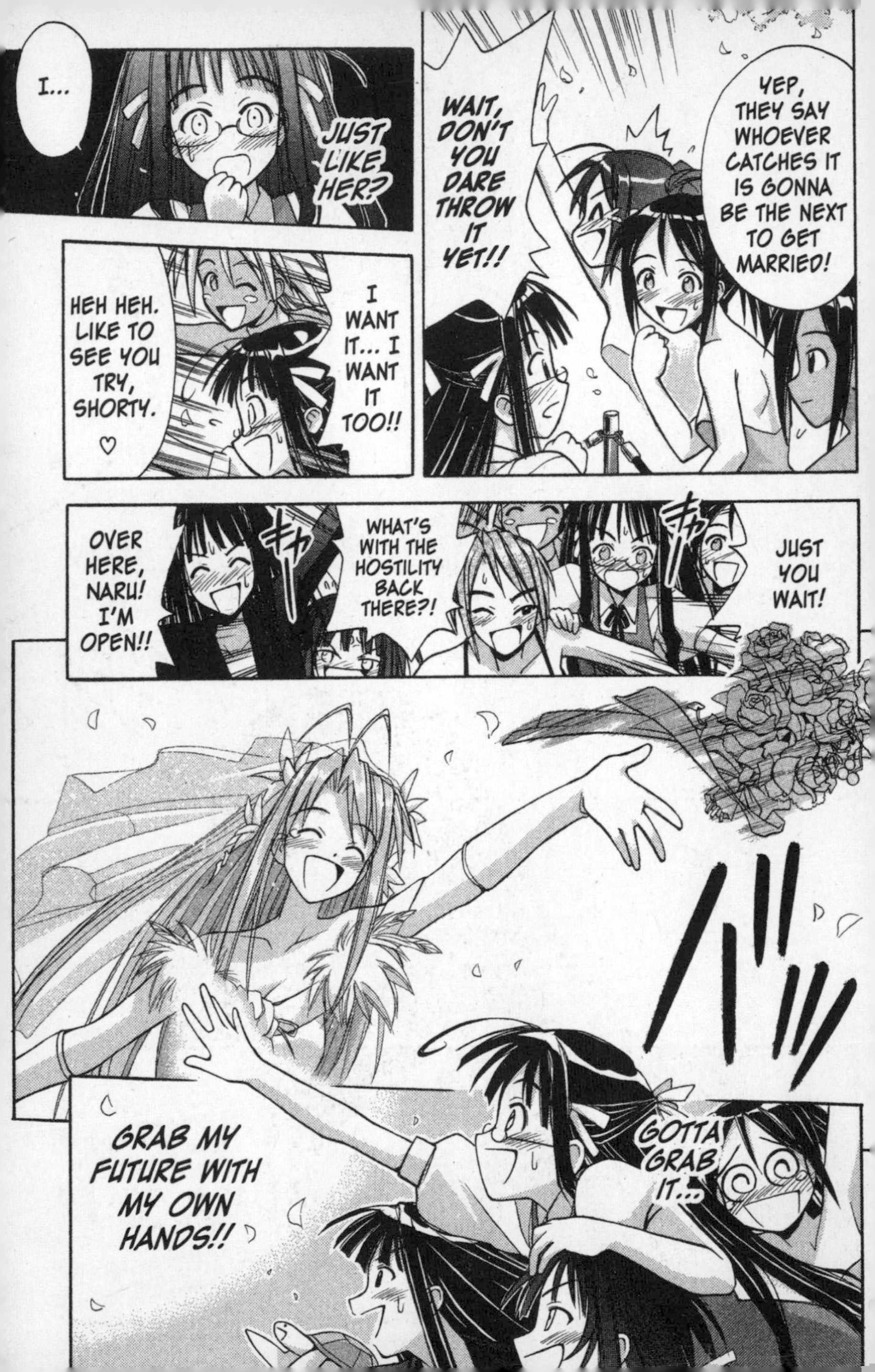
YEP, THEY SAY WHOEVER CATCHES IT IS GONNA BE THE NEXT TO GET MARRIED!
WAIT, DON'T YOU DARE THROW IT YET!!
JUST LIKE HER?
I...
I WANT IT... I WANT IT TOO!!
HEH HEH. LIKE TO SEE YOU TRY, SHORTY. ♡
JUST YOU WAIT!
キャ
WHAT'S WITH THE HOSTILITY BACK THERE?!
キャ
OVER HERE, NARU! I'M OPEN!!
GOTTA GRAB IT...
GRAB MY FUTURE WITH MY OWN HANDS!!

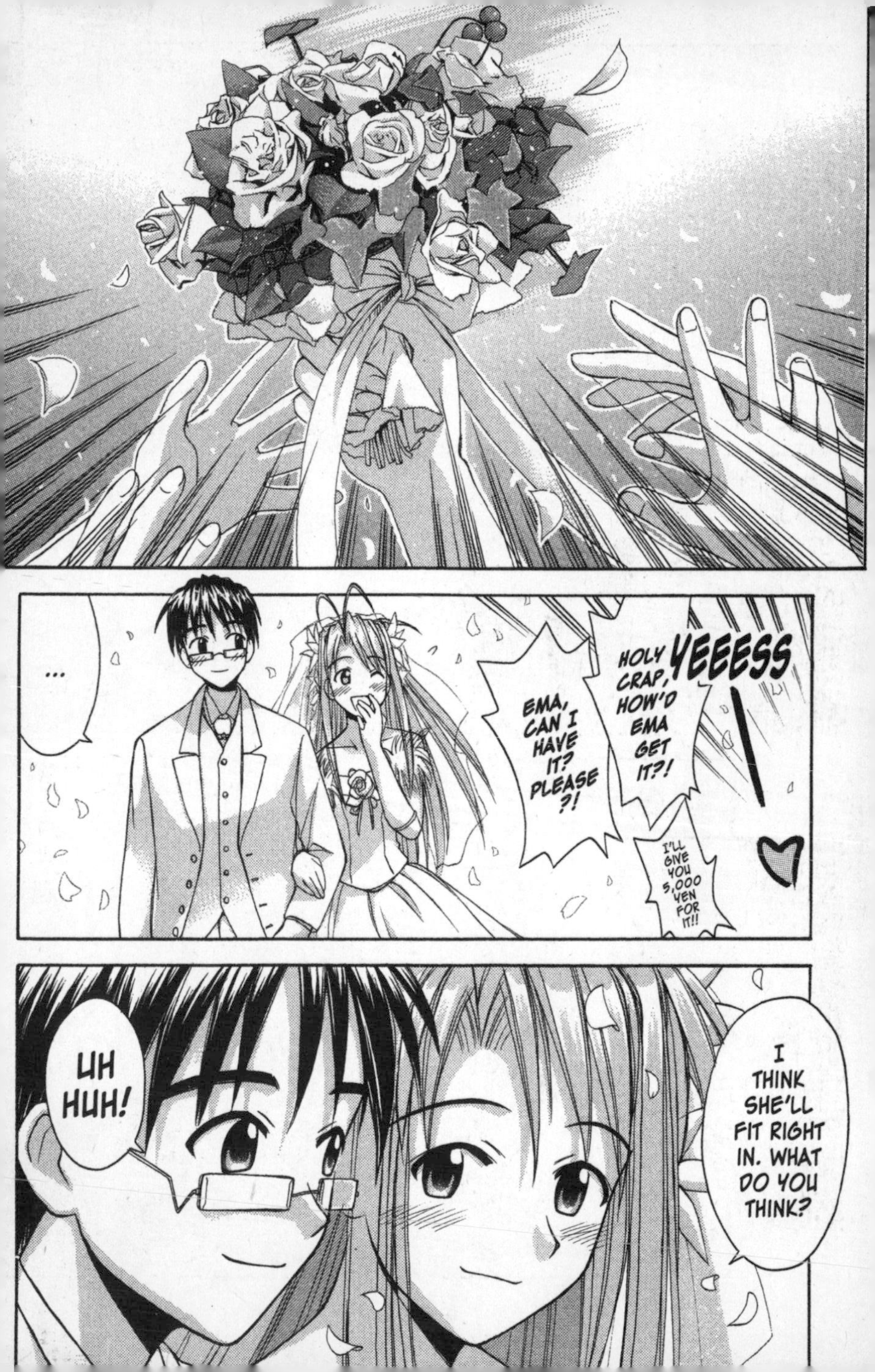
YEEESS!
HOLY CRAP, HOW'D EMA GET IT?!
I'LL GIVE YOU 5,000 YEN FOR IT!!
EMA, CAN I HAVE IT? PLEASE?!
...
I THINK SHE'LL FIT RIGHT IN. WHAT DO YOU THINK?
UH HUH!

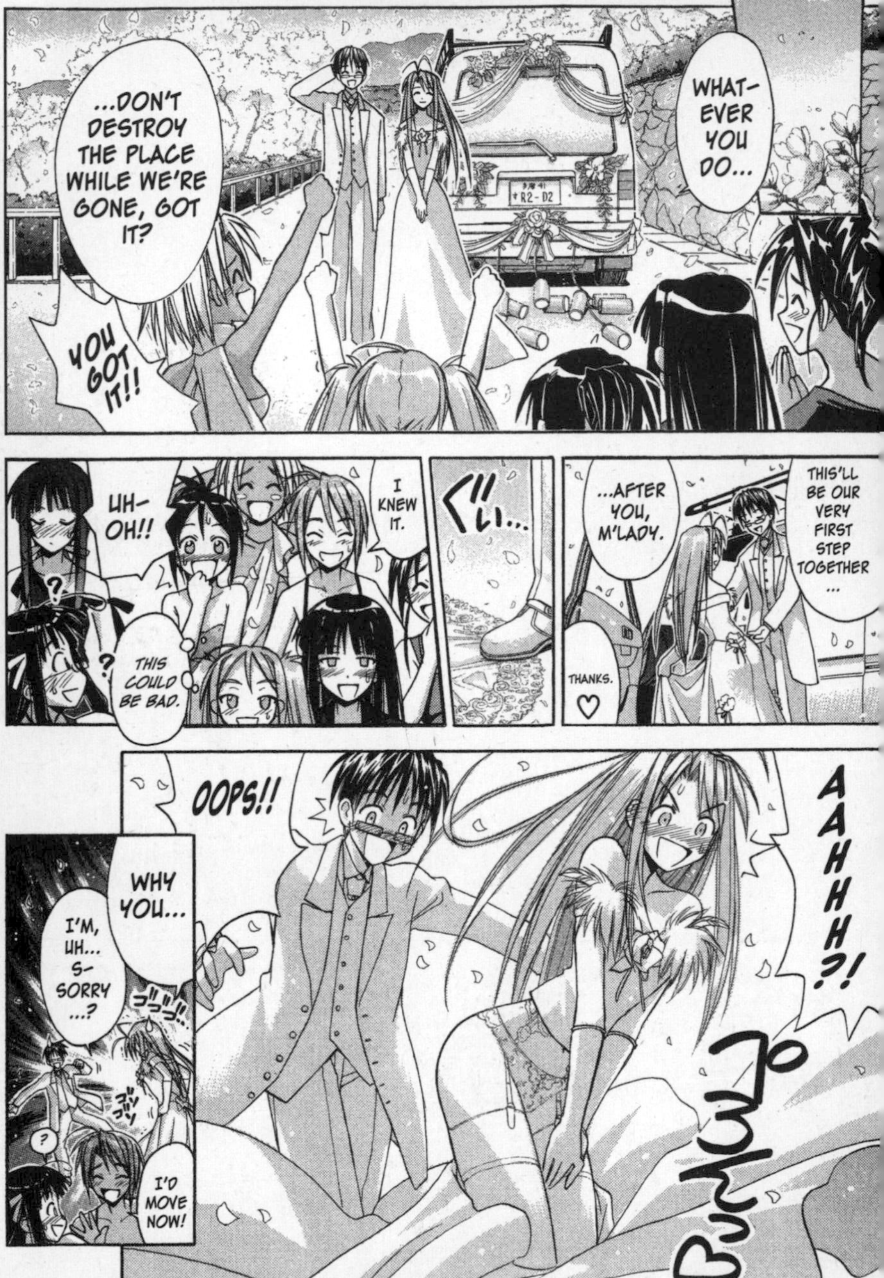
WHAT-EVER YOU DO...
...DON'T DESTROY THE PLACE WHILE WE'RE GONE, GOT IT?
YOU GOT IT!!
THIS'LL BE OUR VERY FIRST STEP TOGETHER ...
...AFTER YOU, M'LADY.
THANKS. ♡
ぐい...
I KNEW IT.
UH-OH!!
THIS COULD BE BAD.
AAHHH?!
ぷるん♡
OOPS!!
WHY YOU...
I'M, UH... S-SORRY ...?
ゴゴゴ!!
ゴツゴツ
I'D MOVE NOW!

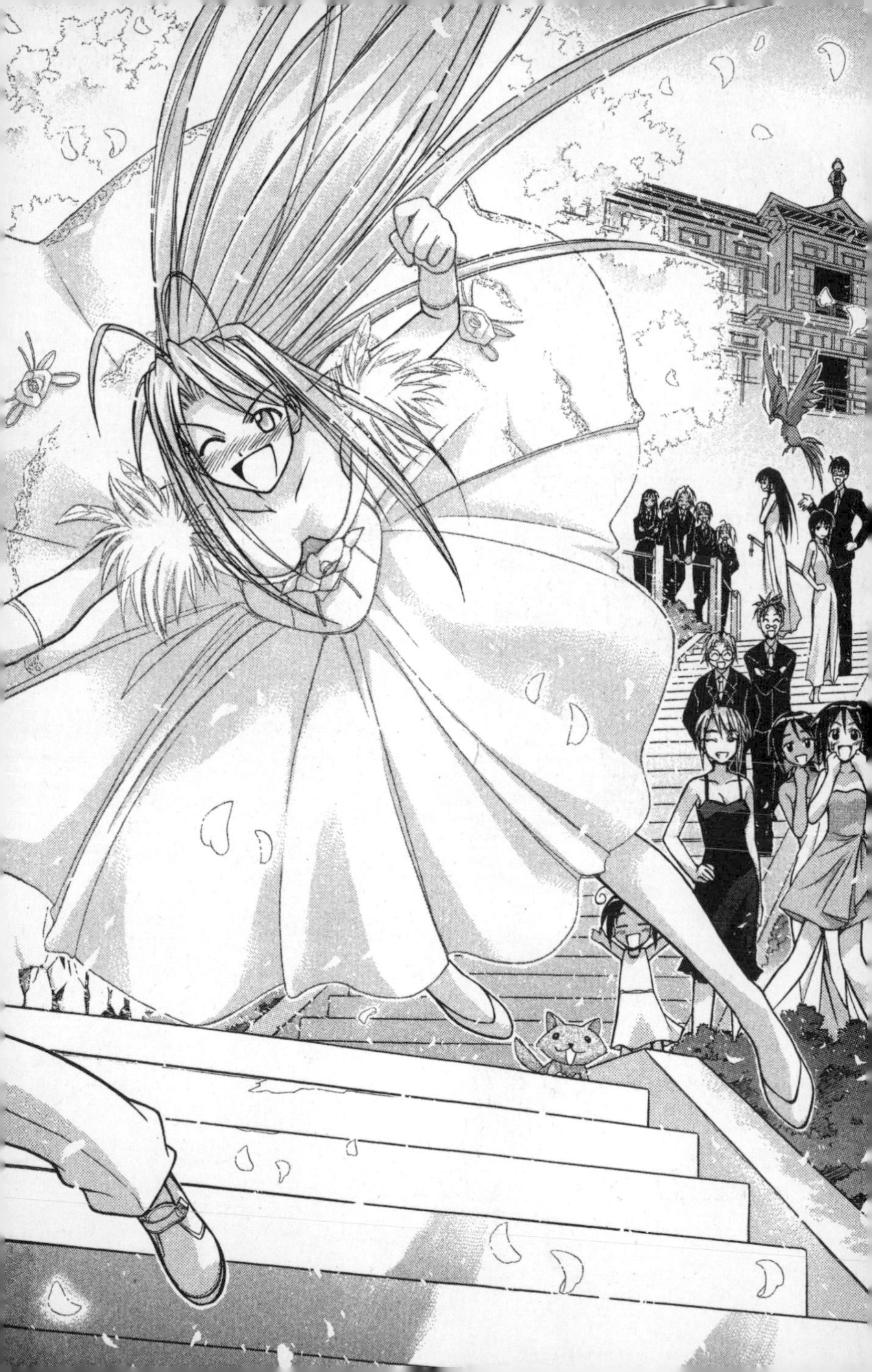

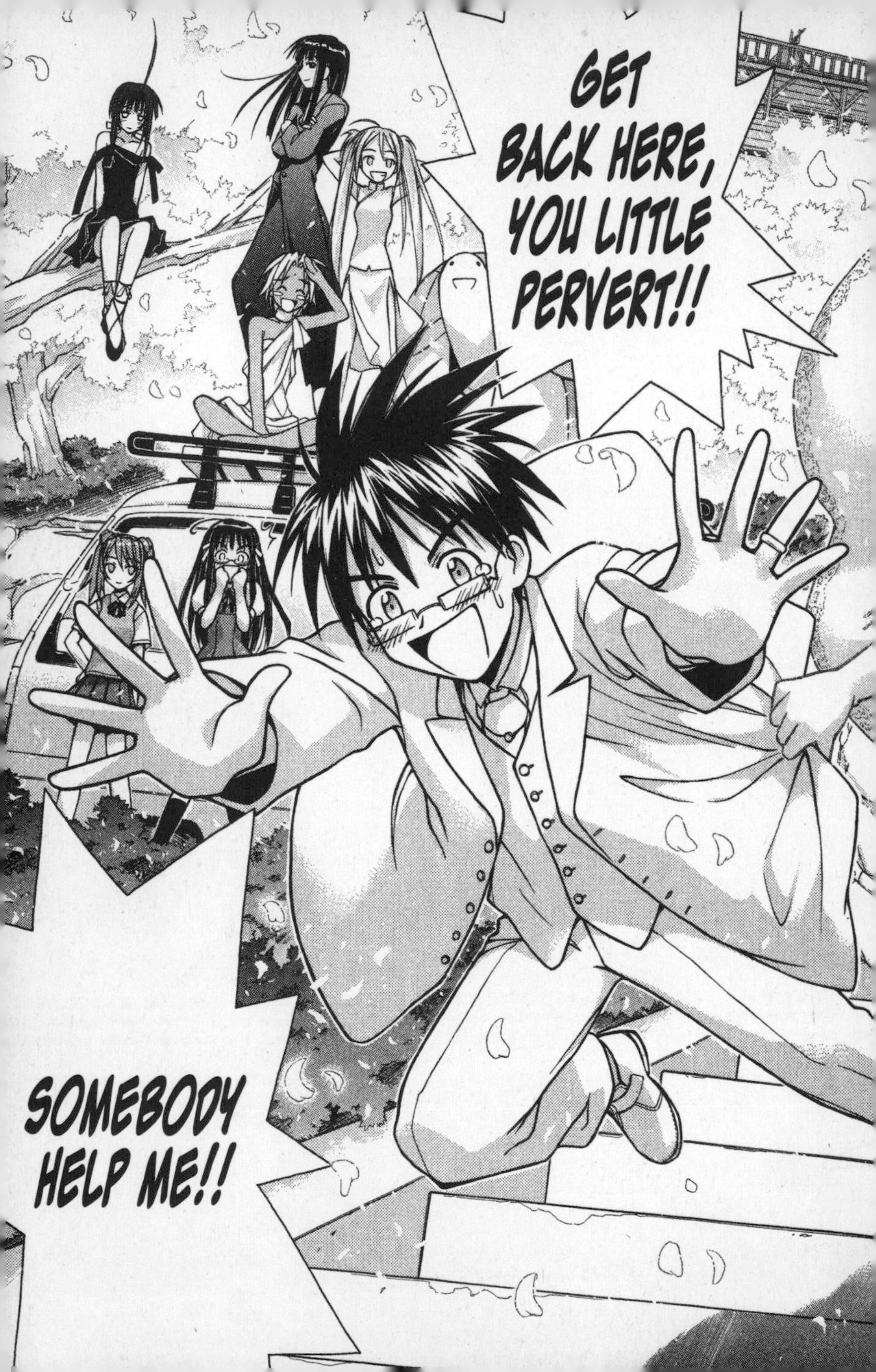
GET BACK HERE, YOU LITTLE PERVERT!!
SOMEBODY HELP ME!!

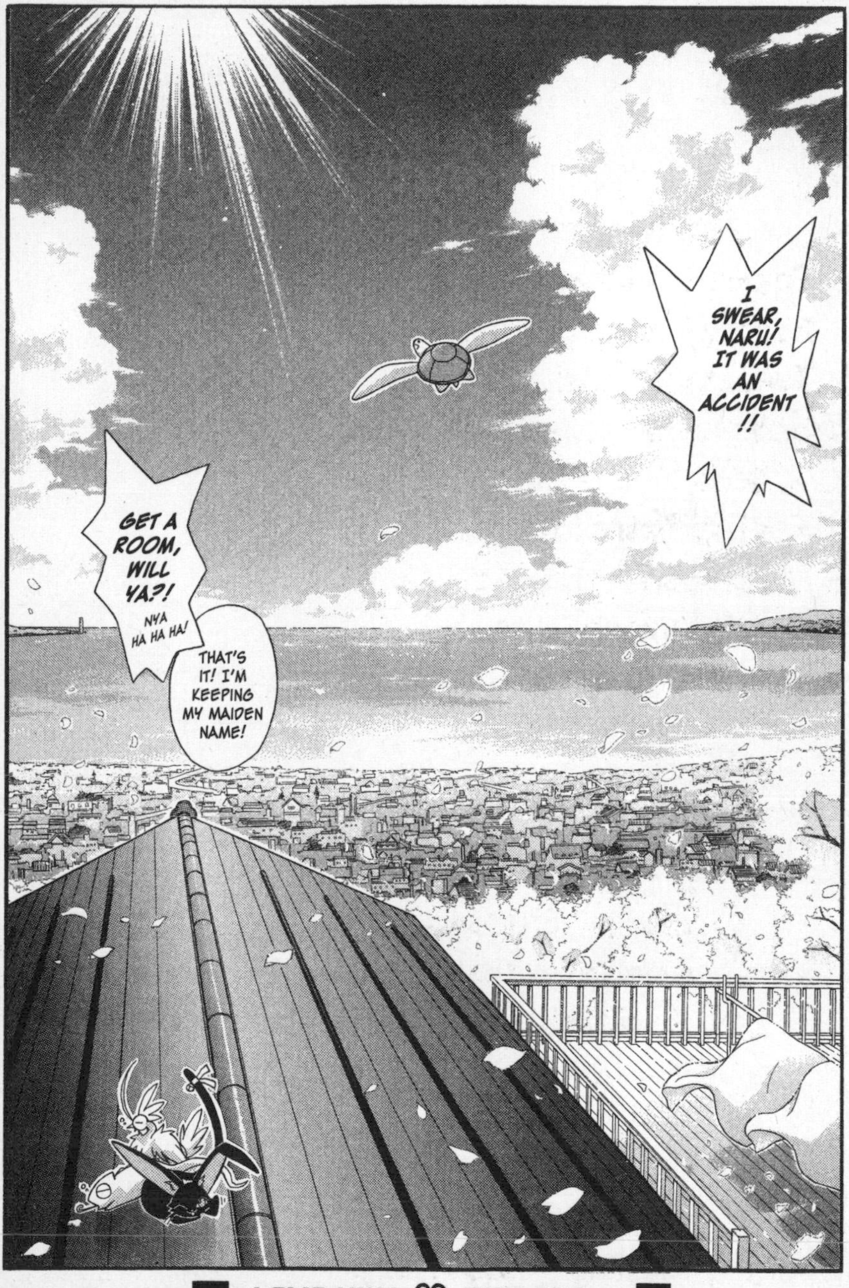
I SWEAR, NARU! IT WAS AN ACCIDENT!!
GET A ROOM, WILL YA?!
NYA HA HA HA!
THAT'S IT! I'M KEEPING MY MAIDEN NAME!

■ LOVE HINA ♡ THE END ■

STAFF

Ken Akamatsu (HINATA. 1~120)
Takashi Takemoto (HINATA. 1~120)
Kenichi Nakamura (HINATA. 1~120)
Takaaki Miyahara (HINATA. 1~120)
Tomohiko Saito (HINATA. 1~20, 78~120)
Masaki Ohyama (HINATA. 16~120)
Yumiko Shinohara (HINATA. 30~73)
Satoshi Yamaura (HINATA. 29)
Mitsuyoshi Arai (HINATA. 29)
Ran Ayanaga (HINATA. 82~120)

Editor

Noboru Ohno
Tomoyuki Shiratsuchi
Masakazu Yoshimoto
Yasushi Yamanaka

KC Editor

Mitsuei Ishii
Shinichiro Yoshihara

Afterword

Ahh, yes! It's finally over. Yep, *Love Hina* has left the building!

But then again, there's that whole *Love Hina* Again OVA series, a couple of novels, the *Love Hina* fan guides, and a ton of CD-ROMs to keep you busy. If you think about it, *Love Hina*'s still got a few more years left in it. As for me, I'm already in the penciling phase of my new project, and... actually, I made that last part up. After all, I've finally gotten my first taste of freedom in three years and I intend to enjoy it for as long as I possibly can!! (Heh heh.) Ah, and getting to sleep as much as I want...could there be any greater joy?

Now, I'd like to take this opportunity to thank anyone and everyone who has been involved in the *Love Hina* project over these past few years.

First, to all my editors at Weekly Shonen Magazine:
Love Hina would only have been half of what it was without all your critical input and creativity. I thank you all so very, very much for everything that you've done for *Love Hina* and me.

To my assistants:
The other complementary half of *Love Hina* was only truly possible thanks to your undying efforts and commitment. Thank you for sleeping over every night for the last three long years! Go get some rest now!!

To the animation staff:
Because of you guys, the anime DVDs have been great sellers, and as the original author, I couldn't have felt safer entrusting my work to your capable hands. I truly cannot wait for the opportunity to work with all of you again on future projects.

To the game staff:
I can't even begin to tell you how exhilarating it was to see *Love Hina* video games start appearing in the weekly rankings every now and then. Thank you so much for all that you've done. And please don't hesitate to contact me any time you need any help with a new project!!

To those in charge of merchandising:
I'm so so sorry that I was never able to show up at any of your new product unveilings during the serial comic run. As the author, I truly enjoyed and appreciated all the wonderful, top-notch designs you crafted for all the *Love Hina* swag. Thank you so much.

To the readers and netizens:
Thank you so much for your overwhelming support. I'm sure the residents of Hinata House feel just as appreciative for all your support as I do. And to those readers overseas, thank you for all your wonderful fan mail. I'm really sorry I wasn't able to respond to any of it, though.

Last but not least, to all of the manga-ka whose names became the basis for those of my characters: Keitaro Arima-san, Kitsune Ayasaka-san, Noriyasu Seta-san and everyone else...thank you. (Heh heh.)

And for the readers, thank you so much for your magnanimous support during this unworthy comic's run! I promise I'll try to do my best on my next project too (if there is one). So please keep up the great support!

Until then, goodbye for now!
And see you again!

Ken Akamatsu
2002 / 1 / 17

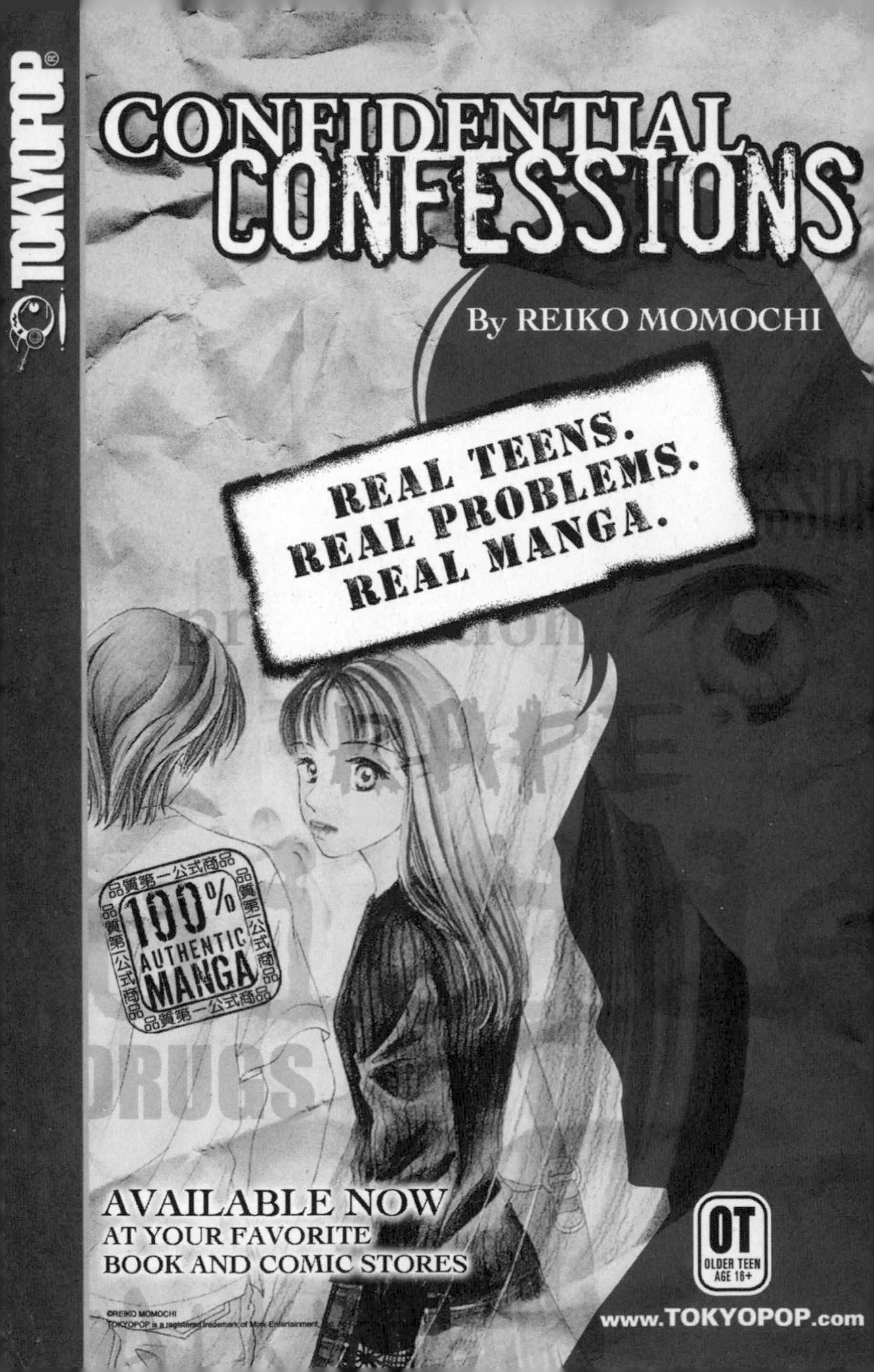
TOKYOPOP®
CONFIDENTIAL CONFESSIONS
By REIKO MOMOCHI
REAL TEENS.
REAL PROBLEMS.
REAL MANGA.
100% AUTHENTIC MANGA
品質第一公式商品
DRUGS
AVAILABLE NOW
AT YOUR FAVORITE
BOOK AND COMIC STORES
OT
OLDER TEEN
AGE 16+
©REIKO MOMOCHI
www.TOKYOPOP.com

-FAKE-

by SANAMI MATOH

They Started as Partners...

They Became *Much* More.

Available NOW at Your
Favorite Book and Comic Stores

So you wanna be
a Rock 'n' Roll star...

Gravitation

by Maki Murakami

Rock 'n' Roll & manga collide with superstar
dreams in this hit property from Japan!
**VOL. 1 IN YOUR FAVORITE
BOOK & COMIC STORES NOW!**

T
TEEN
AGE 13+

www.TOKYOPOP.com

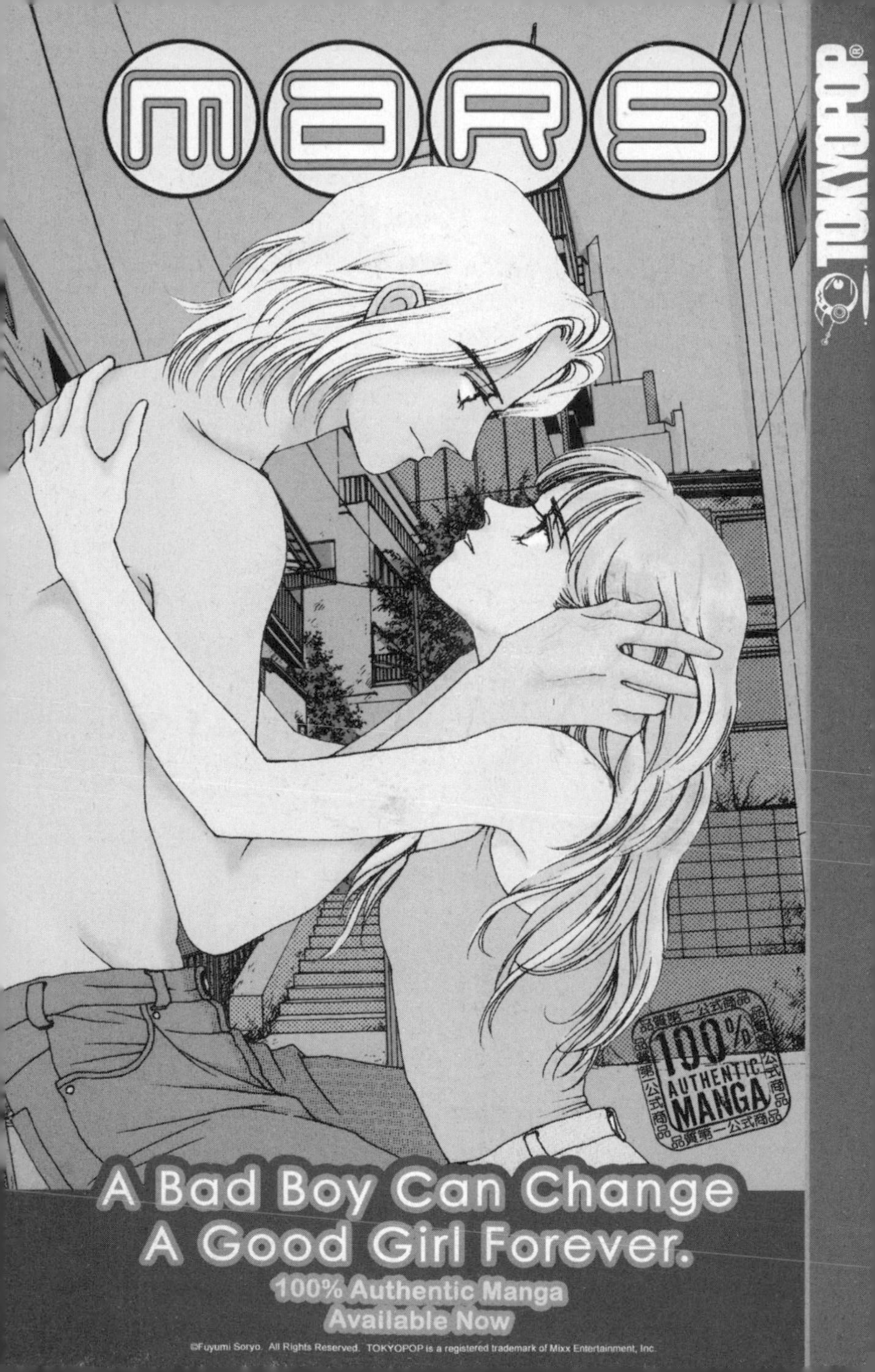
MARS
TOKYOPOP®
100% AUTHENTIC MANGA
A Bad Boy Can Change
A Good Girl Forever.
100% Authentic Manga
Available Now
©Fuyumi Soryo. All Rights Reserved. TOKYOPOP is a registered trademark of Mixx Entertainment, Inc.

STOP!

This is the back of the book.
You wouldn't want to spoil a great ending!

This book is printed "manga-style," in the authentic Japanese right-to-left format. Since none of the artwork has been flipped or altered, readers get to experience the story just as the creator intended. You've been asking for it, so TOKYOPOP® delivered: authentic, hot-off-the-press, and far more fun!

DIRECTIONS

1
2
3
4
5
6
7
8
9
10

If this is your first time reading manga-style, here's a quick guide to help you understand how it works.

It's easy... just start in the top right panel and follow the numbers. Have fun, and look for more 100% authentic manga from TOKYOPOP®!

100% AUTHENTIC MANGA
品質第一公式商品